Key Issues

AGNOSTICISM
Contemporary Responses to Spencer and Huxley

Key Issues

AGNOSTICISM

Contemporary Responses to
SPENCER AND HUXLEY

Series Editor

ANDREW PYLE

University of Bristol

THOEMMES PRESS

© Thoemmes Press 1995

Published in 1995 by
Thoemmes Press
11 Great George Street
Bristol BS1 5RR
England

ISBN
Paper : 1 85506 404 9
Cloth : 1 85506 405 7

Agnosticism: Contemporary Responses to Spencer and Huxley
Key Issues No. 4

British Library Cataloguing-in-Publication Data

A catalogue record of this title is available
from the British Library

Printed in Great Britain by Antony Rowe Ltd., Chippenham

CONTENTS

Contents vii

The pieces reprinted in this book have been taken from original copies and the different grammatical and stylistic arrangement of each has been preserved.

INTRODUCTION

S1. Agnosticism: The Basic Idea.
The central tenet of agnosticism, we are sometimes told, is simply a personal admission of ignorance. The agnostic is the person who frankly admits his or her ignorance regarding the existence and nature of God. The agnostic creed, on this interpretation, amounts to little more than the single article, 'I don't know'. What, we are then asked, could be more innocent or more modest?

Although the agnostics sometimes wrote in such a way as to permit – and even encourage – this reading, it is a gross distortion of their position. There are, after all, any number of subjects on which I am ignorant. I don't know the correct translation of the German word *Geratewohl*, the dates of King Louis XI of France, or the electron configuration of the cobalt atom. But in all these cases I am confident that there is a fact of the matter which is known to the respective experts. If I want to know, all I need to do is ask.

Now in matters theological, there is of course no shortage of authorities. If I confess my ignorance, many such self-proclaimed experts will rush to enlighten me. (Unfortunately, of course, they will all contradict one another.) If I then *continue* to proclaim my ignorance, I am tacitly denying that any of these people know what they are talking about. Instead of the modest 'I don't know', I have advanced to the more aggressive and challenging assertion, 'We don't know'.

This in turn raises further questions of interpretation. What is the scope of the 'we' in the claim 'we don't know'? All presently existing human beings, perhaps? But then we don't know whether there is intelligent life in the Andromeda system, or whether cold fusion is possible. In such cases, however, we know – at least in principle – how to find out. In a hundred year's time, our descendants may know the answers to both questions. This isn't the sort of ignorance that the agnostics had in mind.[1] What

---

[1] Robert Flint's *Agnosticism* (Edinburgh, Blackwoods, 1903), otherwise a

they meant, clearly, was that we – i.e. *all human beings at all times* – are ignorant as to whether there is a God. No observation or experiment *could* settle the issue.

We are now getting close to the heart of the agnostics' position. They do not regard it as a contingent fact that we don't know the truth about the existence and nature of God. It is not that we expect our grandchildren to be as much wiser and better-informed than ourselves in theology as we hope they will be in astrophysics. In theology, further observations and experiments will not aid them. Here we encounter not just the unknown but the *unknowable*, a permanent and insuperable barrier to our enquiries.

The agnostic's logic thus leads him from the modest 'I don't know', *via* the more challenging 'we don't know' to his final position, 'there is a reason of principle why human beings as such *can't* know'. If this is true, then the babble of the self-appointed experts is just empty noise, and we have a principled reason for ignoring the *minutiae* of their eternal squabbles. But the agnostic has now been led to assert a strong and controversial epistemological thesis. How might that thesis be defended?

S.2. Metaphysical Origins: Hume and Kant.

The 'founding fathers' of agnosticism, as a considered and reflective philosophical position, were the eighteenth century philosophers David Hume and Immanuel Kant. Both men subjected the traditional 'proofs' of God's existence to a rigorous and ultimately destructive critique; both set out accounts of human knowledge which saw it as essentially restricted to the world of phenomena; both would have vigorously rejected the label of 'atheist'. For all the profound differences that divide their respective philosophies, it is this common ground that makes them the joint ancestors of agnosticism.

David Hume (1711-1776) argued, in his famous *Treatise* and *Enquiry*, that all our ideas (concepts) can be traced back to our impressions of sensation and reflection.[2] Strictly speaking, this would imply that any attempt to talk about a 'Reality' that

perceptive account, errs by assimilating agnosticism too closely to scepticism in general.

2   David Hume, *Treatise of Human Nature* (1739-1740), Oxford, O.U.P., 1978; *Enquiry Concerning Human Understanding* (1748), Oxford, O.U.P., 1975.

exists 'behind' the veil of appearances must be literally meaningless. The noises uttered by theologians (and by atheists too!) would have no more meaning than Lewis Carroll's nonsense poem, Jabberwocky.[3] Only a few of Hume's disciples have accepted this extreme meaning-empiricism; most have interpreted his empiricism as placing strict limits on what we can *know* rather than on what we can intelligibly *claim*. On either reading, our knowledge is confined to the world of phenomena, of how things appear to beings like us. It is no surprise to find that the prince of the agnostics, Thomas Huxley, wrote a book on Hume acknowledging substantial intellectual debts.[4]

Immanuel Kant (1724–1804) argued in his *Critique of Pure Reason*[5] that the world that we experience – the phenomenal world – is in part a construction of our own minds. This justifies certain knowledge-claims about the phenomenal world, while at the same time disqualifying metaphysicians' claims to knowledge of the 'noumenal' world, the world of things-in-themselves. It is therefore, he concluded, vain to try to prove the existence of God by philosophical argument.[6] A deeply pious man, Kant thought that the *idea* of God would naturally occur both to the natural scientist and to the moralist. To the natural scientist, he thought, the world will appear as if designed; to the moralist, conscience will seem as if it were the voice of God. In neither case, however, are we entitled to move from 'we find it natural to think as if there were a God' to 'there is a God'. The limits of our knowledge are the limits of our actual and possible experience.

The history of the reception of Kant's thought in England would make a fascinating story.[7] The barriers to overcome were formidable: few Englishmen read German; Kant's prose proved hard to read and almost impossible to translate; his

3 See A. J. Ayer, *Language, Truth, and Logic* (1936), Harmondsworth, Penguin, 1971, especially Chapter 6, 'Critique of Ethics and Theology'.

4 T. H. Huxley, *Hume: With helps to the Study of Berkeley*, London, Macmillan, 1897.

5 I Kant, *Critique of Pure Reason*, 2nd edition (1787), translated by Norman Kemp Smith, London, Macmillan, 1933.

6 *ibid*, Transcendental Dialectic, Book 2 Chapter 3, 'The Ideal of Pure Reason',

7 See George MacDonald Ross and Tony McWalter, eds. *Kant and his Influence*, Bristol, Thoemmes, 1990, for a part of this story.

reputation for impenetrable obscurity went ahead of him and ensured that few even bothered to try. (Herbert Spencer, for example, read no German and had to absorb Kant at second hand.) For our purposes, the crucial 'missing links' between Kant and British agnosticism were Sir William Hamilton and Henry Mansel.[8]

Sir William Hamilton (1788–1856) was professor of logic and metaphysics at the University of Edinburgh. His 'Philosophy of the Conditioned' shows significant differences from Kant, and reflects equally the Scottish 'Common Sense' philosophy of Thomas Reid. With Kant, however, Hamilton insists that *our* knowledge is confined to the relative and the conditioned, and thus cannot extend to the Absolute and Unconditioned (God). This line of argument was taken up by Hamilton's English disciple Henry Longueville Mansel (1820–1871). In his influential Bampton Lectures, *The Limits of Religious Thought* (1858), Mansel attempted a sort of philosophical conjuring trick, trying to use an extreme philosophical scepticism to justify traditional Christianity.[9] He soon found the tactic to be a double-edged sword: the agnostics (Spencer, Stephen, Huxley) all cite Mansel as evidence that the most 'advanced' Christian thinkers were coming over to their position. If 'The Unconditioned' is, as Mansel claims, absolutely beyond our ken, why should we abide by the formulae and rituals of traditional *Christian* worship?

S3. Science and Religion.

The gradual assimilation of the message of Hume and Kant was by no means the only cause of the rise of agnosticism. The mid-to-late nineteenth century saw three great scientific syntheses: the conservation of energy (Helmholtz), the electromagnetic theory (Maxwell), and the theory of evolution by natural selection (Darwin). Together, these theories offered the prospect of a complete naturalistic account of the physical world. One could, of course, continue to defend a 'God of the gaps', trying to find a role for God wherever scientific knowledge remained gappy and incomplete. Darwin's theory,

---

8   For Kant's influence on Hamilton and Mansel, see Bernard Lightman, *The Origins of Agnosticism*, Baltimore and London, Johns Hopkins University Press, 1987, Chapter 2, pp. 32–67.

9   H. L. Mansel, *The Limits of Religious Thought*, Oxford, John Murray, 1858.

for example, did not account for the origin of life: one could defend a role for God within the natural world at this point. But it was becoming clear to the more intelligent and far-sighted theologians that such a strategy was doomed to be one of gradual retreat and ultimate surrender. A more radical rethink was required.

The agnostics' suggestion was that the world of Nature should be handed over, lock, stock, and barrel, to the natural sciences. This is the burden of Spencer's argument in his *First Principles*, and of Tyndall's oratory in his famous *Belfast Address*. Religion, both men thought, can only benefit from this tactical withdrawal: rather than compete with the natural sciences on their own ground, it should confine itself to the noumenal world. But the noumenal world, according to Spencer, is unknowable – we know that it exists, but can make no positive claims about it. Religion, therefore, must abandon its creeds and dogmas, and amount in the end to little more than a sort of reverence or awe in the face of the Unknowable. Few theologians were happy with this so-called 'reconciliation' between science and religion: even with a capital U, 'the Unknowable' was a poor substitute for God.

Not surprisingly, it was the scientists who were most enthusiastic about Spencer's 'reconciliation': it gave them all they wanted, and enabled them to set aside certain nagging questions about ultimate origins and real essences as 'meta-physical'. In Germany, the great physiologist Emil Du-Bois Reymond (1818–1896) proclaimed that there were seven 'World-Riddles' to which science would never be able to find answers.[10] These were the essence of force and matter, the origin of movement, the origin of life, the teleology of Nature, the origins of sensation, the origin of thought, and free will. To these questions, Du-Bois Reymond thought, science can only answer, '*ignoramus et ignorabimus*', that is, we are and will remain ignorant.

Other scientists disagreed with particular items on Reymond's list – one or two of them do seem to be amenable to the methods of science – while sympathizing with his general position. Tyndall and Huxley, for example, were both keen to extend the methods of science to the whole of the natural world, including questions about life and mind. The result,

[10] For Du Bois Reymond, see K. E. Rothschuh's article in the *Dictionary of Scientific Biography*, Vol 4, pp. 200–204.

they both felt, will be a uniform mechanistic materialism. But if asked whether our universe *really is* just a colossal machine, both men would have returned a brusque and decided negative. Science, they would have replied, is a system of symbols and concepts we have developed to help us make sense of the world of experience; it does not tell us how things are in themselves. This tension between the materialism implicit in Huxley's science and the idealism of his metaphysics is acutely pointed out by critics such as Barry and Ward.

It is surely no accident that the birth of agnosticism coincides closely with the publication of Charles Darwin's *Origin of Species* in 1859.[11] Darwin's work was widely perceived as having overthrown the traditional argument for design, and thus shown that natural science can do without natural theology.[12] Although Hume had criticized the argument for design in his *Dialogues concerning Natural Religion*,[13] and Kant had respectfully set it aside as persuasive but not conclusive,[14] their criticisms were largely ignored. In Britain in particular, the tradition of natural theology was still strong, from Paley's classic *Natural Theology* of 1802[15] down to the Bridgwater Treatises of the 1830s.[16] The evidence of design in a bird's wing or a cat's eye was considered to be so striking as to disarm sceptical doubts. Even Darwin admitted that such 'organs of extreme perfection' posed a *prima facie* objection to

11   C. Darwin, *The Origin of Species* (1859). For a modern edition with an introduction by J. W. Burrow, see the Pelican version, Harmondsworth, 1968. For the resulting controversy, see David Hull, ed, *Darwin and His Critics*, Harvard University Press, Cambridge, Massachusetts, 1973.

12   See Michael Ruse, *The Darwinian Revolution*, Chicago and London, University of Chicago Press, especially Chapter 9, pp. 234–267; and William Irvine, *Apes, Angels, and Victorians*, Cleveland and New York, Meridian Books, 1959, especially Chapter 8, pp. 101–126.

13   David Hume, *Dialogues Concerning Natural Religion* (1779). For a modern version with an introduction and a selection of secondary literature, see Stanley Tweyman's edition in the Routledge 'In Focus' series (London, Routledge, 1991).

14   The physico-theological proof, says Kant in the *Critique of Pure Reason*, p. 520, must always be mentioned with respect, as it is 'the oldest, the clearest, and the most accordant with the common reason of mankind'.

15   William Paley, *Natural Theology* (1802), in his *Collected Works*, Volume 4, London, Rivington, 1819.

16   For the survival of Natural Theology in Britain in the nineteenth century, see J. H. Brooke, *Science and Religion: Some Historical Perspectives*, Cambridge, C.U.P., 1991, pp. 192–225.

his theory.[17] The theory of natural selection offered, however, a purely naturalistic account of apparent 'design' – it was no longer necessary to posit a divine designer. It also accounted for apparent lapses in design that the natural theologians could not explain.

While many theologians fulminated against Darwin's theories, others sought to accommodate Darwinism *within* Natural Theology, either by positing a 'God of the gaps' to breathe life into the first forms, or by suggesting that evolution could not proceed without a certain divine guidance, exerted invisibly from behind the scenes. Darwin's theory, such theologians remind us, overthrows only the crudest versions of the argument for design; it is still compatible with teleological conceptions of Nature. (William Barry takes just this line against Huxley.) Darwin himself was clearly unimpressed: from an early age, he found it hard to see evidence in Nature of intelligent and benevolent design. A public avowal of atheism would, however, have given too much of a shock to pious relatives and clerical friends. In later life he came to accept Huxley's word 'agnostic' as an appropriate expression of his own religious views.[18] For him, as for other Victorian philosophers, writers, and scientists, this was the respectable face of unbelief, far removed from the militant atheism of men such as Bradlaugh and Holyoake.

S4. *Shades of Meaning.*

Was agnosticism supposed to provide an alternative to traditional faiths? Was 'the Unknowable' meant as a substitute for God? Strange though it may sound, this does indeed seem to have been the avowed position of some agnostics.[19] Herbert Spencer even presents his agnosticism as the inevitable next phase in the evolution of religion. The religious beliefs of a society, he claims, reflect its degree of mental sophistication. Starting with primitive 'ghost' theories, religious conceptions have become progressively more advanced, moving from polytheism to monotheism and from anthropomorphic to more abstract conceptions of God. Even in Christianity, however,

---

[17] Darwin, *Origin of Species*, Chapter 6, 'Difficulties', pp. 217–224.

[18] For Darwin's agnosticism, see Adrian Desmond and James Moore, *Darwin*, London, Michael Joseph, p. 636, p. 657.

[19] For this positive form of agnosticism, see Lightman, especially chapters 5 and 6.

God is still conceived in *personal* terms – that is, some remnant of primitive anthropomorphism remains. Agnosticism, by substituting 'the Unknowable' for 'God', represents the next step forward, perhaps the final stage in the evolution of religion. It is certainly hard to think of anything more abstract and less anthropomorphic than Spencer's 'Unknowable'.

In answer to his critics, Spencer insists that this is still a positive creed.[20] We know that the Unknowable exists – a phenomenal world *requires* a noumenal world. If we try to arrive at a positive conception of it, however, our faculties fail us: all we can say is that, behind the scenes of the familiar phenomenal world, there is an incomprehensible but omnipresent power. In his article, 'Religion, A Retrospect and A Prospect', he borrows still more of the theologian's terminology and speaks of 'an Infinite and Eternal Energy, from which all things proceed'. To disciples and critics alike, it looked as if 'the Unknowable' was intended to take the place of God.

What would agnostic worship be like? Without positive doctrinal content, an agnostic creed must consist almost entirely of negations. Gladstone asked Samuel Laing to formulate such a creed (reprinted here), but the very notion of a fixed creed, whether of eight articles or thirty nine, was dismissed by Huxley as an absurdity. His essay, 'Agnosticism', was written largely to correct such misapprehensions. The word was coined, says Huxley, around 1869, when he needed a convenient label for the metaphysical and epistemological views he found himself defending in the debates of the Metaphysical Society. 'Agnostic', Huxley explains, is simply the negation of 'gnostic'.[21] The gnostics claim to be in possession of a special sort of insight into the nature and properties of God; the agnostic explicitly denies that he has any such insight. The word was never intended to be name of a creed or of any fixed body of doctrine; rather, it stands essentially for the method of doubt itself. The agnostic, on this view, is the critical thinker, the partial sceptic, the person who refuses to believe anything without adequate reasons.

[20]   See, for example, Spencer's reply to Frederic Harrison, 'Last Words about Agnosticism and the Religion of Humanity', *The Nineteenth Century*, Vol XVI, 1884, pp. 826–839.

[21]   For the origins of the term 'agnostic', see Lightman, pp. 10–13. Huxley insists that 'agnostic' is just the negation of 'gnostic'; it does not signify worship of the 'unknown god' of *Acts*, 17, 23.

We now find ourselves faced with two significantly different interpretations of what agnosticism means. There is the more positive interpretation, according to which the agnostic is committed to the existence of something real but unknowable 'behind' the phenomenal world; and there is the more negative interpretation, in which 'the unknowable' might as well, for all practical purposes, be nothing at all. Spencer and his disciples take the positive view, and seek to assimilate their agnosticism to the views of sceptically-minded Christians like Mansel. Tyndall takes a similarly positive view, representing agnosticism as anti-clerical but not at all anti-religious. Agnostic worship is conceived as a sort of emotionally charged awe or reverence in the face of natural beauty or grandeur. (It is no accident that both Tyndall and Leslie Stephen were devout Alpinists.) On the other hand, Huxley registers his protest against the notion that agnosticism is any sort of surrogate for religion. If one takes the method of doubt at all seriously, one can't justify turning 'the unknowable' into an object of worship. As the idealist metaphysician F. H. Bradley was to say, 'Mr Spencer's attitude towards the unknowable seems a proposal to take something for God simply because we do not know what the devil it can be'[22]

S5. Seizing the Moral High Ground.

For most of recorded history, the intellectual defenders of established religions have sought to portray their particular creeds as essential pillars of the moral and political order. Christian apologists poured forth streams of books, pamphlets, and sermons on the theme. Take away belief in God and the afterlife, they warned, and moral chaos will soon follow. Even the eighteenth-century *philosophes* had their doubts, and wondered whether Christianity, although obviously false, might not be useful for keeping the lower classes in their place. The moral high ground, it seemed, belonged by divine right to the priests, who never ceased to portray the freethinkers as dissolute and licentious rogues.

All this was to change in the middle of the nineteenth century. Two key events help us to fix the precise date of the change. In 1860 Huxley clashed with Bishop ('Soapy Sam')

[22] See John Passmore, *A Hundred Years of Philosophy*, Harmondsworth, Penguin, 1957, pp. 62–63.

Wilberforce over Darwinism and its implications for human origins.[23] Huxley won a famous propaganda victory by successfully portraying himself as an honest searcher after truth, and the bishop as a time-serving and prejudiced defender of vested interests. Then in 1865, in his *Examination of Sir William Hamilton's Philosophy*, John Stuart Mill took issue with Mansel over the moral properties of God.[24] Mansel had argued that, although we are completely ignorant of the nature of God, we can still call him 'good' and 'just', although these words will no longer have their usual human meanings. Mill was outraged, and said so in one of his rare purple passages. To play fast and loose with the meanings of words, he insisted, is not just intellectually but morally bankrupt.

In many respects, this seizing of the moral high ground by the anti-clerical party represents the heart of the debate over agnosticism. From the beginning, the agnostics appeal explicitly to such moral values as personal integrity, unselfishness, honesty, frankness, humility, and tolerance. The agnostics seek to portray themselves as intellectually honest in following the arguments wherever they may lead, as humble in frankly admitting their limitations, and as tolerant of the weaknesses of their fellow men. The defenders of the established Churches are represented, in sharp contrast, as standing for little more than pride and prejudice.

A few examples must suffice here. Leslie Stephen speaks of a 'sacred duty' to face facts, and accuses the theologians of shirking this duty. The gnostics, he claims, are guilty of the sin of pride; it is we agnostics who honestly admit 'that there are limits to the sphere of human intelligence', and face the consequences of that fact. The Christian Church, argues Huxley, has tried to turn 'honest disbelief' into a *sin* – this is the single greatest fault in Christian doctrine and practice. As for Clifford's famous article, 'The Ethics of Belief', it is one long lay sermon *against* faith. To question and to doubt, Clifford insists, is not a sin but a *duty*; to believe any proposition whatever on inadequate grounds is a sin against mankind. 'It is wrong always, everywhere, and for any one, to believe anything upon insufficient evidence.'

[23]   See Desmond and Moore's *Darwin*, pp. 492–499.

[24]   J. S. Mill, *Examination of Sir William Hamilton's Philosophy*, London, 1865. For perceptive remarks, see David Berman, *A History of Atheism in Britain*, London, Routledge, 1988, pp. 235–247.

The critics of agnosticism must therefore *either* take up arms in defence of faith, *or* insist that the evidence for Christianity really is sufficient after all. Both views are represented in this volume. W. H. Mallock admits that agnostic conclusions (indistinguishable in practice from atheism) follow from agnostic methods (universal doubt), and reacts with a vigorous reaffirmation of faith. Charles Coupe, a Jesuit priest writing in the Catholic *Dublin Review*, insists that the evidence for theism is there in the world all around us. According to the authorities of the Church, God 'has not left himself without witness'; the agnostic is therefore inexcusable and bound inevitably for the flames of Hell.

Unfortunately for the defenders of orthodoxy, this tactic can easily backfire. If the moral credibility of the agnostics is by now assured – if they are widely regarded as intellectually honest and morally upright citizens – then arguments such as that of Coupe will only cast doubt on the authority of Popes, Councils, and even Saint Paul himself! A *just* God, people began to argue, would *not* condemn a man to eternal damnation for honestly expressing his doubts about what, if anything, exists behind the veil of phenomena. Herbert Spencer notes that the moral sentiments of his Victorian contemporaries could no longer accept the traditional doctrine of eternal punishment. In the evolution of religion, he predicts, the notion of hell will be quietly abandoned as an embarrassment by Christian theologians.

S6. The Agnostics.

Six of the contributors to this volume can properly be labelled agnostics. Who were these men, and how did they arrive at their agnosticism?

Herbert Spencer (1820–1903) was one of the intellectual giants of late Victorian Britain.[25] His *First Principles* (1862) is the first part of his monumental ten-volume *System of Synthetic Philosophy*, which presented an evolutionary and naturalistic account of the known universe, taking in biology, psychology, sociology, and even ethics. By confining religion to the realm of the unknowable, Spencer leaves the knowable world free for

---

[25] For Spencer, see his own *Autobiography*, 2 volumes, London, Williams and Norgate, 1904, and Rudolf Metz, *A Hundred Years of British Philosophy*, London, Allen & Unwin, 1938, especially pp. 104–106.

the sciences, and for the higher synthesis offered by his own philosophy. In *First Principles* Spencer argues that the human mind falls inevitably into paradoxes when it tries to address questions about the relation between God and the World. These paradoxes bear a striking relation to Kant's antinomies in his 'Dialectic of Pure Reason';[26] Spencer probably derived them from Hamilton and Mansel. Agnosticism thus appears both as the inevitable result of the failure of metaphysics and as the next phase in the evolution of religion. In the two pieces included here, Spencer argues first that his theory of 'the Unknowable' provides the only workable reconciliation between the claims of science and those of religion; then claims that nineteenth century Christianity is gradually but visibly evolving into agnosticism.

John Tyndall (1820–1893) was an Irish physicist with special interests in heat radiation, optics, and acoustics.[27] In his presidential address before the Belfast meeting of the British Association in 1874, he presented in outline an account of the triumphs of atomism and materialism from Democritus down to Maxwell. Science, Tyndall proclaims, has the right to extend its theories and methods to the whole of Nature. Going beyond Darwin's caution and the *ignorabimus* of Du Bois Reymond, Tyndall suggests that a materialistic explanation of life itself may be possible. Matter contains 'the promise and potency of all terrestrial life'. But what *is* this matter? The phenomena testify to a mysterious and inscrutable power, but tell us nothing about what it is like in itself. Here it is metaphysical reflection on the methods and conclusions of the physical sciences that is leading to agnosticism. Tyndall also seems keen to preserve a role for some sort of non-doctrinal religion in our *emotional* lives.

Leslie Stephen (1832–1904) was one of the great Victorian men of letters – critic, essayist, historian of ideas, and founder of the *Dictionary of National Biography*. Stephen had been ordained a priest in the Church of England, but found himself unable to continue preaching doctrine he could no longer believe, and left the church in 1870. 'An Agnostic's Apology' is, above all else, a plea for intellectual honesty. It is also the only major agnostic

---

26   I. Kant, *Critique of Pure Reason*, 'First Antinomy', pp. 396–402.

27   For Tyndall, see A. S. Eve and C. H. Creasey, *The Life and Work of John Tyndall*, London, Macmillan, 1945.

work to discuss the problem of evil.[28] For Stephen, the metaphysical doctrines of Christianity were obviously fantastic and unreal, but it was not the metaphysics that really mattered. Written shortly after the death of his first wife, the article focuses sharply on the *failure* of orthodox Christian doctrine to provide emotional support and solace to the suffering and the distressed. What is the use of talking of 'the sure and certain hope of the Resurrection to come', when no honest and intelligent person can have such certainty? Many churchmen, Stephen argued, are now agnostics in all but name: they should say so frankly and honestly.

William Kingdom Clifford (1845-1879) was a precociously gifted mathematician who became professor at University College London in 1871, but died of tuberculosis while still in his 30s. His *Lectures and Essays* were collected and edited after his death by Leslie Stephen and Frederick Pollock.[29] In 'The Ethics of Belief' Clifford delights in turning the tables against his clerical opponents and representing them as profoundly immoral, and the much vaunted theological virtue of faith as a dangerous and anti-social vice. The famous article, 'The Will to Believe', by the American pragmatist William James,[30] is in large part a reply to 'The Ethics of Belief'.

Samuel Laing (1812-1897) was a barrister, an official of the Board of Trade, a Liberal MP, and chairman of the London, Brighton, and South Coast Railway.[31] Although he acknowledged intellectual debts to both Spencer and Huxley, his brand of agnosticism seems closer to the former than to the latter. He clearly thought of agnosticism as a positive doctrine, and was even sympathetic to the notion that there could be such a thing as 'Christian Agnosticism'. Asked by Gladstone to formulate an 'agnostic's creed', Laing came up with a set of eight propositions. Some of these would have been accepted by all our agnostics; but one of them – Laing's own curious

---

[28] For Stephen's agnosticism, see Noel Annan, *Leslie Stephen: the Godless Victorian*, New York, Random House, 1984, Chapter 9, pp. 234-266.

[29] W. K. Clifford, *Lectures and Essays*, 2 Volumes, ed L. Stephen and F. Pollock, London, Macmillan, 1879.

[30] William James, 'The Will to Believe', in *Pragmatism: the Classic Writings*, ed H. S. Thayer, Indianapolis, Hackett, 1982, pp. 186-208.

[31] For Samuel Laing, see Lightman, pp. 143-144.

principle of 'polarity' – was pronounced completely incomprehensible by Huxley.

Thomas Henry Huxley (1825–1895) was a major figure both in the biological sciences and in the popularization of science.[32] He was widely read in science and metaphysics, both in English and in German. The influence of Hume and Kant, Hamilton and Mansel had made him an agnostic even before he became famous – from 1860 – as the great champion of Darwinism in late Victorian Britain. The grounds for Huxley's agnosticism are thus both metaphysical (stemming from Hume and Kant) *and* implicit in his science. The word 'agnostic' was coined by Huxley around 1869, and served him as a convenient label when articulating and defending his views in the lively meetings of the Metaphysical Society. His article 'Agnosticism' explains the origin of the word, and protests against its misuse by Spencer, Laing, and others. It also takes issue with the attacks on agnostics by the positivist Frederick Harrison and the churchman Henry Wace.

S7. The Critics.

John Bernard Dalgairns (1818–1876) was educated at Oxford, where he graduated BA in 1839 and MA in 1842. While at Oxford, he fell under the influence of J. H. Newman, and was received into the Roman Catholic Church in 1845. In 1846 he was admitted to holy orders as a priest of the oratory. Like Newman, Dalgairns saw the world of external nature as largely 'deserted' by God, showing little or no sign of the divine presence. The study of external nature alone, he admitted, might well lead men to agnosticism.[33] But to focus on external nature alone is to ignore a crucial source of evidence. God makes himself manifest to us, Dalgairns insists, in religious and moral experience. Even the atheist feels the pangs of conscience, thus providing an indirect proof of the existence of God. (A moral law requires a lawgiver.) The issue between Dalgairns and his agnostic opponents will thus turn on the

---

[32] For Huxley, see Cyril Bibby, *Scientist Extraordinary: the Life and Scientific Work of Thomas Henry Huxley*, Oxford and New York, Pergamon Press, 1972.

[33] See Lee H. Yearley, *The Ideas of Newman*, Pennsylvania State University Press, 1978, especially Chapter 1, 'Natural Religion'.

adequacy of their purely naturalistic accounts of the origin and – more crucially – the authority of our moral sentiments.[34]

Frederic Harrison (1831–1923) was a lawyer and a prolific writer on a wide variety of political, religious, and cultural subjects. He was also the leading English disciple of Comte in the late nineteenth century, and president of the English Positivist Committee from 1880 to 1905.[35] As a positivist, Harrison was dismissive of the old and – to his mind – completely discredited metaphysics of Christianity. The agnostics, Harrison claims, have dealt a death blow to *theology*. But religion is much more than just theology, and Spencer's attempts to offer agnosticism as a substitute for the Christian religion are dismissed with scorn. A religion, Harrison argues, must play a vital unifying role within a society; it must provide shared meaning and purpose and a sense of community. Judged by this *human* criterion, the worship of 'The Unknowable' is an abject failure. Agnosticism, Harrison concludes, marks a mere transitional phase between the collapse of Christianity and the triumph of the 'Religion of Humanity'. Harrison's attack prompted a lively controversy with Spencer over the respective merits of 'The Unknowable' and 'Humanity' as objects of our religious emotions.[36]

Henry Wace (1836–1924) was an Anglican minister, basically conservative and traditionalist in his theology, who eventually rose to become Dean of Canterbury in 1903. His characterization of the agnostics as mere atheists or infidels, too cowardly to show their true colours, drew Huxley's polemical counterblast in 1889. Wace then replied to Huxley, defending

---

[34] For evolutionary-naturalist accounts of the origin of our moral sentiments, see H. Spencer, *The Data of Ethics*, London, Williams and Norgate, 1879; and L. Stephen, *The Science of Ethics*, London, Smith, Elder, & Co, 1882, reprinted Bristol, Thoemmes, 1991.

[35] See Martha S. Vogeler, *Frederic Harrison: the Vocations of a Positivist*, Oxford, Clarendon, 1984; and T. R. Wright, *The Religion of Humanity: The Impact of Comtean Positivism on Victorian Britain*, Cambridge, C.U.P., 1986.

[36] For Spencer's reply to Harrison, see his 'Retrogressive Religion', *The Nineteenth Century*, Vol XVI, 1884, pp. 3-26. Harrison replied in 'Agnostic Metaphysics', *The Nineteenth Century*, Vol XVI, 1884, pp. 353-378. Spencer came back in turn with 'Last Words about Agnosticism and the Religion of Humanity', *The Nineteenth Century*, Vol XVI, 1884, pp. 826-839.

the Christian revelation against doubters. There can be no doubt, Wace insists, that Jesus Christ lived and died in – and for – his convictions about the nature and reality of the spiritual world. Huxley must therefore regard him as a mere dreamer, a man who lived and died under illusions. It must, Wace thinks, be 'very unpleasant' for anyone to say that he does not believe Christ. The controversy between Wace and Huxley dragged on, but drifted into the realms of Biblical criticism and the reliability of the gospels as records of Christ's life and thought.[37] This is peripheral territory for the agnostic. Huxley could grant that Christ said and did everything (miracles excepted) reported of him in the New Testament, and still ask why he should accept that this particular man had any special knowledge of the spirit world.

William Hurrell Mallock (1849–1923), novelist and essayist, was the son of a Devonshire clergyman, educated first by a private tutor, then at Balliol College Oxford. His *New Republic* (1877) was a series of dialogues, modelled on Plato, on contemporary social and religious issues.[38] By basing his principal characters on such well-known figures as Jowett, Pater, Arnold, and Ruskin, Mallock was able to achieve a considerable literary success. He went on to write on philosophy, theology, and politics, defending private property and the private possession of land against the socialists. He was accepted into the Roman Catholic Church on his deathbed. In his article, 'Cowardly Agnosticism', he insists that the agnostics are, for all practical purposes, atheists, and asks what the consequences of this practical atheism are for conduct. Spencer and Harrison, he notes, at least attempt to provide some positive substitute (however inadequate) for God; Huxley does not. Mallock thinks that an attenuated ethics, based on social utility, will survive the demise of Christianity, but that *ideal* morality will collapse. Huxley is a coward because he refuses to face the terrible fact that his agnosticism has undermined the moral law itself.

---

[37] Wace replied to Huxley with 'Agnosticism: A Reply to Professor Huxley', *The Nineteenth Century*, Vol XXV, 1889, pp. 351-368. Huxley's 'Agnosticism: A Rejoinder' (reprinted in his *Collected Essays*, London, Macmillan, 1897 Volume 5, pp. 262-308) provided a swift reaction; Wace replied again with 'Christianity and Agnosticism', *The Nineteenth Century*, Vol XXV, 1889, pp. 700-721.

[38] W. H. Mallock, *The New Republic*, London, Chatto and Windus, 1877. The early editions appeared anonymously.

Charles Coupe (1853-1910) was a Jesuit priest, author of *Where is the Church?* (1900) and *Lectures on the Holy Eucharist* (1906). In his article in the Catholic *Dublin Review*, he seeks to show that, according to the normal methods of theology - that is, consulting the authority of Scripture, the Church Fathers, Popes, and Councils - the agnostics cannot be in good faith. Their blindness to the Christian evidences must be at least in part wilful, and therefore culpable. Coupe's task is complicated by the presence within the Church of Christians who seem to be essentially in agreement with the agnostics, i.e. who believe that without a special divine gift of grace men are *incapable* of seeing the evidence in Nature for God. Coupe thus has to insist, against such 'traditionalists' and agnostics alike, that the verdict of the Church is that of Saint Paul, that 'God has not left Himself without witness', and that unbelievers are 'fools' and 'inexcusable'. Coupe is even doubtful of the claim that the agnostics are morally upright men: in practice, he thinks, agnosticism must lead either to pessimism or to Epicureanism.

William Barry (1849-1930) was another Catholic priest, educated first at Birmingham and then in Rome. He was ordained in Rome, and was present at the Vatican Council of 1870. He then returned to England, and became professor of philosophy at the Birmingham theological college from 1873 to 1877. He was a prolific author, writing about eighty periodical articles as well as more substantial works of philosophy and theology. Barry cites Spencer, Darwin, Tyndall, and Huxley as the four prophets of the 'gospel of unbelief', but it is Huxley who provides his primary target. Huxley is accused of misunderstanding the implications of his own science. It is only superficial minds, in Barry's view, who see an antagonism between science and religion. Science *assumes* a rational and comprehensible order; religion explains this order as the product of intelligence. Darwin's theory of evolution by natural selection, for example, refutes only the crudest forms of natural theology. Teleology is displaced but not abandoned; evolution still testifies to God. Instead of an *ignoramus*, science itself must ultimately issue in a *te deum*. As regards the soul, Barry argues, Huxley falls into even deeper confusions. His science is pure materialism; his official philosophy is idealist; he never manages to overcome the ensuing contradictions. But it is in ethics, Barry insists, that Huxley's creed fails altogether. Huxley's ethics is based on the 'social sanction', but this is unequal to the task. Without a transcendental support, the bonds of morality will become feeble and mere self-indulgence reign.

James Ward (1843–1925) was a philosopher and psychologist, a fellow of Trinity College Cambridge from 1875, and professor of mental philosophy and logic at Cambridge from 1897. He came from a Congregationalist family, and was brought up a strict Calvinist, educated for the Nonconformist ministry in England and Germany. He later broke with established religion, though he remained fundamentally sympathetic to religion and hostile to atheism and agnosticism. In his Gifford Lectures, *Naturalism and Agnosticism*, delivered at the University of Aberdeen between 1895 and 1898, he argued that scientific naturalism and religious agnosticism were, when thought through, really incompatible in their fundamental assumptions.[39] If the materialist picture of the world offered by Huxley and Tyndall were ever to be *completed*, he asked, would there not be an irresistible impulse to conclude that that was all there was? Or, to put the same question the other way round, can one assert that souls are real, yet then add that their existence makes no difference to anything we can observe and measure? The very idea of a sharp demarcation between the knowable and the unknowable (but nevertheless equally real) is dismissed by Ward as a fundamental error.[40] Science, he goes on to argue, does *not* lead to the materialistic naturalism of Huxley. Physics deals in mere abstractions; reality is knowable but is spiritual in nature. Ward is thus led eventually to a metaphysical monadism akin in some respects to that of Leibniz. You may drive metaphysics out with a pitchfork, but she will return!

Andrew Pyle
University of Bristol
October 1994

[39]   James Ward, *Naturalism and Agnosticism*, The Gifford Lectures for 1896–1898, 2 volumes, London, Adam and Charles Black, 1899.

[40]   For similar criticisms of any attempt to draw a sharp distinction between 'the knowable' and 'the unknowable', see Henry Sidgwick, *Lectures on the Philosophy of Kant*, especially his assault on Spencer's metaphysics and epistemology at p. 267ff.

THE RECONCILIATION
[Herbert Spencer]

§27. Thus do all lines of argument converge to the same conclusion. Those imbecilities of the understanding which disclose themselves when we try to answer the highest questions of objective science, subjective science proves to be necessitated by the laws of that understanding. Finally, we discover that this conclusion which, in its unqualified form, seems opposed to the instinctive convictions of mankind, falls into harmony with them when the missing qualification is supplied.

Here, then, is that basis of agreement we set out to seek. This conclusion which objective science illustrates and subjective science shows to be unavoidable, – this conclusion which brings the results of speculation into harmony with those of common sense; is also the conclusion which reconciles Religion with Science. Common Sense asserts the existence of a reality; Objective Science proves that this reality cannot be what we think it; Subjective Science shows why we cannot think of it as it is, and yet are compelled to think of it as existing; and in this assertion of a Reality utterly inscrutable in nature, Religion finds an assertion essentially coinciding with her own. We are obliged to regard every phenomenon as a manifestation of some Power by which we are acted upon; though Omnipresence is unthinkable, yet, as experience discloses no bounds to the diffusion of phenomena, we are unable to think of limits to the presence of this Power; while the criticisms of Science teach us that this Power is Incomprehensible. And this consciousness of an Incomprehensible Power, called Omnipresent from inability to assign its limits, is just that consciousness on which Religion dwells.

To understand fully how real is the reconciliation thus reached, it will be needful to look at the respective attitudes that Religion and Science have all along maintained towards this conclusion.

§28. In its earliest and crudest forms Religion manifested, however vaguely and inconsistently, an intuition forming the germ of this highest belief in which philosophies finally unite. The consciousness of a mystery is traceable in the rudest ghost theory. Each higher creed, rejecting those definite and simple interpretations of Nature previously given, has become more religious by doing this. As the concrete and conceivable agencies assigned as the causes of things, have been replaced by agencies less concrete and conceivable, the element of mystery has necessarily become more predominant. Through all its phases the disappearance of those dogmas by which the mystery was made unmysterious, has formed the essential change delineated in religious history. And so Religion has been approaching towards that complete recognition of this mystery which is its goal.

For its essentially valid belief Religion has constantly done battle. Gross as were the disguises under which it first espoused this belief, and cherishing this belief, even still, under disfiguring vestments, it has never ceased to maintain and defend it. Though from age to age Science has continually defeated it wherever they have come in collision, and has obliged it to relinquish one or more of its positions, it has held the remaining ones with undiminished tenacity. After criticism has abolished its arguments, there has still remained with it the indestructible consciousness of a truth which, however faulty the mode in which it had been expressed, is yet a truth beyond cavil.

But while from the beginning, Religion has had the all-essential office of preventing men from being wholly absorbed in the relative or immediate, and of awakening them to a consciousness of something beyond it, this office has been but very imperfectly discharged. In its early stages the consciousness of supernature being simply the consciousness of numerous supernatural persons essentially manlike, was not far removed from the ordinary consciousness. As thus constituted, Religion was and has ever been more or less irreligious; and indeed continues to be largely irreligious even now. In the first place (restricting ourselves to Religion in its more developed form), it has all along professed to have some knowledge of that which transcends knowledge, and has so contradicted its own teachings. While with one breath it has asserted that the Cause of all things passes understanding, it has, with the next breath, asserted that the Cause of all things possesses such or such attributes – can be in so far understood. In the second place, while in great part sincere in its fealty to the great truth it has had to uphold, it has often been insincere, and consequently irreligious, in maintaining the untenable doctrines by which it has obscured this great truth. Each assertion respecting the nature, acts, or motives of that Power which the Universe manifests to us, has been repeatedly called in question, and proved to be inconsistent with itself, or with accompanying assertions. Yet each of them has been age after age insisted on. Just as though unaware that its central position was impregnable, Religion has obstinately held every outpost long after it was obviously indefensible. And this introduces us to the third and most serious form of irreligion which Religion has displayed; namely, an imperfect belief in that which it especially professes to believe. How truly its central position *is* impregnable, Religion has never adequately realized. In the devoutest faith as we commonly see it, there lies hidden a core of scepticism; and it is this scepticism which causes that dread of inquiry shown by Religion when face to face with Science. Obliged to abandon one by one the superstitions it once tenaciously held, and daily finding other cherished beliefs more and more shaken, Religion secretly fears that all things may some day be explained; and thus itself betrays a lurking doubt whether that Incomprehensible Cause of which it is conscious, is really incomprehensible.

Of Religion then, we must always remember, that amid its many errors and corruptions it has asserted and diffused a supreme verity. From the first, the recognition of this supreme verity, in however imperfect a manner, has been its vital element; and its chief defects, once extreme but gradually diminishing, have been its failures to recognize in full that which it recognized in part. The truly religious element of Religion has always been good; that which has proved untenable in doctrine and vicious in practice, has been its irreligious element; and from this it has been undergoing purification.

§29. And now observe that the agent which has effected the purification has been Science. On both sides this fact is overlooked. Religion ignores its immense debt to Science; and Science is scarcely at all conscious how much Religion owes it.

Yet it is demonstrable that every step by which Religion has progressed from its first low conception to the comparatively high one now reached, Science has helped it, or rather forced it, to take; and that even now, Science is urging further steps in the same direction.

When we include under the name Science all definite knowledge of the order existing among phenomena, it becomes manifest that from the outset, the discovery of an established order has modified that conception of disorder, or undetermined order, which underlies every superstition. As fast as experience proves that certain familiar changes always present the same sequences, there begins to fade from the mind the conception of special personalities to whose variable wills they were before ascribed. And when, step by step, accumulating observations do the like with the less familiar changes, a similar modification of belief takes place respecting them.

While this process seems to those who effect it, and those who undergo it, an anti-religious one, it is really the reverse. Instead of the specific comprehensible agency before assigned, there is substituted a less specific and less comprehensible agency; and though this, standing in opposition to the previous one, cannot at first call forth the same feeling, yet, as being less comprehensible, it must eventually call forth this feeling more fully. Take an instance. Of old the Sun was regarded as the chariot of a god, drawn by horses. How far the idea thus grossly expressed was idealized, we need not inquire. It suffices to remark that this accounting for the apparent motion of the Sun by an agency like certain visible terrestrial agencies, reduced a daily wonder to the level of the commonest intellect. When, many centuries after, Copernicus having enunciated the heliocentric theory of the solar system, Kepler discovered that the orbits of the planets are ellipses, and that the planets describe equal areas in equal times, he concluded that in each of them there must exist a spirit to guide its movements. Here we see that with the progress of Science, there had disappeared the idea of a gross mechanical traction, such as was first assigned in the case of the Sun; but that while for the celestial motions there was substituted a less-easily conceivable force, it was still thought needful to assume personal agents as causes of the regular irregularity of the motions. When, finally, it was proved that these planetary revolutions with all their variations and disturbances, conform to one universal law – when the presiding spirits which Kepler conceived were set aside, and the force of gravitation put in their places; the change was really the abolition of an imaginable agency, and the substitution of an unimaginable one. For though the *law* of gravitation is within our mental grasp, it is impossible to realize in thought the *force* of gravitation. Newton himself confessed the force of gravitation to be incomprehensible without the intermediation of an ether; and, as we have already seen, (§ 18,) the assumption of an ether does not help us. Thus it is with Science in general. Its progress in grouping particular relations of phenomena under laws, and these special laws under laws more and more general, is of necessity a progress to causes more and more abstract. And causes more and more abstract, are of necessity causes less and less conceivable; since the formation of an abstract conception involves the dropping of certain concrete elements of thought. Hence the most abstract conception, to which Science is slowly approaching, is one that merges into the inconceivable or unthinkable, by the dropping of all concrete elements of thought. And so is justified the assertion that the beliefs which Science has forced upon Religion, have been intrinsically more religious than those which they supplanted.

Science, however, like Religion, has but very incompletely fulfilled its office. As Religion has fallen short of its function in so far as it has been irreligious; so has Science fallen short of its function in so far as it has been unscientific. Let us note the several parallelisms. In its earlier stages Science, while it began to teach the constant relations of phenomena, and thus discredited the belief in separate personalities as the causes of them, itself substituted the belief in causal agencies which, if not personal, were yet concrete. When certain facts were said to show "Nature's abhorrence of a vacuum," when the properties of gold were explained as due to some entity called "aureity," and when the phenomena of life were attributed to "a vital principle"; there was set up a mode of interpreting the facts which, while antagonistic to the religious mode, because assigning other agencies was also unscientific, because it assumed a knowledge of that about which nothing was known. Having abandoned these metaphysical agencies – having seen that they are not independent existences, but merely special combinations of general causes, Science has more recently ascribed extensive groups of phenomena to electricity, chemical affinity, and other like general powers. But in speaking of these as ultimate and independent entities, Science has preserved substantially the same attitude as before. Accounting thus for all phenomena, it has not only maintained its seeming antagonism to Religion, by alleging agencies of a radically unlike kind; but, in so far as it has tacitly implied its comprehension of these agencies, it has continued unscientific. At the present time, however, the most advanced men of science are abandoning these later conceptions, as their predecessors abandoned the earlier ones. Magnetism, heat, light, &c., which were early in the century spoken of as so many distinct imponderables, physicists now regard as different modes of manifestation of some one universal force; and in so regarding them are ceasing to think of this force as comprehensible. In each phase of its progress, Science has thus stopped short with superficial solutions – has unscientifically neglected to ask what were the natures of the agents it familiarly invoked. Though in each succeeding phase it has gone a little deeper, and merged its supposed agents in more general and abstract ones, it has still, as before, rested content with these as if they were ascertained realities. And this, which has all along been an unscientific characteristic of Science, has all along been a part-cause of its conflict with Religion.

§30. Thus from the outset the faults of both Religion and Science have been the faults of imperfect development. Originally a mere rudiment, each has been growing more complete; the vice of each has in all times been its incompleteness; the disagreements between them have been consequences of their incompleteness; and as they reach their final forms they come into harmony.

The progress of intelligence has throughout been dual. Though it has not seemed so to those who made it, every step in advance has been a step towards both the natural and the supernatural. The better interpretation of each phenomenon has been, on the one hand, the rejection of a cause that was relatively conceivable in its nature but unknown in the order of its actions, and, on the other hand, the adoption of a cause that was known in the order of its actions but relatively inconceivable in its nature. The first advance involved the conception of agencies less assimilable to the familiar agencies of men and animals, and therefore less understood; while, at the same time, such newly-conceived agencies, in so far as they were distinguished by their uniform effects, were better understood than those they replaced. All subsequent advances display the same double result; and thus the progress has been as much towards the establishment of a positively unknown as towards the establishment of a positively known. Though as knowledge advances, unaccountable and seemingly supernatural facts are brought into the category of facts that are accountable or natural; yet, at the same time, all accountable or natural facts are proved to be in their ultimate genesis unaccountable and supernatural. And so there arise two antithetical states of mind, answering to the opposite sides of that existence about which we think. While our consciousness of Nature under the one aspect constitutes Science, our consciousness of it under the other aspect constitutes Religion.

In other words, Religion and Science have been undergoing a slow differentiation, and their conflicts have been due to the imperfect separation of their spheres and functions. Religion has, from the first, struggled to unite more or less science with its nescience; Science has, from the first, kept hold of more or less nescience as though it were a part of science. So long as the process of differentiation is incomplete, more or less of antagonism must continue. Gradually as the limits of possible cognition are established, the causes of conflict will diminish. And a permanent peace will be reached when Science becomes fully convinced that its explanations are proximate and relative, while Religion becomes fully convinced that the mystery it contemplates is ultimate and absolute.

Religion and Science are therefore necessary correlatives. To carry further a metaphor before used, – they are the positive and negative poles of thought; of which neither can gain in intensity without increasing the intensity of the other.

§31. Some do indeed allege that though the Ultimate Cause of things cannot really be conceived by us as having specified attributes, it is yet incumbent upon us to assert those attributes. Though the forms of our consciousness are such that the Absolute cannot in any manner or degree be brought within them, we are nevertheless told that we must represent the Absolute to ourselves as having certain characters. As writes Mr. Mansel, in the work from which I have already quoted largely – "It is our duty, then, to think of God as personal; and it is our duty to believe that He is infinite."

Now if there be any meaning in the foregoing arguments, duty requires us neither to affirm nor deny personality. Our duty is to submit ourselves to the established limits of our intelligence, and not perversely to rebel against them. Let those who can, believe that there is eternal war set between our intellectual faculties and our moral obligations. I, for one, admit no such radical vice in the constitutions of things.

This which to most will seem an essentially irreligious position, is an essentially religious one – nay is *the* religious one, to which, as already shown, all others are but approximations. In the estimate it implies of the Ultimate Cause, it does not fall short of the alternative position, but exceeds it. Those who espouse this alternative position, assume that the choice is between personality and something lower than personality; whereas the choice is rather between personality and something that may be higher. Is it not possible that there is a mode of being as much transcending Intelligence and Will, as these transcend mechanical motion? Doubtless we are totally unable to imagine any such higher mode of being. But this is not a reason for questioning its existence; it is rather the reverse. Have we not seen how utterly unable our minds are to form even an approach to a conception of that which underlies all phenomena? Is it not proved that we fail because of the incompetency of the Conditioned to grasp the Unconditioned? Does it not follow that the Ultimate Cause cannot in any respect be conceived because it is in every respect greater than can be conceived? And may we not therefore rightly refrain from assigning to it any attributes whatever, on the ground that such attributes, derived as they must be from our own natures, are not elevations but degradations? Indeed it seems strange that men should suppose the highest worship to lie in assimilating the object of their worship to themselves. Not in asserting a transcendent difference, but in asserting a certain likeness, consists the element of their creed which they think essential. It is true that from the time when the rudest savages imagined the causes of things to be persons like themselves but invisible, down to our own time, the degree of assumed likeness has been diminishing. But though a bodily form and substance similar to that of man, has long since ceased, among cultivated races, to be a literally-conceived attribute of the Ultimate Cause – though the grosser human desires have been also rejected as unfit elements of the conception – though there is some hesitation in ascribing even the higher human feelings, save in idealized shapes; yet it is still thought not only proper, but imperative, to ascribe the most abstract qualities of our nature. To think of the Creative Power as in all respects anthropomorphous, is now considered impious by men who yet hold themselves bound to think of the Creative Power as in some respects anthropomorphous; and who do not see that the one proceeding is but an evanescent form of the other. And then, most marvellous of all, this course is persisted in even by those who contend that we are wholly unable to frame any conception whatever of the Creative Power. After it has been shown that every supposition respecting the genesis of the Universe commits us to alternative impossibilities of thought – after it has been shown why, by the very constitution of our minds, we are debarred from thinking of the Absolute; it is still asserted that we ought to think of the Absolute thus and thus. In all ways we find thrust on us the truth, that we are not permitted to know – nay are not even permitted to conceive – that Reality which is behind the veil of Appearance; and yet it is said to be our duty to believe (and in so far to conceive) that this Reality exists in a certain defined manner. Shall we call this reverence? or shall we call it the reverse?

Volumes might be written upon the impiety of the pious. Through the printed and spoken thoughts of religious teachers, may everywhere be traced a professed familiarity with the ultimate mystery of things, which, to say the least of it, is anything but congruous with the accompanying expressions of humility. The attitude thus assumed can be fitly represented only by further developing a simile long current in theological controversies – the simile of the watch. If for a moment we made the grotesque supposition that the tickings and other movements of a watch constituted a kind of consciousness; and that a watch possessed of such a consciousness, insisted on regarding the watchmaker's actions as determined like its own by springs and escapements; we should simply complete a parallel of which religious teachers think much. And were we to suppose that a watch not only formulated the cause of its existence in these mechanical terms, but held that watches were bound out of reverence so to formulate this cause, and even vituperated, as atheistic watches, any that did not venture so to formulate it; we should merely illustrate the presumption of

theologians by carrying their own argument a step further. A few
extracts will bring home to the reader the justice of this
comparison. We are told, for example, by one of high repute
among religious thinkers, that the Universe is "the manifestation
and abode of a Free Mind, like our own; embodying His personal
thought in its adjustments, realizing His own ideal in its
phenomena, just as we express our inner faculty and character
through the natural language of an external life. In this view, we
interpret Nature by Humanity; we find the key to her aspects in
such purposes and affections as our own consciousness enables us
to conceive; we look everywhere for physical signals of an ever-
living Will; and decipher the universe as the autobiography of an
Infinite Spirit, repeating itself in miniature within our Finite
Spirit." The same writer goes still further. He not only thus
parallels the assimilation of the watchmaker to the watch, – he
not only thinks the created can "decipher" "the autobiography" of
the Creating; but he asserts that the necessary limits to the one
are necessary limits to the other. The primary qualities of bodies,
he says, "belong eternally to the material datum objective to
God" and control his acts; while the secondary ones are
"products of pure Inventive Reason and Determining Will" –
constitute "the realm of Divine originality." * * * "While on this
Secondary field His Mind and ours are thus contrasted, they meet
in resemblance again upon the Primary; for the evolutions of
deductive Reason there is but one track possible to all
intelligences; no *merum arbitrium* can interchange the false and
true, or make more than one geometry, one scheme of pure
Physics, for all worlds; and the Omnipotent Architect Himself, in
realizing the Kosmical conception, in shaping the orbits out of
immensity and determining seasons out of eternity, could but
follow the laws of curvature, measure and proportion." That is
to say, the Ultimate Cause is like a human mechanic, not only as
"shaping" the "material datum objective to" Him, but also as
being obliged to conform to the necessary properties of that
datum. Nor is this all. There follows some account of "the Divine
psychology," to the extent of saying that "we learn" "the
character of God – the order of affections in Him" from "the
distribution of authority in the hierarchy of our impulses." In
other words, it is alleged that the Ultimate Cause has desires that
are to be classed as higher and lower like our own.[1] Every

---

[1]   These extracts are from an article entitled "Nature and God," published in
the *National Review* for October, 1860, by Dr. Martineau.

one has heard of the king who wished he had been present at the creation of the world, that he might have given good advice. He was humble, however, compared with those who profess to understand not only the relation of the Creating to the created, and also how the Creating is constituted. And yet this transcendent audacity, which thinks to penetrate the secrets of the Power manifested through all existence – nay, even to stand behind that Power and note the conditions to its action – this it is which passes current as piety! May we not affirm that a sincere recognition of the truth that our own and all other existence is a mystery absolutely beyond our comprehension, contains more of true religion than all the dogmatic theology ever written?

Meanwhile let us recognize whatever of permanent good there is in these persistent attempts to frame conceptions of that which cannot be conceived. From the beginning it has been only through the successive failures of such conceptions to satisfy the mind, that higher and higher ones have been gradually reached; and doubtless, the conceptions now current are indispensable as transitional modes of thought. Even more than this may be willingly conceded. It is possible, nay probable, that under their most abstract forms, ideas of this order will always continue to occupy the background of our consciousness. Very likely there will ever remain a need to give shape to that indefinite sense of an Ultimate Existence, which forms the basis of our intelligence. We shall always be under the necessity of contemplating it as *some* mode of being; that is – of representing it to ourselves in *some* form of thought, however vague. And we shall not err in doing this so long as we treat every notion we thus frame as merely a symbol. Perhaps the constant formation of such symbols and constant rejection of them as inadequate, may be hereafter, as it has hitherto been, a means of discipline. Perpetually to construct ideas requiring the utmost stretch of our faculties, and perpetually to find that such ideas must be abandoned as futile imaginations, may realize to us more fully than any other course, the greatness of that which we vainly strive to grasp. By continually seeking to know and being continually thrown back with a deepened conviction of the impossibility of knowing, we may keep alive the consciousness that it is alike our highest wisdom and our highest duty to regard that through which all things exist as The Unknowable.

§32. An immense majority will refuse, with more or less of indignation, a belief seeming to them so shadowy and indefinite. "You offer us," they will say, "an unthinkable abstraction in place of a Being towards whom we may entertain definite feelings. Though we are told that the Absolute is the only reality, yet since we are not allowed to conceive it, it might as well be a pure negation. Instead of a Power which we can regard as having some sympathy with us, you would have us contemplate a Power to which no emotion whatever can be ascribed. And so we are to be deprived of the very substance of our faith."

This kind of protest of necessity accompanies every change from a lower creed to a higher. The belief in a community of nature between himself and the object of his worship, has always been to Man a satisfactory one; and he has always accepted with reluctance those successively less concrete conceptions which have been forced upon him. Doubtless, in all times and places, it has consoled the barbarian to think of his deities as so like himself in nature, that they might be bribed by offerings of food; and the assurance that deities could not be so propitiated must have been repugnant, because it deprived him of an easy method of gaining supernatural protection. To the Greeks it was manifestly a source of comfort that on occasions of difficulty they could obtain, through oracles, the advice of their gods, - nay, might even get the personal aid of their gods in battle; and it was probably a very genuine anger which they visited upon philosophers who called in question these gross ideas of their mythology. A religion which teaches the Hindoo that it is impossible to purchase eternal happiness by placing himself under the wheel of Juggernaut, can scarcely fail to seem a cruel one to him; since it deprives him of the pleasurable consciousness that he can at will exchange miseries for joys. Nor is it less clear that to our Catholic ancestors, the beliefs that crimes could be compounded for by the building of churches, that their own punishments and those of their relatives could be abridged by the saying of masses, and that divine aid or forgiveness might be gained through the intercession of saints, were highly solacing ones; and that Protestantism, in substituting the conception of a God so comparatively unlike themselves as not to be influenced by such methods, must have appeared hard and cold. Naturally, therefore, we must expect a further step in the same direction to meet with a similar resistance from outraged sentiments. No mental revolution can be accomplished without more or less laceration. Be it a change of habit or a change of conviction, it must, if the habit or conviction be strong, do violence to some of the feelings; and these must of course oppose it. For long-experienced, and therefore definite, sources of satisfaction, have to be substituted sources of satisfaction that have not been experienced, and are therefore indefinite. That which is relatively well known and real, has to be given up for that which is relatively unknown and ideal. And of course such an exchange cannot be made without a conflict involving pain. Especially, then, must there arise a strong antagonism to any alteration in so deep and vital a conception as that with which we are here dealing. Underlying, as this conception does, all ideas concerning the established order of things, a modification of it threatens to reduce the superstructure to ruins. Or to change the metaphor – being the root with which are connected our ideas of goodness, rectitude, or duty, it appears impossible that it should be transformed without causing these to wither away and die. The whole higher part of the nature takes up arms against a change which seems to eradicate morality.

This is by no means all that has to be said for such protests. There is a deeper meaning in them. They do not simply express the natural repugnance to a revolution of belief, here made specially intense by the vital importance of the belief to be revolutionized; but they also express an instinctive adhesion to a belief that is in one sense the best – the best for those who thus cling to it, though not abstractedly the best. For here it is to be remarked that what were above spoken of as the imperfections of Religion, at first great but gradually diminishing, have been imperfections as measured by an absolute standard, and not as measured by a relative one. Speaking generally, the religion current in each age and among each people, has been as near an approximation to the truth as it was then and there possible for men to receive. The concrete forms in which it has embodied the truth, have been the means of making thinkable what would otherwise have been unthinkable; and so have for the time being served to increase its impressiveness. If we consider the conditions of the case, we shall find this to be an unavoidable conclusion. During each stage of progress men must think in such terms of thought as they possess. While all the conspicuous changes of which they can observe the origins, have men and animals as antecedents, they are unable to think of antecedents in general under any other shapes; and hence creative agencies are almost of necessity conceived by them in these shapes. If, during this phase, these concrete conceptions were taken from them and the attempt made to give them comparatively abstract conceptions, the result would be to leave their minds with none at all; since the substituted ones could not be mentally represented. Similarly with every successive stage of religious belief, down to the last. Though, as accumulating experiences slowly modify the earliest ideas of causal personalities, there grow up more general and vague ideas of them; yet these cannot be at once replaced by others still more general and vague. Further experiences must supply the needful further abstractions, before the mental void left by the destruction of such inferior ideas can be filled by ideas of a superior order. And at the present time, the refusal to abandon a relatively concrete consciousness for a relatively abstract one, implies the inability to frame the relatively abstract one; and so implies that the change would be premature and injurious. Still more clearly shall we see the injuriousness of any such premature change, on observing that the effects of a belief upon conduct must be diminished in proportion as the vividness with which it is realized becomes less. Evils and benefits akin to those which the savage has personally felt, or learned from those who have felt them, are the only evils and benefits he can understand; and these must be looked for as coming in ways like those of which he has had experience. His deities must be imagined to have like motives and passions and methods with the beings around him; for motives and passions and methods of a higher character, being unknown to him, and in great measure unthinkable by him, cannot be so represented in thought as to influence his deeds. During every phase of civilization, the actions of the Unseen Reality, as well as the resulting rewards and punishments, being conceivable only in such forms as experience furnishes, to supplant them by higher ones before wider experiences have made higher ones conceivable, is to set up vague and uninfluential motives for definite and influential ones. Even now, for the great mass of men, unable to trace out with clearness those good and bad consequences which conduct brings round through the established order of things, it is well that there should be depicted future punishments and future joys – pains and pleasures of definite kinds, produced in ways direct and simple enough to be clearly imagined. Nay still more must be conceded. Few are as yet wholly fitted to dispense with such conceptions as are current. The highest abstractions take so great a mental power to realize with any vividness, and are so inoperative on conduct unless they are vividly realized, that their regulative effects must for a long period to come be appreciable on but a small minority. To see clearly how a right or wrong act generates consequences, internal and external, that go on branching out more widely as years progress, requires a rare power of analysis. And to estimate these consequences in their totality requires a grasp of thought possessed by none. Were it not that throughout the progress of the race, men's experiences of the effects of conduct have been slowly generalized into principles – were it not that these principles have been from generation to generation insisted on by parents, upheld by public opinion, sanctified by religion, and enforced by threats of eternal damnation for disobedience – were it not that under these potent influences habits have been modified, and the feelings proper to them made innate; disastrous results would follow the removal of those strong and distinct motives which the current belief supplies. Even as it is, those who relinquish the faith in which they have been brought up, for this most abstract faith in which Science and Religion unite, may not uncommonly fail to act up to their convictions. Left to their organic morality, enforced only be general reasonings difficult to keep before the mind, their defects of nature will often come out more strongly than they would have done under their previous creed. The substituted creed can become adequately operative only when it becomes, like the present one, an element in early education, and has the support of a strong social sanction. Nor will men be quite ready for it until, through the continuance of a discipline which has partially moulded them to the conditions of social existence, they are completely moulded to those conditions.

We must therefore recognize the resistance to a change of theological opinion, as in great measure salutary. Forms of religion, like forms of government, must be fit for those who live under them; and in the one case as in the other, the form which is fittest is that for which there is an instinctive preference. As a barbarous race needs a harsh terrestrial rule, and shows attachment to a despotism capable of the necessary rigour; so does such a race need a belief in a celestial rule that is similarly harsh, and shows attachment to such a belief. And as the sudden substitution of free institutions for despotic ones, is sure to be followed by a reaction; so, if a creed full of dreadful ideal penalties is all at once replaced by one presenting ideal penalties that are comparatively gentle, there will inevitably be a return to some modification of the old belief. The parallelism holds yet further. During those early stages in which there is extreme incongruity between the relatively best and the absolutely best, both political and religious changes, when at rare intervals they occur, are violent; and they entail violent retrogressions. But as the incongruity between that which is and that which should be, diminishes, the changes become more moderate, and are succeeded by more moderate counter-movements; until, as these movements and counter-movements decrease in amount and increase in frequency, they merge into an almost continuous growth. This holds true of religious creeds and forms, as of civil ones. And so we learn that theological conservatism, like political conservatism, has an important function.

§33. That spirit of toleration which is so marked a trait of modern times, has thus a deeper meaning than is supposed. What we commonly regard simply as a due respect for the right of private judgment, is really a necessary condition to the balancing of the progressive and conservative tendencies – is a means of maintaining the adaptation between men's beliefs and their natures. It is therefore a spirit to be fostered; and especially by the catholic thinker, who perceives the functions of these conflicting creeds. Doubtless whoever feels the greatness of the error his fellows cling to and the greatness of the truth they reject, will find it hard to show a due patience. It is hard to listen calmly to the futile arguments used in support of irrational doctrines, and to the misrepresentations of antagonist doctrines. It is hard to bear the display of that pride of ignorance which so far exceeds the pride of science. Naturally such a one will be indignant when charged with irreligion because he declines to accept the carpenter theory of creation as the most worthy one. He may think it needless, as it is difficult, to conceal his repugnance to a creed which tacitly ascribes to The Unknowable a love of adulation such as would be despised in a human being. Convinced as he is that pain, as we see it in the order of nature, is an aid to the average welfare, there will perhaps escape from him an angry condemnation of the belief that punishment is a divine vengeance, and that divine vengeance is eternal. He may be tempted to show his contempt when he is told that actions instigated by an unselfish sympathy or by a pure love of rectitude, are intrinsically sinful; and that conduct is truly good only when it is due to a faith whose openly-professed motive is other-worldliness. But he must restrain such feelings. Though he may be unable to do this during the excitement of controversy, he must yet qualify his antagonism in calmer moments; so that his mature judgment and resulting conduct may be without bias.

To this end let him bear in mind three cardinal facts – two of them already dwelt on, and one still to be pointed out. The first is that with which we commenced; namely, the existence of a fundamental verity under all forms of religion, however degraded. In each of them there is a soul of truth. The second, set forth at length in the foregoing section, is that while those concrete elements in which each creed embodies this soul of truth are bad as measured by an absolute standard, they are good as measured by a relative standard. The remaining one is that these various beliefs are parts of the constituted order of things, and, if not in their special forms yet in their general forms, necessary parts. Seeing how one or other of them is everywhere present, is of perennial growth, and when cut down redevelops in a form but slightly modified, we cannot avoid the inference that they are needful accompaniments of human life, severally fitted to the societies in which they are indigenous. We must recognize them as elements in that great evolution of which the beginning and end are beyond our knowledge or conception – as modes of manifestation of The Unknowable, and as having this for their warrant.

Our toleration therefore should be the widest possible. In dealing with alien beliefs our endeavour must be, not simply to refrain from injustice of word or deed, but also to do justice by an open recognition of positive worth. We must qualify our disagreement with as much as may be of sympathy.

§34. These admissions will perhaps be held to imply that the current theology should be passively accepted, or, at any rate, should not be actively opposed. "Why," it may be asked, "if creeds are severally fit for their times and places, should we not rest content with that to which we are born? If the established belief contains an essential truth – if the forms under which it presents this truth, though intrinsically bad, are extrinsically good – if the abolition of these forms would be at present detrimental to the great majority – nay, if there are scarcely any to whom the ultimate and most abstract belief can furnish an adequate rule of life; surely it is wrong, for the present at least, to propagate this ultimate and most abstract belief."

The reply is that though existing religious ideas and institutions have an average adaptation to the characters of the people who live under them, yet, as these characters are ever changing, the adaptation is ever becoming imperfect; and the ideas and institutions need remodelling with a frequency proportionate to the rapidity of the change. Hence, while it is requisite that free play should be given to conservative thought and action, progressive thought and action must also have free play. Without the agency of both there cannot be those continual re-adaptations which orderly progress demands.

Whoever hesitates to utter that which he thinks the highest truth, lest it should be too much in advance of the time, may reassure himself by looking at his acts from an impersonal point of view. Let him remember that opinion is the agency through which character adapts external arrangements to itself, and that his opinion rightly forms part of this agency – is a unit of force constituting, with other such units, the general power which works out social changes; and he will perceive that he may properly give utterance to his innermost conviction: leaving it to produce what effect it may. It is not for nothing that he has in him these sympathies with some principles and repugnance to others. He, with all his capacities, and aspirations, and beliefs, is not an accident but a product of the time. While he is a descendant of the past he is a parent of the future; and his thoughts are as children born to him, which he may not carelessly let die. Like every other man he may properly consider himself as one of the myriad agencies through whom works the Unknown Cause; and when the Unknown Cause produces in him a certain belief, he is thereby authorized to profess and act out that belief. For, to render in their highest sense the words of the poet –

——————— Nature is made better by no mean,
But nature makes that mean: over that art
Which you say adds to nature, is an art
That nature makes.

Not as adventitious therefore will the wise man regard the faith
which is in him. The highest truth he sees he will fearlessly
utter; knowing that, let what may come of it, he is thus playing
his right part in the world – knowing that if he can effect the
change he aims at – well; if not – well also; though not *so* well.

IS GOD UNKNOWABLE?
[John Bernard Dalgairns]

We have never heard in this society[1] any one assert, "There is no God." We have, however, very often heard that God is unknowable. The mouths of the advocates of Theism are thus stopped at once, and God is thrust out of court. This disability, however, God shares with many things. He is only a portion of the great Unknowable, of which, as I must be brief, I will say at once that to me it is very unintelligible. The curious thing is that the Unknowable, in the system to which I refer, takes precisely the place of the Infinite and the Absolute in other systems. Nay, it is the Absolute. The argument by which the impossibility of knowledge is asserted is the hopeless relativity of the human intellect. The Unknowable, then, is such, because it is the Absolute. It is printed in capital letters. It is mentioned with bated breath. Now, I cannot understand total blindness in such a case. Blind men are not afraid in the dark. It comes to this, then. Existence is predicated of that of which we know nothing whatsoever.

To come, however, more closely to the point, I find the ultimate reason why Unknowableness is asserted is the fact that we can know nothing but our own states of consciousness. Now, I ask whether it can possibly be said that we do not know something of the states of consciousness of our friends. If so, I shall be quite satisfied if I am allowed to say I know God as I know my friend. Let Him be neither more nor less of a phantom than my next-door neighbour, and I am content. The object of this paper is to show that my knowledge of God is as real as my knowledge of man.

I begin by observing that I have here, almost unwittingly, been using words very like those of an author whom no one will suspect of mysticism, or of any inclination to transcendentalism – I mean Mr. Mill. I mention this because it is remarkable that on the subject of God, the language of the

1 The greater part of this paper was read before a Philosophical Society.

patriarch of the psychology of the Unknowable is very different from that of the Agnosticism which I am now considering. Mr. Mill has never said that God is Unknowable. On the contrary, he always avers that God can be known as anything else is known. "The relativity of human knowledge, the compossibility of the Absolute, and the contradictions which follow the attempt to conceive a Being with all, or without any, attributes, are no obstacles to our having the same kind of knowledge of God which we have of other things, namely, not as they exist absolutely, but relatively." Again, "If I talk of a Being who is absolute in wisdom and goodness, that is, who knows everything, and at all times intends what is best for every sentient creature, I understand perfectly what I mean." This conception is not adequate, but "who will pretend that it is unmeaning?" I shall not despair of showing that Mr. Mill believes in some sort of a God. Most certainly he entertains the question of the possibility of His existence, and would not put God out of court on the ground of the incompetency of human faculties. God is not to him an unmeaning term. Now, it may be that I am mistaken, but as far as I can make out, the Agnosticism of physical science goes deeper than this. It certainly does wish altogether to exclude Atheism; most sincerely it would disavow the assertion that there is no God. It would not allow a probability to make out either in His favour, or against Him. This results immediately from the rigid exclusion of all knowledge but of "our own states of consciousness." This is by no means the same thing as Mr. Mill's definition of "knowing;" a thing is knowable when it impresses our intelligence in some specific way. From this follow at once the knowableness of God; for why should not God impress Himself on my intelligence?

Whatever stress, then, Mr. Mill may lay upon the value of the experience of consciousness, he evidently does not consider that the mind of each of us is hermetically sealed to knowledge of the action of other minds and other things upon it. Yet this total ignorance is necessary to the position of Agnosticism. According to Professor Huxley, everything beyond our own states of consciousness is utterly unmeaning. Thus, "if I say that impenetrability is a property of matter, all that I can really mean is that the consciousness which I call extension, and the consciousness I call resistance, constantly accompany one another." God, I suppose, in this view, might perhaps rise to the dignity of a working hypothesis, but certainly no higher. If the word God cannot convey any meaning to my mind, then it is simply absurd to argue for or against His existence. As well argue about the existence of X Y Z, or Abracadabra. This system has of course great polemical advantages. It enables its authors to use language of all kinds, materialistic and spiritual, by turns. They reap the profit at once of both knowledge and ignorance. To them ignorance is a harbour of refuge from which they may issue on piratical expeditions into the realm of knowledge. Its enormous and incurable weakness is that it excludes from the circle of knowledge what the common sense of mankind will never consent to give up to ignorance. If God is unknowable on the ground that we know nothing but our own states of consciousness, so is our neighbour. If God is a working hypothesis, so is also my friend.

In what I have further to say upon the school which I venture to criticise, I shall henceforth principally use the works of Mr. Herbert Spencer. It is true that a man downright and earnest, as is Professor Huxley, leaves no doubt as to his meaning, yet he does not draw out the theory so much at length as that writer. I should gather, then, that Mr. Spencer's view is that the Unknowable really exists, but to assign any quality whatsoever to it is simply unmeaning, on the ground that the human mind can attach no real thought to any name which may be framed about it. Now to meet this assertion it is a sufficient answer to show that if we examine the thought of God itself, it is not outside the conditions of human intelligence. On the contrary, both the process and the product, the way in which it is obtained, and the thought itself, – we shall find that it has all the elements which fit it to be a piece of real knowledge. After that all theories about the Unknowable are beside the point. Whatever is beyond human knowledge, God is knowable, and is known as everything else is known. You may put Humanity down on its knees before a scientific Inquisition, and force it to say that God is Unknowable; it will rise up again and say, "For all that I know Him."

It is evident that a great deal turns upon the notion attached to knowledge, and in the uncertainty of what is meant by it in the school of thinkers whom I am criticising, I am obliged to look for an explanation, and I find a great consensus, in some respects, as to the meaning of the term. If we first turn to Germany, where, as usual, the subject has been more scientifically treated than in England, we find there a special branch of mental science reserved for knowledge; while logic contains the theory of thought, dialectic treats of the theory of cognition. To ascertain this, the act of cognition itself is examined, and in the case of Kant the result is as follows: – "Thought, according to him, is one thing; knowledge is another. Knowledge contains two elements, the category by which a thing is thought, and the intuition by which it is given. But all intuitions possible to man being sensible, it follows that the thought of an object, by means of a pure concept of understanding, is only knowledge in as far as that concept is applied to objects of sense."[2] The illustration which he gives is remarkable. He even seems to deny the name of objective knowledge to mathematics. Being a pure product of the mind, mathematical concepts only deserve the name of such knowledge because they are capable of being applied to the real intuitions of sense. The point to which I would draw attention here is that, according to Kant's view, knowledge implies a variety of elements, some from within, others from without; all knowledge of reality involves a mixture of products of the mind and of experience. His very reason for denying that God is an object of knowledge is that He is not an object of experience. I now turn to the very apostle of the Unknowable, Mr. Herbert Spencer. Amidst all that is destructive in his philosophy, he is most anxious to vindicate real knowledge to the human mind. Now, what is the criterion by which, amidst all human delusions, he recognises truth? Amidst all our hollow thoughts, which have the ring which indicates that they are a reality? In a remarkable passage in which he asks how the human intellect can have a consciousness of the Unknowable, the real existence of which he vehemently affirms, he answers that this consciousness is the "product of many mental acts," and is "necessitated by the persistence of one element under successive changes." "The measure of relative validity among our beliefs is the degree of their persistence in opposition to the effort made to change them"[3] Again, his criterion of the reality of symbolic conceptions is that they are legitimate, "provided that *by some cumulative or indirect processes of thought*, or by the fulfilment of predictions based upon them, we can assure

---

[2] Kritik der reinen Vernunft, p. 124, Hartenstein's ed.

[3] First Principles, 94, 96.

ourselves that they stand for actualities." Here we may remark this much agreement with Kant; real knowledge is the result of multiplicity. That may be considered as real which comes to us from many sides, and which conveys under all changes a persistent unity of impression. I find the same principle stated in Professor Tyndall's answer to Dr. Mozley. He treats with scorn all doubts thrown upon the reality of Science, and he claims for it a certainty on the ground that it is knowledge conveyed to us through a mixture of what he elsewhere, in a brilliant essay, calls imagination and experience. What is this but to say that when the same truth comes to us from various parts of our nature, and retains its identity under all, it may be considered as a real addition to our stock of knowledge. The principle here laid down is that the coincidence of diversity of origin with unity of result forces conviction upon us.

This demand for cumulative proof may be considered to be a characteristic of modern thought. We seem all of us to have a suspicion of any one proof which claims to be peremptory and necessary. This seems to be at once a result of our love of facts and of the feeling of the vastness of the Universe, together with our inability to express it in adequate thoughts. This is, I suppose, what is meant by our dislike of what has been called paper logic. As long as the terms of our syllogism are A B C our argument goes on swimmingly, but as soon as we substitute concepts for symbols, then we begin to ask how far they can express the things which they represent. In fact, all truth seems to come to us something in the same way as the objects of sense. No one sense is adequate to convey the whole properties of an object. The notion of it comes in like a flood upon us from every sense, and each impression of sense is utterly different from every other. The melody of its voice is non-existent for the eye, while its brilliant colouring is not even chaos for the ear. Each impression is, therefore, manifestly inadequate, because of its utter unlikeness to the rest; yet this very diversity is a proof of the reality of the one force which thus impresses its truth upon us. This cumulativeness of knowledge is a result of the principle of its relativity, which, to a great extent at least, is certainly modern. What is meant by this principle is that things are known to me primarily by their power of impressing me; and as my being is made up of various faculties, things make themselves known through various channels; thus the truth is the cumulative result of that which rushes in upon me through all these different avenues. In this way everything concrete is known to me. It must first make itself known before I can know it, and announce its presence in many ways before I recognize it. I am willing to argue on these principles, though they may be exaggerated; and my very proof that God is really known to us is, that, while the thought of Him comes persistently before us through external proofs of every kind, He also announces Himself to us personally in our inmost being. What Kant denies is the very thing which I maintain; we experience God. Mr. Herbert Spencer maintains that God is unknowable, because He can come under no known genus; but what if He be a concrete Fact? What I affirm is that our consciousness is made up from a threefold influence. In our thoughts, then, besides the two factors, sense and mind, we are conscious of a third, the contact of an infinite Will and Intellect.

It is quite plain, from the very nature of the argument, that it can only be most imperfectly exposed in a paper such as this. A mere fragment of the subject must be selected as a specimen of what is meant. I will therefore occupy myself in drawing out the knowledge of God which we gather from the Moral Law.

It is very often said that conscience is the voice of God. That this contains a great truth, I gladly admit. Yet I cannot accept the statement in that crude form. On the contrary, it forces itself upon us that conscience is the dictate of our own reason. Otherwise I cannot see how it could be a moral law at all. Even supposing it to be imposed upon us from without, I must make it thoroughly my own before it can bind me. I must see that it is right, else can it have no authority. Of course, a superior can command me, but not till I know that he, too, is a moral being. He, too, must have an intellect, and must know right from wrong; else, he is a tyrant, and I rebel, and have a right to do so. So thoroughly personal is law, so absolutely is it a product of an intellect, so certain is it that it must be contained in a mind and spring out of it. The same truth comes upon us in every possible shape. Of course, conscience is something more than reason. It is intellect exercised upon a definite subject-matter, and in a definite way. It contemplates actions, but not external material actions, nor in as far as they are objects of thought, but as things to be done, and with a relation to will. Thus conscience is exercised upon a quality in actions which results out of a relation to a living will and intellect. Again, a moral law has not only freedom for its condition, but results from it. I see that I am free, that I am exempted from the iron law of natural necessity, which binds me so inexorably on every side, at the very moment that, by virtue of that very freedom which tells me that I can choose one of two things, I feel myself bound to choose one. For all these reasons I cannot but think that conscience is a part of my own consciousness – nay, its inmost core. It is the voice of my intellect and free-will. Above all, it is my own reason, because it can make a mistake. In intricate cases I am conscious of a syllogism and a process. My conscience, indeed, is faithful to its inevitable intuition that the right must be done, irrespective of its consequences; it falters in pronouncing what in this particular instance is right. It is on this very fallibility of conscience that I found my argument. We have arrived thus far, the moral law can only exist in a personality. It is rooted in an intellect and a will. That an intellect should see an action as wrong is a condition of wrongness not only in the sense that it makes the doer wrong, but that the material action could not be wrong if there was no one in the Universe to see that it is wrong. I am not arguing that a law implies an imposing will (though that may be true), but that whether it be a copy or an original, wherever it exists, a law implies a person in which it lives. The lawgiver and he to whom the law is addressed must both be moral beings. This, then, is the question. That I am a law to myself is certain; is my reason, however, the original or the shadow; is it primary or derived? I can conceive but one answer to the question. The very changes and variations, the falterings and hesitations, in the dictates of conscience which are adduced to prove its empiric character, only show that the original impersonated law is not in us, but elsewhere.

Let us take but one peculiarity of the human Conscience, its strange combination of absoluteness and relativity. If one thing is certain about conscience, it is that it considers its own dictates to be universal. I do not think that any one would assert that falsehood, injustice, or cruelty would be right in heaven. I pass by the whole question as to the origin of conscience. We intuitionalists indeed argue that a law so absolute as to be binding on all conceivable beings, could never have issued from experience, for experience can never rise above its level. But I do not insist upon this; however you may account for conscience, such is the avowed truth. Let but a child take in the fact that a thing is wrong, he will say to his little sister. "You must not do that, for it is wicked." Nor, I think, can it be said that this is an argument drawn from the similarity of beings, for the very point is that we hold that the moral law is especially distinguished from physical, in that it binds all possible beings. We know that ginger would not be hot to an angel, but we know also that God, if He exists, is as much bound not to be unjust as man, for He is not a lawgiver in the sense that He makes any law according to arbitrary will. Now, what right has the conscience of man to bind the universe? What right have we to import our casuistry into Paradise, and to seat our conscience on the throne of God? Plainly none whatever. Yet whenever we are certain that we are right, and in all the grand lines of morality we are absolutely certain, as certain as that two and two make four, we say at once without hesitation, this law is binding in Heaven. If it is not right for God, it is not right for me. What is the consequence? One of two things, either there exists a Being whose intellect and will are identical with absolute moral truth and impersonated law, or morality itself is a great mistake. While all law has its life in a personal being, absolute law can only live in a Personal Being who is identical with it, because His will is ever right, so that His nature is a law at once to Himself and to all beings. My reason tells me that there is an absolute obligation of which it cannot itself be the ground; if there be not an absolute reason, then that obligation itself is groundless. Herein, and here alone, lies the ground of the possibility of a categorical imperative; there is somewhat whose existence has in itself an absolute worth. That somewhat is not man, who is not an end to all possible being, but God.[4]

To all this a well-known objection has been made. After all, it is said, this conclusion rests upon a hypothesis. If morals are to have a foundation in a real obligation, then there is a God. But what if they are groundless? For all practical purposes, it is enough that men should inevitably conceive themselves bound. Furthermore, the idea God is a necessity emerging from the want of a hypothesis, and for that very reason has no objective force other than a hypothetical one. As for myself, I must own even such a hypothetical necessity would be enough to prove

---

4 Kant's Metaphysic of Ethics. Mahaffy's Translation, p. 41.

the existence of God. In the case before us, the obligation is so inseparable a part of morality, that whatever is necessary to the reality of the obligation has to me an objective force. God is not necessary only to my conception of morality: His existence is necessary to the existence of an obligation. I do not call Him into account for the idea but for the fact of morality. Thus far, however, I feel the power of the objection. The argument is too roundabout, too indirect to be an account of the mode in which anything so immediate as the relation between God and morals comes with such overwhelming might on the mind of man. I allow it to be hypothetical; to me it is an indispensable hypothesis; to many here probably it is a supposition, and nothing more. But the wonder is that this same hypothesis, to you so thin and intangible as to be unreal, suddenly transfers itself from the region of à priori intuition to that of pleasure and pain. This abstract God proves His concreteness by a sharp pang felt in the depths of the emotional parts of my being. I know it to be He by the cumulative process, of which we have heard so much. On the one hand, my analysis of moral law throws me upon a Personal Being in whom it lives; on the other, I experience a sensible pain, which is a direct consequence of the same moral law. Here is a combination of intuition and experience which is Kant's condition of knowledge. If there be a God, our imagination would present Him to us as inflicting pain on a violator of His law, and lo! the imagination turns out to be an experimental fact. The Unknowable suddenly stabs me to the heart.

I do not think that it can be said that this argument is a mere trick of subtle logic. The strangeness of the connection between duty and feeling had already struck Kant. He says that "this energy of a naked intellectual idea upon the sensory is quite uninvestigable by reason." "Man," he adds, "must content himself with comprehending à priori thus much, that such a feeling attaches inseparably to the representation of the law by every finite intelligent." I must confess that I do not comprehend this à priori. I doubt whether we should know wrong to be hateful, unless we felt the emotion of hate. Kant's account seems to me a wonderful instance of the great defects in his psychology which have so often been pointed out. He does not take into account that part of the phenomena to which I am now referring; I mean the pain of conscience on account of a broken law. He only contemplates the sentiment of reverence which is intuitively felt towards the moral law, and refers it to the humbling of self which necessarily accompanies the idea of duty. In the same place, however, he quite allows that this sentiment will not account for the "pathologic, internal sense of pleasure" which accompanies it. It affords, then, no reason for the pain which follows a violated law. Humility is not always a pleasant feeling, and, on the other hand, emancipation from law would be just as likely to naturally produce pleasure as pain. Again, it is quite conceivable that there should be a cold, passionless, moral being, in whom goodness would produce no feeling. For pleasure and pain it requires a separate apparatus from intuition. This is precisely what we find in man; though conscience is the dictate of reason, yet the term "moral sense" is by no means a misnomer. With all the sharpness and instantaneousness of a sense, anguish unutterable, of a kind distinguishable from any other, follows at once on wrong-doing, and that feeling gives us notice of the presence of evil, as sense reveals to us poison. Considered as a perception, it depends as little on the human will as sight or sound. What I have already said is sufficient to point out God as the immediate author of this wholesome misery. Among the many ways in which this may be effected, I will now dwell on one, rather as an answer to objectors than for the sake of the theory itself, which I only propound with hesitation.

The obvious objection to what I have said is the observation that the phenomenon is simply accounted for by the very hypothetical connection between the idea of God and of obligation on which I have insisted. Man having conceived the idea of God as the author of the moral law, out of that idea itself would naturally arise the emotion of fear. I cannot, however, think this is tenable, for a simple reason. This anguish of a bad conscience exists in the case of those who do not believe in God. An Atheist who committed murder would feel it to the full. We all know that those to whom God is unknowable may be conscientious men. The phenomenon of conscience, then, is quite separable from the notion of God. Again, it may be argued with more plausibility that the feeling of self-degradation will account for the pain of conscience. That this enters into it, I do not doubt, yet I cannot think that it accounts for it. It is plain that the pain of conscience arises specifically from the representation, "I have done wrong." Now the degradation of self is not the essence of wrong-doing, any more than self-respect is virtue. He who did what is materially right out of a notion of self-love would not be virtuous at all. Besides which degradation only accompanies certain classes of sins with which shame is more immediately connected. Lady Macbeth feels remorse, but does not feel degraded by the crimes which were the steps to her throne. If this be so, no way of accounting for this peculiar anguish appears but to refer it to the direction action of God. It has its source not in the idea of God, but in God Himself. It is easy to point out the mode of this action in accordance with what has been said.

The implicit end of all right moral action is the absolute good or Summum Bonum, not as an idea, but as actually existing. We have seen that this absolute good is identical with a Personal Being who is the highest moral good; at the same time, I need fear no contradiction from a Utilitarian when I affirm that the highest moral good is also the highest happiness. No wonder, then, that a man who has separated himself by wrong from the Absolute Good simultaneously feels unhappiness. He has suffered an actual loss. Of course a man who imagines a loss which he has not actually sustained may suffer actually; but here the reality is too certain; he has done wrong. In other words, the Being who is the highest good, and contact with whom is the highest happiness, has withdrawn Himself from him. He has suffered, then, a real loss; if he knows God, he understands it; but whether he knows Him or not, he is profoundly sad. There is anarchy in the whole realm of ends, since that which is a desirable end in itself is away. As his whole intellectual being would be in a state of preternatural agony if, through some malevolent influence, falsehood all at once became its aim instead of truth, so his will is all confused if the absolutely desirable, which is its root and its foundation, is taken away, and a moral falsehood held up before it.

There is not one of the phenomena of conscience which does not more than fit into the view that the emotional part of it comes directly from the action of a Personal Being, of a marked character, the inmost core of which is Love. I have already adverted to that most merciful provision by which the pang of conscience outlives the denial of God. If the action of God in the soul of man ceased the instant that His existence was denied, the darkness would be eternal and return hopeless. On the contrary, the emotion of conscience is the passionate cry of the Father coming to claim the child, who denies that He exists. If the reproach were openly directed against Atheism itself, endless syllogisms would marshal themselves against it; but God consents to come under the thin disguise of some broken moral law, against which no reasoning avails, in order to spare the pride of the erring spirit, whose first impulse is "ever to deny." Wonderful mercy! in this, as in all other cases, out of the very violated law rises the cry of wrath. Yet this does not last for ever; it is a fact that the sharpest pain accompanies the first steps into vice, and the emotion is deadened as a man goes deeper into guilt. For this there are two causes. Subjectively considered, this pain is the loss of God; objectively, it is God withdrawing Himself. The sharp pain then comes from the first wrench, and from the miserable *ennui* of aimlessness which ensues when the great good of life is torn away and the will left in solitude without its legitimate end. Like all other losses, it is loss felt as time goes on. But on the other side, God goes further and further into the distance, and His voice comes in muffled accents as though stifled by a thickening medium. If the character of God were, as is supposed, simple absolute benevolence and nothing else, this would not be. The heart of this being is passionate love, and it turns in disappointment from an obstinate free-will which will not be educated, and which Omnipotence cannot break or bend. It was a profound saying of the poet of Christianity that the everlasting pit was the creation of eternal love.

Fecemi la divina Potestate
La somma sapienza e'l primo amore.[5]

The natural hell of a dumb conscience is a frightful God-abandoned solitude, the result of holy love, turned into anger by despair at the hardness of the heart which it has wooed in vain.

I began by saying that the knowledge which we have of God is as real as that which we have of man. In one respect, however, we come much nearer to knowing God as He is than is ever possible in the case of a creature. God always comes to us, it is true, under some disguise. However immediate may be the inference by which we obtain a knowledge of God, an inference or a process there always is. Thus, though it might be

---

[5] Dante, Inf., canto 3.

quite true to say that the Universe is a vision of God, yet it must never be forgotten that it is the vision of Him under a veil, and that the veil, however thin, is a substance. It is not simply God working on our senses, but the world consists of powers intermediate between ourselves and the Being who works through them. Our knowledge of Him is thus phenomenal, through this effect, just as we know our fellow-creatures by "broken gleams" of their inmost selves which we obscurely gather from their features and their movements, through the impression which they make upon us. Furthermore, in the case of God there is this additional difficulty, that He is infinitely beyond us, while creatures are within our powers. We have the further disadvantage that we are relative beings contemplating the Absolute, who has chosen voluntarily to enter into relations with us. We are, therefore, forced to make partial mistakes; which, however, right themselves, because we know that they are mistakes, and allow for them as such.[6] The only fatal mistake would be twofold. We might either, in despair at the refracting medium through which we view Him, consider that our knowledge of Him is false, and that He is utterly different from the vision which we have of Him, or we may transfer the process of development from our minds to Him, and subject the Immutable to a law of changeful progress. We might either be Agnostics or Hegelians. When, however, we regard God as identical with the Moral Law, these dangers all but vanish. The inference is more immediate, and the veil is at its very thinnest. The atmosphere through which we see God is least charged with the vapours of earth and transfused with its colours. We have but allowance to make for the tremulousness and idiosyncracies of the organ by which we view Him. We have passed beyond phenomena. Can that be called a phenomenal view of God, when I can undoubtingly declare what it must be, and, therefore, what it is? Then human consciousness comes nearest to the divine. I have now reached a height when contradictions vanish, and obtained a standard by which all mistakes can be set right. If I am obliged to think this act of creation in terms of time, the necessities of the moral law oblige me to think God Himself as eternal. Moreover, this eternity is no prolongation of time, but forces time to vanish altogether

---

[6]   It is quite true that there are degrees in sin, but even venial sins can never become right any more than mortal.

from His being. Each enactment of that law has the totality of God behind it, and the same obligation, which, immutable and undivided, is coincident with each moment of time, since each is valid for all time and space. I have no difficulty in thinking time away from a Being whose intellect is pure intuition, and who is not forced to think through concepts; but I defy any thought to separate eternity from the moral law, and from the Being in whom it lies, and with whom it is identical.

We are now in a condition to consider whether the notion of a First Canon really involves the contradictions which are supposed in the "First Principles" of the philosophy of the Unknowable to be inherent to it. It is thought the idea of a self-existent Being (which a First Canon must necessarily be) is inconceivable because "it involves the conception of infinite past-time – which is an impossibility;" but we have discovered that God has not existed in infinite past-time, but in eternity. It is thought that the First Canon could not be Absolute, because "the Absolute means that which has no necessary relation to any other being." No doubt; but suppose that the Absolute God enters into the relations of Creator with created beings from the sole motive of pure and simple love, then these relations cease at once to be necessary. In man, indeed, love implies a want, because we love a goodness which we find and do not make; but if creatures are loved by God, their very lovableness is His gift, and the pale shadow of that beauty which He possessed in fulness from all eternity. I do not mean, of course, that any cumulative argument can give us the power of believing in any real contradiction in terms, but it does give us a right to say that the apparent inconceivableness arises from an inadequate conception of the terms, since on further examination it turns out that there is more in them than we perceived at first. It is not that any such argument can destroy real fallacies, but it does demonstrate that what looked like fallacy is but partial truth, by bringing further light to bear upon the subject. It does not mechanically superimpose one probability on another to make a certainty; but it creates certainty, because the mind is convinced that the agreement of so many various witnesses from so many different sides to the same truth cannot be the effect of chance.

The more we examine the Agnostic position the more untenable it seems. It is not only that there is a logical inconsistency in the assertion that the existence of the Absolute is asserted to be known and yet that the Absolute is utterly unknowable. The mistake is neither verbal nor technical. The fact is, that three-fourths of the phenomena of the case are boldly ignored. Of course, if you leave out the whole moral nature of man, God is unknowable. Of course, if you hang, draw, and quarter man, burn his heart before his eyes, and disperse the several portions of his being, you will lose the power of knowing the God, of whom man is the chief natural revelation. If you persist in looking only at the physical side of God and forget His dealings with the conscience, no wonder that He is unknowable. Who ever said that He was knowable thus? If you take only the metaphysical notion of First Cause and stop there, you do not exclude the possibility of a mere immanent substance of the universe. You are putting on the argument of a weight which it cannot bear if you attempt to extract from it our God, a personal Being, the only one worthy of the name of God. So far I agree with Mr. Herbert Spencer. He by no means ignores some arguments for God's existence. He holds the unthinkableness of Atheism and Pantheism. Sometimes he uses all but scholastic language about a First unbeginning Cause. We hold our breath, and expect him to pronounce the name of God. We are disappointed when he rejects him on account of supposed contradictions, and stops short of God to take refuge in the Unknowable. I maintain that these contradictions are neutralized if we go beyond the notion of a First Cause and take in the cumulative proof to be derived from man's whole being. We require the right, not indeed to pass them over (for God is still incomprehensible, though not unknowable), but to transcend and correct them. For this, all that is necessary is, after looking at the arguments one by one as they crowd in upon us from various sides, to exhibit their accumulated force. To do this we do not beg the question, and we require no assumption. There is proof enough that the great First Cause of the physical universe is also the Personal Being who speaks to the individual conscience. I must confess that I have never felt the difficulties which others feel about the antagonism between Physical Science and Religion. Mind and Matter play into each other's hands. I grant indeed what I think is perfectly obvious, that there is an ultimate irreducible difference between the autocratic free will and the unvarying phenomena of nature; but the difference only makes their working together the more remarkable. In many ways I find intellect and matter most wonderfully pointing to a unity of origin. Look, for instance, at mathematics, the most purely mental of all our intellectual creations. Solely out of the depths of our consciousness we spin theories about lines, angles, and circles. Without the slightest admixture of experience we think out their truths; but when we come to look at the external universe, we find that it is constructed precisely on those *à priori* principles of our own minds. There are no lines or circles in the sky, yet we can reconstruct the universe and find out its laws by their help. We might be tempted to turn Pantheist, and look upon Mind and Matter as two aspects of the same identical substance, if the chasm between them did not force us to find the reason of this marvellous correspondence combined with diversity in the notion of the oneness of their Creator. The mental figures drawn by the human mind turn out to be, not identical with, but shadows of the thoughts of Him who made the outward world. I find the same reconciliation of the antagonism between Nature and Free-Will in the moral nature of the Creator. The immensity and unvarying laws of the external world render human morals possible. The phenomena and the ascertainable properties of physical substances subserve other and higher purposes than the admiration of the scientific observer and the utility of man. If we could not predict infallibly the consequences of our actions, they would cease to be moral. If poison did not destroy nor steel pierce, it would be superfluous to enact "Thou shalt not kill." What would become of the decalogue, if the laws of physics were capricious? The cold neutrality and the indifference to ethics of nature when brought into contact with free-will become at once transfigured and minister matter to right and wrong. We need not assume the existence of a knowable Creator, of a Demiurge or an Ahriman. A good Being did not impose a moral meaning on the creation of another. External actions are not the arbitrary and conventional symbols of moral qualities, but their formal objects. If the desires of the heart are evil, it is because the acts which are passionately desired are wrong. Just as man's physical organization ministers to the sanctities of wedded love and renders society possible, so in a thousand ways does nature, by virtue of its fixed laws, enter into the very substance of what I may call the ordinary supernatural. The transference of conscience from the purely moral to the emotional part of our being is only one instance of the same principle. It is thus proved to be unphilosophical to separate the Absolute of logic and the First Cause required by the physical world from the Personal Being who gives a sanction to the moral law. If this be the case, He ceases to be unknowable.

It is such considerations as these which explain and justify the ineradicable belief of mankind in the love of God. There are more terrible difficulties in the way than any doctrines of evolution or metaphysical inconceivabilities. The more a man realizes the agony of moral suffering and the power of evil, the more difficulty he will feel in reconciling it with the goodness of the God who permits it. Let it be observed, however, that this is a difficulty which comes, not from our ignorance, but our knowledge. There is so much provision for innocent joyousness in the universe, such facilities for cheap happiness in its beauty and in human feelings, that we see everywhere marks of benevolence, and we feel tempted to have recourse to the hypothesis of a good Being limited in power. This is to misread the phenomena of the universe; it does not bear the aspect of weak benevolence; it wears the sad look of yearning, unrequited love. There is a power against which Omnipotence itself is shattered; I mean the power of the free-will. I can walk up to all the difficulties of the universe and look them full in the face, when I feel within myself the splendid power of loving God, which can only be bestowed upon me by one who loves me. I know that life is worth living on such terms as these, and I am even willing to endure the terrible possibilities of evil, because they are essential to the free gift of my spontaneous love. That the Being who has given me this capability should not love me, that is the true inconceivable; I care not for the inconceivabilities of the Infinite, though I shudder at the scandals of the universe. The former exist only on paper, and vanish before the realities of concrete being; but the power of evil is too real to be ignored. I can find no consolation in a vague Most High or in a Divine Personality to be elaborated out of a universe of evil as well as good. The fact is, that there are souls perishing apparently without a chance of safety, sinking into an abyss of sin with their whole freight of human feelings and desires. It is but cold comfort to talk of general laws or of a universe righting itself. Yet when I look into myself and hear the loving voice of God in my conscience, even recalling me to Himself, – when I think that this is no privilege of a favourite, but the birthright of every child of man, then I feel that, in spite of all appearances to the contrary, God does love each individual soul and strains it to His bosom. A Being who can touch the heart and work in the depths of the spirit has an invisible power of compensation, which it is unphilosophical to ignore when we wish to calculate the chances of virtue in the terrible fight. Yet, after all, men and women fall, you will say. I know it; but then there is the Cross.

Finally, I hold it to be not a piece of mysticism, but of excellent metaphysic, that God is knowable and known to me by a mixture of intuition and experience. It is the only key to what otherwise is inexplicable, the mixture of the emotional and the intuitional in morals. He is virtuous who loves the right, and the right is lovable because it is identical with a Personal Being. We have heard much of the inability of the human mind to embrace the Infinite. What if the Infinite embraces me? No analysis of concepts will persuade me that I cannot know Him. Let us be consistent in holding the doctrine of the relativity of the human intellect. If for this reason I do not know God, then I know nothing whatsoever, for my knowledge of the Finite is also relative. I know Him as I know everything else, through the effects of His immediate action, experienced in my spirit. I do not know Him adequately; but then I am not deceived, for I am conscious of the inadequacy of my thoughts. I do not know Him by one concept, but by a number of concepts, mutually correcting one another. They are all relative; but none are untrue, and at the bottom of all lies the consciousness of which we cannot rid ourselves, that the Absolute Good exists. I fear not the reproach of holding an anthropomorpous view of God. According to this theory, God is not drawn after the likeness of man, but man is Deiform, for God is the archetype of all that is good. You will never persuade mankind that God cannot be known as Infinite Love.

ADDRESS DELIVERED BEFORE THE BRITISH ASSOCIATION AT BELFAST
[John Tyndall]

At the outset of this Address it was stated that physical theories which lie beyond experience are derived by a process of abstraction from experience. It is instructive to note from this point of view the successive introduction of new conceptions. The idea of the attraction of gravitation was preceded by the observation of the attraction of iron by a magnet, and of light bodies by rubbed amber. The polarity of magnetism and electricity appealed to the senses; and thus became the substratum of the conception that atoms and molecules are endowed with definite, attractive, and repellent poles, by the play of which definite forms of crystalline architecture are produced. Thus molecular force becomes *structural*. It required no great boldness of thought to extend its play into organic nature, and to recognize in molecular force the agency by which both plants and animals are built up. In this way out of experience arise conceptions which are wholly ultra-experiential. None of the atomists of antiquity had any notion of this play of molecular polar force, but they had experience of gravity as manifested by falling bodies. Abstracting from this, they permitted their atoms to fall eternally through empty space. Democritus assumed that the larger atoms moved more rapidly than the smaller ones, which they therefore could overtake, and with which they could combine. Epicurus, holding that empty space could offer no resistance to motion, ascribed to all the atoms the same velocity; but he seems to have overlooked the consequence that under such circumstances the atoms could never combine. Lucretius cut the knot by quitting the domain of physics altogether, and causing the atoms to move together by a kind of volition.

Was the instinct utterly at fault which caused Lucretius thus to swerve from his own principles? Diminishing gradually the number of progenitors, Mr. Darwin comes at length to one 'primordial form;' but he does not say, as far as I remember, how he supposes this form to have been introduced. He quotes with satisfaction the words of a celebrated author and divine who had 'gradually learnt to see that it is just as noble a conception of the Deity to believe He created a few original forms, capable of self-development into other and needful forms, as to believe that He required a fresh act of creation to supply the voids caused by the action of His laws.' What Mr. Darwin thinks of this view of the introduction of life I do not know. But the anthropomorphism, which it seemed his object to set aside, is as firmly associated with the creation of a few forms as with the creation of a multitude. We need clearness and thoroughness here. Two courses and two only, are possible. Either let us open our doors freely to the conception of creative acts, or, abandoning them, let us radically change our notions of matter. If we look at matter as pictured by Democritus, and as defined for generations in our scientific text-books, the notion of any form of life whatever coming out of it is utterly unimaginable. The argument placed in the mouth of Bishop Butler suffices, in my opinion, to crush all such materialism as this. But those who framed these definitions of matter were not biologists but mathematicians, whose labours referred only to such accidents and properties of matter as could be expressed in their formulae. The very intentness with which they pursued mechanical science turned their thoughts aside from the science of life. May not their imperfect definitions be the real cause of our present dread? Let us reverently, but honestly, look the question in the face. Divorced from matter, where is life to be found? Whatever our *faith* may say, our *knowledge* shows them to be indissolubly joined. Every meal we eat, and every cup we drink, illustrates the mysterious control of Mind by Matter.

Trace the line of life backwards, and see it approaching more and more to what we call the purely physical condition. We come at length to those organisms which I have compared to drops of oil suspended in a mixture of alcohol and water. We reach the *protogenes* of Haeckel, in which we have 'a type distinguishable from a fragment of albumen only by its finely granular character.' Can we pause here? We break a magnet and find two poles in each of its fragments. We continue the process of breaking, but, however small the parts, each carries with it, though enfeebled, the polarity of the whole. And when we can break no longer, we prolong the intellectual vision to the polar molecules. Are we not urged to do *something* similar in the case of life? Is there not a temptation to close to some extent with Lucretius, when he affirms that 'nature is seen to do all things spontaneously of herself without the meddling of the gods?' or with Bruno, when he declares that Matter is not 'that mere empty capacity which philosophers have pictured her to be, but the universal mother who brings forth all things as the fruit of her own womb?' Believing as I do in the continuity of Nature, I cannot stop abruptly where our microscopes cease to be of use. Here the vision of the mind authoritatively supplements the vision of the eye. By an intellectual necessity I cross the boundary of the experimental evidence, and discern in that Matter which we, in our ignorance of its latent powers, and notwithstanding our professed reverence for its Creator, have hitherto covered with opprobrium, the promise and potency of all terrestrial Life.

If you ask me whether there exists the least evidence to prove that any form of life can be developed out of matter, without demonstrable antecedent life, my reply is that evidence considered perfectly conclusive by many has been adduced; and that were some of us who have pondered this question to follow a very common example, and accept testimony because it falls in with our belief, we also should eagerly close with the evidence referred to. But there is in the true man of science a wish stronger than the wish to have his beliefs upheld; namely, the wish to have them true. And this stronger wish causes him to reject the most plausible support if he has reason to suspect that it is vitiated by error. Those to whom I refer as having studied this question, believing the evidence offered in favour of 'spontaneous generation' to be thus vitiated, cannot accept it. They know full well that the chemist now prepares from inorganic matter a vast array of substances which were some time ago regarded as the sole products of vitality. They are intimately acquainted with the structural power of matter as evidenced in the phenomena of crystallization. They can justify scientifically their *belief* in its potency, under the proper conditions, to produce organisms. But in reply to your question they will frankly admit their inability to point to any satisfactory experimental proof that life can be developed save from demonstrable antecedent life. As already indicated, they draw the line from the highest organisms through lower ones down to the lowest, and it is the prolongation of this line by the intellect beyond the range of the senses that leads them to the conclusion which Bruno so boldly enunciated.[1]

The 'materialism' here professed may be vastly different from what you suppose, and I therefore crave your gracious patience to the end. 'The question of an external world,' says Mr. J. S. Mill, 'is the great battleground of metaphysics.'[2] Mr. Mill himself reduces external phenomena to 'possibilities of sensation.' Kant, as we have seen, made time and space 'forms' of our own intuitions. Fichte, having first by the inexorable logic of his understanding proved himself to be a mere link in that chain of eternal causation which holds so rigidly in Nature, violently broke the chain by making Nature, and all that it inherits, an apparition of his own mind.[3] And it is by no means easy to combat such notions. For when I say I see you, and that I have not the least doubt about it, the reply is, that what I am really conscious of is an affection of my own retina. And if I urge that I can check my sight of you by touching you, the retort would be that I am equally transgressing the limits of fact; for what I am really conscious of is, not that you are there, but that the nerves of my hand have undergone a change. All we hear, and see, and touch, and taste, and smell, are, it would be urged, mere variations of our own condition, beyond which, even to the extent of a hair's breadth, we cannot go. That anything answering to our impressions exists outside of ourselves is not a *fact*, but an *inference*, to which all validity would be denied by an idealist like Berkeley, or by a sceptic like Hume. Mr. Spencer takes another line. With him, as with the uneducated man, there is no doubt or question as to the existence of an external world. But he differs from the uneducated, who think that the world really *is* what consciousness represents it to be. Our states of consciousness are mere *symbols* of an outside entity which produces them and determines the order of their succession, but the real nature of which we can never know.[4] In fact, the whole process of

---

1 'Bruno was a 'Pantheist' not an 'Atheist' or a 'Materialist.'

2 *Examination of Hamilton*, p. 154.

3 *Bestimmung des Menschen.*

4 In a paper, at once popular and profound, entitled *Recent Progress in the Theory of Vision*, contained in the volume of Lectures by Helmholtz, published by Longmans, this symbolism of our states of consciousness is also dwelt upon. The impressions of sense are the mere *signs* of external

evolution is the manifestation of a Power absolutely inscrutable to the intellect of man. As little in our day as in the days of Job can man by searching find this Power out. Considered fundamentally, then, it is by the operation of an insoluble mystery that life on earth is evolved, species differentiated, and mind unfolded from their prepotent elements in the immeasurable past. There is, you will observe, no very rank materialism here.

The strength of the doctrine of evolution consists, not in an experimental demonstration (for the subject is hardly accessible to this mode of proof), but in its general harmony with scientific thought. From contrast, moreover, it derives enormous relative strength. On the one side we have a theory (if it could with any propriety be so called) derived, as were the theories referred to at the beginning of this Address, not from the study of Nature, but from the observation of men – a theory which converts the Power whose garment is seen in the visible universe into an Artificer, fashioned after the human model, and acting by broken efforts, as man is seen to act. On the other side, we have the conception that all we see around us, and all we feel within us – the phenomena of physical nature as well as those of the human mind – have their unsearchable roots in a cosmical life, if I dare apply the term, an infinitesimal span of which is offered to the investigation of man. And even this span is only knowable in part. We can trace the development of a nervous system, and correlate with it the parallel phenomena of sensation and thought. We see with undoubting certainty that they go hand in hand. But we try to soar in a vacuum the moment we seek to comprehend the connexion between them. An Archimedean fulcrum is here required which the human mind cannot command; and the effort to solve the problem, to borrow a comparison from an

things. In this paper Helmholtz contends strongly against the view that the consciousness of space in inborn; and he evidently doubts the power of the chick to pick up grains of corn without preliminary lessons. On this point, he says, further experiments are needed. Such experiments have been since made by Mr. Spalding, aided, I believe, in some of his observations by the accomplished and deeply lamented Lady Amberly; and they seem to prove conclusively that the chick does not need a single moment's tuition to enable it to stand, run, govern the muscles of its eyes, and to peck. Helmholtz, however, is contending against the notion of pre-established harmony; and I am not aware of his views as to the organisation of experiences of race or breed.

illustrious friend of mine, is like the effort of a man trying to lift himself by his own waistband. All that has been here said is to be taken in connexion with this fundamental truth. When 'nascent senses' are spoken of, when 'the differentiation of a tissue at first vaguely sensitive all over' is spoken of, and when these processes are associated with 'the modification of an organism by its environment,' the same parallelism, without contact, or even approach to contact, is implied. Man the *object* is separated by an impassable gulf from man the *subject*. There is no motor energy in intellect to carry it without logical rupture from the one to the other.

Further, the doctrine of evolution derives man in his totality from the inter-action of organism and environment through countless ages past. The Human Understanding, for example – that faculty which Mr. Spencer has turned so skilfully round upon its own antecedents – is itself a result of the play between organism and environment through cosmic ranges of time. Never surely did prescription plead so irresistible a claim. But then it comes to pass that, over and above his understanding, there are many other things appertaining to man whose perspective rights are quite as strong as those of the under-standing itself. It is a result, for example, of the play of organism and environment that sugar is sweet and that aloes are bitter, that the smell of henbane differs from the perfume of a rose. Such facts of consciousness (for which, by the way, no adequate reason has yet been rendered) are quite as old as the understanding; and many other things can boast an equally ancient origin. Mr. Spencer at one place refers to that most powerful of passions – the amatory passion – as one which, when it first occurs, is antecedent to all relative experience whatever; and we may pass its claim as being at least as ancient and valid as that of the understanding. Then there are such things woven into the texture of man as the feeling of Awe, Reverence, Wonder – and not alone the sexual love just referred to, but the love of the beautiful, physical, and moral, in Nature, Poetry, and Art. There is also that deep-set feeling which, since the earliest dawn of history, and probably for ages prior to all history, incorporated itself in the Religions of the world. You who have escaped from these religions into the high-and-dry light of the intellect may deride them; but in so doing you deride accidents of form merely, and fail to touch the immovable basis of the religious sentiment in the nature of man. To yield this sentiment reasonable satisfaction is the problem of problems at the present hour. And grotesque in relation to scientific culture as many of the religions of the world have been and are – dangerous, nay destructive, to the dearest privileges of freemen as some of them undoubtedly have been, and would, if they could, be again – it will be wise to recognize them as the forms of a force, mischievous, if permitted to intrude on the region of *knowledge*, over which it holds no command, but capable of being guided to noble issues in the region of *emotion*, which is its proper and elevated sphere.

All religious theories, schemes and systems, which embrace notions of cosmogony, or which otherwise reach into the domain of science, must, *in so far as they do this*, submit to the control of science, and relinquish all thought of controlling it. Acting otherwise proved disastrous in the past, and it is simply fatuous to-day. Every system which would escape the fate of an organism too rigid to adjust itself to its environment must be plastic to the extent that the growth of knowledge demands. When this truth has been thoroughly taken in, rigidity will be relaxed, exclusiveness diminished, things now deemed essential will be dropped, and elements now rejected will be assimilated. The lifting of the life is the essential point; and as long as dogmatism, fanaticism, and intolerance are kept out, various modes of leverage may be employed to raise life to a higher level. Science itself not unfrequently derives motive power from an ultra-scientific source. Whewell speaks of enthusiasm of temper as a hindrance to science; but he means the enthusiasm of weak heads. There is a strong and resolute enthusiasm in which science finds an ally; and it is to the lowering of this fire, rather than to the diminution of intellectual insight, that the lessening productiveness of men of science in their mature years is to be ascribed. Mr. Buckle sought to detach intellectual achievement from moral force. He gravely erred; for without moral force to whip it into action, the achievements of the intellect would be poor indeed.

It has been said that science divorces itself from literature: but the statement, like so many others, arises from lack of knowledge. A glance at the less technical writings of its leaders – of its Helmholtz, its Huxley, and its Du Bois-Reymond – would show what breadth of literary culture they command. Where among modern writers can you find their superiors in clearness and vigour of literary style? Science desires not isolation, but freely combines with every effort towards the bettering of man's estate. Single-handed, and supported not by outward sympathy, but by inward force, it has built at least one great wing of the many-mansioned home which man in his totality demands. And if rough walls and protruding rafter-ends indicate that on one side the edifice is still incomplete, it is only by wise combination of the parts required with those already irrevocably built that we can hope for completeness. There is no necessary incongruity between what has been accomplished, and what remains to be done. The moral glow of Socrates, which we all feel by ignition, has in it nothing incompatible with the physics of Anaxagoras which he so much scorned, but which he would hardly scorn to-day.

And here I am reminded of one amongst us, hoary, but still strong, whose prophet-voice some thirty years ago, far more than any other of his age, unlocked whatever of life and nobleness lay latent in its most gifted minds – one fit to stand beside Socrates or the Maccabean Eleazar, and to dare and suffer all that they suffered and dared – fit, as he once said of Fichte, 'to have been the teacher of the Stoa, and to have discoursed of Beauty and Virtue in the groves of Academe.' With a capacity to grasp physical principles which his friend Goethe did not possess, and which even total lack of exercise has not been able to reduce to atrophy, it is the world's loss that he, in the vigour of his years, did not open his mind and sympathies to science, and make its conclusions a portion of his message to mankind. Marvellously endowed as he was – equally equipped on the side of the Heart and of the Understanding – he might have done much towards teaching us how to reconcile the claims of both, and to enable them in coming times to dwell together in unity of spirit and in the bond of peace.

And now the end is come. With more time, or greater strength and knowledge, what has been here said might have been better said, while worthy matters here omitted might have received fit expression. But there would have been no material deviation from the views set forth. As regards myself, they are not the growth of a day; and as regards you, I thought you ought to know the environment which, with or without your consent, is rapidly surrounding you, and in relation to which some adjustment on your part may be necessary. A hint of

Hamlet's, however, teaches us all how the troubles of common life may be ended; and it is perfectly possible for you and me to purchase intellectual peace at the price of intellectual death. The world is not without refuges of this description; nor is it wanting in persons who seek their shelter and try to persuade others to do the same. The unstable and the weak will yield to this persuasion, and they to whom repose is sweeter than the truth. But I would exhort you to refuse the offered shelter and to scorn the base repose – to accept, if the choice be forced upon you, commotion before stagnation, the leap of the torrent before the stillness of the swamp.

In the course of this Address I have touched on debatable questions and led you over what will be deemed dangerous ground – and this partly with the view of telling you that as regards these questions science claims unrestricted right of search. It is not to the point to say that the views of Lucretius and Bruno, of Darwin and Spencer, may be wrong. Here I should agree with you, deeming it indeed certain that these views will undergo modification. But the point is, that, whether right or wrong, we ask the freedom to discuss them. For science, however, no exclusive claim is here made; you are not urged to erect it into an idol. The inexorable advance of man's understanding in the path of knowledge, and those unquenchable claims of his moral and emotional nature which the understanding can never satisfy, are here equally set forth. The world embraces not only a Newton, but a Shakespeare – not only a Boyle, but a Raphael – not only a Kant, but a Beethoven – not only a Darwin, but a Carlyle. Not in each of these, but in all is human nature whole. They are not opposed, but supplementary – not mutually exclusive, but reconcilable. And if, unsatisfied with them all, the human mind, with the yearning of a pilgrim for his distant home, will turn to the Mystery from which it has emerged, seeking so to fashion it as to give unity to thought and faith; so long as this is done, not only without intolerance or bigotry of any kind, but with the enlightened recognition that ultimate fixity of conception is here unattainable, and that each succeeding age must be held free to fashion the Mystery in accordance with its own needs – then, casting aside all the restrictions of Materialism, I would affirm this to be a field for the noblest exercise of what, in contrast with the *knowing* faculties, may be called the *creative* faculties of man.

'Fill thy heart with it,' said Goethe, 'and then name it as thou wilt.' Goethe himself did this in untranslatable language.[5] Wordsworth did it in words known to all Englishmen, and which may be regarded as a forecast and religious vitalization of the latest and deepest scientific truth, –

> 'For I have learned
> To look on nature; not as in the hour
> Of thoughtless youth; but hearing oftentimes
> The still, sad music of humanity,
> Nor harsh nor grating, though of ample power
> To chasten and subdue. *And I have felt*
> *A presence that disturbs me with the joy*
> *Of elevated thoughts; a sense sublime*
> *Of something far more deeply interfused,*
> *Whose dwelling is the light of setting suns,*
> *And the round ocean, and the living air,*
> *And the blue sky, and in the mind of man:*
> *A motion and a spirit, that impels*
> *All thinking things, all objects of all thought,*
> *And rolls through all things.'*[6]

5 Procemium to 'Gott und Welt.'
6 Tintern Abbey.

AN AGNOSTIC'S APOLOGY
[Leslie Stephen]

The name Agnostic, originally coined by Professor Huxley about 1869, has gained general acceptance. It is sometimes used to indicate the philosophical theory which Mr. Herbert Spencer, as he tells us, developed from the doctrine of Hamilton and Mansel. Upon that theory I express no opinion. I take the word in a vaguer sense, and am glad to believe that its use indicates an advance in the courtesies of controversy. The old theological phrase for an intellectual opponent was Atheist – a name which still retains a certain flavour as of the stake in this world and hell-fire in the next, and which, moreover, implies an inaccuracy of some importance. Dogmatic Atheism – the doctrine that there is no God, whatever may be meant by God – is, to say the least, a rare phase of opinion. The word Agnosticism, on the other hand, seems to imply a fairly accurate appreciation of a form of creed already common and daily spreading. The Agnostic is one who asserts – what no one denies – that there are limits to the sphere of human intelligence. He asserts, further, what many theologians have expressly maintained, that those limits are such as to exclude at least what Lewes called 'metempirical' knowledge. But he goes further, and asserts, in opposition to theologians, that theology lies within this forbidden sphere. This last assertion raises the important issue; and, though I have no pretension to invent an opposition nickname, I may venture, for the purposes of this article, to describe the rival school as Gnostics.

The Gnostic holds that our reason can, in some sense, transcend the narrow limits of experience. He holds that we can attain truths not capable of verification, and not needing verification, by actual experiment or observation. He holds, further, that a knowledge of those truths is essential to the highest interests of mankind, and enables us in some sort to solve the dark riddle of the universe. A complete solution, as everyone admits, is beyond our power. But some answer may be given to the doubts which harass and perplex us when we try to frame any adequate conception of the vast order of which we form an insignificant portion. We cannot say why this or that arrangement is what it is; we can say, though obscurely, that some answer exists, and would be satisfactory, if we could only find it. Overpowered, as every honest and serious thinker is at times overpowered, by the sight of pain, folly, and helplessness, by the jarring discords which run through the vast harmony of the universe, we are yet enabled to hear at times a whisper that all is well, to trust to it as coming from the most authentic source, and to know that only the temporary bars of sense prevent us from recognising with certainty that the harmony beneath the discords is a reality and not a dream. This knowledge is embodied in the central dogma of theology. God is the name of the harmony; and God is knowable. Who would not be happy in accepting this belief, if he could accept it honestly? Who would not be glad if he could say with confidence, the evil is transitory, the good eternal: our doubts are due to limitations destined to be abolished, and the world is really an embodiment of love and wisdom, however dark it may appear to our faculties? And yet, if the so-called knowledge be illusory, are we not bound by the most sacred obligations to recognise the facts? Our brief path is dark enough on any hypothesis. We cannot afford to turn aside after every *ignis fatuus* without asking whether it leads to sounder footing or to hopeless quagmires. Dreams may be pleasanter for the moment than realities; but happiness must be won by adapting our lives to the realities. And who, that has felt the burden of existence, and suffered under well-meant efforts at consolation, will deny that such consolations are the bitterest of mockeries? Pain is not an evil; death is not a separation; sickness is but a blessing in disguise. Have the gloomiest speculations of avowed pessimists ever tortured sufferers like those kindly platitudes? Is there a more cutting piece of satire in the language than the reference in our funeral service to the 'sure and certain hope of a blessed resurrection'? To dispel genuine hopes might be painful, however salutary. To suppress these spasmodic efforts to fly in the face of facts would be some comfort, even in the distress which they are meant to alleviate.

Besides the important question whether the Gnostic can prove his dogmas, there is, therefore, the further question whether the dogmas, if granted, have any meaning. Do they answer our doubts, or mock us with the appearance of an answer? The Gnostics rejoice in their knowledge. Have they anything to tell us? They rebuke what they call the 'pride of reason' in the name of a still more exalted pride. The scientific reasoner is arrogant because he sets limits to the faculty in which he trusts, and denies the existence of any other faculty. They are humble because they dare to tread in the regions which he declares to be inaccessible. But without bandying such accusations, or asking which pride is the greatest, the Gnostics are at least bound to show some ostensible justification for their complacency. Have they discovered a firm resting-place from which they are entitled to look down in compassion or contempt upon those who hold it to be a mere edifice of moonshine? If they have diminished by a scruple the weight of one passing doubt, we should be grateful: perhaps we should be converts. If not, why condemn Agnosticism?

I have said that our knowledge is in any case limited. I may add that, on any showing, there is a danger in failing to recognise the limits of possible knowledge. The word Gnostic has some awkward associations. It once described certain heretics who got into trouble from fancying that men could frame theories of the Divine mode of existence. The sects have been dead for many centuries. Their fundamental assumptions can hardly be quite extinct. Not long ago, at least, there appeared in the papers a string of propositions framed – so we were assured – by some of the most candid and most learned of living theologians. These propositions defined by the help of various languages the precise relations which exist between the persons of the Trinity. It is an odd, though far from an unprecedented, circumstance that the unbeliever cannot quote them for fear of profanity. If they were transplanted into the pages of the 'Fortnightly Review,' it would be impossible to convince anyone that the intention was not to mock the simple-minded persons who, we must suppose, were not themselves intentionally irreverent. It is enough to say that they defined the nature of God Almighty with an accuracy from which modest naturalists would shrink in describing the genesis of a black-beetle. I know not whether these dogmas were put forward as articles of faith, as pious conjectures, or as tentative contribu-tions to a sound theory. At any rate, it was supposed that they were interesting to beings of flesh and blood. If so, one can only ask in wonder whether an utter want of reverence is most strongly implied in this mode of dealing with sacred mysteries; or an utter ignorance of the existing state of the world in the assumption that the question which really divides mankind is the double procession of the Holy Ghost; or an utter incapacity for speculation in the confusion of these dead exuviae of long-past modes of thought with living intellectual tissue; or an utter want of imagination, or of even a rudimentary sense of humour, in the hypothesis that the promulgation of such dogmas could produce anything but the laughter of sceptics and the contempt of the healthy human intellect?

The sect which requires to be encountered in these days is not one which boggles over the *filioque*, but certain successors of those Ephesians who told Paul that they did not even know 'whether there were any Holy Ghost.' But it explains some modern phenomena when we find that the leaders of theology hope to reconcile faith and reason, and to show that the old symbols have still a right to the allegiance of our hearts and brains, by putting forth these portentous propositions. We are struggling with hard facts, and they would arm us with the forgotten tools of scholasticism. We wish for spiritual food, and are to be put off with these ancient mummeries of forgotten dogma. If Agnosticism is the frame of mind which summarily rejects these imbecilities, and would restrain the human intellect from wasting its powers on the attempt to galvanise into sham activity this *caput mortuum* of old theology, nobody need be afraid of the name. Argument against such adversaries would be itself a foolish waste of time. Let the dead bury their dead, and Old Catholics decide whether the Holy Ghost proceeds from the Father and the Son, or from the Father alone. Gentlemen, indeed, who still read the Athanasian Creed, and profess to attach some meaning to its statements, have no right to sneer at their brethren who persist in taking things seriously. But for men who long for facts instead of phrases, the only possible course is to allow such vagaries to take their own course to the limbo to which they are naturally destined, simply noting, by the way, that modern Gnosticism may lead to puerilities which one blushes even to notice.

It is not with such phenomena that we have seriously to deal. Nobody maintains that the unassisted human intellect can discover the true theory of the Trinity; and the charge of Agnosticism refers, of course, to the sphere of reason, not to the sphere of revelation. Yet those who attack the doctrine are chiefly believers in revelation; and as such they should condescend to answer one important question. Is not the denunciation of reason a commonplace with theologians? What could be easier than to form a catena of the most philosophical defenders of Christianity who have exhausted language in declaring the impotence of the unassisted intellect? Comte has not more explicitly enounced the incapacity of man to deal with the Absolute and the Infinite than a whole series of orthodox writers. Trust your reason, we have been told till we are tired of the phrase, and you will become Atheists or Agnostics. We take you at your word: we become Agnostics. What right have you to turn round and rate us for being a degree more logical than yourselves? Our right, you reply, is founded upon a Divine revelation to ourselves or our Church. Let us grant – it is a very liberal concession – that the right may conceivably be established; but still you are at one with us in philosophy. You say, as we say, that the natural man can know nothing of the Divine nature. That is Agnosticism. Our fundamental principle is not only granted, but asserted. By what logical device you succeed in overleaping the barriers which you have declared to be insuperable is another question. At least you have no *primâ facie* ground for attacking our assumption that the limits of the human intellect are what you declare them to be. This is no mere verbal retort. Half, or more than half, of our adversaries agree formally with our leading principle. They cannot attack us without upsetting the very ground upon which the ablest advocates of their own case rely. The last English writer who professed to defend Christianity with weapons drawn from wide and genuine philosophical knowledge was Dean Mansel. The whole substance of his argument was simply and solely the assertion of the first principles of Agnosticism. Mr. Herbert Spencer, the prophet of the Unknowable, the foremost representative of Agnosticism, professes in his programme to be carrying 'a step further the doctrine put into shape by Hamilton and Mansel.' Nobody, I suspect would now deny, nobody except Dean Mansel himself, and the 'religious' newspapers, ever denied very seriously, that the 'further step' thus taken was the logical step. Opponents both from within and without the Church, Mr. Maurice and Mr. Mill, agreed that this affiliation was legitimate. The Old Testament represents Jehovah as human, as vindictive, as prescribing immoralities; therefore, Jehovah was not the true God; that was the contention of the infidel. We know nothing whatever about the true God was the reply, for God means the Absolute and the Infinite. Any special act may come from God, for it may be a moral miracle; any attribute may represent the character of God to man, for we know nothing whatever of His real attributes, and cannot even conceive Him as endowed with attributes. The doctrine of the Atonement cannot be revolting, because it cannot have any meaning. Mr. Spencer hardly goes a step beyond his original, except, indeed, in candour.

Most believers repudiate Dean Mansel's arguments. They were an anachronism. They were fatal to the decaying creed of pure Theism, and powerless against the growing creed of Agnosticism. When theology had vital power enough to throw out fresh branches, the orthodox could venture to attack the Deist, and the Deist could assail the traditional beliefs. As the impulse grows fainter, it is seen that such a warfare is suicidal. The old rivals must make an alliance against the common enemy. The theologian must appeal for help to the metaphysician whom he reviled. Orthodoxy used to call Spinoza an Atheist; it is now glad to argue that even Spinoza is a witness on its own side. Yet the most genuine theology still avows its hatred of reason and distrusts sham alliances. Newman was not, like Dean Mansel, a profound metaphysician, but his admirable rhetoric expressed a far finer religious instinct. He felt more keenly, if he did not reason so systematically; and the force of one side of his case is undeniable. He holds that the unassisted reason cannot afford a sufficient support for a belief in God. He declares, as innumerable writers of less power have declared, that there is 'no medium, in true philosophy, between Atheism and Catholicity, and that a perfectly consistent mind, under those circumstances in which it finds itself here below, must embrace either the one or the other.'[1] He looks in vain for any antagonist, except the Catholic Church, capable of baffling and withstanding 'the fierce energy of passion, and the all-corroding, all-dissolving scepticism of the intellect in religious matters.'[2] Some such doctrine is in fact but a natural corollary from the doctrine of human corruption held by all genuine theologians. The very basis of orthodox theology is the actual

---

[1]   *History of my Religious Opinions*, pp. 322–3.

[2]   *Ibid*, p. 379.

separation of the creation from the Creator. In the 'Grammar of Assent,' Newman tells us that we 'can only glean from the surface of the world some faint and fragmentary views' of God. 'I see,' he proceeds, 'only a choice of alternatives in view of so critical a fact; either there is no Creator, or He has disowned His creatures.'[3] The absence of God from His own world is the one prominent fact which startles and appals him. Newman, of course, does not see or does not admit the obvious consequence. He asserts most emphatically that he believes in the existence of God as firmly as in his own existence; and he finds the ultimate proof of this doctrine – a proof not to be put into mood and figure – in the testimony of the conscience. But he apparently admits that Atheism is as logical, that is, as free from self-contradiction, as Catholicism. He certainly declares that though the ordinary arguments are conclusive, they are not in practice convincing. Sound reason would, of course, establish theology; but corrupt man does not and cannot reason soundly. Newman, however, goes further than this. His Theism can only be supported by help of his Catholicity. If, therefore, Newman had never heard of the Catholic Church – if, that is, he were in the position of the great majority of men now living, and of the overwhelming majority of the race which has lived since its first appearance, he would be driven to one of two alternatives. Either he would be an Atheist or he would be an Agnostic. His conscience might say, there is a God; his observation would say, there is no God. Moreover, the voice of conscience has been very differently interpreted. Newman's interpretation has no force for anyone who, like most men, does not share his intuitions. To such persons, therefore, there can be, on Newman's own showing, no refuge except the admittedly logical refuge of Atheism. Even if they shared his intuitions, they would be necessarily sceptics until the Catholic Church came to their aid, for their intuitions would be in hopeless conflict with their experience. I need hardly add that, to some minds, the proposed alliance with reason of a Church which admits that its tenets are corroded and dissolved wherever free reason is allowed to play upon them, is rather suspicious. At any rate, Newman's arguments go to prove that man, as guided by reason, ought to be an Agnostic, and that, at the present moment, Agnosticism is the only reasonable faith for at least three-quarters of the race.

3   *Grammar of Assent*, p. 392.

All, then, who think that men should not be dogmatic about matters beyond the sphere of reason or even conceivability, who hold that reason, however weak, is our sole guide, or who find that their conscience does not testify to the divinity of the Catholic God, but declares the moral doctrines of Catholicity to be demonstrably erroneous, are entitled to claim such orthodox writers as sharing their fundamental principles, though refusing to draw the legitimate inferences. The authority of Dean Mansel and Newman may of course be repudiated. In one sense, however, they are simply stating an undeniable fact. The race collectively is agnostic, whatever may be the case with individuals. Newton might be certain of the truth of his doctrines, whilst other thinkers were still convinced of their falsity. It could not be said that the doctrines were certainly true, so long as they were doubted in good faith by competent reasoners. Newman may be as much convinced of the truth of his theology as Professor Huxley of its error. But speaking of the race, and not of the individual, there is no plainer fact in history than the fact that hitherto no knowledge has been attained. There is not a single proof of natural theology of which the negative has not been maintained as vigorously as the affirmative.

You tell us to be ashamed of professing ignorance. Where is the shame of ignorance in matters still involved in endless and hopeless controversy? Is it not rather a duty? Why should a lad who has just run the gauntlet of examinations and escaped to a country parsonage be dogmatic, when his dogmas are denounced as erroneous by half the philosophers of the world? What theory of the universe am I to accept as demonstrably established? At the very earliest dawn of philosophy men were divided by earlier forms of the same problems which divide them now. Shall I be a Platonist or an Aristotelian? Shall I admit or deny the existence of innate ideas? Shall I believe in the possibility or in the impossibility of transcending experience? Go to the mediaeval philosophy, says one controversialist. To which mediaeval philosophy, pray? Shall I be a nominalist or a realist? And why should I believe you rather than the great thinkers of the seventeenth century, who agreed with one accord that the first condition of intellectual progress was the destruction of that philosophy? There would be no difficulty if it were a question of physical science. I might believe in Galileo and Newton and their successors down to

Adams and Leverrier without hesitation, because they all substantially agree. But when men deal with the old problems there are still the old doubts. Shall I believe in Hobbes or in Descartes? Can I stop where Descartes stopped, or must I go on to Spinoza? Or shall I follow Locke's guidance, and end with Hume's scepticism? Or listen to Kant, and, if so, shall I decide that he is right in destroying theology, or in reconstructing it, or in both performances? Does Hegel hold the key of the secret, or is he a mere spinner of jargon? May not Feuerbach or Schopenhauer represent the true development of metaphysical inquiry? Shall I put faith in Hamilton and Mansel, and, if so, shall I read their conclusions by the help of Mr. Spencer, or shall I believe in Mill or in Green? State any one proposition in which all philosophers agree, and I will admit it to be true; or any one which has a manifest balance of authority, and I will agree that it is probable. But so long as every philosopher flatly contradicts the first principles of his predecessors, why affect certainty? The only agreement I can discover is, that there is no philosopher of whom his opponents have not said that his opinions lead logically either to Pantheism or to Atheism.

When all the witnesses thus contradict each other, the *primâ facie* result is pure scepticism. There is no certainty. Who am I, if I were the ablest of modern thinkers, to say summarily that all the great men who differed from me are wrong, and so wrong that their difference should not even raise a doubt in my mind? From such scepticism there is indeed one, and, so far as I can see, but one, escape. The very hopelessness of the controversy shows that the reasoners have been transcending the limits of reason. They have reached a point where, as at the pole, the compass points indifferently to every quarter. Thus there is a chance that I may retain what is valuable in the chaos of speculation, and reject what is bewildering by confining the mind to its proper limits. But has any limit ever been suggested, except a limit which comes in substance to an exclusion of all ontology? In short, if I would avoid utter scepticism, must I not be an Agnostic?

Let us suppose, however, that this difficulty can be evaded. Suppose that, after calling witnesses from all schools and all ages, I can find ground for excluding all the witnesses who make against me. Let me say, for example, that the whole school which refuses to transcend experience errs from the wickedness of its heart and the consequent dulness of its intellect. Some people seem to think that a plausible and happy suggestion. Let the theologian have his necessary laws of thought, which enable him to evolve truth beyond all need of verification from experience. Where will the process end? The question answers itself. The path has been trodden again and again, till it is as familiar as the first rule of arithmetic. Admit that the mind can reason about the Absolute and the Infinite, and you will get to Spinoza. No refutation of his arguments, starting from his premises, has ever been even apparently successful. In fact, the chain of reasoning is substantially too short and simple to be for a moment doubtful. Theology, if logical, leads straight to Pantheism. The Infinite God is everything. All things are bound together as cause and effect. God, the first cause, is the cause of all effects down to the most remote. In one form or other, that is the conclusion to which all theology approximates as it is pushed to its legitimate result.

Here, then, we have an apparent triumph over Agnosticism. But nobody can accept Spinoza without rejecting all the doctrines for which the Gnostics really contend. In the first place, revelation and the God of revelation disappear. The argument according to Spinoza against supernaturalism differs from the argument according to Hume in being more peremptory. Hume only denies that a past miracle can be proved by evidence: Spinoza denies that it could ever have happened. As a fact, miracles and a local revelation were first assailed by Deists more effectually than by sceptics. The old Theology was seen to be unworthy of the God of nature, before it was said that nature could not be regarded through the theological representation. And, in the next place, the orthodox assault upon the value of Pantheism is irresistible. Pantheism can give no ground for morality, for nature is as much the cause of vice as the cause of virtue; it can give no ground for an optimist view of the universe, for nature causes evil as much as it causes good. We no longer doubt, it is true, whether there be a God, for our God means all reality; but every doubt which we entertained about the universe is transferred to the God upon whom the universe is moulded. The attempt to transfer to pure being or to the abstraction of Nature the feelings with which we are taught to regard a person of transcendent wisdom and benevolence is, as theologians assert, hopeless. To deny the existence of God is in this sense the same as to deny the existence of no-God. We keep the old word; we have altered the whole of its contents. A Pantheist is, as a rule, one who looks upon the universe through his feelings instead of his reason, and who regards it with love because his habitual frame of mind is amiable. But he has no logical argument as against the Pessimist, who regards it with dread unqualified by love, or the Agnostic, who finds it impossible to regard it with any but a colourless emotion.

The Gnostic, then, gains nothing by admitting the claims of a faculty which at once overturns his conclusions. His second step is invariably to half-retract his first. We are bound by a necessary law of thought, he tells us, to believe in universal causation. Very well, then, let us be Pantheists. No, he says; another necessary law of thought tells us that causation is not universal. We know that the will is free, or, in other words, that the class of phenomena most important to us are not caused. This is the position of the ordinary Deist; and it is of vital importance to him, for otherwise the connection between Deism and morality is, on his own ground, untenable. The ablest and most logical thinkers have declared that the free-will doctrine involves a fallacy, and have unravelled the fallacy to their own satisfaction. Whether right or wrong, they have at least this advantage, that, on their showing, reason is on this point consistent with itself. The advocate of free-will, on the other hand, declares that an insoluble antinomy occurs at the very threshold of his speculations. An uncaused phenomenon is unthinkable; yet consciousness testifies that our actions, so far as they are voluntary, are uncaused. In face of such a contradiction, the only rational state of mind is scepticism. A mind balanced between two necessary and contradictory thoughts must be in a hopeless state of doubt. The Gnostic, therefore, starts by proclaiming that we must all be Agnostics in regard to a matter of primary philosophical importance. If by free-will he means anything else than a denial of causation, his statement is irrelevant.

For, it must be noticed, this is not one of the refined speculative problems which may be neglected in our ordinary reasoning. The ancient puzzles about the one and the many, or the infinite and the finite, may or may not be insoluble. They do not affect our practical knowledge. Familiar difficulties have been raised as to our conceptions of motion: the hare and tortoise problem may be revived by modern metaphysicians; but the mathematician may continue to calculate the movements of the planets and never doubt whether the quicker body will, in fact, overtake the slower. The free-will problem cannot be thus shirked. We all admit that a competent reasoner can foretell the motions of the moon; and we admit it because we know that there is no element of objective chance in the problem. But the determinist asserts, whilst the libertarian denies, that it would be possible for an adequate intelligence to foretell the actions of a man or a race. There is or is not an element of objective chance in the question; and whether there is or is not must be decided by reason and observation, independently of those puzzles about the infinite and the finite, which affect equally the man and the planet. The anti-determinist asserts the existence of chance so positively, that he doubts whether God Himself can foretell the future of humanity; or, at least, he is unable to reconcile Divine prescience with his favourite doctrine.

In most practical questions, indeed, the difference is of little importance. The believer in free-will admits that we can make an approximate guess; the determinist admits that our faculty of calculation is limited. But when we turn to the problems with which the Gnostic desires to deal, the problem is of primary importance. Free-will is made responsible for all the moral evil in the world. God made man perfect, but He gave His creatures free-will. The exercise of that free-will has converted the world into a scene in which the most striking fact, as Newman tells us, is the absence of the Creator. It follows, then, that all this evil, the sight of which leads some of us to Atheism, some to blank despair, and some to epicurean indifference, and the horror of which is at the root of every vigorous religious creed, results from accident. If even God could have foretold it, He foretold it in virtue of faculties inconceivable to finite minds; and no man, however exalted his faculties, could by any possibility have foretold it. Here, then, is Agnosticism in the highest degree. An inexorable necessity of thought makes it absolutely impossible for us to say whether this world is the ante-room to heaven or hell. We do not know, nay, it is intrinsically impossible for us to know, whether the universe is to be a source of endless felicity or a ghastly and everlasting torture-house. The Gnostic invites us to rejoice because the existence of an infinitely good and wise Creator is a guarantee for our happiness. He adds, in the same breath, that this good and wise Being has left it to chance whether His creatures shall all, or in any proportion, go straight to the devil. He reviles the Calvinist, who dares to think that God has settled the point by His arbitrary will. Is an arbitrary decision better or worse than a trusting to chance? We know that there is a great First Cause; but we add that there are at this moment in the world some twelve hundred million little first causes which may damn or save themselves as they please.

The free-will hypothesis is the device by which theologians try to relieve God of the responsibility for the sufferings of His creation. It is required for another purpose. It enables the Creator to be also the judge. Man must be partly independent of God, or God would be at once pulling the wires and punishing the puppets. So far the argument is unimpeachable; but the device justifies God at the expense of making the universe a moral chaos. Grant the existence of this arbitrary force called free-will, and we shall be forced to admit that, if justice is to be found anywhere, it is at least not to be found in this strange anarchy, where chance and fate are struggling for the mastery.

The fundamental proposition of the anti-determinist, that which contains the whole pith and substance of his teaching, is this: that a determined action cannot be meritorious. Desert can only accrue in respect of actions which are self-caused, or in so far as they are self-caused; and self-caused is merely a periphrasis for uncaused. Now no one dares to say that our conduct is entirely self-caused. The assumption is implied in every act of our lives and every speculation about history that men's actions are determined, exclusively or to a great extent, by their character and their circumstances. Only so far as that doctrine is true can human nature be the subject of any reasoning whatever; for reason is but the reflection of external regularity, and vanishes with the admission of chance. Our conduct, then, is the resultant of the two forces, which we may call fate and free-will. Fate is but the name for the will of God. He is responsible for placing us with a certain character in a certain position; He cannot justly punish us for the conse-quences; we are responsible to Him for the effects of our free-will alone, if free-will exists. That is the very contention of the anti-determinist; let us look for a moment at the consequences.

The ancient difficulty which has perplexed men since the days of Job is this: Why are happiness and misery arbitrarily distributed? Why do the good so often suffer, and the evil so often flourish? The difficulty, says the determinist, arises entirely from applying the conception of justice where it is manifestly out of place. The advocate of free-will refuses this escape, and is perplexed by a further difficulty. Why are virtue and vice arbitrarily distributed? Of all the puzzles of this dark world, or of all forms of the one great puzzle, the most appalling is that which meets us at the corner of every street. Look at the children growing up amidst moral poison; see the brothel and the public-house turning out harlots and drunkards by the thousand; at the brutalised elders preaching cruelty and shamelessness by example; and deny, if you can, that lust and brutality are generated as certainly as scrofula and typhus. Nobody dares to deny it. All philanthropists admit it; and every hope of improvement is based on the assumption that the moral character is determined by its surroundings. What does the theological advocate of free-will say to reconcile such a spectacle with our moral conceptions? Will God damn all these wretches for faults due to causes as much beyond their power as the shape of their limbs or as the orbits of the planets? Or will He make some allowance, and decline to ask for grapes from thistles, and exact purity of life from beings born in corruption, breathing corruption, and trained in corruption? Let us try each alternative.

To Job's difficulty it has been replied that, though virtue is not always rewarded and vice punished, yet virtue *as such* is rewarded, and vice *as such* is punished. If that be true, God, on the free-will hypothesis, must be unjust. Virtue and vice, as the facts irresistibly prove, are caused by fate or by God's will as well as by free-will – that is, our own will. To punish a man brought up in a London slum by the rule applicable to a man brought up at the feet of Christ is manifestly the height of injustice. Nay, for anything we can tell – for we know nothing of the circumstances of their birth and education – the effort which Judas Iscariot exerted in restoring the price of blood may have required a greater force of free-will than would have saved Peter from denying his Master. Moll Flanders may put forth more power to keep out of the lowest depths of vice than a girl brought up in a convent to kill herself by ascetic austerities. If, in short, reward is proportioned to virtue, it cannot be proportioned to merit, for merit, by the hypothesis, is proportioned to the free-will, which is only one of the factors of virtue. The apparent injustice may, of course, be remedied by some unknowable compensation; but for all that appears, it is the height of injustice to reward equally equal attainments under entirely different conditions. In other words, the theologian has raised a difficulty from which he can only escape by the help of Agnosticism. Justice is not to be found in the visible arrangements of the universe.

Let us, then, take the other alternative. Assume that rewards are proportioned, not to virtue, but to merit. God will judge us by what we have done for ourselves, not by the tendencies which He has impressed upon us. The difficulty is disguised, for it is not diminished, and morality is degraded. A man should be valued, say all the deepest moralists, by his nature, not by his external acts; by what he is, not by how he came to be what he is. Virtue is heaven, and vice is hell. Divine rewards and punishments are not arbitrarily annexed, but represent the natural state of a being brought into harmony with the supreme law, or in hopeless conflict with it. We need a change of nature, not a series of acts unconnected with out nature. Virtue is a reality precisely in so far as it is a part of nature, not of accident; of our fate, not of our free-will. The assertion in some shape of these truths has been at the bottom of all great moral and religious reforms. The attempt to patch up some compromise between this and the opposite theory has generated those endless controversies about grace and free-will on which no Christian Church has ever been able to make up its mind, and which warn us that we are once more plunging into Agnosticism. In order to make the Creator the judge, you assume that part of man's actions are his own. Only on that showing can he have merit as against his Maker. Admitting this, and only if we admit this, we get a footing for the debtor and creditor theories of morality – for the doctrine that man runs up a score with Heaven in respect of that part of his conduct which is uncaused. Thus we have a ground for the various theories of merit by which priests have thriven and Churches been corrupted; but it is at the cost of splitting human nature in two, and making happiness depend upon those acts which are not really part of our true selves.

It is not, however, my purpose to show the immorality or the unreasonableness of the doctrine. I shall only remark that it is essentially agnostic. Only in so far as phenomena embody fixed 'laws' can we have any ground for inference in this world, and, à fortiori, from this world to the next. If happiness is the natural consequence of virtue, we may plausibly argue that the virtuous will be happy hereafter. If heaven be a bonus arbitrarily bestowed upon the exercise of an inscrutable power, all analogies break down. The merit of an action as between men depends upon the motives. The actions for which God rewards and punishes are the actions or those parts of actions which are independent of motive. Punishment amongst men is regulated by some considerations of its utility to the criminal or his fellows. No conceivable measure of Divine punishment can even be suggested when once we distinguish between divine and natural; and the very essence of the theory is that such a distinction exists. For whatever may be true of the next world, we begin by assuming that new principles are to be called into play hereafter. The new world is summoned into being to redress the balance of the old. The fate which here too often makes the good miserable and the bad happy, which still more strangely fetters our wills and forces the strong will into wickedness and strengthens the weak will to goodness, will then be suspended. The motive which persuades us to believe in the good arrangement hereafter is precisely the badness of this. Such a motive to believe cannot itself be a reason for belief. That would be to believe because belief was unreasonable. This world, once more, is a chaos, in which the most conspicuous fact is the absence of the Creator. Nay, it is so chaotic that, according to theologians, infinite rewards and penalties are required to square the account and redress the injustice here accumulated. What is this, so far as the natural reason is concerned, but the very superlative of Agnosticism? The appeal to experience can lead to nothing, for our very object is to contradict experience. We appeal to facts to show that facts are illusory. The appeal to *à priori* reason is not more hopeful, for you begin by showing that reason on these matters is self-contradictory, and you insist that human nature is radically irregular, and therefore beyond the sphere of reason. If you could succeed in deducing any theory by reason, reason would, on your showing, be at hopeless issue with experience.

There are two questions, in short, about the universe which must be answered to escape from Agnosticism. The great fact which puzzles the mind is the vast amount of evil. It may be answered that evil is an illusion, because God is benevolent; or it may be answered that evil is deserved, because God is just. In one case the doubt is removed by denying the existence of the difficulty, in the other it is made tolerable by satisfying our consciences. We have seen what natural reason can do towards justifying these answers. To escape from Agnosticism we become Pantheists; then the divine reality must be the counterpart of phenomenal nature, and all the difficulties recur. We escape from Pantheism by the illogical device of free-will. Then God is indeed good and wise, but God is no longer omnipotent. By His side we erect a fetish called free-will, which is potent enough to defeat all God's good purposes, and to make His absence from His own universe the most conspicuous fact given by observation; and which, at the same time, is by its own nature intrinsically arbitrary in its action. Your Gnosticism tells us that an almighty benevolence is watching over everything, and bringing good out of all evil. Whence, then, comes the evil? By free-will; that is, by chance! It is an exception, an exception which covers, say, half the pheno-mena, and includes all that puzzle us. Say boldly at once no explanation can be given, and then proceed to denounce Agnosticism. If, again, we take the moral problem, the Pantheist view shows desert as before God to be a contradic-tion in terms. We are what He has made us; nay, we are but manifestations of Himself – how can He complain? Escape from the dilemma by making us independent of God, and God, so far as the observed universe can tell us, becomes systemati-cally unjust. He rewards the good and the bad, and gives equal reward to the free agent and the slave of fate. Where are we to turn for a solution?

Let us turn to revelation; that is the most obvious reply. By all means, though this is to admit that natural reason cannot help us; or, in other words, it directly produces more Agnosticism, though indirectly it makes an opening for revelation. There is, indeed, a difficulty here. Pure theism, as we have observed, is in reality as vitally opposed to historical revelation as simple scepticism. The word God is used by the metaphysician and the savage. It may mean anything, from 'pure Being' down to the most degraded fetish. The 'universal consent' is a consent to use the same phrase for antagonistic conceptions – for order and chaos, for absolute unity or utter heterogeneity, for a universe governed by a human will, or by a will of which man cannot form the slightest conception. This is, of course, a difficulty which runs off the orthodox disputant like water from a duck's back. He appeals to his conscience, and his conscience tells him just what he wants. It reveals a Being just at that point in the scale between the two extremes which is convenient for his purposes. I open, for example, a harmless little treatise by a divine who need not be named. He knows intuitively, so he says, that there is a God, who is benevolent and wise, and endowed with personality, that is to say, conceived anthropomorphically enough to be capable of acting upon the universe, and yet so far different from man as to be able to throw a decent veil of mystery over His more questionable actions. Well, I reply, my intuition tells me of no such Being. Then, says the divine, I can't prove my statements, but you would recognise their truth if your heart or your intellect were not corrupted: that is, you must be a knave or a fool. This is a kind of argument to which one is perfectly accustomed in theology. I am right, and you are wrong; and I am right because I good and wise. By all means; and now let us see what your wisdom and goodness can tell us.

The Christian revelation makes statements which, if true, are undoubtedly of the very highest importance. God is angry with man. Unless we believe and repent we shall all be damned. It is impossible, indeed, for its advocates even to say this without instantly contradicting themselves. Their doctrine frightens them. They explain in various ways that a great many people will be saved without believing, and that eternal damnation is not eternal nor damnation. It is only the vulgar who hold such views, and who, of course, must not be disturbed in them; but they are not for the intelligent. God grants 'uncovenanted mercies' – that is, He sometimes lets a sinner off, though He has not made a legal bargain about it – an explanation calculated to exalt our conceptions of the Deity! But let us pass over these endless shufflings from the horrible to the meaningless. Christianity tells us in various ways how the wrath of the Creator may be appeased and His goodwill ensured. The doctrine is manifestly important to believers; but does it give us a clearer or happier view of the universe? That is what is required for the confusion of Agnostics; and, if the mystery were in part solved, or the clouds thinned in the slightest degree, Christianity would triumph by its inherent merits. Let us, then, ask once more, Does Christianity exhibit the ruler of the universe as benevolent or as just?

If I were to assert that of every ten beings born into this world nine would be damned, that all who refused to believe what they did not hold to be proved, and all who sinned from overwhelming temptation, and all who had not had the good-fortune to be the subjects of a miraculous conversion or the recipients of a grace conveyed by a magical charm, would be tortured to all eternity, what would an orthodox theologian reply? He could not say, 'That is false'; I might appeal to the highest authorities for my justification; nor, in fact, could he on his own showing deny the possibility. Hell, he says, exists; he does not know who will be damned; though he does know that all men are by nature corrupt and liable to be damned if not saved by supernatural grace. He might, and probably would, now say, 'That is rash. You have no authority for saying how many will be lost and how many saved: you cannot even say what is meant by hell or heaven: you cannot tell how far God may be better than His word, though you may be sure that He won't be worse than His word.' And what is all this but to say, We know nothing about it? In other words, to fall back on Agnosticism. The difficulty, as theologians truly say, is not so much that evil is eternal, as that evil exists. That is in substance a frank admission that, as nobody can explain evil, nobody can explain anything. Your revelation, which was to prove the benevolence of God, has proved only that God's benevolence may be consistent with the eternal and infinite misery of most of His creatures; you escape only by saying that it is also consistent with their not being eternally and infinitely miserable. That is, the revelation reveals nothing.

But the revelation shows God to be just. Now, if the free-will hypothesis be rejected – and it is rejected, not only by infidels, but by the most consistent theologians – this question cannot really arise at all. Jonathan Edwards will prove that there cannot be a question of justice as between man and God. The creature has no rights against his Creator. The question of justice merges in the question of benevolence; and Edwards will go on to say that most men are damned, and that the blessed will thank God for their tortures. That is logical, but not consoling. Passing this over, can revelation prove that God is just, assuming that justice is a word applicable to dealings between the potter and the pot?

And here we are sent to the 'great argument of Butler.' Like some other theological arguments already noticed, that great argument is to many minds – those of James Mill and of Dr. Martineau, for example – a direct assault upon Theism, or, in other words, an argument for Agnosticism. Briefly stated, it comes to this. The God of revelation cannot be the God of nature, said the Deists, because the God of revelation is unjust. The God of revelation, replied Butler, may be the God of nature, for the God of nature is unjust. Stripped of its various involutions, that is the sum and substance of this celebrated piece of reasoning. Butler, I must say in passing, deserves high credit for two things. The first is that he is the only theologian who has ever had the courage to admit that any difficulty existed when he was struggling most desperately to meet the difficulty; though even Butler could not admit that such a difficulty should affect a man's conduct. Secondly, Butler's argument really rests upon a moral theory, mistaken indeed in some senses, but possessing a stoical grandeur. To admit, however, that Butler was a noble and a comparatively candid thinker is not to admit that he ever faced the real difficulty. It need not be asked here by what means he evaded it. His position is in any case plain. Christianity tells us, as he thinks, that God damns men for being bad, whether they could help it or not; and that He lets them off, or lets some of them off, for the sufferings of others. He damns the helpless and punishes the innocent. Horrible! exclaims the infidel. Possibly, replies Butler, but nature is just as bad. All suffering is punishment. It strikes the good as well as the wicked. The father sins, and the son suffers. I drink too much, and my son has the gout. In another world we may suppose that the same system will be carried out more thoroughly. God will pardon some sinners because He punished Christ, and He will damn others everlastingly. That is His way. A certain degree of wrongdoing here leads to irremediable suffering, or rather to suffering remediable by death alone. In the next world there is no death; therefore, the suffering won't be remediable at all. The world is a scene of probation, destined to fit us for a better life. As a matter of fact, most men make it a discipline of vice instead of a discipline of virtue; and most men, therefore, will presumably be damned. We see the same thing in the waste of seeds and animal life, and may suppose, therefore, that it is part of the general scheme of Providence.

This is the Christian revelation according to Butler. Does it make the world better? Does it not, rather, add indefinitely to the terror produced by the sight of all its miseries, and justify James Mill for feeling that rather than such a God he would have no God? What escape can be suggested? The obvious one: it is all a mystery; and what is mystery but the theological phrase for Agnosticism? God has spoken, and endorsed all our most hideous doubts. He has said, let there be light, and there is no light – no light, but rather darkness visible, serving only to discover sights of woe.

The believers who desire to soften away the old dogmas – in other words, to take refuge from the unpleasant results of their doctrine with the Agnostics, and to retain the pleasant results with the Gnostics – have a different mode of escape. They know that God is good and just; that evil will somehow disappear and apparent injustice be somehow redressed. The practical objection to this amiable creed suggests a sad comment upon the whole controversy. We fly to religion to escape from our dark forebodings. But a religion which stifles these forebodings always fails to satisfy us. We long to hear that they are groundless. As soon as we are told that they are groundless we mistrust our authority. No poetry lives which reflects only the cheerful emotions. Our sweetest songs are those which tell of saddest thought. We can bring harmony out of melancholy; we cannot banish melancholy from the world. And the religious utterances, which are the highest form of poetry, are bound by the same law. There is a deep sadness in the world. Turn and twist the thought as you may, there is no escape. Optimism would be soothing if it were possible; in fact, it is impossible, and therefore a constant mockery; and of all dogmas that ever were invented, that which has least vitality is the dogma that whatever is, is right.

Let us, however, consider for a moment what is the net result of this pleasant creed. Its philosophical basis may be sought in pure reason or in experience; but, as a rule, its adherents are ready to admit that the pure reason requires the support of the emotions before such a doctrine can be established, and are therefore marked by a certain tinge of mysticism. They feel rather than know. The awe with which they regard the universe, the tender glow of reverence and love with which the bare sight of nature affects them, is to them the ultimate guarantee of their beliefs. Happy those who feel such emotions! Only, when they try to extract definite statements of fact from these impalpable sentiments, they should beware how far such statements are apt to come into terrible collision with reality. And, meanwhile, those who have been disabused with

Candide, who have felt the weariness and pain of all 'this unintelligible world,' and have not been able to escape into any mystic rapture, have as much to say for their own version of the facts. Is happiness a dream, or misery, or is it all a dream? Does not our answer vary with our health and with our condition? When, rapt in the security of a happy life, we cannot even conceive that our happiness will fail, we are practical optimists. When some random blow out of the dark crushes the pillars round which our life has been entwined as recklessly as a boy sweeps away a cobweb, when at a single step we plunge through the flimsy crust of happiness into the deep gulfs beneath, we are tempted to turn to Pessimism. Who shall decide, and how? Of all questions that can be asked, the most important is surely this: Is the tangled web of this world composed chiefly of happiness or of misery? And of all questions that can be asked, if is surely the most unanswerable. For in no other problem is the difficulty of discarding the illusions arising from our own experience, of eliminating 'the personal error' and gaining an outside standing-point, so hopeless.

In any case the real appeal must be to experience. Ontologists may manufacture libraries of jargon without touching the point. They have never made, or suggested the barest possibility of making, a bridge from the world of pure reason to the contingent world in which we live. To the thinker who tries to construct the universe out of pure reason, the actual existence of error in our minds and disorder in the outside world presents a difficulty as hopeless as that which the existence of vice and misery presents to the optimist who tries to construct the universe out of pure goodness. To say that misery does not exist is to contradict the primary testimony of consciousness; to argue on *à priori* grounds that misery or happiness predominates, is as hopeless a task as to deduce from the principle of the excluded middle the distance from St. Paul's to Westminster Abbey. Questions of fact can only be solved by examining facts. Perhaps such evidence would show – and if a guess were worth anything, I should add that I guess that it would show – that happiness predominates over misery in the composition of the known world. I am, therefore, not prejudiced against the Gnostic's conclusion; but I add that the evidence is just as open to me as to him. The whole world in which we live may be an illusion – a veil to be withdrawn in some higher state of being. But be it what it may, it supplies all the evidence upon which we can rely. If evil predominates here, we have no reason to suppose that good predominates elsewhere. All the ingenuity of theologians can never shake our conviction that facts are what we feel them to be, nor invert the plain inference from facts; and facts are just as open to one school of thought as to another.

What, then, is the net result? One insoluble doubt has haunted men's minds since thought began in the world. No answer has ever been suggested. One school of philosophers hands it to the next. It is denied in one form only to reappear in another. The question is not which system excludes the doubt, but how it expresses the doubt. Admit or deny the competence of reason in theory, we all agree that it fails in practice. Theologians revile reason as much as Agnostics; they then appeal to it, and it decides against them. They amend their plea by excluding certain questions from its jurisdiction, and those questions include the whole difficulty. They go to revelation, and revelation replies by calling doubt, mystery. They declare that their consciousness declares just what they want it to declare. Ours declares something else. Who is to decide? The only appeal is to experience, and to appeal to experience is to admit the fundamental dogma of Agnosticism.

Is it not, then, the very height of audacity, in face of a difficulty which meets us at every turn, which has perplexed all the ablest thinkers in proportion to their ability, which vanishes in one shape only to show itself in another, to declare roundly, not only that the difficulty can be solved, but that it does not exist? Why, when no honest man will deny in private that every ultimate problem is wrapped in the profoundest mystery, do honest men proclaim in pulpits that unhesitating certainty is the duty of the most foolish and ignorant? Is it not a spectacle to make the angels laugh? We are a company of ignorant beings, feeling our way through mists and darkness, learning only by incessantly-repeated blunders, obtaining a glimmering of truth by falling into every conceivable error, dimly discerning light enough for our daily needs, but hopelessly differing whenever we attempt to describe the ultimate origin or end of our paths; and yet, when one of us ventures to declare that we don't know the map of the universe as well as the map of our infinitesimal parish, he is hooted, reviled, and perhaps told that he will be damned to all eternity for his faithlessness. Amidst all the endless and hopeless controversies which have left nothing but bare husks of meaningless words, we have been able to discover certain reliable truths. They don't take us very far, and the condition of discovering them has been distrust of *à priori* guesses, and the systematic interrogation of experience. Let us, say some of us, follow at least this clue. Here we shall find sufficient guidance for the needs of life, though we renounce for ever the attempt to get behind the veil which no one has succeeded in raising; if, indeed, there be anything behind. You miserable Agnostics! is the retort; throw aside such rubbish, and cling to the old husks. Stick to the words which profess to explain everything; call your doubts mysteries, and they won't disturb you any longer; and believe in those necessary truths of which no two philosophers have ever succeeded in giving the same version.

Gentlemen, we can only reply, wait till you have some show of agreement amongst yourselves. Wait till you can give some answer, not palpably a verbal answer, to some one of the doubts which oppress us as they oppress you. Wait till you can point to some single truth, however trifling, which has been discovered by your method, and will stand the test of discussion and verification. Wait till you can appeal to reason without in the same breath vilifying reason. Wait till your Divine revelations have something more to reveal than the hope that the hideous doubts which they suggest may possibly be without foundation. Till then we shall be content to admit openly, what you whisper under your breath or hide in technical jargon, that the ancient secret is a secret still; that man knows nothing of the Infinite and Absolute; and that, knowing nothing, he had better not be dogmatic about his ignorance. And, meanwhile, we will endeavour to be as charitable as possible, and whilst you trumpet forth officially your contempt for our scepticism, we will at least try to believe that you are imposed upon by your own bluster.

THE ETHICS OF BELIEF[1]
[William Kingdom Clifford]

I. *The Duty of Inquiry*

A shipowner was about to send to sea an emigrant-ship. He knew that she was old, and not over-well built at the first; that she had seen many seas and climes, and often had needed repairs. Doubts had been suggested to him that possibly she was not seaworthy. These doubts preyed upon his mind and made him unhappy; he thought that perhaps he ought to have her thoroughly overhauled and refitted, even though this should put him to great expense. Before the ship sailed, however, he succeeded in overcoming these melancholy reflections. He said to himself that she had gone safely through so many voyages and weathered so many storms that it was idle to suppose she would not come safely home from this trip also. He would put his trust in Providence, which could hardly fail to protect all these unhappy families that were leaving their father-land to seek for better times elsewhere. He would dismiss from his mind all ungenerous suspicions about the honesty of builders and contractors. In such ways he acquired a sincere and comfortable conviction that his vessel was thoroughly safe and seaworthy; he watched her departure with a light heart, and benevolent wishes for the success of the exiles in their strange new home that was to be; and he got his insurance-money when she went down in mid-ocean and told no tales.

What shall we say of him? Surely this, that he was verily guilty of the death of those men. It is admitted that he did sincerely believe in the soundness of his ship; but the sincerity of his conviction can in no wise help him, because *he had no right to believe on such evidence as was before him*. He had acquired his belief not by honestly earning it in patient investigation, but by stifling his doubts. And although in the end he may have felt so sure about it that he could not think

---

[1] *Contemporary Review*, January 1877.

otherwise, yet inasmuch as he had knowingly and willingly worked himself into that frame of mind, he must be held responsible for it.

Let us alter the case a little, and suppose that the ship was not unsound after all; that she made her voyage safely, and many others after it. Will that diminish the guilt of her owner? Not one jot. When an action is once done, it is right or wrong for ever; no accidental failure of its good or evil fruits can possibly alter that. The man would not have been innocent, he would only have been not found out. The question of right or wrong has to do with the origin of his belief, not the matter of it; not what it was, but how he got it; not whether it turned out to be true or false, but whether he had a right to believe on such evidence as was before him.

There was once an island in which some of the inhabitants professed a religion teaching neither the doctrine of original sin nor that of eternal punishment. A suspicion got abroad that the professors of this religion had made use of unfair means to get their doctrines taught to children. They were accused of wresting the laws of their country in such a way as to remove children from the care of their natural and legal guardians; and even of stealing them away and keeping them concealed from their friends and relations. A certain number of men formed themselves into a society for the purpose of agitating the public about this matter. They published grave accusations against individual citizens of the highest position and character, and did all in their power to injure these citizens in the exercise of their professions. So great was the noise they made, that a Commission was appointed to investigate the facts; but after the Commission had carefully inquired into all the evidence that could be got, it appeared that the accused were innocent. Not only had they been accused on insufficient evidence, but the evidence of their innocence was such as the agitators might easily have obtained, if they had attempted a fair inquiry. After these disclosures the inhabitants of that country looked upon the members of the agitating society, not only as persons whose judgment was to be distrusted, but also as no longer to be counted honourable men. For although they had sincerely and conscientiously believed in the charges they had made, *yet they had no right to believe on such evidence as was before them.* Their sincere convictions, instead of being honestly earned by patient inquiring, were stolen by listening to the voice of prejudice and passion.

Let us vary this case also, and suppose, other things remaining as before, that a still more accurate investigation proved the accused to have been really guilty. Would this make any difference to the guilt of the accusers? Clearly not; the question is not whether their belief was true or false, but whether they entertained it on wrong grounds. They would no doubt say, "Now you see that we were right after all; next time perhaps you will believe us." And they might be believed, but they would not thereby become honourable men. They would not be innocent, they would only be not found out. Every one of them, if he chose to examine himself *in foro conscientiae*, would know that he had acquired and nourished a belief, when he had no right to believe on such evidence as was before him; and therein he would know that he had done a wrong thing.

It may be said, however, that in both of these supposed cases it is not the belief which is judged to be wrong, but the action following upon it. The shipowner might say, "I am perfectly certain that my ship is sound, but still I feel it my duty to have her examined, before trusting the lives of so many people to her." And it might be said to the agitator, "However convinced you were of the justice of your cause and the truth of your convictions, you ought not to have made a public attack upon any man's character until you had examined the evidence on both sides with the utmost patience and care."

In the first place, let us admit that, so far as it goes, this view of the case is right and necessary; right, because even when a man's belief is so fixed that he cannot think otherwise, he still has a choice in regard to the action suggested by it, and so cannot escape the duty of investigating on the ground of the strength of his convictions; and necessary, because those who are not yet capable of controlling their feelings and thoughts must have a plain rule dealing with overt acts.

But this being premised as necessary, it becomes clear that it is not sufficient, and that our previous judgment is required to supplement it. For it is not possible so to sever the belief from the action it suggests as to condemn the one without condemning the other. No man holding a strong belief on one side of a question, or even wishing to hold a belief on one side, can investigate it with such fairness and completeness as if he were really in doubt and unbiassed; so that the existence of a belief not founded on fair inquiry unfits a man for the performance of this necessary duty.

Nor is that truly a belief at all which has not some influence upon the actions of him who holds it. He who truly believes that which prompts him to an action has looked upon the action to lust after it, he has committed it already in his heart. If a belief is not realised immediately in open deeds, it is stored up for the guidance of the future. It goes to make a part of that aggregate of beliefs which is the link between sensation and action at every moment of all our lives, and which is so organised and compacted together that no part of it can be isolated from the rest, but every new addition modifies the structure of the whole. No real belief, however trifling and fragmentary it may seem, is ever truly insignificant; it prepares us to receive more of its like, confirms those which resembled it before, and weakens others; and so gradually it lays a stealthy train in our inmost thoughts, which may some day explode into overt action, and leave its stamp upon our character for ever.

And no one man's belief is in any case a private matter which concerns himself alone. Our lives are guided by that general conception of the course of things, which has been created by society for social purposes. Our words, our phrases, our forms and processes and modes of thought, are common property, fashioned and perfected from age to age; an heirloom which every succeeding generation inherits as a precious deposit and a sacred trust to be handed on to the next one, not unchanged but enlarged and purified, with some clear marks of its proper handiwork. Into this, for good or ill, is woven every belief of every man who has speech of his fellows. An awful privilege, and an awful responsibility, that we should help to create the world in which posterity will live.

In the two supposed cases which have been considered, it has been judged wrong to believe on insufficient evidence, or to nourish belief by suppressing doubts and avoiding investigation. The reason of this judgment is not far to seek: it is that in both these cases the belief held by one man was of great importance to other men. But forasmuch as no belief held by one man, however seemingly trivial the belief, and however obscure the believer, is every actually insignificant or without its effect on the fate of mankind, we have no choice but to extend our judgment to all cases of belief whatever. Belief, that sacred faculty which prompts the decisions of our will, and knits into harmonious working all the compacted energies of our being, is ours not for ourselves, but for humanity. It is rightly used on truths which have been established by long experience and waiting toil, and which have stood in the fierce light of free and fearless questioning. Then it helps to bind men together, and to strengthen and direct their common action. It is desecrated when given to unproved and unquestioned statements, for the solace and private pleasure of the believer; to add a tinsel splendour to the plain straight road of our life and display a bright mirage beyond it; or even to drown the common sorrows of our kind by a self-deception which allows them not only to cast down, but also to degrade us. Whoso would deserve well of his fellows in this matter will guard the purity of his belief with a very fanaticism of jealous care, lest at any time it should rest on an unworthy object, and catch a stain which can never be wiped away.

It is not only the leader of men, statesman, philosopher, or poet, that owes this bounden duty to mankind. Every rustic who delivers in the village alehouse his slow, infrequent sentences, may help to kill or keep alive the fatal superstitions which clog his race. Every hard-worked wife of an artisan may transmit to her children beliefs which shall knit society together, or rend it in pieces. No simplicity of mind, no obscurity of station, can escape the universal duty of questioning all that we believe.

It is true that this duty is a hard one, and the doubt which comes out of it is often a very bitter thing. It leaves us bare and powerless where we thought that we safe and strong. To know all about anything is to know how to deal with it under all circumstances. We feel much happier and more secure when we think we know precisely what to do, no matter what happens, than when we have lost our way and do not know where to turn. And if we have supposed ourselves to know all about anything, and to be capable of doing what is fit in regard to it, we naturally do not like to find that we are really ignorant and powerless, that we have to begin again at the beginning, and try to learn what the thing is and how it is to be dealt with – if indeed anything can be learnt about it. It is the sense of power attached to a sense of knowledge that makes men desirous of believing, and afraid of doubting.

This sense of power is the highest and best of pleasures when the belief on which it is founded is a true belief, and has been fairly earned by investigation. For then we may justly feel that it is common property, and holds good for others as well as for ourselves. Then we may be glad, not that *I* have learned secrets by which I am safer and stronger, but that *we men* have got mastery over more of the world; and we shall be strong, not for ourselves, but in the name of Man and in his strength. But if the belief has been accepted on insufficient evidence, the pleasure is a stolen one. Not only does it deceive ourselves by giving us a sense of power which we do not really possess, but it is sinful, because it is stolen in defiance of our duty to mankind. That duty is to guard ourselves from such beliefs as from a pestilence, which may shortly master our own body and then spread to the rest of the town. What would be thought of one who, for the sake of a sweet fruit, should deliberately run the risk of bringing a plague upon his family and his neighbours?

And, as in other such cases, it is not the risk only which has to be considered; for a bad action is always bad at the time when it is done, no matter what happens afterwards. Every time we let ourselves believe for unworthy reasons, we weaken our powers of self-control, of doubting, of judicially and fairly weighing evidence. We all suffer severely enough from the maintenance and support of false beliefs and the fatally wrong actions which they lead to, and the evil born when one such belief is entertained is great and wide. But a greater and wider evil arises when the credulous character is maintained and supported, when a habit of believing for unworthy reasons is fostered and made permanent. If I steal money from any person, there may be no harm done by the mere transfer of possession; he may not feel the loss, or it may prevent him from using the money badly. But I cannot help doing this great wrong towards Man, that I make myself dishonest. What hurts society is not that it should lose its property, but that it should become a den of thieves; for then it must cease to be society. This is why we ought not to do evil that good may come; for at any rate this great evil has come, that we have done evil and are made wicked thereby. In like manner, if I let myself believe anything on insufficient evidence, there may be no great harm done by the mere belief; it may be true after all, or I may never have occasion to exhibit it in outward acts. But I cannot help doing this great wrong towards Man, that I make myself credulous. The danger to society is not merely that it should believe wrong things, though that is great enough; but that it should become credulous, and lose the habit of testing things and inquiring into them; for then it must sink back into savagery.

The harm which is done by credulity in a man is not confined to the fostering of a credulous character in others, and consequent support of false beliefs. Habitual want of care about what I believe leads to habitual want of care in others about the truth of what is told to me. Men speak the truth to one another when each reveres the truth in his own mind and in the other's mind; but how shall my friend revere the truth in my mind when I myself am careless about it, when I believe things because I want to believe them, and because they are comforting and pleasant? Will he not learn to cry "Peace," to me, when there is no peace? By such a course I shall surround myself with a thick atmosphere of falsehood and fraud, and in that I must live. It may matter little to me, in my cloud-castle of sweet illusions and darling lies; but it matters much to Man that I have made my neighbours ready to deceive. The credulous man is father to the liar and the cheat; he lives in the bosom of this his family, and it is no marvel if he should become even as they are. So closely are our duties knit together, that whoso shall keep the whole law, and yet offend in one point, he is guilty of all.

To sum up: it is wrong always, everywhere, and for any one, to believe anything upon insufficient evidence.

If a man, holding a belief which he was taught in childhood or persuaded of afterwards, keeps down and pushes away any doubts which arise about it in his mind, purposely avoids the reading of books and the company of men that call in question or discuss it, and regards as impious those questions which cannot easily be asked without disturbing it – the life of that man is one long sin against mankind.

If this judgment seems harsh when applied to those simple souls who have never known better, who have been brought up from the cradle with a horror of doubt, and taught that their eternal welfare depends on *what* they believe, then it leads to the very serious question, *Who hath made Israel to sin?*

It may be permitted me to fortify this judgment with the sentence of Milton[2] –

"A man may be a heretic in the truth; and if he believe things only because his pastor says so, or the assembly so determine,

---

[2] *Areopagitica.*

without knowing other reason, though his belief be true, yet the very truth he holds becomes his heresy."

And with this famous aphorism of Coleridge[3] –

"He who begins by loving Christianity better than Truth, will proceed by loving his own sect or Church better than Christianity, and end in loving himself better than all."

Inquiry into the evidence of a doctrine is not to be made once for all, and then taken as finally settled. It is never lawful to stifle a doubt; for either it can be honestly answered by means of the inquiry already made, or else it proves that the inquiry was not complete.

"But," says one, "I am a busy man; I have no time for the long course or study which would be necessary to make me in any degree a competent judge of certain questions, or even able to understand the nature of the arguments." Then he should have no time to believe.

II. *The Weight of Authority*

Are we then to become universal sceptics, doubting everything afraid always to put one foot before the other until we have personally tested the firmness of the road? Are we to deprive ourselves of the help and guidance of that vast body of knowledge which is daily growing upon the world, because neither we nor any other one person can possibly test a hundredth part of it by immediate experiment or observation, and because it would not be completely proved if we did? Shall we steal and tell lies because we have had no personal experience wide enough to justify the belief that it is wrong to do so?

There is no practical danger that such consequences will ever follow from scrupulous care and self-control in the matter of belief. Those men who have most nearly done their duty in this respect have found that certain great principles, and these most fitted for the guidance of life, have stood out more and more clearly in proportion to the care and honesty with which they were tested, and have acquired in this way a practical certainty. The beliefs about right and wrong which guide our actions in dealing with men in society, and the beliefs about physical nature which guide our actions in dealing with animate and inanimate bodies, these never suffer from investigation; they can take care of themselves, without being propped up by "acts

---

[3] *Aids to Reflection.*

of faith," the clamour of paid advocates, or the suppression of contrary evidence. Moreover there are many cases in which it is our duty to act upon probabilities, although the evidence is not such as to justify present belief; because it is precisely by such action, and by observation of its fruits, that evidence is got which may justify future belief. So that we have no reason to fear lest a habit of conscientious inquiry should paralyse the actions of our daily life.

But because it is not enough to say, "It is wrong to believe on unworthy evidence," without saying also what evidence is worthy, we shall now go on to inquire under what circumstances it is lawful to believe on the testimony of others; and then, further, we shall inquire more generally when and why we may believe that which goes beyond our own experience, or even beyond the experience of mankind.

In what cases, then, let us ask in the first place, is the testimony of a man unworthy of belief? He may say that which is untrue either knowingly or unknowingly. In the first case he is lying, and his moral character is to blame; in the second case he is ignorant or mistaken, and it is only his knowledge or his judgment which is in fault. In order that we may have the right to accept his testimony as ground for believing what he says, we must have reasonable grounds for trusting his *veracity*, that he is really trying to speak the truth so far as he knows it; his *knowledge*, that he has had opportunities of knowing the truth about this matter; and his *judgment*, that he has made proper use of those opportunities in coming to the conclusion which he affirms.

However plain and obvious these reasons may be, so that no man of ordinary intelligence, reflecting upon the matter, could fail to arrive at them, it is nevertheless true that a great many persons do habitually disregard them in weighing testimony. Of the two questions, equally important to the trustworthiness of a witness, "Is he dishonest?" and "May he be mistaken?" the majority of mankind are perfectly satisfied if *one* can, with some show of probability, be answered in the negative. The excellent moral character of a man is alleged as ground for accepting his statements about things which he cannot possibly have known. A Mohammedan, for example, will tell us that the character of his Prophet was so noble and majestic that it commands the reverence even of those who do not believe in his mission. So admirable was his moral teaching, so wisely put together the great social machine which he created, that his precepts have not only been accepted by a great portion of mankind, but have actually been obeyed. His institutions have on the one hand rescued the negro from savagery, and on the other hand have taught civilisation to the advancing West; and although the races which held the highest forms of his faith, and most fully embodied his mind and thought, have all been conquered and swept away by barbaric tribes, yet the history of their marvellous attainments remains as an imperishable glory to Islam. Are we to doubt the word of a man so great and so good? Can we suppose that this magnificent genius, this splendid moral hero, has lied to us about the most solemn and sacred matters? The testimony of Mohammed is clear, that there is but one God, and that he, Mohammed, is his Prophet; that if we believe in him we shall enjoy everlasting felicity, but that if we do not we shall be damned. This testimony rests on the most awful of foundations, the revelation of heaven itself; for was he not visited by the angel Gabriel, as he fasted and prayed in his desert cave, and allowed to enter into the blessed fields of Paradise? Surely God is God and Mohammed is the Prophet of God.

What should we answer to this Mussulman? First, no doubt, we should be tempted to take exception against his view of the character of the Prophet and the uniformly beneficial influence of Islam: before we could go with him altogether in these matters it might seem that we should have to forget many terrible things of which we have heard or read. But if we chose to grant him all these assumptions, for the sake of argument, and because it is difficult both for the faithful and for the infidels to discuss them fairly and without passion, still we should have something to say which takes away the ground of his belief, and therefore shows that it is wrong to entertain it. Namely this: the character of Mohammed is excellent evidence that he was honest and spoke the truth so far as he knew it; but it is no evidence at all that he knew what the truth was. What means could he have of knowing that the form which appeared to him to be the angel Gabriel was not a hallucination, and that his apparent visit to Paradise was not a dream? Grant that he himself was fully persuaded and honestly believed that he had the guidance of heaven, and was the vehicle of a supernatural revelation, how could he know that this strong conviction was not a mistake? Let us put ourselves in his place; we shall find that the more completely we endeavour to realise what passed through his mind, the more clearly we shall perceive that the Prophet could have had no adequate ground for the belief in his own inspiration. It is most probable that he himself never doubted of the matter, or thought of asking the question; but we are in the position of those to whom the question has been asked, and who are bound to answer it. It is known to medical observers that solitude and want of food are powerful means of producing delusion and of fostering a tendency to mental disease. Let us suppose, then, that I, like Mohammed, go into desert places to fast and pray; what things can happen to me which will give me the right to believe that I am divinely inspired? Suppose that I get information, apparently from a celestial visitor, which upon being tested is found to be correct. I cannot be sure, in the first place, that the celestial visitor is not a figment of my own mind, and that the information did not come to me, unknown at the time to my consciousness, through some subtle channel of sense. But if my visitor were a real visitor, and for a long time gave me information which was found to be trustworthy, this would indeed be good ground for trusting him in the future as to such matters as fall within human powers of verification; but it would not be ground for trusting his testimony as to any other matters. For although his tested character would justify me in believing that he spoke the truth so far as he knew, yet the same question would present itself – what ground is there for supposing that he knows?

Even if my supposed visitor had given me such information, subsequently verified by me, as proved him to have means of knowledge about verifiable matters far exceeding my own; this would not justify me in believing what he said about matters that are not at present capable of verification by man. It would be ground for interesting conjecture, and for the hope that, as the fruit of our patient inquiry, we might by and by attain to such a means of verification as should rightly turn conjecture into belief. For belief belongs to man, and to the guidance of human affairs: no belief is real unless it guide our actions, and those very actions supply a test of its truth.

But, it may be replied, the acceptance of Islam as a system is just that action which is prompted by belief in the mission of the Prophet, and which will serve for a test of its truth. Is it possible to believe that a system which has succeeded so well is really founded upon a delusion? Not only have individual saints found joy and peace in believing, and verified those spiritual experiences which are promised to the faithful, but nations also have been raised from savagery or barbarism to a higher social state. Surely we are at liberty to say that the belief has been acted upon, and that it has been verified.

It requires, however, but little consideration to show that what has really been verified is not at all the supernal character of the Prophet's mission, or the trustworthiness of his authority in matters which we ourselves cannot test, but only his practical wisdom in certain very mundane things. The fact that believers have found joy and peace in believing gives us the right to say that the doctrine is a comfortable doctrine, and pleasant to the soul; but it does not give us the right to say that it is true. And the question which our conscience is always asking about that which we are tempted to believe is not, "Is it comfortable and pleasant?" but, "Is it true?" That the Prophet preached certain doctrines, and predicted that spiritual comfort would be found in them, proves only his sympathy with human nature and his knowledge of it; but it does not prove his superhuman knowledge of theology.

And if we admit for the sake of argument (for it seems that we cannot do more) that the progress made by Moslem nations in certain cases was really due to the system formed and sent forth into the world by Mohammed, we are not at liberty to conclude from this that he was inspired to declare the truth about things which we cannot verify. We are only at liberty to infer the excellence of his moral precepts, or of the means which he devised for so working upon men so as to get them obeyed, or of the social and political machinery which he set up. And it would require a great amount of careful examination into the history of those nations to determine which of these things had the greater share in the result. So that here again it is the Prophet's knowledge of human nature, and his sympathy with it, that are verified; not his divine inspiration or his knowledge of theology.

If there were only one Prophet, indeed, it might well seem a difficult and even an ungracious task to decide upon what points we would trust him, and on what we would doubt his authority; seeing what help and furtherance all men have gained in all ages from those who saw more clearly, who felt more strongly, and who sought the truth with more single heart than their weaker brethren. But there is not only one Prophet;

and while the consent of many upon that which, as men, they had real means of knowing and did know, has endured to the end, and been honourably built into the great fabric of human knowledge, the diverse witness of some about that which they did not and could not know remains as a warning to us that to exaggerate the prophetic authority is to misuse it, and to dishonour those who have sought only to help and further us after their power. It is hardly in human nature that a man should quite accurately gauge the limits of his own insight; but it is the duty of those who profit by his work to consider carefully where he may have been carried beyond it. If we must needs embalm his possible errors along with his solid achievements, and use his authority as an excuse for believing what he cannot have known, we make of his goodness an occasion to sin.

To consider only one other such witness: the followers of the Buddha have at least as much right to appeal to individual and social experience in support of the authority of the Eastern saviour. The special mark of his religion, it is said, that in which it has never been surpassed, is the comfort and consolation which it gives to the sick and sorrowful, the tender sympathy with which it soothes and assuages all the natural griefs of men. And surely no triumph of social morality can be greater or nobler than that which has kept nearly half the human race from persecuting in the name of religion. If we are to trust the accounts of his early followers, he believed himself to have come upon earth with a divine and cosmic mission to set rolling the wheel of the law. Being a prince, he divested himself of his kingdom, and of his free will became acquainted with misery, that he might learn how to meet and subdue it. Could such a man speak falsely about solemn things? And as for his knowledge, was he not a man miraculous with powers more than man's? He was born of woman without the help of man; he rose into the air and was transfigured before his kinsmen; at last he went up bodily into heaven from the top of Adam's Peak. Is not his word to be believed in when he testifies of heavenly things?

If there were only he, and no other, with such claims! But there is Mohammed with his testimony; we cannot choose but listen to them both. The Prophet tells us that there is one God, and that we shall live for ever in joy or misery, according as we believe in the Prophet or not. The Buddha says that there is no

God, and that we shall be annihilated by and by if we are good enough. Both cannot be infallibly inspired; one or other must have been the victim of a delusion, and thought he knew that which he really did not know. Who shall dare to say which? and how can we justify ourselves in believing that the other was not also deluded?

We are led, then to these judgments following. The goodness and greatness of a man do not justify us in accepting a belief upon the warrant of his authority, unless there are reasonable grounds for supposing that he knew the truth of what he was saying. And there can be no grounds for supposing that a man knows that which we, without ceasing to be men, could not be supposed to verify.

If a chemist tells me, who am no chemist, that a certain substance can be made by putting together other substances in certain proportions and subjecting them to a known process, I am quite justified in believing this upon his authority, unless I know anything against his character or his judgment. For his professional training is one which tends to encourage veracity and the honest pursuit of truth, and to produce a dislike of hasty conclusions and slovenly investigation. And I have reasonable ground for supposing that he knows the truth of what he is saying, for although I am no chemist, I can be made to understand so much of the methods and processes of the science as makes it conceivable to me that, without ceasing to be man, I might verify the statement. I may never actually verify it, or even see any experiment which goes towards verifying it; but still I have quite reason enough to justify me in believing that the verification is within the reach of human appliances and powers, and in particular that it has been actually performed by my informant. His result, the belief to which he has been led by his inquiries, is valid not only for himself but for others; it is watched and tested by those who are working in the same ground, and who know that no greater service can be rendered to science than the purification of accepted results from the errors which may have crept into them. It is in this way that the result becomes common property, a right object of belief, which is a social affair and matter of public business. Thus it is to be observed that his authority is valid because there are those who question it and verify it; that it is precisely this process of examining and purifying that keeps alive among investigators the love of that which shall stand all possible tests, the sense of public responsibility as of those whose work, if well done, shall remain as the enduring heritage of mankind.

But if my chemist tells me that an atom of oxygen has existed unaltered in weight and rate of vibration through all time I have no right to believe this on his authority, for it is a thing which he cannot know without ceasing to be man. He may quite honestly believe that this statement is a fair inference from his experiments, but in that case his judgment is at fault. A very simply consideration of the character of experiments would show him that they never can lead to results of such a kind; that being themselves only approximate and limited, they cannot give us knowledge which is exact and universal. No eminence of character and genius can give a man authority enough to justify us in believing him when he makes statements implying exact or universal knowledge.

Again, an Arctic explorer may tell us that in a given latitude and longitude he has experienced such and such a degree of cold that the sea was of such a depth, and the ice of such a character. We should be quite right to believe him, in the absence of any stain upon his veracity. It is conceivable that we might, without ceasing to be men, go there and verify his statement; it can be tested by the witness of his companions, and there is adequate ground for supposing that he knows the truth of what he is saying. But if an old whaler tells us that the ice is 300 feet thick all the way up to the Pole, we shall not be justified in believing him. For although the statement may be capable of verification by man, it is certainly not capable of verification by *him*, with any means and appliances which he has possessed; and he must have persuaded himself of the truth of it by some means which does not attach any credit to his testimony. Even if, therefore, the matter affirmed is within the reach of human knowledge, we have no right to accept it upon authority unless it is within the reach of our informant's knowledge.

What shall we say of that authority, more venerable and august than any individual witness, the time-honoured tradition of the human race? An atmosphere of beliefs and conceptions has been formed by the labours and struggles of our forefathers, which enables us to breathe amid the various and complex circumstances of our life. It is around and about us and within us; we cannot think except in the forms and processes of thought which it supplies. Is it possible to doubt and to test it? and if possible, is it right?

We shall find reason to answer that it is not only possible and right, but our bounden duty; that the main purpose of the tradition itself is to supply us with the means of asking questions, of testing and inquiring into things; that if we misuse it, and take it as a collection of cut-and-dried statements to be accepted without further inquiry, we are not only injuring ourselves here, but, by refusing to do our part towards the building up of the fabric which shall be inherited by our children, we are tending to cut off ourselves and our race from the human line.

Let us first take care to distinguish a kind of tradition which especially requires to be examined and called in question, because it especially shrinks from inquiry. Suppose that a medicine-man in Central Africa tells his tribe that a certain powerful medicine in his tent will be propitiated if they kill their cattle, and that the tribe believe him. Whether the medicine was propitiated or not there are no means of verifying, but the cattle are gone. Still the belief may be kept up in the tribe that propitiation has been effected in this way; and in a later generation it will be all the easier for another medicine-man to persuade them to a similar act. Here the only reason for belief is that everybody has believed the thing for so long that it must be true. And yet the belief was founded on fraud, and had been propagated by credulity. That man will undoubtedly do right, and be a friend of men, who shall call it in question and see that there is no evidence of it, help his neighbours to see as he does, and even, if need be, go into the holy tent and break the medicine.

The rule which should guide us in such cases is simple and obvious enough: that the aggregate testimony of our neighbours is subject to the same conditions as the testimony of any one of them. Namely, we have no right to believe a thing true because everybody says so unless there are good grounds for believing that some one person at least has the means of knowing what is true, and is speaking the truth so far as he knows it. However many nations and generations of men are brought into the witness-box they cannot testify to anything which they do not know. Every man who has accepted the statement from somebody else, without himself testing and verifying it, is out of court; his word is worth nothing at all.

And when we get back at last to the true birth and beginning of the statement, two serious questions must be disposed of in regard to him who first made it: was he mistaken in thinking that he *knew* about this matter, or was he lying?

This last question is unfortunately a very actual and practical one even to us at this day and in this country. We have no occasion to go to La Salette, or to Central Africa, or to Lourdes, for examples of immoral and debasing superstition. It is only too possible for a child to grow up in London surrounded by an atmosphere of beliefs fit only for the savage, which have in our own time been founded in fraud and propagated by credulity.

Laying aside, then, such tradition as is handed on without testing by successive generations, let us consider that which is truly built up out of the common experience of mankind. This great fabric is for the guidance of our thoughts, and through them of our actions, both in the moral and in the material world. In the moral world, for example, it gives us the conceptions of right in general, of justice, of truth, of beneficence, and the like. These are given as conceptions, not as statements or propositions; they answer to certain definite instincts which are certainly within us, however they came there. That it is right to be beneficent is matter of immediate personal experience; for when a man retires within himself and there finds something, wider and more lasting than his solitary personality, which says, "I want to do right," as well as, "I want to do good to man," he can verify by direct observation that one instinct is founded upon and agrees fully with the other. And it is his duty so to verify this and all similar statements.

The tradition says also, at a definite place and time, that such and such actions are just, or true, or beneficent. For all such rules a further inquiry is necessary, since they are sometimes established by an authority other than that of the moral sense founded on experience. Until recently, the moral tradition of our own country – and indeed of all Europe – taught that it was beneficent to give money indiscriminately to beggars. But the questioning of this rule, and investigation into it, led men to see that true beneficence is that which helps a man to do the work which he is most fitted for, not that which keeps and encourages him in idleness; and that to neglect this distinction in the present is to prepare pauperism and misery for the future. By this testing and discussion not only has practice been purified and made more beneficent, but the very conception of beneficence has been made wider and wiser. Now here the great social heirloom consists of two parts: the instinct of beneficence, which makes a certain side of our nature, when predominant, wish to do good to men; and the intellectual conception of beneficence, which we can compare with any proposed course of conduct and ask, "Is this beneficent or not?" By the continual asking and answering of such questions the conception grows in breadth and distinctness, and the instinct becomes strengthened and purified. It appears then, that the great use of the conception, the intellectual part of the heirloom, is to enable us to ask questions; that it grows and is kept straight by means of these questions; and if we do not use it for that purpose we shall gradually lose it altogether, and be left with a mere code of regulations which cannot rightly be called morality at all.

Such considerations apply even more obviously and clearly, if possible, to the store of beliefs and conceptions which our fathers have amassed for us in respect of the material world. We are ready to laugh at the rule of thumb of the Australian who continues to tie his hatchet to the side of the handle, although the Birmingham fitter has made a hole on purpose for him to put the handle in. His people have tied up hatchets so for ages: who is he that he should set himself up against their wisdom? He has sunk so low that he cannot do what some of them must have done in the far distant past – call in question an established usage, and invent or learn something better. Yet here, in the dim beginning of knowledge, where science and art are one, we find only the same simple rule which applies to the highest and deepest growths of that cosmic Tree; to its loftiest flower-tipped branches as well as to the profoundest of its hidden roots; the rule, namely, that what is stored up and handed down to us is rightly used by those who act as the makers acted, when they stored it up; those who use it to ask further questions, to examine, to investigate; who try honestly and solemnly to find out what is the right way of looking at things and of dealing with them.

A question rightly asked is already half answered, said Jacobi; we may add that the method of solution is the other half of the answer, and that the actual result counts for nothing by the side of these two. For an example let us go to the telegraph, where theory and practice, grown each to years of discretion, are marvellously wedded for the fruitful service of men. Ohm found that the strength of an electric current is directly proportional to the strength of the battery which produces it, and inversely as the length of the wire along which it has to travel. This is called Ohm's law; but the result, regarded as a statement to be believed, is not the valuable part of it. The first half is the question: what relation holds good between these quantities? So put, the question involves already the conception of strength of current, and of strength of battery, as quantities to be measured and compared; it hints clearly that these are the things to be attended to in the study of electric currents. The second half is the method of investigation; how to measure these quantities, what instruments are required for the experiment, and how are they to be used? The student who begins to learn about electricity is not asked to believe in Ohm's law: he is made to understand the question, he is placed before the apparatus, and he is taught to verify it. He learns to do things, not to think he knows things; to use instruments and to ask questions, not to accept a traditional statement. The question which required a genius to ask it rightly is answered by a tiro. If Ohm's law were suddenly lost and forgotten by all men, while the question and the method of solution remained, the result could be rediscovered in an hour. But the result by itself, if known to a people who could not comprehend the value of the question or the means of solving it, would be like a watch in the hands of a savage who could not wind it up, or an iron steamship worked by Spanish engineers.

In regard, then, to the sacred tradition of humanity, we learn that it consists, not in propositions or statements which are to be accepted and believed on the authority of the tradition, but in questions rightly asked, in conceptions which enable us to ask further questions, and in methods of answering questions. The value of all these things depends on their being tested day by day. The very sacredness of the precious deposit imposes upon us the duty and the responsibility of testing it, of purifying and enlarging it to the utmost of our power. He who makes use of its results to stifle his own doubts, or to hamper the inquiry of others, is guilty of a sacrilege which centuries shall never be able to blot out. When the labours and questionings of honest and brave men shall have built up the fabric of known truth to a glory which we in this generation can neither hope for nor imagine, in that pure and holy temple he shall have no part nor lot, but his name and his works shall be cast out into the darkness of oblivion for ever.

III. *The Limits of Inference*

The question in what cases we may believe that which goes beyond our experience, is a very large and delicate one, extending to the whole range of scientific method, and requiring a considerable increase in the application of it before it can be answered with anything approaching to completeness. But one rule, lying on the threshold of the subject, of extreme simplicity and vast practical importance, may here be touched upon and shortly laid down.

A little reflection will show us that every belief, even the simplest and most fundamental, goes beyond experience when regarded as a guide to our actions. A burnt child dreads the fire, because it believes that the fire will burn it to-day just as it did yesterday; but this belief goes beyond experience, and assumes that the unknown fire of to-day is like the known fire of yesterday. Even the belief that the child was burnt yesterday goes beyond *present* experience, which contains only the memory of a burning, and not the burning itself; it assumes, therefore, that this memory is trustworthy, although we know that a memory may often be mistaken. But if it is to be used as a guide to action, as a hint of what the future is to be, it must assume something about that future, namely, that it will be consistent with the supposition that the burning really took place yesterday; which is going beyond experience. Even the fundamental "I am," which cannot be doubted, is no guide to action until it takes to itself "I shall be," which goes beyond experience. The question is not, therefore, "May we believe what goes beyond experience?" for this is involved in the very nature of belief; but " How far and in what manner may we add to our experience in forming our beliefs?"

And an answer, of utter simplicity and universality, is suggested by the example we have taken: a burnt child dreads the fire. We may go beyond experience by assuming that what we do not know is like what we do know; or, in other words, we may add to our experience on the assumption of a uniformity in nature. What this uniformity precisely is, how we grow in the knowledge of it from generation to generation, these are questions which for the present we lay aside, being content to examine two instances which may serve to make plainer the nature of the rule.

From certain observations made with the spectroscope, we infer the existence of hydrogen in the sun. By looking into the spectroscope when the sun is shining on its slit, we see certain definite bright lines: and experiments made upon bodies on the earth have taught us that when these bright lines are seen hydrogen is the source of them. We assume, then, that the unknown bright lines in the sun are like the known bright lines of the laboratory, and that hydrogen in the sun behaves as hydrogen under similar circumstances would behave on the earth.

But are we not trusting our spectroscope too much? Surely, having found it to be trustworthy for terrestrial substances, where its statements can be verified by man, we are justified in accepting its testimony in other like cases; but not when it gives us information about things in the sun, where its testimony cannot be directly verified by man?

Certainly, we want to know a little more before this inference can be justified; and fortunately we do know this. The spectroscope testifies to exactly the same thing in the two cases; namely, that light-vibrations of a certain rate are being sent through it. Its construction is such that if it were wrong about this in one case, it would be wrong in the other. When we come to look into the matter, we find that we have really assumed the matter of the sun to be like the matter of the earth, made up of a certain number of distinct substances; and that each of these, when very hot, has a distinct rate of vibration, by which it may be recognised and singled out from the rest. But this is the kind of assumption which we are justified in using when we add to our experience. It is an assumption of uniformity in nature, and can only be checked by comparison with many similar assumptions which we have to make in other such cases.

But is this a true belief, of the existence of hydrogen in the sun? Can it help in the right guidance of human action?

Certainly not, if it is accepted on unworthy grounds, and without some understanding of the process by which it is got at. But when this process is taken in as the ground of the belief, it becomes a very serious and practical matter. For if there is no hydrogen in the sun, the spectroscope – that is to say, the measurement of rates of vibration – must be an uncertain guide in recognising different substances; and consequently it ought not to be used in chemical analysis – in assaying, for example – to the great saving of time, trouble, and money. Whereas the acceptance of the spectroscopic method as trustworthy has enriched us not only with new metals, which is a great thing, but with new processes of investigation, which is vastly greater.

For another example, let us consider the way in which we infer the truth of an historical event – say the siege of Syracuse in the Peloponnesian war. Our experience is that manuscripts exist which are said to be and which call themselves manuscripts of the history of Thucydides; that in other manuscripts, stated to be by later historians, he is described as living during the time of the war; and that books, supposed to date from the revival of learning, tell us how these manuscripts had been preserved and were then acquired. We find also that men do not, as a rule, forge books and histories without a special motive; we assume that in this respect men in the past were like men in the present; and we observe that in this case no special motive was present. That is, we add to our experience on the assumption of a uniformity in the characters of men. Because our knowledge of this uniformity is far less complete and exact than our knowledge of that which obtains in physics, inferences of the historical kind are more precarious and less exact than inferences in many other sciences.

But if there is any special reason to suspect the character of the persons who wrote or transmitted certain books, the case becomes altered. If a group of documents give internal evidence that they were produced among people who forged books in the names of others, and who, in describing events, suppressed those things which did not suit them, while they amplified such as did suit them; who not only committed these crimes, but gloried in them as proofs of humility and zeal; then we must say that upon such documents no true historical inference can be founded, but only unsatisfactory conjecture.

We may, then, add to our experience on the assumption of a uniformity in nature; we may fill in our picture of what is and has been, as experience gives it us, in such a way as to make the whole consistent with this uniformity. And practically demonstrative inference – that which gives us a right to believe in the result of it – is a clear showing that in no other way than by the truth of this result can the uniformity of nature be saved.

No evidence, therefore, can justify us in believing the truth of a statement which is contrary to, or outside of, the uniformity of nature. If our experience is such that it cannot be filled up consistently with uniformity, all we have a right to conclude is that there is something wrong somewhere; but the possibility of inference is taken away; we must rest in our experience, and not go beyond it at all. If an event really happened which was not a part of the uniformity of nature, it would have two properties: no evidence could give the right to believe it to any except those whose actual experience it was; and no inference worthy of belief could be founded upon it at all.

Are we then bound to believe that nature is absolutely and universally uniform? Certainly not; we have no right to believe anything of this kind. The rule only tells us that in forming beliefs which go beyond our experience, we may make the assumption that nature is practically uniform so far as we are concerned. Within the range of human action and verification, we may form, by help of this assumption, actual beliefs; beyond it, only those hypotheses which serve for the more accurate asking of questions.

To sum up:-

We may believe what goes beyond our experience, only when it is inferred from that experience by the assumption that what we do not know is like what we know.

We may believe the statement of another person, when there is reasonable ground for supposing that he knows the matter of which he speaks, and that he is speaking the truth so far as he knows it.

It is wrong in all cases to believe on insufficient evidence; and where it is presumption to doubt and to investigate, there it is worse than presumption to believe.

RELIGION: A RETROSPECT AND PROSPECT[1]
[Herbert Spencer]

Unlike the ordinary consciousness, the religious consciousness is concerned with that which lies beyond the sphere of sense. A brute thinks only of things which can be touched, seen, heard, tasted, etc.; and the like is true of the untaught child, the deaf-mute, and the lowest savage. But the developing man has thoughts about existences which he regards as usually intangible, inaudible, invisible; and yet which he regards as operative upon him. What suggests this notion of agencies transcending perception? How do these ideas concerning the supernatural evolve out of ideas concerning the natural? The transition cannot be sudden; and an account of the genesis of religion must begin by describing the steps through which the transition takes place.

The ghost-theory exhibits these steps quite clearly. We are shown by it that the mental differentiation of invisible and intangible beings from visible and tangible beings progresses slowly and unobtrusively. In the fact that the other-self, supposed to wander in dreams, is believed to have actually done and seen whatever was dreamed – in the fact that the other-self when going away at death, but expected presently to return, is conceived as a double equally material with the original; we see that the supernatural agent in its primitive form diverges very little from the natural agent – is simply the original man with some added powers of going about secretly and doing good or evil. And the fact that when the double of the dead man ceases to be dreamed about by those who knew him, his non-appearance in dreams is held to imply that he is finally dead, shows that these earliest supernatural agents are conceived as having but a temporary existence: the first tendencies to a permanent consciousness of the supernatural prove abortive.

[1] The statements concerning matters of fact in the first part of this article are based on the contents of Part I. of *The Principles of Sociology*.

In many cases no higher degree of differentiation is reached. The ghost-population, recruited by deaths on the one side, but on the other side losing its members as they cease to be recollected and dreamed about, does not increase; and no individuals included in it come to be recognised through successive generations as established supernatural powers. Thus the Unkulunkulu, or old-old one, of the Zulus, the father of the race, is regarded as finally or completely dead; and there is propitiation only of ghosts of more recent date. But where circumstances favour the continuance of sacrifices at graves, witnessed by members of each new generation, who are told about the dead and transmit the tradition, there eventually arises the conception of a permanently-existing ghost or spirit. A more marked contrast in thought between supernatural beings and natural beings is thus established. There simultaneously results a great increase in the number of these supposed supernatural beings, since the aggregate of them is now continually added to; and there is a strengthening tendency to think of them as everywhere around, and as causing all unusual occurrences.

Differences among the ascribed powers of ghosts soon arise. They naturally follow from observed differences among the powers of living individuals. Hence it results that while the propitiations of ordinary ghosts are made only by their descendants, it comes occasionally to be thought prudent to propitiate also the ghosts of the more dreaded individuals, even though they have no claims of blood. Quite early there thus begin those grades of supernatural beings which eventually become so strongly marked.

Habitual wars, which more than all other causes initiate these first differentiations, go on to initiate further and more decided ones. For with those compoundings of small societies into greater ones, and re-compounding of these into still greater, which war effects, there, of course, with the multiplying gradations of power among living men, arises the conception of multiplying gradations of power among their ghosts. Thus in course of time are formed the conceptions of the great ghosts or gods, the more numerous secondary ghosts or demi-gods, and so on downwards – a pantheon: there being still, however, no essential distinction of kind; as we see in the calling of ordinary ghosts *manes*-gods by the Romans and *elohim* by the Hebrews. Moreover, repeating as the other life in the other world does the life in this world, in its needs, occupations, and social organisation, there arises not only a differentiation of grades among supernatural beings in respect of their powers, but also in respect of their characters and kinds of activity. There come to be local gods, and gods reigning over this or that order of phenomena; there come to be good and evil spirits of various qualities; and where there has been by conquest a superposing of societies one upon another, each having its own system of ghost-derived beliefs, there results an involved combination of such beliefs, constituting a mythology.

Of course ghosts primarily being doubles like the originals in all things; and gods (when not the living members of a conquering race) being doubles of the more powerful men; it results that they, too, are originally no less human than other ghosts in their physical characters, their passions, and their intelligences. Like the doubles of the ordinary dead, they are supposed to consume the flesh, blood, bread, wine, given to them: at first literally, and later in a more spiritual way by consuming the essences of them. They not only appear as visible and tangible persons, but they enter into conflicts with men, are wounded, suffer pain: the sole distinction being that they have miraculous powers of healing and consequent immortality. Here, indeed, there needs a qualification; for not only do various peoples hold that the gods die a first death (as naturally happens where they are members of a conquering race, called gods because of their superiority), but, as in the case of Pan, it is supposed, even among the cultured, that there is a second and final death of a god, like that second and final death of a man supposed among existing savages. With advancing civilisation the divergence of the supernatural being from the natural being becomes more decided. There is nothing to check the gradual de-materialisation of the ghost and of the god; and this de-materialisation is insensibly furthered in the effort to reach consistent ideas of supernatural action: the god ceases to be tangible, and later he ceases to be visible or audible. Along with this differentiation of physical attributes from those of humanity, there goes on more slowly the differentiation of mental attributes. The god of the savage, represented as having intelligence scarcely, if at all, greater than that of the living man, is deluded with ease. Even the gods of the semi-civilised are deceived, make mistakes, repent of their plans; and only in the course of time does there arise the conception of unlimited vision and universal knowledge. The emotional nature simultaneously undergoes a parallel transformation. The grosser passions, originally conspicuous and carefully ministered to by devotees, gradually fade, leaving only the passions less related to corporeal satisfactions; and eventually these, too, become partially de-humanised.

These ascribed characters of deities are continually adapted and re-adapted to the needs of the social state. During the militant phase of activity, the chief god is conceived as holding insubordination the greatest crime, as implacable in anger, as merciless in punishment; and any alleged attributes of a milder kind occupy but small space in the social consciousness. But where militancy declines and the harsh, despotic form of government appropriate to it is gradually qualified by the form appropriate to industrialism, the foreground of the religious consciousness is increasingly filled with those ascribed traits of the divine nature which are congruous with the ethics of peace: divine love, divine forgiveness, divine mercy, are now the characteristics enlarged upon.

To perceive clearly the effects of mental progress and changing social life thus stated in the abstract, we must glance at them in the concrete. If, without foregone conclusions, we contemplate the traditions, records, and monuments of the Egyptians, we see that out of their primitive ideas of gods, brute or human, there were evolved spiritualised ideas of gods, and finally of a god; until the priesthoods of later times, repudiating the earlier ideas, described them as corruptions: being swayed by the universal tendency to regard the first state as the highest – a tendency traceable down to the theories of existing theologians and mythologists. Again, if, putting aside speculations, and not asking what historical value the *Iliad* may have, we take it simply as indicating the early Greek notion of Zeus, and compare this with the notion contained in the Platonic dialogues; we see that Greek civilisation had greatly modified (in the better minds, at least) the purely anthropomorphic conception of him: the lower human attributes being dropped and the higher ones transfigured. Similarly, if we contrast the Hebrew God described in primitive traditions, manlike in appearance, appetites, and emotions, with the Hebrew God as characterised by the prophets, there is shown a widening range of power along with a nature increasingly remote from that of man. And on passing to the conceptions of him which are now entertained, we are made aware of an extreme transfiguration. By a convenient obliviousness, a deity who in early times is represented as hardening men's hearts so that they may commit punishable acts, and as employing a lying spirit to deceive them, comes to be mostly thought of as an embodiment of virtues transcending the highest we can imagine.

Thus, recognising the fact that in the primitive human mind there exists neither religious idea nor religious sentiment, we find that in the course of social evolution and the evolution of intelligence accompanying it, there are generated both the ideas and sentiments which we distinguish as religious; and that through a process of causation clearly traceable, they traverse those stages which have brought them, among civilised races, to their present forms.

And now what may we infer will be the evolution of religious ideas and sentiments throughout the future? On the one hand it is irrational to suppose that the changes which have brought the religious consciousness to its present form will suddenly cease. On the other hand, it is irrational to suppose that the religious consciousness, naturally generated as we have seen, will disappear and leave an unfilled gap. Manifestly it must undergo further changes; and however much changed it must continue to exist. What then are the transformations to be expected? If we reduce the process above delineated to its lowest terms, we shall see our way to an answer.

As pointed out in *First Principles*, §96, Evolution is throughout its course habitually modified by that Dissolution which eventually undoes it: the changes which become manifest being usually but the differential results of opposing tendencies towards integration and disintegration. Rightly to understand the genesis and decay of religious systems, and the probable future of those now existing, we must take this truth into account. During those earlier changes by which there is created a hierarchy of gods, demi-gods, manes-gods, and spirits of various kinds and ranks, evolution goes on with but little qualification. The consolidated mythology produced, while growing in the mass of supernatural beings composing it, assumes increased heterogeneity along with increased definiteness in the arrangement of its parts and the attributes of its members. But the antagonist Dissolution eventually gains predominance. The spreading recognition of natural causation conflicts with this mythological evolution, and insensibly weakens those of its beliefs which are most at variance with advancing knowledge. Demons and the secondary divinities presiding over divisions of Nature, become less thought of as the phenomena ascribed to them are more commonly observed to follow a constant order; and hence these minor components of the mythology slowly dissolve away. At the same time, with growing supremacy of the great god heading the hierarchy, there goes increasing ascription to him of actions which were before distributed among numerous supernatural beings: there is integration of power. While in proportion as there arises the consequent conception of an omnipotent and omnipresent deity, there is a gradual fading of his alleged human attributes: dissolution begins to affect the supreme personality in respect of ascribed form and nature.

Already, as we have seen, this process has in the more advanced societies, and especially among their higher members, gone to the extent of merging all minor supernatural powers in one supernatural power; and already this one supernatural power has, by what Mr. Fiske aptly calls de-anthropomorphisation, lost the grosser attributes of humanity. If things hereafter are to follow the same general course as heretofore, we must infer that this dropping of human attributes will continue. Let us ask what positive changes are hence to be expected.

Two factors must unite in producing them. There is the development of those higher sentiments which no longer tolerate the ascription of inferior sentiments to a divinity; and there is the intellectual development which causes dissatisfaction with the crude interpretations previously accepted. Of course in pointing out the effects of these factors, I must name some which are familiar; but it is needful to glance at them along with others.

The cruelty of a Fijian god who, represented as devouring the souls of the dead, may be supposed to inflict torture during the process, is small compared with the cruelty of a god who condemns men to tortures which are eternal; and the ascription of this cruelty, though habitual in ecclesiastical formulas, occasionally occurring in sermons, and still sometimes pictorially illustrated, is becoming so intolerable to the better-natured, that while some theologians distinctly deny it, others quietly drop it out of their teachings. Clearly, this change cannot cease until the beliefs in hell and damnation disappear.[2] Disappearance of them will be aided by an increasing repugnance to injustice. The visiting on Adam's descendants through hundreds of generations dreadful penalties for a small transgression which they did not commit; the damning of all men who do not avail themselves of an alleged mode of obtaining forgiveness, which most men have never heard of; and the effecting a reconciliation by sacrificing a son who was perfectly innocent, to satisfy the assumed necessity for a propitiatory victim; are modes of action which, ascribed to a human ruler, would call forth expressions of abhorrence; and the ascription of them to the Ultimate Cause of things, even now felt to be full of difficulties, must become impossible. So, too, must die out the belief that a Power present in innumerable worlds throughout infinite space, and who during millions of years of the Earth's earlier existence needed no honouring by its inhabitants, should be seized with a craving for praise; and having created mankind, should be angry with them if they do not perpetually tell him how great he is. As fast as men escape from that glamour of early impressions which prevents them from thinking, they will refuse to imply a trait of character which is the reverse of worshipful.

Similarly with the logical incongruities more and more conspicuous to growing intelligence. Passing over the familiar difficulties that sundry of the implied divine traits are in contradiction with the divine attributes otherwise ascribed – that a god who repents of what he has done must be lacking either in power or in foresight; that his anger presupposes an occurrence which has been contrary to intention, and so indicates defect of means; we come to the deeper difficulty that such emotions, in common with all emotions, can exist only in a consciousness which is limited. Every emotion has its antecedent ideas, and antecedent ideas are habitually supposed to occur in God: he is represented as seeing and hearing this or the other, and as being emotionally affected thereby. That is to say, the conception of a divinity possessing these traits of character, necessarily continues anthropomorphic; not only in the sense that the emotions ascribed are like those of human

[2]   To meet a possible criticism, it may be well to remark that whatever force they may have against deists (and they have very little), Butler's arguments concerning these and allied beliefs do not tell at all against agnostics.

beings, but also in the sense that they form parts of a consciousness which, like the human consciousness, is formed of successive states. And such a conception of the divine consciousness is irreconcilable both with the unchangeableness otherwise alleged, and with the omniscience otherwise alleged. For a consciousness constituted of ideas and feelings caused by objects and occurrences, cannot be simultaneously occupied with all objects and all occurrences throughout the universe. To believe in a divine consciousness, men must refrain from thinking what is meant by consciousness – must stop short with verbal propositions; and propositions which they are debarred from rendering into thoughts will more and more fail to satisfy them. Of course like difficulties present themselves when the will of God is spoken of. So long as we refrain from giving a definite meaning to the word will, we may say that it is possessed by the Cause of All Things, as readily as we may say that love of approbation is possessed by a circle; but when from the words we pass to the thoughts they stand for, we find that we can no more unite in consciousness the terms of the one proposition than we can those of the other. Whoever conceives any other will than his own must do so in terms of his own will, which is the sole will directly known to him – all other wills being only inferred. But will, as each is conscious of it, presupposes a motive – a prompting desire of some kind: absolute indifference excludes the conception of will. More-over will, as implying a prompting desire, connotes some end contemplated as one to be achieved, and ceases with the achievement of it: some other will, referring to some other end, taking its place. That is to say, will, like emotion, necessarily supposes a series of states of consciousness. The conception of a divine will, derived from that of the human will, involves, like it, localisation in space and time: the wiling of each end, excluding from consciousness for an interval the willing of other ends, and therefore being inconsistent with that omni-present activity which simultaneously works out an infinity of ends. It is the same with the ascription of intelligence. Not to dwell on the seriality and limitation implied as before, we may note that intelligence, as alone conceivable by us, presupposes existences independent of it and objective to it. It is carried on in terms of changes primarily wrought by alien activities – the impressions generated by things beyond consciousness, and the ideas derived from such impressions. To speak of an intelligence which exists in the absence of all such alien activities, is to use a meaningless word. If to the corollary that the First Cause, considered as intelligent, must be continually affected by independent objective activities, it is replied that these have become such by act of creation, and were previously included in the First Cause; then the reply is that in such case the First Cause could, before this creation, have had nothing to generate in it such changes as those constituting what we call intelligence, and must therefore have been unintelligent at the time when intelligence was most called for. Hence it is clear that the intelligence ascribed, answers in no respect to that which we know by the name. It is intelligence out of which all the characters constituting it have vanished.

These and other difficulties, some of which are often discussed but never disposed of, must force men hereafter to drop the higher anthropomorphic characters given to the First Cause, as they have long since dropped the lower. The conception which has been enlarging from the beginning must go on enlarging, until, by disappearance of its limits, it becomes a consciousness which transcends the forms of distinct thought, though it for ever remains a consciousness.

'But how can such a final consciousness of the Unknowable, thus tacitly alleged to be true, be reached by successive modifications of a conception which was utterly untrue? The ghost-theory of the savage is baseless. The material double of a dead man in which he believes, never had any existence. And if by gradual de-materialisation of this double was produced the conception of the supernatural agent in general – if the conception of a deity, formed by the dropping of some human attributes and transfiguration of others, resulted from continuance of this process; is not the developed and purified conception reached by pushing the process to its limit, a fiction also? Surely if the primitive belief was absolutely false, all derived beliefs must be absolutely false.'

This objection looks fatal; and it would be fatal were its premiss valid. Unexpected as it will be to most readers, the answer here to be made is that at the outset a germ of truth was contained in the primitive conception – the truth, namely, that the power which manifests itself in consciousness is but a differently-conditioned form of the power which manifests itself beyond consciousness.

Every voluntary act yields to the primitive man proof of a source of energy within him. Not that he thinks about his internal experiences; but in these experiences this notion lies latent. When producing motion in his limbs, and through them motion in other things, he is aware of the accompanying feeling of effort. And this sense of effort, which is the perceived antecedent of changes produced by him, becomes the conceived antecedent of changes not produced by him – furnishes him with a term of thought by which to represent the genesis of these objective changes. At first this idea of muscular force as anteceding unusual events around him, carries with it the whole assemblage of associated ideas. He thinks of the implied effort as an effort exercised by a being just like himself. In course of time these doubles of the dead, supposed to be workers of all but the most familiar changes, are modified in conception. Besides becoming less grossly material, some of them are developed into large personalities presiding over classes of phenomena which being comparatively regular in their order, suggest a belief in beings who, while more powerful than men, are less variable in their modes of action. So that the idea of force as exercised by such beings, comes to be less associated with the idea of a human ghost. Further advances, by which minor supernatural agents are merged in one general agent, and by which the personality of this general agent is rendered vague while becoming widely extended, tend still further to dissociate the notion of objective force from the force known as such in consciousness; and the dissociation reaches its extreme in the thoughts of the man of science, who interprets in terms of force not only the visible changes of sensible bodies, but all physical changes whatever, even up to the undulations of the ethereal medium. Nevertheless, this force (be it force under that statical form by which matter resists, or under that dynamical form distinguished as energy) is to the last thought of in terms of that internal energy which he is conscious of as muscular effort. He is compelled to symbolise objective force in terms of subjective force from lack of any other symbol.

See now the implications. That internal energy which in the experiences of the primitive man was always the immediate antecedent of changes wrought by him – that energy which, when interpreting external changes, he thought of along with those attributes of a human personality connected with it in himself; is the same energy which, freed from anthropo-morphic accompaniments, is now figured as the cause of all external phenomena. The last stage reached is recognition of the truth that force as it exists beyond consciousness, cannot be like what we know as force within consciousness; and that yet, as either is capable of generating the other, they must be different modes of the same. Consequently, the final outcome of that speculation commenced by the primitive man, is that the Power manifested throughout the Universe distinguished as material, is the same power which in ourselves wells up under the form of consciousness.

It is untrue, then, that the foregoing argument proposes to evolve a true belief from a belief which was wholly false. Contrariwise, the ultimate form of the religious consciousness is the final development of a consciousness which at the outset contained a germ of truth obscured by multitudinous errors.

Those who think that science is dissipating religious beliefs and sentiments, seem unaware that whatever of mystery is taken from the old interpretation is added to the new. Or rather, we may say that transference from the one to the other is accompanied by increase; since, for an explanation which has a seeming feasibility, science substitutes an explanation which, carrying us back only a certain distance, there leaves us in presence of the avowedly inexplicable.

Under one of its aspects scientific progress is a gradual transfiguration of Nature. Where ordinary perception saw perfect simplicity it reveals great complexity; where there seemed absolute inertness it discloses intense activity; and in what appears mere vacancy it finds a marvellous play of forces. Each generation of physicists discovers in so-called 'brute matter' powers which, but a few years before, the most instructed physicists would have thought incredible; as instance the ability of a mere iron plate to take up the complicated aërial vibrations produced by articulate speech, which, translated into multitudinous and varied electric pulses, are retranslated a thousand miles off by another iron plate and again heard as articulate speech. When the explorer of Nature sees that, quiescent as they appear, surrounding solid bodies are thus sensitive to forces which are infinitesimal in their amounts – when the spectroscope proves to him that molecules on the Earth pulsate in harmony with molecules in the stars – when there is forced on him the inference that every point in space thrills with an infinity of vibrations passing through it in all directions; the conception to which he tends is much less that of a Universe of dead matter than that of a Universe everywhere alive: alive if not in the restricted sense, still in a general sense.

This transfiguration, which the inquiries of physicists continually increase, is aided by that other transfiguration resulting from metaphysical inquiries. Subjective analysis compels us to admit that our scientific interpretations of the phenomena which objects present, are expressed in terms of our own variously-combined sensations and ideas – are expressed, that is, in elements belonging to consciousness, which are but symbols of the something beyond consciousness. Though analysis afterwards reinstates our primitive beliefs, to the extent of showing that behind every group of phenomenal manifestations there is always a *nexus*, which is the reality that remains fixed amid appearances which are variable; yet we are shown that this *nexus* of reality is for ever inaccessible to consciousness. And when, once more, we remember that the activities constituting consciousness, being rigorously bounded, cannot bring in among themselves the activities beyond the bounds, which therefore seem unconscious, though production of either by the other seems to imply that they are of the same essential nature; this necessity we are under to think of the external energy in terms of the internal energy, gives rather a spiritualistic than a materialistic aspect to the Universe: further thought, however, obliging us to recognise the truth that a conception given in phenomenal manifestations of this ultimate energy can in no wise show us what it is.

While the beliefs to which analytic science thus leads are such as do not destroy the object-matter of religion, but simply transfigure it, science under its concrete forms enlarges the sphere for religious sentiment. From the very beginning the progress of knowledge has been accompanied by an increasing capacity for wonder. Among savages, the lowest are the least surprised when shown remarkable products of civilised art: astonishing the traveller by their indifference. And so little of the marvellous do they perceive in the grandest phenomena of Nature, that any inquiries concerning them they regard as childish trifling. This contrast in mental attitude between the lowest human beings and the higher human beings around us, is paralleled by the contrasts among the grades of these higher human beings themselves. It is not the rustic, nor the artisan, nor the trader, who sees something more than a mere matter of course in the hatching of a chick; but it is the biologist, who, pushing to the uttermost his analysis of vital phenomena, reaches his greatest perplexity when a speck of protoplasm under the microscope shows him life in its simplest form, and makes him feel that however he formulates its processes the actual play of forces remains unimaginable. Neither in the ordinary tourist nor in the deer-stalker climbing the mountains above him, does a highland glen rouse ideas beyond those of sport or of the picturesque; but it may, and often does, in the geologist. He, observing that the glacier-rounded rock he sits on has lost by weathering but half-an-inch of its surface since a time far more remote than the beginnings of human civilisation, and then trying to conceive the slow denudation which has cut out the whole valley, has thoughts of time and of power to which they are strangers – thoughts which, already utterly inadequate to their objects, he feels to be still more futile on noting the contorted beds of gneiss around, which tell him of a time, immeasurably more remote, when far beneath the Earth's surface they were in a half-melted state, and again tell him of a time, immensely exceeding this in remoteness, when their components were sand and mud on the shores of an ancient sea. Nor is it in the primitive peoples who supposed that the heavens rested on the mountain tops, any more than in the modern inheritors of their cosmogony who repeat that 'the heavens declare the glory of God,' that we find the largest conceptions of the Universe or the greatest amount of wonder excited by contemplation of it. Rather, it is in the astronomer, who sees in the Sun a mass so vast that even into one of his spots our Earth might be plunged without touching its edges; and who by every finer telescope is shown an increased multitude of such suns, many of them far larger.

Hereafter, as heretofore, higher faculty and deeper insight will raise rather than lower this sentiment. At present the most powerful and most instructed mind has neither the knowledge nor the capacity required for symbolising in thought the totality of things. Occupied with one or other division of Nature, the man of science usually does not know enough of the other divisions even rudely to conceive the extent and complexity of their phenomena; and supposing him to have adequate knowledge of each, yet he is unable to think of them as a whole. Wider and stronger intellect may hereafter help him to form a vague consciousness of them in their totality. We may say that just as an undeveloped musical faculty, able only to appreciate a simple melody, cannot grasp the variously-entangled passages and harmonies of a symphony, which in the minds of composer and conductor are unified into involved musical effects awakening far greater feeling than is possible to the musically uncultured; so, by future more evolved intelligences, the course of things now apprehensible only in parts may be apprehensible all together, with an accompanying feeling as much beyond that of the present cultured man, as his feeling is beyond that of the savage.

And this feeling is not likely to be decreased but to be increased by that analysis of knowledge which, while forcing him to agnosticism, yet continually prompts him to imagine some solution of the Great Enigma which he knows cannot be solved. Especially must this be so when he remembers that the very notions, beginning and end, cause and purpose, are relative notions belonging to human thought which are probably irrelevant to the Ultimate Reality transcending human thought; and when, though suspecting that explanation is a word without meaning when applied to this Ultimate Reality, he yet feels compelled to think that there must be an explanation.

But amid the mysteries which become the more mysterious the more they are thought about, there will remain the one absolute certainty, that he is ever in presence of an Infinite and Eternal Energy, from which all things proceed.

THE GHOST OF RELIGION
[Frederic Harrison]

In the January number of this Review is to be found an article on Religion which has justly awakened a profound and sustained interest. The creed of Agnosticism was there formulated anew by the acknowledged head of the Evolution philosophy, with a definiteness such as perhaps it never wore before. To my mind there is nothing in the whole range of modern religious discussion more cogent and more suggestive than the array of conclusions the final outcome of which is marshalled in those twelve pages. It is the last word of the Agnostic philosophy in its long controversy with Theology. That word is decisive, and it is hard to conceive how Theology can rally for another bout from such a *sorites* of dilemma as is there presented. My own humble purpose is not to criticise this paper, but to point its practical moral, and, if I may, to add to it a rider of my own. As a summary of philosophical conclusions on the theological problem, it seems to me frankly unanswerable. Speaking generally, I shall now dispute no part of it but one word, and that is the title. It is entitled 'Religion.' To me it is rather the Ghost of Religion. Religion as a living force lies in a different sphere.

The essay, which is packed with thought to a degree unusual even with Mr. Herbert Spencer, contains evidently three parts. The first (pp. 1–5) deals with the historical Evolution of Religion, of which Mr. Spencer traces the germs in the primitive belief in ghosts. The second (pp. 6–8) arrays the moral and intellectual dilemmas involved in all anthropomorphic theology into one long catena of difficulty, out of which it is hard to conceive any free mind emerging with success. The third part (pp. 8–12) deals with the evolution of Religion in the future, and formulates, more precisely than has ever yet been effected, the positive creed of Agnostic philosophy.

Has, then, the Agnostic a positive creed? It would seem so; for Mr. Spencer brings us at last 'to the one absolute certainty, the presence of an Infinite and Eternal Energy, from which all things proceed.' But let no one suppose that this is merely a new name for the Great First Cause of so many theologies and metaphysics. In spite of the capital letters, and the use of theological terms as old as Isaiah or Athanasius, Mr. Spencer's Energy has no analogy with God. It is Eternal, Infinite, and Incomprehensible; but still it is not He, but It. It remains always Energy, Force, nothing anthropomorphic; such as electricity, or anything else that we might conceive as the ultimate basis of all the physical forces. None of the positive attributes which have ever been predicated of God can be used of this Energy. Neither goodness, nor wisdom, nor justice, nor consciousness, nor will, nor life, can be ascribed, even by analogy, to this Force. Now a force to which we cannot apply the ideas of goodness, wisdom, justice, consciousness, or life, any more than we can to a circle, is certainly not God, has no analogy with God, nor even with what Pope has called the 'Great First Cause, least understood.' It shares some of the negative attributes of God and First Cause, but no positive one. It is, in fact, only the Unknowable a little more defined; though I do not remember that Mr. Spencer, or any evolution philosopher, has ever formulated the Unknowable in terms with so deep a theological ring as we hear in the phrase 'Infinite and Eternal Energy, from which all things proceed.'

The terms do seem, perhaps, rather needlessly big and absolute. And fully accepting Mr. Spencer's logical canons, one does not see why it should be called an 'absolute certainty.' 'Practical belief' satisfies me; and I doubt the legitimacy of substituting for it 'absolute certainty.' 'Infinite' and 'Eternal,' also, can mean to Mr. Spencer nothing more than 'to which we know no limits, no beginning or end,' and, for my part, I prefer to say this. Again, 'an Energy' - why AN Energy? The Unknowable may certainly consist of more than one energy. To assert the presence of one uniform energy is to profess to know something very important about the Unknowable: that it is homogeneous, and even identical, throughout the Universe. And the, 'from which all things proceed' is perhaps a rather equivocal reversion to the theologic type. In the Athanasian Creed the Third Person 'proceeds' from the First and the Second. But this process has always been treated as a mystery; and it would be safer to avoid the phrases of mysticism. Let us keep the old words, for we all mean much the same thing; and I prefer to put it thus. All observation and meditation, Science and Philosophy, bring us 'to the *practical belief* that man is ever in the presence of *some energy or energies*, of which he knows nothing, and to which therefore he would be wise to assign no limits, conditions, or functions.' This is, doubtless, what Mr. Spencer himself means. For my part, I prefer his old term, the Unknowable. Though I have always thought that it would be more philosophical not to assert of the Unknown that it is Unknowable. And, indeed, I would rather not use the capital letter, but stick literally to our evidence, and say frankly 'the unknown.'

Thus viewed, the attempt, so to speak, to put a little unction into the Unknowable is hardly worth the philosophical inaccuracy it involves; and such is the drawback to any use of picturesque language. So stated, the positive creed of Agnosticism still retains its negative character. It has a series of propositions and terms, every one of which is a negation. A friend of my own, who was much pressed to say how much of the Athanasian Creed he still accepted, once said that he clung to the idea 'that there was a sort of a something.' In homely words such as the unlearned can understand, that is precisely what the religion of the Agnostic comes to, 'the belief that there is a sort of a something, about which we can know nothing.'

Now let us profess that, as a philosophical answer to the theological problem, that is entirely our own position. The Positivist answer is of course the same as the Agnostic answer. Why, then, do we object to be called Agnostics? Simply because Agnostic is only dog-Greek for 'don't know,' and we have no taste to be called 'don't knows.' The *Spectator* calls us Agnostics, but that is only by way of prejudice. Our religion does not consist in a comprehensive negation; we are not for ever replying to the theological problem; we are quite unconcerned by the theological problem, and have something that we do care for, and do know. Englishmen are Europeans, and many of them are Christians, and they usually prefer to call themselves Englishmen, Christians, or the like, rather than non-Asiatics or anti-Mahometans. Some people still prefer to call themselves Protestants rather than Christians, but the taste is dying out, except among Irish Orangemen, and even the Nonconformist newspaper has been induced by Mr. Matthew Arnold to drop its famous motto: 'The dissidence of Dissent, and the Protestantism of the Protestant religion.' For a man to say that his religion is Agnosticism is simply the sceptical equivalent of saying that his religion is Protestantism. Both mean that his religion is to deny and to differ. But this is not religion. The business of religion is to affirm and to unite, and nothing can be religion but that which at once affirms truth and unites men.

The purpose of the present paper is to show that Agnosticism, though a valid and final answer to the theological or ontological problem – 'what is the ultimate cause of the world and of man?' – is not a religion nor the shadow of a religion. It offers none of the rudiments or elements of religion, and religion is not to be found in that line at all. It is the mere disembodied spirit of dead religion: as we said at the outset, it is the ghost of religion. Agnosticism, perfectly legitimate as the true answer of science to an effete question, has shown us that religion is not to be found anywhere within the realm of Cause. Having brought us to the answer, 'no cause that we know of,' it is laughable to call that negation religion. Mr. Mark Pattison, one of the acutest minds of modern Oxford, rather oddly says that the idea of deity has now been 'defecated to a pure transparency'. The evolution philosophy goes a step further and defecates the idea of cause to a pure transparency. Theology and ontology alike end in the Everlasting No with which science confronts all their assertions. But how whimsical is it to tell us that religion, which cannot find any resting-place in theology or ontology, is to find its true home in the Everlasting No! That which is defecated to a pure transparency can never supply a religion to any human being but a philosopher constructing a system. It is quite conceivable that religion is to end with theology, and both might in the course of evolution become an anachronism. But if religion there is still to be, it cannot be found in this No-man's-land and Know-nothing creed. Better bury religion at once than let its ghost walk uneasy in our dreams.

The true lesson is that we must hark back, and leave the realm of cause. The accident of religion has been mistaken for the essence of religion. The essence of religion is not to answer a question, but to govern and unite men and societies by giving them common beliefs and duties. Theologies tried to do this, and long did it, by resting on certain answers to certain questions. The progress of thought has upset one answer after another, and now the final verdict of philosophy is that all the answers are unmeaning, and that no rational answer can be given. It follows then that questions and answers, both but the accident of religion, must both be given up. A base of belief and duty must be looked for elsewhere, and when this has been found, then again religion will succeed in governing and uniting men. Where is this base to be found? Since the realm of Cause has failed to give us foothold, we must fall back upon the realm of Law – social, moral, and mental law, and not merely physical. Religion consists, not in answering certain questions, but in making men of a certain quality. And the law, moral, mental, social, is pre-eminently the field wherein men may be governed and united. Hence to the religion of Cause there succeeds the religion of Law. But the religion of Law or Science is Positivism.

It is no part of my purpose to criticise Mr. Spencer's memorable essay, except so far as it is necessary to show that that which is a sound philosophical conclusion is not religion, simply by reason that it relates to the subject-matter of theology. But a few words may be suffered as to the historical evolution of religion. To many persons it will sound rather whimsical, and possibly almost a sneer, to trace the germs of religion to the ghost-theory. Our friends of the Psychical Research will prick up their ears, and expect to be taken *au grand sérieux*. But the conception is a thoroughly solid one, and of most suggestive kind. Beyond all doubt, the hypothesis of quasi-human immaterial spirits working within and behind familiar phenomena did take its rise from the idea of the other self which the imagination continually presents to the early reflections of man. And, beyond all doubt, the phenomena of dreams, and the gradual construction of a theory of ghosts, is a very impressive and vivid form of the notion of the other self. It would, I think, be wrong to assert that it is the only form of the notion, and one can hardly suppose that Mr. Spencer would limit himself to that. But, in any case, the construction of a coherent theory of ghosts is a typical instance of a belief in a quasi-human spirit-world. Glorify and amplify this idea, and apply it to the whole of nature, and we get a god-world, a multitude of superhuman divine spirits.

That is the philosophical explanation of the rise of theology, of the peopling of Nature with divine spirits. But does it explain the rise of Religion? No, for theology and religion are not conterminous. Mr. Spencer has unwittingly conceded to the divines that which they assume so confidently – that theology is the same thing as religion, and that there was no religion at all until there was a belief in super-human spirits within and behind Nature. This is obviously an oversight. We have to go very much further back for the genesis of religion. There were countless centuries of time, and there were, and there are, countless millions of men for whom no doctrine of superhuman spirits ever took coherent form. In all these ages and races, probably by far the most numerous that our planet has witnessed, there was religion in all kinds of definite form. Comte calls it Fetichism – terms are not important: roughly, we may call it Nature-worship. The religion in all these types was the belief and worship not of spirits of any kind, not of any immaterial, imagined being *inside* things, but of the actual visible things themselves – trees, stones, rivers, mountains, earth, fire, stars, sun, and sky. Some of the most abiding and powerful of all religions have consisted in elaborate worship of these physical objects treated frankly as physical objects, without trace of ghost, spirit, or god. To say nothing of fire-worship, river, and tree-worship, the venerable religion of China, far the most vast of all systematic religions, is wholly based on reverence for Earth, Sky, and ancestors treated objectively, and not as the abode of subjective immaterial spirits.

Hence the origin of religion is to be sought in the countless ages before the rise of theology; before spirits, ghosts, or gods ever took definite form in the human mind. The primitive uncultured man frankly worshipped external objects in love and in fear, ascribing to them quasi-human powers and feelings. All that we read about Animism, ghosts, spirits, and universal ideas of godhead in this truly primitive stage are metaphysical assumptions of men trying to read the ideas of later epochs into the facts of an earlier epoch. Nothing is more certain than that man everywhere started with a simple worship of natural objects. And the bearing of this on the future of religion is decisive. The religion of man in the vast cycles of primitive ages was reverence for Nature as influencing Man. The religion of man in the vast cycles that are to come will be the reverence for Humanity as supported by Nature. The religion of man in the twenty or thirty centuries of Theology was reverence for the assumed authors or controllers of Nature. But, that assumption having broken up, religion does not break up with it. On the contrary, it enters on a far greater and more potent career, inasmuch as the natural emotions of the human heart are now combined with the certainty of scientific knowledge. The final religion of en-lightened man is the systematised and scientific form of the spontaneous religion of natural man. Both rest on the same element – belief in the Power which controls his life, and grateful reverence for the Power so acknowledged. The primitive man thought that Power to be the object of Nature affecting Man. The cultured man knows that Power to be Humanity itself, controlling and controlled by nature accord-ing to natural law. The transitional and perpetually changing creed of Theology has been an interlude. Agnosticism has uttered its epilogue. But Agnosticism is no more religion than differentiation or the nebular hypothesis is religion.

We have only to see what are the elements and ends of religion to recognise that we cannot find it in the negative and the unknown. In any reasonable use of language religion implies some kind of belief in a Power outside ourselves, some kind of awe and gratitude felt for that Power, some kind of influence exerted by it over our lives. There are always in some sort these three elements – belief, worship, conduct. A religion which gives us nothing in particular to believe, nothing as an object of awe and gratitude, which has no special relation to human duty, is not a religion at all. It may be formula, a generalisation, a logical postulate; but it is not a religion. The universal presence of the unknowable (or rather of the unknown) substratum is not a religion. It is a logical postulate. You may call it, if you please, the first axiom of science, a law of the human mind, or perhaps better the universal postulate of philosophy. But try it by every test which indicates religion and you will find it wanting.

The points which the Unknowable has in common with the object of any religion are very slight and superficial. As the universal substratum it has some analogy with other super-human objects of worship. But Force, Gravitation, Atom, Undulation, Vibration, and other abstract notions have much the same kind of analogy, but nobody every dreamed of a religion of gravitation, or the worship of molecules. The Unknowable has managed to get itself spelt with a capital U; but Carlyle taught us to spell the Everlasting No with capitals also. The Unknowable is no doubt mysterious, and Godhead is mysterious. It certainly appeals to the sense of wonder, and the Trinity appeals to the sense of wonder. It suggests vague and infinite extension, as does the idea of deity: but then Time and Space equally suggest vague and infinite extension. Yet no one but a delirious Kantist every professed that Time and Space were his religion. These seem all the qualities which the Unknowable has in common with objects of worship – ubiquity, mystery, and immensity. But these qualities it shares with some other postulates of thought.

But try it by all the other recognised tests of religion. Religion is not made up of wonder, or of a vague sense of immensity, unsatisfied yearning after infinity. Theology, seeking a refuge in the unintelligible, has no doubt accustomed this generation to imagine that a yearning after infinity is the sum and substance of religion. But that is a metaphysical disease of the age. And there is no reason that philosophers should accept this hysterical piece of transcendentalism, and assume that they have found the field of religion when they have found a field for unquenchable yearning after infinity. Wonder has its place in religion, and so has mystery; but it is a subordinate place. The roots and fibres of religion are to be found in love, awe, sympathy, gratitude, consciousness of inferiority and of dependence, community of will, acceptance of control, manifestation of purpose, reverence for majesty, goodness, creative energy, and life. Where these things are not, religion is not.

Let us take each one of these three elements of religion – belief, worship, conduct – and try them all in turn as applicable to the Unknowable. How mere a phrase must any religion be of which neither belief, nor worship, nor conduct can be spoken! Imagine a religion which can have no believers, because, *ex hypothesi*, its adepts are forbidden to believe anything about it. Imagine a religion which excludes the idea of worship, because its sole dogma is the infinity of Nothingness. Although the Unknowable is logically said to be Something, yet the something of which we neither know nor conceive anything is practically nothing. Lastly, imagine a religion which can have no relation to conduct; for obviously the Unknowable can give us no intelligible help to conduct, and *ex vi termini* can have no bearing on conduct. A religion which could not make any one any better, which would leave the human heart and human society just as it found them, which left no foothold for devotion, and none for faith; which could have no creed, no doctrines, no temples, no priests, no teachers, no rites, no morality, no beauty, no hope, no consolation; which is summed up in one dogma – the Unknowable is everywhere, and Evolution is its prophet – this is indeed 'to defecate religion to a pure transparency.'

The growing weakness of religion has long been that it is being thrust inch by inch off the platform of knowledge; and we watch with sympathy the desperate efforts of all religious spirits to maintain the relations between knowledge and religion. And now it hears the invitation of Evolution to abandon the domain of knowledge, and to migrate to the domain of no-knowledge. The true Rock of Ages, says the philosopher, is the Unknowable. To the eye of Faith all things are henceforth ἀκαταληψία, as Cicero calls it. The paradox would hardly be greater if we were told that true religion consisted in unlimited Vice.

What is religion for? Why do we want it? And what do we expect it to do for us? If it can give us no sure ground for our minds to rest on, nothing to purify the heart, to exalt the sense of sympathy, to deepen our sense of beauty, to strengthen our resolves, to chasten us into resignation, and to kindle a spirit of self-sacrifice – what is the good of it? The Unknowable, *ex hypothesi*, can do none of these things. The object of all religion, in any known variety of religion, has invariably had some quasi-human and sympathetic relation to man and human life. It follows from the very meaning of religion that it could not effect any of its work without such quality or relation. It would be hardly sane to make a religion out of the Equator or the Binomial theorem. Whether it was the religion of the lowest savage, of the Polytheist, or of the Hegelian Theist; whether the object of the worship were a river, the Moon, the Sky, Apollo, Thor, God, or First Cause, there has always been some chain of sympathy – influence on the one side, and veneration on the other. However rudimentary, there must be a belief in some Power influencing the believer, and whose influence he repays with awe and gratitude and a desire to confirm his life thereto. But to make a religion out of the Unknowable is far more extravagant than to make it out of the Equator. We know something of the Equator; it influences seamen, equatorial peoples, and geographers not a little, and we all hesitate, as was once said, to speak disrespectfully of the Equator. But would it be blasphemy to speak disrespectfully of the Unknowable? Our minds are a blank about it. As to acknowledging the Unknowable, or trusting in it, or feeling its influence over us, or paying gratitude to it, or conforming our lives to it, or looking to it for help – the use of such words about it is unmeaning. We can wonder at it, as the child wonders at the 'twinkling star,' and that is all. It is a religion only to stare at.

Religion is not a thing of star-gazing and staring, but of life and action. And the condition of any such effect on our lives and our hearts is some sort of vital quality in that which is the object of the religion. The mountain, sun, or sky which untutored man worships is thought to have some sort of vital quality, some potency of the kind possessed by organic beings. When mountain, sun, and sky cease to have this vital potency, educated man ceases to worship them. Of course all sorts and conditions of divine spirits are assumed in a pre-eminent degree to have this quality, and hence the tremendous force exerted by all religions of divine spirits. Philosophy and the euthanasia of theology have certainly reduced this vital quality to a minimum in our day, and I suppose Dean Mansel's Bampton Lectures touched the low-water mark of vitality as predicated of the Divine Being. Of all modern theologians, the Dean came the nearest to the Evolution negation. But there is a gulf which separates even his all-negative deity from Mr. Spencer's impersonal, unconscious, unthinking, and unthinkable Energy.

Knowledge is of course wholly within the sphere of the Known. Our moral and social science is, of course, within the sphere of knowledge. Moral and social well-being, moral and social education, progress, perfection naturally rest on moral and social science, Civilisation rests on moral and social progress. And happiness can only be secured by both. But if religion has its sphere in the Unknown and Unknowable, it is thereby outside all this field of the Known. In other words Religion (of the Unknowable type) is *ex hypothesi* outside the sphere of knowledge, of civilisation, of social discipline, of morality, of progress, and of happiness. It has no part or parcel in human life. It fills a brief and mysterious chapter in a system of philosophy.

By their fruits you shall know them is true of all sorts of religion. And what are the fruits of the Unknowable but the Dead Sea apples? Obviously it can teach us nothing, influence us in nothing, for the absolutely incalculable and unintelligible can give us neither ground for action nor thought. Nor can it touch any one of our feelings but that of wonder, mystery, and sense of human helplessness. Helpless, objectless, apathetic wonder at an inscrutable infinity may be attractive to a metaphysical divine; but it does not sound like a working force in the world. Does the Evolutionist commune with the Unknowable in the secret silence of his chamber? Does he meditate on it, saying, in quietness and confidence shall be your strength? One would like to see the new *Imitatio Ignoti*. It was said of old, *Ignotum omne pro magnifico*. But the new version is to be *Ignotum omne pro divino*.

One would like to know how much of the Evolutionist's day is consecrated to seeking the Unknowable in a devout way, and what the religious exercises might be. How does the man of science approach the All-Nothingness? and the microscopist, and the embryologist, and the vivisectionist? What do they learn about it, what strength or comfort does it give them? Nothing – nothing: it is an ever-present conundrum to be everlastingly given up, and perpetually to be asked of oneself and one's neighbours, but without waiting for the answer. Tantalus and Sisyphus bore their insoluble tasks, and the Evolutionist carries about his riddle without an answer, his unquenchable thirst to know that which he only knows he can never know. *Quisque suos patimur Manes.* But Tantalus and Sisyphus called it Hell and the retribution of the Gods. The Evolutionist calls it Religion, and one might almost say Paradise.

A child comes up to our Evolutionist friend, looks up in his wise and meditative face, and says, 'Oh! wise and great Master, what is religion?' And he tells that child, It is the presence of the Unknowable. 'But what,' asks the child, 'am I to believe about it?' 'Believe that you can never know anything about it.' 'But how am I to learn to do my duty?' 'Oh! for duty you must turn to the known, to moral and social science.' And a mother wrung with agony for the loss of her child, or the wife crushed by the death of her children's father, or the helpless and the oppressed, the poor and the needy, men, women, and children, in sorrow, doubt, and want, longing for something to comfort them and to guide them, something to believe in, to hope for, to love, and to worship – they come to our philosopher and they say, 'Your men of science have routed our priests, and have silenced our old teachers. What religious faith do you give us in its place?' And the philosopher replies (his full heart bleeding for them) and he says, 'Think on the Unknowable.'

And in the hour of pain, danger, or death, can any one think of the Unknowable, hope anything of the Unknowable, or find any consolation therein? Altars might be built to some Unknown God, conceived as a real being, knowing us, though not known by us yet. But altars to the unknowable infinity, even metaphorical altars, are impossible, for this unknown can never be known, and we have not the smallest reason to imagine that it either knew us, or affects us, or anybody, or anything. As the Unknowable cannot bring men together in a common belief, or for common purposes, or kindred feeling, it can no more unite men than the precession of the equinoxes can unite them. So there can never be congregations of Unknowable worshippers, nor churches dedicated to the Holy Unknowable, nor images nor symbols of the Unknowable mystery. Yes! there is one symbol of the Infinite Unknowable, and it is perhaps the most definite and ultimate word that can be said about it. The precise and yet inexhaustible language of mathematics enables us to express, in a common algebraic formula, the exact combination of the unknown raised to its highest power of infinity. That formula is (x^n), and here we have the beginning and perhaps the end of a symbolism for the religion of the Infinite Unknowable. Schools, academies, temples of the Unknowable, there cannot be. But where two or three are gathered together to worship the Unknowable, there the algebraic formula may suffice to give form to their emotions: they may be heard to profess their unwearying belief in (x^n), even if no weak brother with ritualist tendencies be heard to cry, 'O x^n, love us, help us, make us one with thee!'

These things have their serious side, and suggest the real difficulties in the way of the theory. The alternative is this: Is religion a mode of answering a question in ontology, or is it an institution for affecting human life by acting on the human spirit? If it be the latter, then there can be no religion of the Unknowable, and the sphere of religion must be sought elsewhere in the Knowable. We may accept with the utmost confidence all that the evolution philosophy asserts and denies as to the perpetual indications of an ultimate energy, omnipresent and unlimited, and, so far as we can see, of inscrutable mysteriousness. That remains an ultimate scientific idea, one

no doubt of profound importance. But why should this idea be
dignified with the name of religion, when it has not one of the
elements of religion, except infinity and mystery? The hallowed
name of religion has meant, in a thousand languages, man's
deepest convictions, his surest hopes, the most sacred yearnings
of his heart, that which can bind in brotherhood generations of
men, comfort the fatherless and the widow, uphold the martyr
at the stake, and the hero in his long battle. Why retain this
magnificent word, rich with the associations of all that is great,
pure, and lovely in human nature, if it is to be henceforth
limited to an idea, that can only be expressed by the formula
(x^n); and which by the hypothesis can have nothing to do with
either knowledge, belief, sympathy, hope, life, duty, or
happiness? It is not religion, this. It is a logician's artifice to
escape from an awkward dilemma.

One word in conclusion to those who would see religion a
working reality, and not a logical artifice. The startling
reductio ad absurdum of relegating religion to the unknowable
is only the last step in the process which has gradually reduced
religion to an incomprehensible *minimum*. And this has been
the work of theologians obstinately fighting a losing battle, and
withdrawing at every defeat into a more impregnable and
narrower fastness. They have thrown over one after another
the claims of religion and the attributes of divinity. They are so
hopeless of continuing the contest on the open field of the
known that they more and more seek to withdraw to the cloud-
world of the transcendental. They are so terribly afraid of an
anthropomorphic God that they have sublimated him into a
metaphorical expression – 'defecated the idea to a pure
transparency,' as one of the most eminent of them puts it. Dean
Mansel is separated from Mr. Spencer by degree, not in kind.
And now they are pushed by Evolution into the abyss, and are
solemnly assured that the reconciliation of Religion and Science
is effected by this religion of the Unknowable – this *chimaera
bombinans in vacuo*. Their Infinites and their Incomprehen-
sibles, their Absolute and their Unconditioned, have brought
them to this. It is only one step from the sublime to the
unknowable.

Practically, so far as it affects the lives of men and women in
the battle of life, the Absolute and Unconditioned Godhead of
learned divines is very much the same thing as the Absolute
Unknowable. You may rout a logician by a 'pure trans-

parency,' but you cannot check vice, crime, and war by it, nor train up men and women in holiness and truth. And the set of all modern theology is away from the anthropomorphic and into the Absolute. In trying to save a religion of the spirit-world, theologians are abandoning all religion of the real world; they are turning religion into formulas and phrases, and are taking out of it all power over life, duty, and society.

I say, in a word, unless religion is to be anthropomorphic, there can be no working religion at all. How strange is this new cry, sprung up in our own generation, that religion is dishonoured by being anthropomorphic! Fetichism, Poly-theism, Confucianism, Mediaeval Christianity, and Bible Puritanism have all been intensely anthropomorphic, and all owed their strength and dominion to that fact. You can have no religion without kinship, sympathy, relation of some human kind between the believer, worshipper, servant, and the object of his belief, veneration, and service. The Neo-Theisms have all the same mortal weakness that the Unknowable has. They offer no kinship, sympathy, or relation whatever between worshipper and worshipped. They too are logical formulas begotten in controversy, dwelling apart from man and the world. If the formula of the Unknowable is (x^n) or the Unknown raised to infinity, theirs is (nx), some unknown expression of Infinity. Neither (x^n) nor (nx) will ever make good men and women.

If we leave the religion of formulas and go back to the practical effect of religion on human conduct, we must be driven to the conclusion that the future of religion is to be, not only what every real religion has ever been, anthropomorphic – but frankly anthropic. The attempted religion of Spiritism has lost one after another every resource of a real religion, until *risu solvuntur tabulae*, and it ends in a religion of Nothingism. It is the Nemesis of Faith in spiritual abstractions and figments. The hypothesis has burst, and leaves the Void. The future will have then to return to the Knowable and the certainly known, to the religion of Realism. It must give up explaining the Universe, and content itself with explaining human life. Humanity is the grandest object of reverence within the region of the real and the known, Humanity with the World on which it rests as its base and environment. Religion, having failed in the super-human world, returns to the human world. Here religion can find again all its certainty, all its depth of human sympathy, all its claim to command and reward the purest self sacrifice and love. We can take our place again with all the great religious spirits who have ever moulded the faith and life of men, and we find ourselves in harmony with the devout of every faith who are manfully battling with sin and discord. The way for us is the clearer as we find the religion of Spiritism, in its long and restless evolution of thirty centuries, ending in the legitimate deduction, the religion of the Unknowable, a paradox as memorable as any in the history of the human mind. The alternative is very plain. Shall we cling to a religion of Spiritism when philosophy is whittling away spirit to Nothing? Or shall we accept a religion of Realism, where all the great traditions and functions of religion are retained unbroken?

ARTICLES OF THE AGNOSTIC CREED, AND REASONS FOR THEM[1]
[Samuel Laing]

Article I
That the subjects which positive creeds profess to define are, for the most part, unknowable – i.e., beyond the scope of human reason or conception.

Reasons
For the philosophical proof of this see Herbert Spencer *passim*; also Huxley on Hume, Kant, Spinoza, etc.

We cannot conceive the First Cause which lies behind the phenomena of the universe, which are all linked together by known or knowable secondary causes (*i.e.*, by laws or invariable successions), either as being finite or infinite, conditioned or unconditioned, created or self-existent. In other words, we cannot conceive it at all, and therefore cannot either affirm or deny any proposition respecting it.

Article II
That Darwinism – or, in other words, Evolution by known or knowable natural laws – affords the true explanation of all that (apart from Revelation) we do or can know respecting this inscrutable First Cause, its attributes and relations to man, and such mysteries as birth, life, and immortality.

Reasons
See the works of Darwin, Lyell, Herbert Spencer, Huxley, and Haeckel. And, above all, note the fact that nearly the whole scientific opinion of the civilised world has come round, in little more than twenty-five years, to this view, as completely as it did from the Ptolemaic to the Copernican Astronomy. Every day adds fresh discoveries of missing links, and fresh evidence confirming this theory.

---

[1] Specially compiled at the request of Mr. Gladstone, to whom they were submitted in the form of a letter.

See, for instance, Huxley's pedigree of the horse, and Professor Cope's discoveries of ancestral forms of almost all the mammalia in the Eocene, Miocene, and Pliocene strata of North America. Also the similar discoveries by Falcomer and Gaudry on the Scwalik hills, and at Pikermi; and the clearly-traced development of birds from reptiles, as shown by the archaeopteryx in the British Museum.

The only remaining controversy in the scientific world is not as to the reality of evolution, but as to the precise laws and methods of the variations which have led to it. All agree on the *fact* of evolution, and all attribute a principal cause of it to Darwin's laws of the struggle for life and the survival of the fittest by natural selection and heredity. But some think these laws sufficient, while others, admitting them to be a true and principal cause, think them insufficient without the aid of other causes, such as use and disuse, which are not yet fully understood. But there is no difference of opinion, as far as I am aware, among competent judges, as to evolution being the true law of the universe.

Nor is this confined to men of science; it has become the general mould of modern thought. Bishop Temple and other eminent Divines practically adopt it, and when they talk of "original impress" they discard secondary supernatural interference, by what I have ventured to call elsewhere a "grandmotherly God," as completely as Darwin or Spencer. When Tennyson, the great poet of modern thought, says,

"Behold I know not anything;"

and in solemn words,

"Behind the veil, behind the veil,"

the words come home to us, with almost a thrill of awe, as the condensed essence of the *true* truth.

Article III
I have said "apart from Revelation," for a revelation, attested by prophecies and miracles, is a conceivable proposition, and might teach us things which, without it, we could never know. But it is a question of evidence, and whereas every fair-minded man must admit that it ought to be extremely strong and almost irresistible, we find it to be extremely weak and wholly insufficient.

Reasons

As regards the first part of this proposition, I think you would agree with me and Huxley. I never could endorse Hume's theory that miracles were impossible; but, looking at the thousands, or rather millions, of cases in which events, formerly accepted as miraculous, have turned out to be either mistaken explanations of natural events, as confounding sickness with spiritual possession; or subjective converted into objective impressions, as in dreams, visions, and hallucinations; or else the product of superstitious fancies and excited imaginations in uncritical ages; I have always felt that the evidence for anything really miraculous ought to be of the most cogent and convincing character.

Here, then, we join issue on a definite fact – whether the evidence for such a miraculous revelation is or is not conclusive.

Article IV

It is insufficient, because it rests solely on the assumed inspiration of the Bible – a theory which breaks down when tested by the ordinary rules of criticism, and examined impartially by the light of modern knowledge, unbiassed by any violent prepossession in its favour from tradition and authority.

Reasons

Both Old and New Testaments are, to a great extent, collections of writings of unknown dates and authorship, compiled no one knows exactly how or when, but certainly long after the events they describe, and containing many passages which are mutually contradictory.

For the best summary of this branch of Biblical criticism see Strauss, Kuenen, and Renan.

Article V

The theory of Revelation breaks down, because an inspired revelation cannot contain falsehoods, and many of the statements in the Bible are demonstrably untrue, generally as regards the facts of the universe, and specially as regards the origin of man.

Reasons

The account of creation in Genesis is obviously inconsistent with the real facts, both as regards the relations of the earth to the sun, moon, and stars; the crystal vault separating the waters; the manner and order of succession of vegetable and animal life, and numerous other points. It can be defended only on the plea that the inspired Revelation was not intended to teach ordinary facts, such as those of Astronomy and Geology, but only the religious facts of the existence of God and of man's relations to Him. Taken in this sense, we may consider it as a poetical and sublime version of the older Chaldean cosmogony, which it closely resembles, revised in a Monotheistic sense, and writing "God" for "Gods," and as an interesting record of the ideas floating in the East at an early period.

In this sense it has a great value, and scientific men like the American you refer to (who, I think, is not Dana)[2] may say that it is not inconsistent with modern science. But, if taken as anything approaching to an inspired narrative, and using words in their natural sense, the account utterly breaks down, as Huxley has conclusively shown. But, as a chain cannot be stronger than its weakest links, I prefer to take as the test of inspiration, instead of the vague and poetical and therefore contestable narrative of Genesis i., those of the Noachian Deluge and the Tower of Babel, which are precise and definite statements forming a part of the Biblical account of creation, as much as the proem of Genesis i.

The account of an universal deluge and the destruction of all life, except that of a few pairs of animals preserved and living together for a year in an ark of limited dimensions, from which the earth was repeopled, involves not only physical impossibilities, but is directly opposed to the most certain conclusions of geological and zoological science. The existence of separate zoological provinces, like those of Australia, South America, and others, is absolutely inconsistent with the theory that all animal life has radiated from a single centre, like Ararat, within a recent period.

Shem, Ham, and Japhet may represent the progenitors of the human races known to the ancient world of Chaldea and Syria; but how of the other races – the yellow Mongolians, the red Americans, and black Negroes, the pigmy Negritos, the olive-coloured Malays, and other races, who could by no possibility have been descended from these patriarchs?

---

[2] Probably Sir William Dawson is here meant. He is the only American scientist of eminence who attempts to reconcile science and the Genesaic cosmogony. - Ed. *S. R.*

Again, can any one read Max Müller's works on the origin of language and believe that all the hundreds of different human languages originated from the confusion of tongues and dispersion of tribes, inflicted as a punishment for attempting to reach Heaven by building a tall tower in Mesopotamia?

The origin of man is, however, the point upon which the radical opposition of the Orthodox and Scientific creeds comes out most sharply. It cannot be true both that man has *fallen* and that he has *risen*; that he was miraculously created, quite recently in the world's history, in God's own image, and in a state of high moral perfection, from which he fell by an act of disobedience, introducing sin and death into the world; and, on the other hand, that he has been evolved, during an immense period of time, from semi-animal palaeolithic ancestors, ruder than the rudest savages. The evidence of perhaps 1,000,000 of human implements, found in strata of great geological antiquity in all quarters of the globe, proves to demonstration that man's cause has been upwards, and not downwards, and that the true history of the human race has been the direct contrary of that given by the Bible.

Whether man, like other mammals, was evolved through millions of years from primitive forms may be as yet uncertain, though every fresh discovery points that way. But this much is absolutely certain: that he existed on earth at the least 50,000, and more probably 200,000 or 300,000, years ago, in a state lower than that of the lowest savages, but already spread over the four continents, and therefore far from his first origin; ignorant of all arts except fire and the rude chipping of stones; and that, as ages rolled on, his progress may be traced, step by step, from rude to finer chipping; to the hafted celt, the arrow, and javelin; the barbed harpoon, the eyed needle, the art of drawing, and finally to polished stone, pottery, bronze, iron, and the other arts of civilisation as we had them in full force at the dawn of history 6,000 years ago in Egypt and Chaldea.

Read Lyell's "Antiquity of Man," Geikie's "Prehistoric Europe," or almost any recent work on the subject, and then go to the British Museum and look at the collection of stone and other human implements, and you will see the answer to the question which perplexes you, why Modern Science and Evolution should be considered as hostile to Genesis and orthodox theology. How can these facts be reconciled with the

Biblical theory of Adam's creation and fall, with its logical consequence of the Atonement and Redemption?

As regards the New Testament, it may be true that, when Strauss and other critics attempt to show a mythical origin for everything in the Gospels, they go too far and may be refuted. But their negative and destructive criticism has never been answered.

It remains true that the prophecy of the end of the world in the lifetime of the existing generation, distinct and precise as it is, was not fulfilled; that no one has been able to show who were the authors of the Gospels as we now receive them, how much was original from eye-witnesses, how much compiled from tradition and older manuscripts, and when and by whom.

Evidently most of the miracles are explicable by natural causes, related in the language of the day; and by far the most important miracles of all, those of the Resurrection and Ascension, are related with a hopeless contradiction of place and circumstance. According to one, they took place in Galilee; according to another, at Jerusalem; while, according to St. Mark (who, if we are to believe tradition and Papias, comes nearest to the fountain head through St. Peter), if we omit the verses at the end which are not found in the oldest manuscripts and are plainly added, there is positively no mention of any miracle at all. We are merely told that the women went to the tomb, found it empty, and saw a young man in white clothing, who gave them a message, which they never delivered, being afraid. Would this evidence prove the signature of a will, much less a miracle?

I do not, however, myself attach so much weight to this element of Biblical criticism, which can always be disputed about, as I do to what seems to me the crushing and conclusive refutation of the whole theory of the creeds and orthodoxy by the incontrovertible facts which have been exhumed from the high level gravels of the Somme and the Thames, the caves of Devonshire and Belgium, and the rock-shelters of the Vezere.

Article VI
Thus far the Articles of the Negative Creed have been purely negative, and I believe that all who are called Agnostics would agree with them. There are, however, certain positive articles which are generally, though perhaps not universally, held. For

instance, the denial of Atheism, and of a purely mechanical Materialism.

Reasons

If we cannot prove an affirmative respecting these mysteries of a First Cause and a Personal God, assuredly we cannot prove a negative. There may be *anything* in the Unknowable, "behind the veil," for aught we know to the contrary. All we know is that, in our present existence and with our present faculties, we do not know it, and that, as all truth is one, any guess at it, which is inconsistent with what we really do know, stands, *ipso facto*, condemned. Thus, if any one tells me in general terms that there is a Heaven or Hell behind the veil, I reply, "It may be so; I do not know." But, if he attempts to define them, and tells me that by going vertically upwards I shall meet the one, and by going vertically downwards the other, I reply, "This is merely an erroneous guess; it is simply impossible."

Article VII
Morals and Religions are products of Evolution.

Reasons

Morals can be clearly traced to the "survival of the fittest," of the ideas and rules of conduct which have proved themselves the best both for individuals, families, and societies in the "struggle for life," and have become more and more fixed by heredity and environment, until, in modern civilised nations, they have become almost instinctive. This is clearly proved by a reference to history, and by the existing state of morals among races in a different stages of civilisation and with different environments. Thus, murder is honourable among Dyaks and Red Indians, but is execrable in England. Polyandry, legitimate in old India (see the Ramayana), and to this day among certain rude Indian tribes, is repugnant in modern Europe. Polygamy, not inconsistent with Divine favour in the days of David, and now thought to be right by all Mohammedan races, is considered as criminal in Christian countries.

This shows that morals are not the result of any implanted instinct or Divine revelation, but rest on a surer basis – that of heredity and environment, making it certain that, with or without creeds and dogmatical religions, the laws of conscience and morality will go on widening, strengthening, and becoming more and more instinctive with each generation of civilised nations.

As to religions, it is even more evident that they are products of evolution. They are all, in effect, "working hypotheses," by which different generations of men, in different ages and countries, seek to represent their hopes and fears, their rude or refined ideas of science and morality, their aspirations after a future life, and even their fancies and poetical feelings. They all, have, or have had, some good in them suited to their environment, and all that have survived have changed with the changes of that environment, brought about by evolution.

Christianity is, on the whole, the best of these religions,[3] as being that of the most civilised and advanced nations; but it has undergone great modifications, and must undergo more if it is to remain a tolerable "working hypothesis" under the altered conditions of modern science and of modern societies. Imprison it in hard-and-fast dogmatic creeds, and it must wither and perish.

Article VIII
Polarity is the great underlying law of all knowable phe-
nomena, whether of the inorganic or organic universe, or of the
spiritual world of conscience, morals, free will, and
determination.

Reasons
This article is, perhaps, rather one personal to myself than generally accepted, though partial statements of it may be found in the works of Herbert Spencer, Emerson, and other writers. For a detailed argument in support of it see my "Modern Zoroastrian." The following is a brief summary of it. The material universe is built up out of atoms and energies by a first Cause, or, as Bishop Temple calls it, an "original impress." How? By a polarity which makes them combine and pass from the simple and homogeneous into the complex and hetero-geneous, in a course of constant change and evolution. This polarity is a part of the "original impress," and, like Space and Time, is what, in Kantian language, we should term an "imperative category" of human thought and conception. How or why, we know not, any more than we know what lies behind the original atoms and energies. But there it is, and it

3   In justice to Buddhism, to this statement we demur. – ED. *A. J.*

extends to all the higher questions of morals and philosophy. Every proposition has two sides. Right becomes wrong and wisdom folly, if pushed to the "falsehood of extremes." Determinism, or mechanical Materialism, may seem to be a necessary consequence of Darwinian Evolution; but it is only one pole of truth. There is another pole, which gives us a conviction of the reality of Free Will. The reconcilement lies beyond our reach, in the law of polarity, which, in its ultimate essence and origin, is part of the great Unknown.

So, again, the Christian virtues of meekness, self-sacrifice, and love, are good; but so also are the sterner virtues of self-reliance, courage, and providence; and it would not work, in practice, to take "no thought for the morrow," and, "if smitten on one cheek, to turn the other." Wise economy and wise liberality are both good; but the one easily degenerates into parsimony, and the other into extravagance. Patriotism, pushed to excess, becomes Jingoism; philanthropy, carried beyond the mark, lapses into weak sentimentality; and so of all things.

This creed is the only one consistent with facts. It makes us tolerant and comprehensive, and teaches us to find –

"Sermons in stones and good in everything."

It has approved itself to me as a good "working hypothesis" to go through life with, and taught me to try to stand firm in the middle, not letting myself be absorbed by the exclusive attraction of either pole, striving to appropriate all that is true and good, whether it be in the discoveries of science, the beauties of art and nature, the calm and serene philosophy of Epicurus and Confucius, the magnanimous stoicism of Marcus Aurelius, or the pure morality and gentle virtues of Jesus. I feel sure that you will applaud the effort, though we may differ as to the best mode of realising it.

AGNOSTICISM
[Thomas Huxley]

Within the last few months, the public has received much and varied information on the subject of agnostics, their tenets, and even their future. Agnosticism exercised the orators of the Church Congress at Manchester.[1] It has been furnished with a set of "articles" fewer, but not less rigid, and certainly not less consistent than the thirty-nine; its nature has been analysed, and its future severely predicted by the most eloquent of that prophetical school whose Samuel is Auguste Comte. It may still be a question, however, whether the pubic is as much the wiser as might be expected, considering all the trouble that has been taken to enlighten it. Not only are the three accounts of the agnostic position sadly out of harmony with one another, but I propose to show cause for my belief that all three must be seriously questioned by any one who employs the term "agnostic" in the sense in which it was originally used. The learned Principle of King's College, who brought the topic of Agnosticism before the Church Congress, took a short and easy way of settling the business:-

> But if this be so, for a man to urge, as an escape from this article of belief, that he has no means of a scientific knowledge of the unseen world, or of the future, is irrelevant. His difference from Christians lies not in the fact that he has no knowledge of these things, but that he does not believe the authority on which they are stated. He may prefer to call himself an Agnostic; but his real name is an older one – he is an infidel; that is to say, an unbeliever. The word infidel, perhaps, carries an unpleasant significance. Perhaps it is right that it should. It is, and it ought to be, an unpleasant thing for a man to have to say plainly that he does not believe in Jesus Christ.[2]

1 See the *Official Report of the Church Congress held at Manchester*, October 1888, pp. 253, 254.

2 [In this place and in the eleventh essay, there are references to the late

So much of Dr. Wace's address either explicitly or implicitly concerns me, that I take upon myself to deal with it; but, in so doing, it must be understood that I speak for myself alone. I am nor aware that there is any sect of Agnostics; and if there be, I am not its acknowledged prophet or pope. I desire to leave to the Comtists the entire monopoly of the manufacture of imitation ecclesiasticism.

Let us calmly and dispassionately consider Dr. Wace's appreciation of agnosticism. The agnostic, according to his view, is a person who says he has no means of attaining a scientific knowledge of the unseen world or of the future; by which somewhat loose phraseology Dr. Wace presumably means the theological unseen world and future. I cannot think this description happy, either in form or substance, but for the present it may pass. Dr. Wace continues, that it is not "his difference from Christians." Are there then any Christians who say that they know nothing about the unseen world and the future? I was ignorant of the fact, but I am ready to accept it on the authority of a professional theologian, and I proceed to Dr. Wace's next proposition.

The real state of the case, then, is that the agnostic "does not believe the authority" on which "these things" are stated, which authority is Jesus Christ. He is simply an old-fashioned "infidel" who is afraid to own to his right name. As "Presbyter is priest writ large," so is "agnostic" the mere Greek equivalent for the Latin "infidel." There is an attractive simplicity about this solution of the problem; and it has that advantage of being somewhat offensive to the persons attacked, which is so dear to the less refined sort of controversialist. The agnostic says, "I cannot find good evidence that so and so is true." "Ah," says his adversary, seizing his opportunity, " then you declare that Jesus Christ was untruthful, for he said so and so;" a very telling method of rousing prejudice. But suppose that the value of the evidence as to what Jesus may have said and done, and as to the exact nature and scope of his authority, is just that which the agnostic finds it most difficult to determine. If I venture to

Archbishop of York which are of no importance to my main argument, and which I have expunged because I desire to obliterate the traces of a temporary misunderstanding with a man of rare ability, candour, and wit, for whom I entertained a great liking and no less respect. I rejoice to think now of the (then) Bishop's cordial hail the first time we met after our little skirmish, "Well, is it to be peace or war?" I replied, " A little of both." But there was only peace when we parted, and ever after.]

doubt that the Duke of Wellington gave the command "Up, Guards, and at 'em!" at Waterloo, I do not think that even Dr. Wace would accuse me of disbelieving the Duke. Yet it would be just as reasonable to do this as to accuse any one of denying what Jesus said, before the preliminary question as to what he did say is settled.

Now, the question as to what Jesus really said and did is strictly a scientific problem, which is capable of solution by no other methods than those practised by the historian and the literary critic. It is a problem of immense difficulty, which has occupied some of the best heads in Europe for the last century; and it is only of late years that their investigations have begun to converge towards one conclusion.[3]

That kind of faith which Dr. Wace describes and lauds is of no use here. Indeed, he takes pains to destroy its evidential value.

"What made the Mahommedan world? Trust and faith in the declarations and assurances of Mahommed. And what made the Christian world? Trust and faith in the declarations and assurances of Jesus Christ and His Apostles" (*l. c.* p. 253). The triumphant tone of this imaginary catechism leads me to suspect that its author has hardly appreciated its full import. Presumably, Dr. Wace regards Mahommed as an unbeliever, or, to use the term which he prefers, infidel; and considers that his assurances have given rise to a vast delusion which has led, and is leading, millions of men straight to everlasting punishment. And this being so, the "Trust and faith" which have "made the Mahommedan world," in just the same sense as they have "made the Christian world," must be trust and faith in falsehood. No man who has studied history, or even

---

[3] Dr. Wace tells us, "It may be asked how far we can rely on the accounts we possess of our Lord's teaching on these subjects." And he seems to think the question appropriately answered by the assertion that it "ought to be regarded as settled by M. Renan's practical surrender of the adverse case." I thought I knew M. Renan's works pretty well, but I have contrived to miss this "practical" (I wish Dr. Wace had defined the scope of that useful adjective) surrender. However, as Dr. Wace can find no difficulty in pointing out the passage of M. Renan's writings, by which he feels justified in making his statement, I shall wait for further enlightenment, contenting myself, for the present, with remarking that if M. Renan were to retract and do penance in Notre-Dame to-morrow for any contributions to Biblical criticism that may be specially his property, the main results of that criticism, as they are set forth in the works of Strauss, Baur, Reuss, and Volkmar, for example, would not be sensibly affected.

attended to the occurrences of everyday life, can doubt the enormous practical value of trust and faith; but as little will he be inclined to deny that this practical value has not the least relation to the reality of the objects of that trust and faith. In examples of patient constancy of faith and of unswerving trust, the "Acta Martyrum" do not excel the annals of Babism.[4]

The discussion upon which we have now entered goes so thoroughly to the root of the whole matter; the question of the day is so completely, as the author of "Robert Elsmere" says, the value of testimony, that I shall offer no apology for following it out somewhat in detail; and, by way of giving substance to the argument, I shall base what I have to say upon a case, the consideration of which lies strictly within the province of natural science, and of that particular part of it known as the physiology and pathology of the nervous system.

I find, in the second Gospel (chap. v.), a statement, to all appearance intended to have the same evidential value as any other contained in that history. It is the well-known story of the devils who were cast out of a man, and ordered, or permitted, to enter into a herd of swine, to the great loss and damage of the innocent Gerasene, or Gadarene, pig owners. There can be no doubt that the narrator intends to convey to his readers his own conviction that this casting out and entering in were effected by the agency of Jesus of Nazareth; that, by speech and action, Jesus enforced this conviction; nor does any inkling of the legal and moral difficulties of the case manifest itself.

On the other hand, everything that I know of physiological and pathological science leads me to entertain a very strong conviction that the phenomena ascribed to possession are as purely natural as those which constitute small-pox; everything that I know of anthropology leads me to think that the belief in demons and demoniacal possession is a mere survival of a once universal superstition, and that its persistence, at the present time, is pretty much in the inverse ratio of the general instruction, intelligence, and sound judgment of the population among whom it prevails. Everything that I know of law and justice convinces me that the wanton destruction of other people's property is a misdemeanour of evil example. Again, the study of history, and especially of that of the fifteenth, sixteenth, and seventeenth centuries, leaves no shadow of

4   [See De Gobineau, *Les Religions et les Philosophies dans l'Asie Centrale*; and the recently published work of Mr. E. G. Browne, *The Episode of the Bab.*]

doubt on my mind that the belief in the reality of possession and of witchcraft, justly based, alike by Catholics and Protestants, upon this and innumerable other passages in both the Old and New Testaments, gave rise, through the special influence of Christian ecclesiastics, to the most horrible persecutions and judicial murders of thousands upon thousands of innocent men, women, and children. And when I reflect that the record of a plain and simple declaration upon such an occasion as this, that the belief in witchcraft and possession is wicked nonsense, would have rendered the long agony of mediaeval humanity impossible, I am prompted to reject, as dishonouring, the supposition that such declaration was withheld out of condescension to popular error.

"Come forth, thou unclean spirit, out of the man" (Mark v. 8)[5] are the words attributed to Jesus. If I declare, as I have no hesitation in doing, that I utterly disbelieve in the existence of "unclean spirits," and, consequently, in the possibility of their "coming forth" out of a man, I suppose that Dr. Wace will tell me I am disregarding the testimony "of our Lord." For, if these words were really used, the most resourceful of reconcilers can hardly venture to affirm that they are compatible with a disbelief "in these things." As the learned and fair-minded, as well as orthodox, Dr. Alexander remarks, in an editorial note to the article "Demoniacs," in the "Biblical Cyclopaedia" (vol. i. p. 664, note):-

> . . . On the lowest grounds on which our Lord and His Apostles can be placed they must, at least, be regarded as *honest* men. Now, though honest speech does not require that words should be used always and only in their etymological sense, it does require that they should not be used so as to affirm what the speaker knows to be false. Whilst, therefore, our Lord and His Apostles might use the word δαιμονίζεσθαι, or the phrase, δαιμόνιον ἔχειν, as a popular description of certain diseases, without giving in to the belief which lay at the source of such a mode of expression, they could not speak of demons entering into a man, or being cast out of him, without pledging themselves to the belief of an actual possession of the man by the demons. (Campbell, *Prel. Diss.* vi, 1, 10.) If, consequently, they did not hold this belief, they spoke not as honest men.

[5] Here, as always, the revised version is cited.

The story which we are considering does not rest on the authority of the second Gospel alone. The third confirms the second, especially in the matter of commanding the unclean spirit to come out of the man (Luke viii. 29); and, although the first Gospel either gives a different version of the same story, or tells another of like kind, the essential point remains: "If thou cast us out, send us away into the herd of swine. And He said unto them: Go!" (Matt. viii. 31, 32).

If the concurrent testimony of the three synoptics, then, is really sufficient to do away with all rational doubt as to a matter of fact of the utmost practical and speculative importance – belief or disbelief in which may affect, and has affected, men's lives and their conduct towards other men, in the most serious way – then I am bound to believe that Jesus implicitly affirmed himself to possess a "knowledge of the unseen world," which afforded full confirmation of the belief in demons and possession current among his contemporaries. If the story is true, the mediaeval theory of the invisible world may be, and probably is, quite correct; and the witch-finders, from Sprenger to Hopkins and Mather, are much-maligned men.

On the other hand, humanity, noting the frightful consequences of this belief; common sense, observing the futility of the evidence on which it is based, in all cases that have been properly investigated; science, more and more seeing its way to inclose all the phenomena of so-called "possession" within the domain of pathology, so far as they are not to be relegated to that of the police – all these powerful influences concur in warning us, at our peril, against accepting the belief without the most careful scrutiny of the authority on which it rests.

I can discern no escape from this dilemma: either Jesus said what he is reported to have said, or he did not. In the former case, it is inevitable that his authority on matters connected with the "unseen world" should be roughly shaken; in the latter, the blow falls upon the authority of the synoptic Gospels. If their report on a matter of such stupendous and far-reaching practical import as this is untrustworthy, how can we be sure of its trustworthiness in other cases? The favourite "earth," in which the hard-pressed reconciler takes refuge, that the Bible does not profess to teach science,[6] is stopped in this

---

[6] Does any one really mean to say that there is any internal or external criterion by which the reader of a biblical statement, in which scientific matter is contained, is enabled to judge whether it is to be taken *au sérieux*

instance. For the question of the existence of demons and of possession by them, though it lies strictly within the province of science, is also of the deepest moral and religious significance. If physical and mental disorders are caused by demons, Gregory of Tours and his contemporaries rightly considered that relics and exorcists were more useful than doctors; the gravest questions arise as to the legal and moral responsibilities of persons inspired by demoniacal impulses; and our whole conception of the universe and of our relations to it becomes totally different from what it would be on the contrary hypothesis.

The theory of life of an average mediaeval Christian was as different from that of an average nineteenth-century Englishman as that of a West African negro is now, in these respects. The modern world is slowly, but surely, shaking off these and other monstrous survivals of savage delusions; and, whatever happens, it will not return to that wallowing in the mire. Until the contrary is proved, I venture to doubt whether, at this present moment, any Protestant theologian, who has a reputation to lose, will say that he believes the Gadarene story.

The choice then lies between discrediting those who compiled the Gospel biographies and disbelieving the Master, whom they, simple souls, thought to honour by preserving such traditions of the exercise of his authority over Satan's invisible world. This is the dilemma. No deep scholarship, nothing but a knowledge of the revised version (on which it is to be supposed all that mere scholarship can do has been done), with the application thereto of the commonest canons of common sense, is needful to enable us to make a choice between its alternatives. It is hardly doubtful that the story, as told in the first Gospel, is merely a version of that told in the second and third. Nevertheless, the discrepancies are serious

or not? Is the account of the Deluge, accepted as true in the New Testament, less precise and specific than that of the call of Abraham, also accepted as true therein? By what mark does the story of the feeding with manna in the wilderness, which involves some very curious scientific problems, show that it is meant merely for edification, while the story of the inscription of the Law on stone by the hand of Jahveh is literally true? If the story of the Fall is not the true record of an historical occurrence, what becomes of Pauline theology? Yet the story of the Fall as directly conflicts with probability, and is as devoid of trustworthy evidence, as that of the Creation or that of the Deluge, with which it forms a harmoniously legendary series.

and irreconcilable; and, on this ground alone, a suspension of judgment, at the least, is called for. But there is a great deal more to be said. From the dawn of scientific biblical criticism until the present day, the evidence against the long-cherished notion that the three synoptic Gospels are the works of three independent authors, each prompted by Divine inspiration, has steadily accumulated, until, at the present time, there is no visible escape from the conclusion that each of the three is a compilation consisting of a groundwork common to all three – the threefold tradition; and of a superstructure, consisting, firstly, of matter common to it with one of the others, and, secondly, of matter special to each. The use of the terms "groundwork" and "superstructure" by no means implies that the latter must be of later date than the former. On the contrary, some parts of it may be, and probably are, older than some parts of the groundwork.[7]

The story of the Gadarene swine belongs to the groundwork; at least, the essential part of it, in which the belief in demoniac possession is expressed, does; and therefore the compilers of the first, second, and third Gospels, whoever they were, certainly accepted that belief (which, indeed, was universal among both Jews and pagans at that time), and attributed it to Jesus.

What, then, do we know about the originator, or originators, of this groundwork – of that threefold tradition which all three witnesses (in Paley's phrase) agree upon – that we should allow their mere statements to outweigh the counter arguments of humanity, of common sense, of exact science, and to imperil the respect which all would be glad to be able to render to their Master?

Absolutely nothing.[8] There is no proof, nothing more than a fair presumption, that any one of the Gospels existed, in the state in which we find it in the authorised version of the Bible, before the second century, or, in other words, sixty or seventy

[7]   See, for an admirable discussion of the whole subject, Dr. Abbott's article on the Gospels in the *Encyclopaedia Britannica*; and the remarkable monograph by Professor Volkmar, *Jesus Nazarenus und die erste christliche Zeit* (1882). Whether we agree with the conclusions of these writers or not, the method of critical investigation which they adopt is unimpeachable.

[8]   Notwithstanding the hard words shot at me from behind the hedge of anonymity by a writer in a recent number of the *Quarterly Review*, I repeat, without the slightest fear of refutation, that the four Gospels, as they have come to us, are the work of unknown writers.

years after the events recorded. And, between that time and the date of the oldest extant manuscripts of the Gospels, there is no telling what additions and alterations and interpolations may have been made. It may be said that this is all mere speculation, but it is a good deal more. As competent scholars and honest men, our revisers have felt compelled to point out that such things have happened even since the date of the oldest known manuscripts. The oldest two copies of the second Gospel end with the 8th verse of the 16th chapter; the remaining twelve verses are spurious, and it is noteworthy that the maker of the addition has not hesitated to introduce a speech in which Jesus promises his disciples that "in My name shall they cast out devils."

The other passage "rejected to the margin" is still more instructive. It is that touching apologue, with its profound ethical sense, of the woman taken in adultery – which, if internal evidence were an infallible guide, might well be affirmed to be a typical example of the teachings of Jesus. Yet, say the revisers, pitilessly, "Most of the ancient authorities emit John vii. 53–viii. 11." Now let any reasonable man ask himself this question. If, after an approximate settlement of the canon of the New Testament, and even later than the fourth and fifth centuries, literary fabricators had the skill and the audacity to make such additions and interpolations as these, what may they have done when no one had thought of a canon; when oral tradition, still unfixed, was regarded as more valuable than such written records as may have existed in the latter portion of the first century? Or, to take the other alternative, if those who gradually settled the canon did not know of the existence of the oldest codices which have come down to us; or if, knowing them, they rejected their authority, what is to be thought of their competency as critics of the text?

People who object to free criticism of the Christian Scriptures forget that they are what they are in virtue of very free criticism; unless the advocates of inspiration are prepared to affirm that the majority of influential ecclesiastics during several centuries were safeguarded against error. For, even granting that some books of the period were inspired, they were certainly few amongst many; and those who selected the canonical books, unless they themselves were also inspired, must be regarded in the light of mere critics, and, from the evidence they have left of their intellectual habits, very uncritical critics. When one thinks that such delicate questions as those involved fell into the hands of men like Papias (who believed in the famous millenarian grape story); of Irenaeus with his "reasons" for the existence of only four Gospels; and of such calm and dispassionate judges as Tertullian, with his "Credo quia impossibile": the marvel is that the selection which constitutes our New Testament is as free as it is from obviously objectionable matter. The apocryphal Gospels certainly deserve to be apocryphal; but one may suspect that a little more critical discrimination would have enlarged the Apocrypha not inconsiderably.

At this point a very obvious objection arises and deserves full and candid consideration. It may be said that critical scepticism carried to the length suggested is historical pyrrhonism; that if we are altogether to discredit an ancient or a modern historian, because he has assumed fabulous matter to be true, it will be as well to give up paying any attention to history. It may be said, and with great justice, that Eginhard's "Life of Charlemagne" is none the less trustworthy because of the astounding revelation of credulity, of lack of judgment, and even of respect for the eighth commandment, which he has unconsciously made in the "History of the Translation of the Blessed Martyrs Marcellinus and Paul." Or, to go no further back than the last number of the *Nineteenth Century*, surely that excellent lady, Miss Strickland, is not to be refused all credence, because of the myth about the second James's remains, which she seems to have unconsciously invented.

Of course this is perfectly true. I am afraid there is no man alive whose witness could be accepted, if the condition precedent were proof that he had never invented and promulgated a myth. In the minds of all of us there are little places here and there, like the indistinguishable spots on a rock which give foothold to moss or stonecrop; on which, if the germ of a myth fall, it is certain to grow, without in the least degree affecting our accuracy or truthfulness elsewhere. Sir Walter Scott knew that he could not repeat a story without, as he said, "giving it a new hat and stick." Most of us differ from Sir Walter only in not knowing about this tendency of the mythopoeic faculty to break out unnoticed. But it is also perfectly true that the mythopoeic faculty is not equally active in all minds, nor in all regions and under all conditions of the same mind. David Hume was certainly not so liable to temptation as the Venerable Bede, or even as some recent historians who could be mentioned; and the most imaginative of debtors, if he owes five pounds, never makes an obligation to pay a hundred out of it. The rule of common sense is *primâ facie* to trust a witness in all matters, in which neither his self-interest, his passions, his prejudices, nor that love of the marvellous, which is inherent to a greater or less degree in all mankind, are strongly concerned; and, when they are involved, to require corroborative evidence in exact proportion to the contravention of probability by the thing testified.

Now, in the Gadarene affair, I do not think I am unreasonably sceptical, if I say that the existence of demons who can be transferred from a man to a pig, does thus contravene probability. Let me be perfectly candid. I admit I have no *a priori* objection to offer. There are physical things, such as *tæniæ* and *trichinæ*, which can be transferred from men to pigs, and *vice versâ*, and which do undoubtedly produce most diabolical and deadly effects on both. For anything I can absolutely prove to the contrary, there may be spiritual things capable of the same transmigration, with like effects. Moreover I am bound to add that perfectly truthful persons, for whom I have the greatest respect, believe in stories about spirits of the present day, quite as improbable as that we are considering.

So I declare, as plainly as I can, that I am unable to show cause why these transferable devils should not exist; nor can I deny that, not merely the whole Roman Church, but many Wacean "infidels" of no mean repute, do honestly and firmly believe that the activity of such like demonic beings is in full swing in this year of grace 1889.

Nevertheless, as good Bishop Butler says, "probability is the guide of life;" and it seems to me that this is just one of the cases in which the canon of credibility and testimony, which I have ventured to lay down, has full force. So that, with the most entire respect for many (by no means for all) of our witnesses for the truth of demonology, ancient and modern, I conceive their evidence on this particular matter to be ridiculously insufficient to warrant their conclusion.[9]

[9] Their arguments, in the long run, are always reducible to one form. Otherwise trustworthy witnesses affirm that such and such events took place. These events are inexplicable, except the agency of "spirits" is admitted. Therefore "spirits" were the cause of the phenomena.

And the heads of the reply are always the same. Remember Goethe's aphorism: "Alles factische is schon Theorie." Trustworthy witnesses are

After what has been said, I do not think that any sensible man, unless he happen to be angry, will accuse me of "contradicting the Lord and His Apostles" if I reiterate my total disbelief in the whole Gadarene story. But, if that story is discredited, all the other stories of demoniac possession fall under suspicion. And if the belief in demons and demoniac possession, which forms the sombre background of the whole picture of primitive Christianity, presented to us in the New Testament, is shaken, what is to be said, in any case, of the uncorroborated testimony of the Gospels with respect to "the unseen world"?

I am not aware that I have been influenced by any more bias in regard to the Gadarene story than I have been in dealing with other cases of like kind the investigation of which has interested me. I was brought up in the strictest school of evangelical orthodoxy; and when I was old enough to think for myself, I started upon my journey of inquiry with little doubt about the general truth of what I had been taught; and with that feeling of the unpleasantness of being called an "infidel" which, we are told, is so right and proper. Near my journey's end, I find myself in a condition of something more than mere doubt about these matters.

In the course of other inquiries, I have had to do with fossil remains which looked quite plain at a distance, and became more and more indistinct as I tried to define their outline by close inspection. There was something there – something which, if I could win assurance about it, might mark a new epoch in the history of the earth; but, study as long as I might, certainty eluded my grasp. So has it been with me in my efforts to define the grand figure of Jesus as it lies in the primary strata of Christian literature. Is he the kindly, peaceful Christ depicted in the Catacombs? Or is he the stern Judge who frowns above the altar of SS. Cosmas and Damianus? Or can he be rightly represented by the bleeding ascetic, broken down by physical pain, of too many mediaeval pictures? Are we

constantly deceived, or deceive themselves, in their interpretation of sensible phenomena. No one can prove that the sensible phenomena, in these cases, could be caused only by the agency of spirits: and there is abundant ground for believing that they may be produced in other ways. Therefore, the utmost that can be reasonably asked for, on the evidence as it stands, is suspension of judgment. And, on the necessity for even that suspension, reasonable men may differ, according to their views of probability.

to accept the Jesus of the second, or the Jesus of the fourth Gospel, as the true Jesus? What did he really say and do; and how much that is attributed to him, in speech and action, is the embroidery of the various parties into which his followers tended to split themselves within twenty years of his death, when even the threefold tradition was only nascent?

If any one will answer these questions for me with something more to the point than feeble talk about the "cowardice of agnosticism," I shall be deeply his debtor. Unless and until they are satisfactorily answered, I say of agnosticism in this matter "*J'y suis, et j'y reste.*"

But, as we have seen, it is asserted that I have no business to call myself an agnostic; that, if I am not a Christian I am an infidel; and that I ought to call myself by that name of "unpleasant significance." Well, I do not care much what I am called by other people, and if I had at my side all those who, since the Christian era, have been called infidels by other folks, I could not desire better company. If these are my ancestors, I prefer, with the old Frank, to be with them wherever they are. But there are several points in Dr. Wace's contention which must be elucidated before I can even think of undertaking to carry out his wishes. I must, for instance, know what a Christian is. Now what is a Christian? By whose authority is the signification of that term defined? Is there any doubt that the immediate followers of Jesus, the "sect of the Nazarenes," were strictly orthodox Jews differing from other Jews not more than the Sadducees, the Pharisees, and the Essenes differed from one another; in fact, only in the belief that the Messiah, for whom the rest of their nation waited, had come? Was not their chief, "James, the brother of the Lord," reverenced alike by Sadducee, Pharisee, and Nazarene? At the famous conference which, according to the Acts, took place at Jerusalem, does not James declare that "myriads" of Jews, who, by that time, had become Nazarenes, were "all zealous for the Law"? Was not the name of "Christian" first used to denote the converts to the doctrine promulgated by Paul and Barnabas at Antioch? Does the subsequent history of Christianity leave any doubt that, from this time forth, the "little rift within the lute" caused by the new teaching, developed, if not inaugurated, at Antioch, grew wider and wider, until the two types of doctrine irreconcilably diverged? Did not the primitive Nazarenism, or Ebionism, develop into the Nazarenism, and Ebionism, and

Elkasaitism of later ages, and finally die out in obscurity and
condemnation, as damnable heresy; while the younger doctrine
throve and pushed out its shoots into that endless variety of
sects, of which the three strongest survivors are the Roman and
Greek Churches and modern Protestantism?

Singular state of things! If I were to profess the doctrine
which was held by "James, the brother of the Lord," and by
every one of the "myriads" of his followers and co-religionists
in Jerusalem up to twenty or thirty years after the Crucifixion
(and one knows not how much later at Pella), I should be
condemned, with unanimity, as an ebionising heretic by the
Roman, Greek, and Protestant Churches! And, probably, this
hearty and unanimous condemnation of the creed, held by
those who were in the closest personal relation with their Lord,
is almost the only point upon which they would be cordially of
one mind. On the other hand, though I hardly dare imagine
such a thing, I very much fear that the "pillars" of the primitive
Hierosolymitan Church would have considered Dr. Wace an
infidel. No one can read the famous second chapter of
Galatians and the book of Revelation without seeing how
narrow was even Paul's escape from a similar fate. And, if
ecclesiastical history is to be trusted, the thirty-nine articles, be
they right or wrong, diverge from the primitive doctrine of the
Nazarenes vastly more than even Pauline Christianity did.

But, further than this, I have great difficulty in assuring
myself that even James, "the brother of the Lord," and his
"myriads" of Nazarenes, properly represented the doctrines of
their Master. For it is constantly asserted by our modern
"pillars" that one of the chief features of the work of Jesus was
the instauration of Religion by the abolition of what our
sticklers for articles and liturgies, with unconscious humour,
call the narrow restrictions of the Law. Yet, if James knew this,
how could the bitter controversy with Paul have arisen; and
why did not one or the other side quote any of the various
sayings of Jesus, recorded in the Gospels, which directly bear
on the question – sometimes, apparently, in opposite
directions?

So, if I am asked to call myself an "infidel," I reply: To what
doctrine do you ask me to be faithful? Is it that contained in the
Nicene and the Athanasian Creeds? My firm belief is that the
Nazarenes, say of the year 40, headed by James, would have
stopped their ears and thought worthy of stoning the audacious

man who propounded it to them. Is it contained in the so-called Apostles' Creed? I am pretty sure that even that would have created a recalcitrant commotion at Pella in the year 70, among the Nazarenes of Jerusalem, who had fled from the soldiers of Titus. And yet, if the unadulterated tradition of the teachings of "the Nazarene" were to be found anywhere, it surely should have been amidst those not very aged disciples who may have heard them as they were delivered.

Therefore, however sorry I may be to be unable to demonstrate that, if necessary, I should not be afraid to call myself an "infidel," I cannot do it. "Infidel" is a term of reproach, which Christians and Mahommedans, in their modesty, agree to apply to those who differ from them. If he had only thought of it, Dr. Wace might have used the term "miscreant," which, with the same etymological signification, has the advantage of being still more "unpleasant" to the persons to whom it is applied. But why should a man be expected to call himself a "miscreant" or an "infidel"? That St. Patrick "had two birthdays because he was a twin" is a reasonable and intelligible utterance beside that of the man who should declare himself to be an infidel, on the ground of denying his own belief. It may be logically, if not ethically, defensible that a Christian should call a Mahommedan an infidel and *vice versâ*; but, on Dr. Wace's principles, both ought to call themselves infidels, because each applies the term to the other.

Now I am afraid that all the Mahommedan world would agree in reciprocating that appellation to Dr. Wace himself. I once visited the Hazar Mosque, the great University of Mahommedanism, in Cairo, in ignorance of the fact that I was unprovided with proper authority. A swarm of angry undergraduates, as I suppose I ought to call them, came buzzing about me and my guide; and if I had known Arabic, I suspect that "dog of an infidel" would have been by no means the most "unpleasant" of the epithets showered upon me, before I could explain and apologise for the mistake. If I had had the pleasure of Dr. Wace's company on that occasion, the undiscriminative followers of the Prophet would, I am afraid, have made no difference between us; not even if they had known that he was the head of an orthodox Christian seminary. And I have not the smallest doubt that even one of the learned mollahs, if his grave courtesy would have permitted him to say anything offensive to men of another mode of belief, would have told us that he wondered we did not find it "very unpleasant" to disbelieve in the Prophet of Islam.

From what precedes, I think it becomes sufficiently clear that Dr. Wace's account of the origin of the name of "Agnostic" is quite wrong. Indeed, I am bound to add that very slight effort to discover the truth would have convinced him that, as a matter of fact, the term arose otherwise. I am loath to go over an old story once more; but more than one object which I have in view will be served by telling it a little more fully than it has yet been told.

Looking back nearly fifty years, I see myself as a boy, whose education has been interrupted, and who, intellectually, was left, for some years, altogether to his own devices. At that time, I was a voracious and omnivorous reader; a dreamer and speculator of the first water, well endowed with that splendid courage in attacking any and every subject, which is the blessed compensation of youth and inexperience. Among the books and essays, on all sorts of topics from metaphysics to heraldry, which I read at this time, two left indelible impressions on my mind. One was Guizot's "History of Civilisation," the other was Sir William Hamilton's essay "On the Philosophy of the Unconditioned," which I came upon, by chance, in an odd volume of the "Edinburgh Review." The latter was certainly strange reading for a boy, and I could not possibly have understood a great deal of it;[10] nevertheless, I devoured it with avidity, and it stamped upon my mind the strong conviction that, on even the most solemn and important of questions, men are apt to take cunning phrases for answers; and that the limitation of our faculties, in a great number of cases, renders real answers to such questions, not merely actually impossible, but theoretically inconceivable.

Philosophy and history having laid hold of me in this eccentric fashion, have never loosened their grip. I have no pretension to be an expert in either subject; but the turn for philosophical and historical reading, which rendered Hamilton and Guizot attractive to me, has not only filled many lawful leisure hours, and still more sleepless ones, with the repose of

---

10   Yet I must somehow have laid hold of the pith of the matter, for, many years afterwards, when Dean Mansel's Bampton Lectures were published, it seemed to me I already knew all that this eminently agnostic thinker had to tell me.

changed mental occupation, but has not unfrequently disputed my proper work-time with my liege lady, Natural Science. In this way I have found it possible to cover a good deal of ground in the territory of philosophy; and all the more easily that I have never cared much about A's or B's opinion's, but have rather sought to know what answer he had to give to the questions I had to put to him – that of the limitation of possible knowledge being the chief. The ordinary examiner, with his "State the views of So-and-so," would have floored me at any time. If he had said what do *you* think about any given problem, I might have got on fairly well.

The reader who has had the patience to follow the enforced, but unwilling, egotism of this veritable history (especially if his studies have led him in the same direction), will now see why my mind steadily gravitated towards the conclusions of Hume and Kant, so well stated by the latter in a sentence, which I have quoted elsewhere.

"The greatest and perhaps the sole use of all philosophy of pure reason is, after all, merely negative, since it serves not as an organon for the enlargement [of knowledge], but as a discipline for its delimitation; and, instead of discovering truth, has only the modest merit of preventing error."[11]

When I reached intellectual maturity and began to ask myself whether I was an atheist, a theist, or a pantheist; a materialist or an idealist; a Christian or a freethinker; I found that the more I learned and reflected, the less ready was the answer; until, at last, I came to the conclusion that I had neither art nor part with any of these denominations, except the last. The one thing in which most of these good people were agreed was the one thing in which I differed from them. They were quite sure they had attained a certain "gnosis," – had, more or less successfully, solved the problem of existence; while I was quite sure I had not, and had a pretty strong conviction that the problem was insoluble. And, with Hume and Kant on my side, I could not think myself presumptuous in holding fast by that opinion. Like Dante,

Nel mezzo del cammin di nostra vita
Mi ritrovai per una selva oscura,

but, unlike Dante, I cannot add,

11   *Kritik der reinen Vernunft.* Edit. Hartenstein, pp. 256.

Che la diritta via era smarrita.

On the contrary, I had, and have, the firmest conviction that I never left the "verace via" – the straight road; and that this road led nowhere else but into the dark depths of a wild and tangled forest. And though I have found leopards and lions in the path; though I have made abundant acquaintance with the hungry wolf, that "with privy paw devours apace and nothing said," as another great poet says of the ravening beast; and though no friendly spectre has even yet offered his guidance, I was, and am, minded to go straight on, until I either come out on the other side of the wood, or find there is no other side to it, at least, none attainable by me.

This was my situation when I had the good fortune to find a place among the members of that remarkable confraternity of antagonists, long since deceased, but of green and pious memory, the Metaphysical Society. Every variety of philosophical and theological opinion was represented there, and expressed itself with entire openness; most of my colleagues were -*ists* of one sort or another; and, however kind and friendly they might be, I, the man without a rag of a label to cover himself with, could not fail to have some of the uneasy feelings which must have beset the historical fox when, after leaving the trap in which his tail remained, he presented himself to his normally elongated companions. So I took thought, and invested what I conceived to be the appropriate title of "agnostic." It came into my head as suggestively antithetic to the "gnostic" of Church history, who professed to know so much about the very things of which I was ignorant; and I took the earliest opportunity of parading it at our Society, to show that I, too, had a tail, like the other foxes. To my great satisfaction, the term took; and when the *Spectator* had stood godfather to it, any suspicion in the minds of respectable people, that a knowledge of its parentage might have awakened was, of course, completely lulled.

That is the history of the origin of the terms "agnostic" and "agnosticism"; and it will be observed that it does not quite agree with the confident assertion of the reverend Principal of King's College, that "the adoption of the term agnostic is only an attempt to shift the issue, and that it involves a mere evasion" in relation to the Church and Christianity.[12]

[12]   *Report of the Church Congress*, Manchester, 1888, p. 252.

The last objection (I rejoice as much as my readers must do, that it is the last) which I have to take to Dr. Wace's deliverance before the Church Congress arises, I am sorry to say, on a question of morality.

"It is, and it ought to be," authoritatively declares this official representative of Christian ethics, "an unpleasant thing for a man to have to say plainly that he does not believe in Jesus Christ" (*l. c.* p. 254).

Whether it is so depends, I imagine, a good deal on whether the man was brought up in a Christian household or not. I do not see why it should be "unpleasant" for a Mahommedan or Buddhist to say so. But that "it ought to be" unpleasant for any man to say anything which he sincerely, and after due deliberation, believes, is, to my mind, a proposition of the most profoundly immoral character, I verily believe that the great good which has been effected in the world by Christianity has been largely counteracted by the pestilent doctrine on which all the Churches have insisted, that honest disbelief in their more or less astonishing creeds is a moral offence, indeed a sin of the deepest dye, deserving and involving the same future retribution as murder and robbery. If we could only see, in one view, the torrents of hypocrisy and cruelty, the lies, the slaughter, the violations of every obligation of humanity, which have flowed from this source along the course of the history of Christian nations, our worst imaginations of Hell would pale beside the vision.

A thousand times, no! It ought *not* to be unpleasant to say that which one honestly believes or disbelieves. That it so constantly is painful to do so, is quite enough obstacle to the progress of mankind in that most valuable of all qualities, honesty of word or of deed, without erecting a sad concomitant of human weakness into something to be admired and cherished. The bravest of soldiers often, and very naturally, "feel it unpleasant" to go into action; but a court-martial which did its duty would make short work of the officer who promulgated the doctrine that his men *ought* to feel their duty unpleasant.

I am very well aware, as I suppose most thoughtful people are in these times, that the process of breaking away from old beliefs is extremely unpleasant; and I am much disposed to think that the encouragement, the consolation, and the peace afforded · to earnest believers in even the worst forms of

Christianity are of great practical advantage to them. What deductions must be made from this gain on the score of the harm done to the citizen by the ascetic other-worldliness of logical Christianity; to the ruler, by the hatred, malice, and all uncharitableness of sectarian bigotry; to the legislator, by the spirit of exclusiveness and domination of those that count themselves pillars of orthodoxy; to the philosopher, by the restraints on the freedom of learning and teaching which every Church exercises, when it is strong enough; to the conscientious soul, by the introspective hunting after sins of the mint and cummin type, the fear of theological error, and the overpowering terror of possible damnation, which have accompanied the Churches like their shadow, I need not now consider; but they are assuredly not small. If agnostics lose heavily on the one side, they gain a good deal on the other. People who talk about the comforts of belief appear to forget its discomforts; they ignore the fact that the Christianity of the Churches is something more than faith in the ideal personality of Jesus, which they create for themselves, *plus* so much as can be carried into practice, without disorganising civil society, of the maxims of the Sermon on the Mount. Trip in morals or in doctrine (especially in doctrine), without due repentance of retraction, or fail to get properly baptized before you die, and a *plébiscite* of the Christians of Europe, if they were true to their creeds, would affirm your everlasting damnation by an immense majority.

Preachers, orthodox and heterodox, din into our ears that the world cannot get on without faith of some sort. There is a sense in which that is as eminently as obviously true; there is another, in which, in my judgment, it is as eminently as obviously false, and it seems to me that the hortatory, or pulpit, mind is apt to oscillate between the false and the true meanings, without being aware of the fact.

It is quite true that the ground of every one of our actions, and the validity of all our reasonings, rest upon the great act of faith, which leads us to take the experience of the past as a safe guide in our dealings with the present and the future. From the nature of ratiocination, it is obvious that the axioms, on which it is based, cannot be demonstrated by ratiocination. It is also a trite observation that, in the business of life, we constantly take the most serious action upon evidence of an utterly insufficient character. But it is surely plain that faith is not necessarily entitled to dispense with ratiocination because ratiocination cannot dispense with faith as a starting-point; and that because we are often obliged, by the pressure of events, to act on very bad evidence, it does not follow that it is proper to act on such evidence when the pressure is absent.

The writer of the epistle to the Hebrews tells us that "faith is the assurance of things hoped for, the proving of things not seen." In the authorised version, "substance" stands for "assurance," and "evidence" for "proving." The question of the exact meaning of the two words, ὑπόστασις and ἔλεγχος, affords a fine field of discussion for the scholar and the metaphysician. But I fancy we shall be not far from the mark if we take the writer to have had in his mind the profound psychological truth, that men constantly feel certain about things for which they strongly hope, but have no evidence, in the legal or logical sense of the word; and he calls this feeling "faith." I may have the most absolute faith that a friend has not committed the crime of which he is accused. In the early days of English history, if my friend could have obtained a few more compurgators of a like robust faith, he would have been acquitted. At the present day, if I tendered myself as a witness on that score, the judge would tell me to stand down, and the youngest barrister would smile at my simplicity. Miserable indeed is the man who has not such faith in some of his fellow-men – only less miserable than the man who allows himself to forget that such faith is not strictly speaking, evidence; and when his faith is disappointed, as will happen now and again, turns Timon and blames the universe for his own blunders. And so, if a man can find a friend, the hypostasis of all his hopes, the mirror of his ethical ideal, in the Jesus of any, or all, of the Gospels, let him live by faith in that ideal. Who shall or can forbid him? But let him not delude himself with the notion that his faith is evidence of the objective reality of that in which he trusts. Such evidence is to be obtained only by the use of the methods of science, as applied to history and to literature, and it amounts at present to very little.

It appears that Mr. Gladstone some time ago asked Mr. Laing if he could draw up a short summary of the negative creed; a body of negative propositions, which have so far been adopted on the negative side as to be what the Apostles' and other accepted creeds are on the positive; and Mr. Laing at once kindly obliged Mr. Gladstone with the desired articles – eight of them.

If any one had preferred this request to me, I should have replied that, if he referred to agnostics, they have no creed; and, by the nature of the case, cannot have any. Agnosticism, in fact, is not a creed, but a method, the essence of which lies in the rigorous application of a single principle. That principle is of great antiquity; it is as old as Socrates; as old as the writer who said, "Try all things, hold fast by that which is good;" it is the foundation of the Reformation, which simply illustrated the axiom that every man should be able to give a reason for the faith that is in him; it is the great principle of Descartes; it is the fundamental axiom of modern science. Positively the principle may be expressed: In matters of the intellect, follow your reason as far as it will take you, without regard to any other consideration. And negatively: In matters of the intellect do not pretend that conclusions are certain which are not demonstrated or demonstrable. That I take to be the agnostic faith, which if a man keep whole and undefiled, he shall not be ashamed to look the universe in the face, whatever the future may have in store for him.

The results of the working out of the agnostic principle will vary according to individual knowledge and capacity, and according to the general condition of science. That which is unproven today may be proven by the help of new discoveries to-morrow. The only negative fixed points will be those negations which flow from the demonstrable limitation of our faculties. And the only obligation accepted is to have the mind always open to conviction. Agnostics who never fail in carrying out their principles are, I am afraid, as rare as other people of whom the same consistency can be truthfully predicated. But, if you were to meet with such a phoenix and to tell him that you had discovered that two and two make five, he would patiently ask you to state your reasons for that conviction, and express his readiness to agree with you if he found them satisfactory. The apostolic injunction to "suffer fools gladly" should be the rule of life of a true agnostic. I am deeply conscious how far I myself fall short of this ideal, but it is my personal conception of what agnostics ought to be.

However, as I began by stating, I speak only for myself; and I do not dream of anathematizing and excommunicating Mr. Laing. But, when I consider his creed and compare it with the

Athanasian, I think I have on the whole a clearer conception of the meaning of the latter. "Polarity," in Article VIII., for example, is a word about which I heard a good deal in my youth, when "Naturphilosophie" was in fashion, and greatly did I suffer from it. For many years past, whenever I have met with "polarity" anywhere but in a discussion of some purely physical topic, such as magnetism, I have shut the book. Mr. Laing must excuse me if the force of habit was too much for me when I read his eighth article.

And now, what is to be said to Mr. Harrison's remarkable deliverance "On the future of agnosticism"?[13] I would that it were not my business to say anything, for I am afraid I can say nothing which shall manifest my great personal respect for this able writer, and for the zeal and energy with which he ever and anon galvanises the weakly frame of Positivism until it looks, more than ever, like John Bunyan's Pope and Pagan rolled into one. There is a story often repeated, and I am afraid none the less mythical on that account, of a valiant and loud-voiced corporal in command of two full privates who, falling in with a regiment of the enemy in the dark, orders it to surrender under pain of instant annihilation by his force; and the enemy surrenders accordingly. I am always reminded of this tale when I read the positivist commands to the forces of Christianity and of Science; only the enemy show no more signs of intending to obey now than they have done any time these forty years.

The allocution under consideration has a certain papal flavour. Mr. Harrison speaks with authority and not as one of the common scribes of the period. He knows not only what agnosticism is and how it has come about, but what will become of it. The agnostic is to content himself with being the precursor of the positivist. In his place, as a sort of navvy levelling the ground and cleansing it of such poor stuff as Christianity, he is a useful creature who deserves patting on the back, on condition that he does not venture beyond his last. But let not these scientific Sanballats presume that they are good enough to take part in the building of the Temple – they are mere Samaritans, doomed to die out in proportion as the Religion of Humanity is accepted by mankind. Well, if that is their fate, they have time to be cheerful. But let us hear Mr. Harrison's pronouncement of their doom.

[13] *Fortnightly Review*, Jan. 1889.

"Agnosticism is a stage in the evolution of religion, an entirely negative stage, the point reached by physicists, a purely mental conclusion, with no relation to things social at all" (p. 154). I am quite dazed by this declaration. Are there, then, any "conclusions" that are not "purely mental"? Is there "no relation to things social" in "mental conclusions" which affect men's whole conception of life? Was that prince of agnostics, David Hume, particularly imbued with physical science? Supposing physical science to be non-existent, would not the agnostic principle, applied by the philologist and the historian, lead to exactly the same results? Is the modern more or less complete suspension of judgment as to the facts of the history of regal Rome, or the real origin of the Homeric poems, anything but agnosticism in history and in literature? And if so, how can agnosticism be the "mere negation of the physicist"?

"Agnosticism is a stage in the evolution of religion." No two people agree as to what is meant by the term "religion"; but if it means, as I think it ought to mean, simply the reverence and love for the ethical ideal, and the desire to realise that ideal in life, which every man ought to feel – then I say agnosticism has no more to do with it than it has to do with music or painting. If, on the other hand, Mr. Harrison, like most people, means by "religion" theology, then, in my judgment, agnosticism can be said to be a stage in its evolution, only as death may be said to be the final stage in the evolution of life.

> When agnostic logic is simply one of the canons of thought, agnosticism, as a distinctive faith, will have spontaneously disappeared (p. 155).

I can but marvel that such sentences as this, and those already quoted, should have proceeded from Mr. Harrison's pen. Does he really mean to suggest that agnostics have a logic peculiar to themselves? Will he kindly help me out of my bewilderment when I try to think of "logic" being anything else than the canon (which, I believe, means rule) of thought? As to agnosticism being a distinctive faith, I have already shown that it cannot possibly be anything of the kind, unless perfect faith in logic is distinctive of agnostics; which, after all, it may be.

> Agnosticism as a religious philosophy *per se* rests on an almost total ignoring of history and social evolution (p. 152).

But neither *per se* nor *per aliud* has agnosticism (if I know anything about it) the least pretension to be a religious philosophy; so far from resting on ignorance of history, and that social evolution of which history is the account, it is and has been the inevitable result of the strict adherence to scientific methods by historical investigators. Our forefathers were quite confident about the existence of Romulus and Remus, of King Arthur, and of Hengist and Horsa. Most of us have become agnostics in regard to the reality of these worthies. It is a matter of notoriety of which Mr. Harrison, who accuses us all so freely of ignoring history, should not be ignorant, that the critical process which has shattered the foundations of orthodox Christian doctrine owes its origin, not to the devotees of physical science, but, before all, to Richard Simon, the learned French Oratorian, just two hundred years ago. I cannot find evidence that either Simon, or any one of the great scholars and critics of the eighteenth and nineteenth centuries who have continued Simon's work, had any particular acquaintance with physical science. I have already pointed out that Hume was independent of it. And certainly one of the most potent influences in the same direction, upon history in the present century, that of Grote, did not come from the physical side. Physical science, in fact, has had nothing directly to do with the criticism of the Gospels; it is wholly incompetent to furnish demonstrative evidence that any statement made in these histories is untrue. Indeed, modern physiology can find parallels in nature for events of apparently the most eminently supernatural kind recounted in some of those histories.

It is a comfort to hear, upon Mr. Harrison's authority, that the laws of physical nature show no signs of becoming "less definite, less consistent, or less popular as time goes on" (p. 154). How a law of nature is to become indefinite, or "inconsistent," passes my poor powers of imagination. But with universal suffrage and the coach-dog theory of premiership in full view; the theory, I mean, that the whole duty of a political chief is to look sharp for the way the social coach is driving, and then run in front and bark loud – as if being the leading noise-maker and guiding were the same things – it is truly satisfactory to me to know that the laws of nature are increasing in popularity. Looking at recent developments of the policy which is said to express the great heart of the people, I have had my doubts of the fact; and my love for my fellow-countrymen has led me to reflect, with dread, on what will happen to them, if any of the laws of nature ever become so unpopular in their eyes, as to be voted down by the transcendent authority of universal suffrage. If the legion of demons, before they set out on their journey in the swine, had had time to hold a meeting to resolve unanimously "That the law of gravitation is oppressive and ought to be repealed," I am afraid it would have made no sort of difference to the result, when their two thousand unwilling porters were once launched down the steep slopes of the fatal shore of Gennesaret.

> The question of the place of religion as an element of human nature, as a force of human society, its origin, analysis, and functions, has never been considered at all from an agnostic point of view (p. 152).

I doubt not that Mr. Harrison knows vastly more about history than I do; in fact, he tells the public that some of my friends and I have had no opportunity of occupying ourselves with that subject. I do not like to contradict any statement which Mr. Harrison makes on his own authority; only, if I may be true to my agnostic principles, I humbly ask how he has obtained assurance on this head. I do not profess to know anything about the range of Mr. Harrison's studies; but as he has thought it fitting to start the subject, I may venture to point out that, on evidence adduced, it might be equally permissible to draw the conclusion that Mr. Harrison's other labours have not allowed him to acquire that acquaintance with the methods and results of physical science, or with the history of philosophy, or of philological and historical criticism, which is essential to any one who desires to obtain a right understanding of agnosticism. Incompetence in philosophy, and in all branches of science except mathematics, is the well-known mental characteristic of the founder of positivism. Faithfulness in disciples is an admirable quality in itself; the pity is that it not unfrequently leads to the imitation of the weaknesses as well as of the strength of the master. It is only such over-faithfulness which can account for a "strong mind really saturated with the historical sense" (p. 153) exhibiting the extraordinary forgetfulness of the historical fact of the existence of David Hume implied by the assertion that it would be difficult to name a single known agnostic who has given to history anything like the amount of thought and study which he brings to a knowledge of the physical world (p. 153).

Whoso calls to mind what I may venture to term the bright side of Christianity – that ideal of manhood, with its strength and its patience, its justice and its pity for human frailty, its helpfulness to the extremity of self-sacrifice, its ethical purity and nobility, which apostles have pictured, in which armies of martyrs have placed their unshakable faith, and whence obscure men and women, like Catherine of Sienna and John Knox, have derived the courage to rebuke popes and kings – is not likely to underrate the importance of the Christian faith as a factor in human history, or to doubt that if that faith should prove to be incompatible with our knowledge, or necessary want of knowledge, some other hypostasis of men's hopes, genuine enough and worthy enough to replace it, will arise. But that the incongruous mixture of bad science with eviscerated papistry, out of which Comte manufactured the positivist religion, will be the heir of the Christian ages, I have too much respect for the humanity of the future to believe. Charles the Second told his brother, "They will not kill me, James, to make you king." And if critical science is remorselessly destroying the historical foundations of the noblest ideal of humanity which mankind have yet worshipped, it is little likely to permit the pitiful reality to climb into the vacant shrine.

That a man should determine to devote himself to the service of humanity – including intellectual and moral self-culture under that name; that this should be, in the proper sense of the word, his religion – is not only an intelligible, but I think, a laudable resolution. And I am greatly disposed to believe that it is the only religion which will prove itself to be unassailably acceptable so long as the human race endures. But when the Comtist asks me to worship "Humanity" – that is to say, to adore the generalised conception of men as they ever have been and probably ever will be – I must reply that I could just as soon bow down and worship the generalised conception of a "wilderness of apes." Surely we are not going back to the days of Paganism, when individual men were deified, and the hard good sense of a dying Vespasian could prompt the bitter jest, "Ut puto Deus fio." No divinity doth hedge a modern man, be he even a sovereign ruler. Nor is there any one, except a municipal magistrate, who is officially declared worshipful. But if there is no spark of worship-worthy divinity in the individual twigs of humanity, whence comes that godlike splendour which the Moses of Positivism fondly imagines to pervade the whole bush?

I know no study which is so unutterably saddening as that of the evolution of humanity, as it is set forth in the annals of history. Out of the darkness of prehistoric ages man emerges with the marks of his lowly origin strong upon him. He is a brute, only more intelligent than the other brutes, a blind prey to impulses, which as often as not lead him to destruction; a victim to endless illusions, which make his mental existence a terror and a burden, and fill his physical life with barren toil and battle. He attains a certain degree of physical comfort, and develops a more or less workable theory of life, in such favourable situations as the plains of Mesopotamia or of Egypt, and then, for thousands and thousands of years, struggles, with varying fortunes, attended by infinite wickedness, bloodshed, and misery, to maintain himself at this point against the greed and the ambition of his fellow-men. He makes a point of killing and otherwise persecuting all those who first try to get him to move on; and when he has moved on a step, foolishly confers post-mortem deification on his victims. He exactly repeats the process with all who want to move a step yet farther. And the best men of the best epochs are simply those who make the fewest blunders and commit the fewest sins.

That one should rejoice in the good man, forgive the bad man, and pity and help all men to the best of one's ability, is surely indisputable. It is the glory of Judaism and of Christianity to have proclaimed this truth, through all their aberrations. But the worship of a God who needs forgiveness and help, and deserves pity every hour of his existence, is no better than that of any other voluntarily selected fetish. The Emperor Julian's project was hopeful in comparison with the prospects of the Comtist Anthropolatry.

When the historian of religion in the twentieth century is writing about the nineteenth, I foresee he will say something of this kind:

The most curious and instructive events in the religious history of the preceding century are the rise and progress of two new sects called Mormons and Positivists. To the student who has carefully considered these remarkable phenomena nothing in the records of religious self-delusion can appear improbable.

The Mormons arose in the midst of the great Republic, which, though comparatively insignificant, at that time, in territory as in the number of its citizens, was (as we know from the fragments of the speeches of its orators which have come down to us) no less remarkable for the native intelligence of its population than for the wide extent of their information, owing to the activity of their publishers in diffusing all that they could invent, beg, borrow, or steal. Nor were they less noted for their perfect freedom from all restraints in thought, or speech, or deed; except, to be sure, the beneficent and wise influence of the majority, exerted, in case of need, through an institution known as "tarring and feathering," the exact nature of which is now disputed.

There is a complete consensus of testimony that the founder of Mormonism, one Joseph Smith, was a low-minded, ignorant scamp, and that he stole the "Scriptures" which he propounded; not being clever enough to forge even such contemptible stuff as they contain. Nevertheless he must have been a man of some force of character, for a considerable number of disciples soon gathered about him. In spite of repeated outbursts of popular hatred and violence – during one of which persecutions Smith was brutally murdered – the Mormon body steadily increased, and became a flourishing community. But the Mormon practices being objectionable to the majority, they were, more than once, without any pretence of law, but by force of riot, arson, and murder, driven away from the land they had occupied. Harried by these persecutions, the Mormon body eventually committed itself to the tender mercies of a desert as barren as that of Sinai; and after terrible sufferings and privations, reached the Oasis of Utah. Here it grew and flourished, sending out missionaries to, and receiving converts from, all parts of Europe, sometimes to the number of 10,000 in a year; until, in 1880, the rich and flourishing community numbered 110,000 souls in Utah alone, while there were probably 30,000 or 40,000 scattered abroad elsewhere. In the whole history of religions there is no more remarkable example of the power of faith; and, in this case, the founder of that faith was indubitably a most despicable creature. It is interesting to observe that the course taken by the great Republic and its citizens runs exactly parallel with that taken by the Roman Empire and its citizens towards the early Christians, except that the Romans had a certain legal excuse for their acts of violence, inasmuch as the Christian "sodalitia" were not licensed, and consequently were, *ipso facto*, illegal assemblages. Until, in the latter part of the nineteenth century, the United States legislature decreed the illegality of polygamy, the Mormons were wholly within the law.

Nothing can present a greater contrast to all this than the history of the Positivists. This sect arose much about the same time as that of the Mormons, in the upper and most instructed stratum of the quick-witted, sceptical population of Paris. The founder, Auguste Comte, was a teacher of mathematics, but of no eminence in that department of knowledge, and with nothing but an amateur's acquaintance with physical, chemical, and biological science. His works are repulsive, on account of the dull diffuseness of their style, and a certain air, as of a superior person, which characterises them; but nevertheless they contain good things here and there. It would take too much space to reproduce in detail a system which proposes to regulate all human life by the promulgation of a Gentile Leviticus. Suffice it to say, that M. Comte may be described as a syncretic, who, like the Gnostics of early Church history, attempted to combine the substance of imperfectly comprehended contemporary science with the form of Roman Christianity. It may be that this is the reason why his disciples were so very angry with some obscure people called Agnostics, whose views, if we may judge by the account left in the works of a great Positivist controversial writer, were very absurd.

To put the matter briefly, M. Comte, finding Christianity and Science at daggers drawn, seems to have said to Science, "You find Christianity rotten at the core, do you? Well, I will scoop out the inside of it." And to Romanism: "You find Science mere dry light – cold and bare. Well, I will put your shell over it, and so, as schoolboys make a spectre out of a turnip and a tallow candle, behold the new religion of Humanity complete!"

Unfortunately neither the Romanists, nor the people who were something more than amateurs in science, could be got to worship M. Comte's new idol properly. In the native country of Positivism, one distinguished man of letters and one of science, for a time, helped to make up a roomful of the faithful, but their love soon grew cold. In England, on the other hand, there appears to be little doubt that, in the ninth decade of the century, the multitude of disciples reached the grand total of several score. They had the advantage of the advocacy of one or two most eloquent and learned apostles, and, at any rate, the sympathy of several persons of light and leading; and, if they were not seen, they were heard, all over the world. On the other hand, as a sect, they laboured under the prodigious disadvantage of being refined, estimable people, living in the midst of the worn-out civilisation of the old work; where any one who had tried to persecute them, as the Mormons were persecuted, would have been instantly hanged. But the majority never dreamed of persecuting them; on the contrary, they were rather given to scold and otherwise try the patience of the majority.

The history of this sects in the closing years of the century is highly instructive. Mormonism . . ..

But I find I have suddenly slipped off Mr. Harrison's tripod, which I had borrowed for the occasion. The fact is, I am not equal to the prophetical business, and ought not to have undertaken it.

[It did not occur to me, while writing the latter part of this essay, that it could be needful to disclaim the intention of putting the religious system of Comte on a level with Mormonism. And I was unaware of the fact that Mr. Harrison rejects the greater part of the Positivist Religion, as taught by Comte. I have, therefore, erased one or two passages, which implied his adherence to the "Religion of Humanity" as developed by Comte, 1893.]

REPLY TO PROFESSOR HUXLEY
[Henry Wace]

It would hardly be reasonable to complain of Professor
Huxley's delay in replying to the Paper on 'Agnosticism' which
I read five months ago, when, at the urgent request of an old
friend, I reluctantly consented to address the Church Congress
at Manchester. I am obliged to him for doing it the honour to
bring it to the notice of a wider circle than that to which it was
directly addressed; and I fear that, for reasons which have been
the occasion of universal regret, he may not have been equal to
literary effort. But, at the same time, it is impossible not to
notice that a writer is at a great advantage in attacking a
fugitive essay a quarter of a year after it was made public. Such
a lapse of time ought, indeed, to enable him to apprehend
distinctly the argument with which he is dealing; and it might,
at least, secure him from any such inaccuracy in quotation as
greater haste might excuse. But if either his idiosyncracy, or his
sense of assured superiority, should lead him to pay no real
attention to the argument he is attacking, or should betray him
into material misquotation, he may at least be sure that
scarcely any of his readers will care to refer to the original
paper, or will have the opportunity of doing so. I can scarcely
hope that Professor Huxley's obliging reference to the *Official
Report of the Church Congress* will induce many of those who
are influenced by his answer to my Paper to purchase that
interesting volume, though they would be well-repaid by some
of its other contents; and I can hardly rely on their spending
even twopence upon the reprint of the Paper, published by the
Society for Promoting Christian Knowledge. I have therefore
felt obliged to ask the editor of this Review to be kind enough
to admit to his pages a brief re-statement of the position which
Professor Huxley has assailed, with such notice of his
arguments as is practicable within the comparatively brief
space which can be afforded me. I could not, indeed, amidst
the pressing claims of a College like this in term time, besides

the chairmanship of a Hospital, a Preachership, and other duties, attempt any reply which would deal as thoroughly as could be wished with an article of so much skill and finish. But it is a matter of justice to my cause and to myself to remove at once the unscientific and prejudiced representation of the case which Professor Huxley has put forward; and fortunately there will be need of no elaborate argument for this purpose. There is no occasion to go beyond Professor Huxley's own Article and the language of my Paper to exhibit his entire misapprehension of the point in dispute; while I am much more than content to rely for the invalidation of his own contentions upon the authorities he himself quotes.

What, then, is the position with which Professor Huxley finds fault? He is good enough to say that what he calls my 'description' of an Agnostic may for the present pass, so that we are so far, at starting, on common ground. The actual description of an Agnostic, which is given in my paper, is indeed distinct from the words he quotes, and is taken from an authoritative source. But what I have said is that, as an escape from such an article of Christian belief as that We have a Father in Heaven, or that Jesus Christ is the Judge of quick and dead, and will hereafter return to judge the world, an Agnostic urges that 'he has no means of a scientific knowledge of the unseen world or of the future;' and I maintain that this plea is irrelevant. Christians do not presume to say that they have a scientific knowledge of such articles of their creed. They say that they believe them, and they believe them mainly on the assurances of Jesus Christ. Consequently their characteristic difference from an Agnostic consists in the fact that they believe those assurances, and that he does not. Professor Huxley's observation, 'are there then any Christians who say that they know nothing about the unseen world and the future? I was ignorant of the fact, but I am ready to accept it on the authority of a professed theologian,' is either a quibble, or one of many indications that he does not recognise the point at issue. I am speaking, as the sentence shows, of scientific knowledge – knowledge which can be obtained by our own reason and observation alone – and no one with Professor Huxley's learning is justified in being ignorant that it is not upon such knowledge, but upon supernatural revelation, that Christian belief rests. However, as he goes on to say, my view of 'the real state of the case is that the Agnostic "does not believe the authority" on which "these things" are stated, which authority is Jesus Christ. He is simply an old-fashioned "infidel" who is afraid to own to his right name.' The argument has nothing to do with his motive, whether it is being afraid or not. It only concerns the fact that that by which he is distinctively separated from the Christian is that he does not believe the assurances of Jesus Christ.

Professor Huxley thinks there is 'an attractive simplicity about this solution of the problem' – he means, of course, this statement of the case – 'and it has that advantage of being somewhat offensive to the persons attacked, which is so dear to the less refined sort of controversialist.' I think Professor Huxley must have forgotten himself and his own feelings in this observation. There can be no question, of course, of his belonging himself to the more refined sort of controversialists; but he has a characteristic fancy for solutions of problems, or statements of cases, which have the 'advantage of being somewhat offensive to the persons attacked.' Without taking this particular phrase into account, it certainly has 'the advantage of being offensive to the persons attacked' that Professor Huxley should speak in this article of 'the pestilent doctrine on which all the churches have insisted, that honest disbelief' – the word 'honest' is not a misquotation – 'honest disbelief in their more or less astonishing creeds is a moral offence, indeed a sin of the deepest dye, deserving and involving the same future retribution as murder or robbery,' or that he should say, 'Trip in morals or in doctrine (especially in doctrine), without due repentance or retractation, or fail to get properly baptized before you die, and a *plébiscite* of the Christians of Europe, if they were true to their creeds, would affirm your ever-lasting damnation by an immense majority.' We have fortunately nothing to do in this argument with *plébiscites*; and as statements of authoritative Christian teaching, the least that can be said of these allegations is that they are offensive exaggerations. It had 'the advantage' again, of being 'offensive to the persons attacked,' when Professor Huxley, in an article in this Review on 'Science and the Bishops,' in November 1887, said that 'Scientific ethics can and does declare that the profession of belief in such narrative as that of the devils entering a herd of swine, or of the fig tree that was blasted for bearing no figs, upon the evidence on which multitudes of Christians believe it, 'is immoral;' and the observation which followed, that 'theological apologists would do well to consider the fact that, in the matter of intellectual veracity, science is already a long way ahead of the churches,' has the same 'advantage.' I repeat that I cannot but treat Professor Huxley as an example of the more refined sort of controversialist; it must be supposed, therefore, that when he speaks of observations or insinuations which are somewhat offensive to the 'persons attacked' being dear to the other sort of controversialists, he is unconscious of his own methods of controversy – or, shall I say, his own temptations?

But I desire as far as possible to avoid any rivalry with Professor Huxley in these refinements – more or less – of controversy; and am, in fact, forced by pressure both of space and of time to keep as rigidly as possible to the points directly at issue. He proceeds to restate the case as follows:– 'The Agnostic says, "I cannot find good evidence that so and so is true." "Ah," says his adversary, seizing his opportunity, "then you declare that Jesus Christ was untruthful, for he said so and so" – a very telling method of rousing prejudice.' Now that superior scientific veracity to which, as we have seen, Professor Huxley lays claim, should have prevented him putting such vulgar words into my mouth. There is not a word in my paper to charge Agnostics with declaring that Jesus Christ was 'untruthful.' I believe it impossible in these days for any man who claims attention – I might say, for any man – to declare our Lord untruthful. What I said, and what I repeat, is that the position of an Agnostic involves the conclusion that Jesus Christ was under an 'illusion' in respect to the deepest beliefs of His life and teaching. The words of my paper are: 'An Agnosticism which knows nothing of the relation of man to God must not only refuse belief to our Lord's most undoubted teaching, but must deny the reality of the spiritual convictions in which He lived and died.' The point is this – that there can, at least, be no reasonable doubt that Jesus Christ lived, and taught, and died, in the belief of certain great principles respecting the existence of God, our relation to God, and His own relation to us, which an Agnostic says are beyond the possibilities of human knowledge; and of course an Agnostic regards Jesus Christ as a man. If so, he must necessarily regard Jesus Christ as mistaken, since the notion of His being untruthful is a supposition which I could not conceive being suggested. The question I have put is not, as Professor Huxley represents, what is the most unpleasant alternative to belief in the primary truths of the Christian religion, but what is the least unpleasant; and all I have maintained is that the least unpleasant alternative necessarily involved is, that Jesus Christ was under an illusion in His most vital convictions.

I content myself with thus rectifying the state of the case, without making the comments which I think would be justified on such a crude misrepresentation of my argument. But Professor Huxley goes on to observe that 'the value of the evidence as to what Jesus may have said and done, and as to the exact nature and scope of his authority, is just that which the Agnostic finds it most difficult to determine.' Undoubtedly, that is a primary question; but who would suppose from Professor Huxley's statement of the case that the argument of the paper he is attacking proceeded to deal with this very point, and that he has totally ignored the chief consideration it alleged? Almost immediately after the words Professor Huxley has quoted, the following passage occurs, which I must needs transfer to these pages, as containing the central point of the argument. 'It may be asked how far we can rely on the accounts we possess of our Lord's teaching on these subjects. Now it is unnecessary for the general argument before us to enter on those questions respecting the authenticity of the Gospel narratives, which ought to be regarded as settled by M. Renan's practical surrender of the adverse case. *Apart from all disputed points of criticism, no one practically doubts that our Lord lived, and that He died on the Cross, in the most intense sense of filial relation to His Father in Heaven, and that He bore testimony to that Father's providence, love, and grace towards mankind. The Lord's Prayer affords sufficient evidence upon these points. If the Sermon on the Mount alone be added, the whole unseen world, of which the Agnostic refuses to know anything, stands unveiled before us. There you see revealed the Divine Father and Creator of all things, in personal relation to His creatures, hearing their prayers, witnessing their actions, caring for them and rewarding them. There you hear of a future judgment administered by Christ Himself, and of a Heaven to be hereafter revealed, in which those who live as the children of that Father, and who suffer in the cause and for the sake of Christ Himself, will be abundantly rewarded. If Jesus Christ preached that Sermon, made those promises, and taught that prayer, then anyone who says that*

we know nothing of God, or of a future life, or of an unseen
world, says that he does not believe Jesus Christ.'

Professor Huxley has not one word to say upon this
argument, though the whole case is involved in it. Let us take
as an example the illustration he proceeds to give. 'If,' he says,
'I venture to doubt that the Duke of Wellington gave the
command, "Up, Guards, and at 'em!" at Waterloo, I do not
think that even Dr. Wace would accuse me of disbelieving the
Duke.' Certainly not. But if Professor Huxley were to maintain
that the pursuit of glory was the true motive of the soldier, and
that it was an illusion to suppose that simple devotion to duty
could be the supreme guide of military life, I should certainly
charge him with contradicting the Duke's teaching and
disregarding his authority and example. A hundred stories like
that of 'Up, Guards, and at 'em!' might be doubted, or
positively disproved, and it would still remain a fact beyond all
reasonable doubt that the Duke of Wellington was essentially
characterised by the sternest and most devoted sense of duty,
and that he had inculcated duty as the very watchword of a
soldier; and even Professor Huxley would not suggest that
Lord Tennyson's ode, which has embodied this characteristic
in immortal verse, was an unfounded poetical romance.

The main question at issue, in a word, is one which Professor
Huxley has chosen to leave entirely on one side – whether,
namely, allowing for the utmost uncertainty on other points of
the criticism to which he appeals, there is any reasonable doubt
that the Lord's Prayer and the Sermon on the Mount afford a
true account of our Lord's essential belief and cardinal
teaching. If they do – then I am not now contending that they
involve the whole of the Christian Creed; I am not arguing, as
Professor Huxley would represent, that he ought for that
reason alone to be a Christian – I simply represent that, as an
Agnostic, he must regard those beliefs and that teaching as
mistaken – the result of an illusion, to say the least. I am not
going, therefore, to follow Professor Huxley's example, and go
down a steep place with the Gadarene swine into a sea of
uncertainties and possibilities, and stake the whole case of
Christian belief as against Agnosticism upon one of the most
difficult and mysterious narratives in the New Testament. I will
state my position on that question presently. But I am first and
chiefly concerned to point out that Professor Huxley has
skilfully evaded the very point and edge of the argument he had

to meet. Let him raise what difficulties he pleases, with the help of his favourite critics, about the Gadarene swine, or even about all the stories of demoniacs. He will find that his critics – and even critics more rationalistic than they – fail him when it comes to the Lord's Prayer and the Sermon on the Mount, and, I will add, the story of the Passion. He will find, or rather he must have found, that the very critics he relies upon recognise that in the Sermon on the Mount and the Lord's Prayer, allowing for variations in form and order, the substance of our Lord's essential teaching is preserved. On a point which, until Professor Huxley shows cause to the contrary, can hardly want argument, the judgment of the most recent of his witnesses may suffice – Professor Reuss of Strasburg. In Professor Huxley's article on the 'Evolution of Theology' in the number of this Review for March 1886, he says: 'As Reuss appears to me to be one of the most learned, acute, and fair-minded of those whose works I have studied, I have made most use of the commentary and dissertations in his splendid French edition of the Bible.' What then is the opinion of the critic for whom Professor Huxley has this regard? In the volume of his work which treats of the first three Gospels, Reuss says at p. 191–2: 'If anywhere the tradition which has preserved to us the reminiscences of the life of Jesus upon earth carries with it certainty and the evidence of its fidelity, it is here;' and again: 'In short, it must be acknowledged that the redactor, in thus concentrating the substance of the moral teaching of the Lord, has rendered a real service to the religious study of this portion of the tradition, and the reserves which historical criticism has a right to make with respect to the form will in no way diminish this advantage.' It will be observed that Professor Reuss thinks, as many good critics have thought, that the Sermon on the Mount combines various distinct utterances of our Lord, but he none the less recognises that it embodies an unquestionable account of the substance of our Lord's teaching.

But it is surely superfluous to argue either this particular point, or the main conclusion which I have founded on it. Can there be any doubt whatever, in the mind of any reasonable man, that Jesus Christ had beliefs respecting God which an Agnostic alleges there is no sufficient ground for? We know something at all events of what His disciples taught; we have authentic original documents, unquestioned by any of Professor Huxley's authorities, as to what St. Paul taught and believed, and of what he taught and believed respecting his Master's teaching; and the central point of this teaching is a direct assertion of knowledge and revelation as against the very Agnosticism from which Professor Huxley manufactured that designation. 'As I passed by,' said St. Paul at Athens, 'I found an altar with this inscription: "To the unknown God." Whom therefore ye ignorantly – or in Agnosticism – worship, Him declare I unto you.' An Agnostic withholds his assent from this primary article of the Christian creed; and though Professor Huxley, in spite of the lack of information he alleges respecting early Christian teaching, knows enough on the subject to have a firm belief 'that the Nazarenes, say of the year 40,' headed by James, would have stoned anyone who propounded the Nicene creed to them, he will hardly contend that they denied that article, or doubted that Jesus Christ believed it. Let us again listen to the authority to whom Professor Huxley himself refers. Reuss says at page 4 of the work already quoted:–

> Historical literature in the primitive Church attaches itself in the most immediate manner to the reminiscences collected by the Apostles and their friends, directly after their separation from their Master. The need of such a return to the past arose naturally from the profound impression which had been made upon them by the teaching, and still more by the individuality itself of Jesus, and on which both their hopes for the future and their convictions were founded. . . . It is in these facts, in this continuity of a tradition which could not but go back to the very morrow of the tragic scene of Golgotha that we have a strong guarantee for its authenticity. . . . We have direct historical proof that the thread of tradition was not interrupted. Not only does one of our Evangelists furnish this proof in formal terms (Luke i. 2); but in many other places besides we perceive the idea, or the point of view, that all which the Apostles know, think, and teach, is at bottom and essentially a reminiscence – a reflection of what they have seen and learnt at another time, a reproduction of lessons and impressions received.

Now let it be allowed for argument's sake that the belief and teaching of the Apostles are distinct from those of subsequent Christianity, yet it is surely a mere paradox to maintain that they did not assert, as taught by their Master, truths which an Agnostic denies. They certainly spoke, as Paul did, of the Love of God; they certainly spoke, as Paul did, of Jesus having been raised from the dead by God the Father (Gal. i. 1); they certainly spoke, as Paul did, of Jesus Christ returning to judge the world; they certainly spoke, as Paul did, of 'The God and Father of our Lord Jesus Christ' (2 Cor. xi. 31). That they could have done this without Jesus Christ having taught God's love, or having said that God was His Father, or having declared that He would judge the world, is a supposition which will certainly be regarded by an overwhelming majority of reasonable men as a mere paradox; and I cannot conceive, until he says so, that Professor Huxley would maintain it. But if so, then all Professor Huxley's argumentation about the Gadarene swine is mere irrelevance to the argument he undertakes to answer. The Gospels might be obliterated as evidence to-morrow, and it would remain indisputable that Jesus Christ taught certain truths respecting God, and man's relation to God, from which an Agnostic withholds his assent. If so, he does not believe Jesus Christ's teaching; he is so far an unbeliever, and 'unbeliever,' Dr. Johnson says, is an equivalent of 'Infidel.'

This consideration will indicate another irrelevance in Professor Huxley's argument. He asks for a definition of what a Christian is, before he will allow that he can be justly called an infidel. But without being able to give an accurate definition of a crayfish, which perhaps only Professor Huxley could do, I may be very well able to say that some creatures are not crayfish; and it is not necessary to frame a definition of a Christian in order to say confidently that a person who does not believe the broad and unquestionable elements of Christ's teachings and convictions is not a Christian. 'Infidel' or 'unbeliever' is of course, as Professor Huxley says, a relative and not a positive term. He makes a great deal of play out of what he seems to suppose will be a very painful and surprising consideration to myself, that to a Mahommedan I am an infidel. Of course I am; and I should never expect a Mahommedan, if he were called upon, as I was, to argue before an assembly of his own fellow-believers, to call me anything else. Professor Huxley is good enough to imagine me in his company on a visit to the Hazar Mosque at Cairo. When he entered that mosque without due credentials, he suspects that, he had understood Arabic, 'dog of an infidel' would have been by no means the most 'unpleasant' of the epithets showered upon him, before he could explain and apologise for the mistake. If, he says, 'I had had the pleasure of Dr. Wace's company on that occasion, the undiscriminative followers of the Prophet would, I am afraid, have made no difference between us; not even if they had known that he was the head of an orthodox Christian seminary.' Probably not; and I will add that I should have felt very little confidence in any attempts which Professor Huxley might have made, in the style of his present Article, to protect me, by repudiating for himself the unpleasant epithets which he deprecates. It would, I suspect, have been of very little avail to attempt a subtle explanation, to one of the learned Mollahs of whom he speaks, that he really did not mean to deny that there was one God, but only that he did not know anything on the subject, and that he desired to avoid expressing any opinion respecting the claims of Mahomet. It would be plain to the learned Mollah that Professor Huxley did not believe either of the articles of the Mahommedan creed – in other words that, for all his fine distinctions, he was at bottom a downright infidel, such as I confessed myself, and that there was an end of the matter. There is no fair way of avoiding the plain matter of fact in either case. A Mahommedan believes and asserts that there is no God but God, and that Mahomet is the Prophet of God. I don't believe Mahomet. In the plain, blunt, sensible phrase people used to use on such subjects, I believe he was a false prophet, and I am a downright infidel about him. The Christian creed might almost be summed up in the assertion that there is one, and but one God, and that Jesus Christ is His Prophet; and whoever denies that creed says that he does not believe Jesus Christ, by whom it was undoubtedly asserted. It is better to look facts in the face, especially from a scientific point of view. Whether Professor Huxley is justified in his denial of that creed is a further question, which demands separate consideration, but which was not, and is not now, at issue. All I say is that his position involves that disbelief or infidelity, and that this is a responsibility which must be faced by Agnosticism.

But I am forced to conclude that Professor Huxley cannot have taken the pains to understand the point I raised, not only by the irrelevance of his argument on these considerations, but by a misquotation which the superior accuracy of a man of science ought to have rendered impossible. Twice over in the article, he quotes me as saying that 'it is, and it ought to be, an unpleasant thing for a man to have to say plainly that he does not believe in Jesus Christ.' As he winds up his attack upon my paper by bringing against this statement his rather favourite charge of 'immorality' – and even 'most profound immorality' – he was the more bound to accuracy in his quotation of my words. But neither in the official report of the Congress to which he refers, nor in any report that I have seen, is this the statement attributed to me. What I said, and what I meant to say, was that it ought to be an unpleasant thing for a man to have to say plainly 'that he does not believe Jesus Christ.' By inserting the little word 'in,' Professor Huxley has, by an unconscious ingenuity, shifted the import of the statement. He goes on (p. 184) to denounce 'the pestilent doctrine on which all the Churches have insisted, that honest disbelief in their more or less astonishing creeds is a moral offence, indeed a sin of the deepest dye.' His interpretation exhibits, in fact, the idea in his own mind, which he has doubtless conveyed to his readers, that I said it ought to be unpleasant to a man to have to say that he does not believe in the Christian Creed. I certainly think it ought, for reasons I will mention; but that is not what I said. I spoke, deliberately, not of the Christian Creed as a whole, but of Jesus Christ as a person, and regarded as a witness to certain primary truths which an Agnostic will not acknowledge. It was a personal consideration to which I appealed, and not a dogmatic one; and I am sorry, for that reason, that Professor Huxley will not allow me to leave it in the reserve with which I hoped it had been sufficiently indicated. I said that 'no criticism worth mentioning doubts the story of the Passion; and that story involves the most solemn attestation, again and again, of truths of which an Agnostic coolly says he knows nothing. An Agnosticism which knows nothing of the relation of man to God must not only refuse belief to our Lord's most undoubted teaching, but must deny the reality of the spiritual convictions in which He lived and died. It must declare that His most intimate, most intense beliefs, and His dying aspirations were an illusion. Is that supposition tolerable?' I do not think this deserves to be called 'a proposition of the most profoundly immoral character.' I think it ought to be unpleasant, and I am sure it always will be unpleasant, for a man to listen to the Saviour on the Cross uttering such words as 'Father, into Thy hands I commend my spirit,' and to say that they are not to be trusted as revealing a real relation between the Saviour and God. In spite of all doubts as to the accuracy of the Gospels, Jesus Christ – I trust I may be forgiven, under the stress of controversy, for mentioning His sacred Name in this too familiar manner – is a tender and sacred figure to all thoughtful minds, and it is, it ought to be, and it always will be, a very painful thing, to say that He lived and died under a mistake in respect to the words which were first and last on His lips. I think, as I have admitted, that it should be unpleasant for a man who has as much appreciation of Christianity, and of its work in the world, as Professor Huxley sometimes shows, to have to say that its belief was founded on no objective reality. The unpleasantness, however, of denying one system of thought may be balanced by the pleasantness, as Professor Huxley suggests, of asserting another and a better one. But nothing, to all time, can do away with the unpleasantness, not only of repudiating sympathy with the most sacred figure of humanity in His deepest beliefs and feelings, but of pronouncing Him under an illusion in His last agony. If it be the truth, let it by all means be said; but if we are to talk of 'immorality' in such matters, I think there must be a lack of moral sensibility in any man who could say it without pain.

The plain fact is that this misquotation would have been as impossible as a good deal else of Professor Huxley's argument, had he, in any degree, appreciated the real strength of the hold which Christianity has over men's hearts and minds. The strength of the Christian Church, in spite of its faults, errors, and omissions, is not in its creed, but in its Lord and Master. In spite of all the critics, the Gospels have conveyed to the minds of millions of men a living image of Christ. They see Him there; they hear His voice; they listen, and they believe Him. It is not so much that they accept certain doctrines as taught by Him, as that they accept Him, Himself, as their Lord and their God. The sacred fire of trust in Him descended upon the Apostles, and has from them been handed on from generation to generation. It is with that living personal figure that agnosticism has to deal; and as long as the Gospels practically produce the effect of making that figure a reality to human hearts, so long will the Christian Faith, and the Christian Church, in their main characteristics, be vital and permanent forces in the world. Professor Huxley tells us, in a melancholy passage, that he cannot define 'the grand figure of Jesus.' Who shall dare to 'define' it? But saints have both written and lived an *imitatio Christi*, and men and women can feel and know what they cannot define. Professor Huxley, it would seem, would have us all wait coolly until we had solved all critical difficulties, before acting on such a belief. 'Because,' he says, 'we are often obliged, by the pressure of events, to act on very bad evidence, it does not follow that it is proper to act on such evidence when the pressure is absent.' Certainly not; but it is strange ignorance of human nature for Professor Huxley to imagine that there is no 'pressure' in this matter. It was a voice which understood the human heart better which said, 'Come unto me, all ye that labour and are heavy laden, and I will give you rest;' and the attraction of that voice outweighs many a critical difficulty under the pressure of the burdens and the sins of life.

Professor Huxley, indeed, admits, in one sentence of his article, the force of this influence on individuals.

> If (he says) a man can find a friend, the hypostasis of all his hopes, the mirror of his ethical ideal, in the pages of any, or of all, of the Gospels, let him live by faith in that ideal. Who shall, or can, forbid him? But let him not delude himself with the notion that his faith is evidence of the objective reality of that in which he trusts. Such evidence is to be obtained only by the use of the methods of science, as applied to history and to literature, and it amounts at present to very little.

Well, a single man's belief in an ideal may be very little evidence of its objective reality. But the conviction of millions of men, generation after generation, of the veracity of the four evangelical witnesses, and of the human and Divine reality of the figure they describe, has at least something of the weight of the verdict of a jury. *Securus judicat orbis terrarum*. Practically the figure of Christ lives. The Gospels have created it; and it subsists as a personal fact in life, alike among believers and unbelievers. Professor Huxley, himself, in spite of all his scepticism, appears to have his own type of this character. The apologue of the woman taken in adultery might, he says, 'if internal evidence were an infallible guide, well be affirmed to be a typical example of the teachings of Jesus.' Internal evidence may not be an infallible guide; but it certainly carries great weight, and no one has relied more upon it in these questions than the critics whom Professor Huxley quotes.

But as I should be sorry to imitate Professor Huxley, on so momentous a subject, by evading the arguments and facts he alleges, I will consider the question of external evidence on which he dwells. I must repeat that the argument of my Paper is independent of this controversy. The fact that our Lord taught and believed what Agnostics ignore is not dependent on the criticism of the four Gospels. In addition to the general evidence to which I have alluded, there is a further consideration which Professor Huxley feels it necessary to mention, but which he evades by an extraordinary inconsequence. He alleges that the story of the Gadarene swine involves fabulous matter, and that this discredits the trustworthiness of the whole Gospel record. But he says:-

> At this point a very obvious objection arises and deserves full and candid consideration. It may be said that critical scepticism carried to the length suggested is historical pyrrhonism; that if we are to altogether discredit an ancient or a modern historian because he has assumed fabulous matter to be true, it will be as well to give up paying any attention to history . . . . Of course (he acknowledges) this is perfectly true. I am afraid there is no man alive whose witness could be accepted, if the condition precedent were proof that he had never invented and promulgated a myth.

The question, then, which Professor Huxley himself raises, and which he had to answer, was this: Why is the general evidence of the Gospels, on the main facts of our Lord's life and teaching, to be discredited, even if it be true that they have invented or promulgated a myth about the Gadarene swine? What is his answer to that simple and broad question? Strange to say, absolutely none at all! He leaves this vital question without any answer, and goes back to the Gadarene swine. The question he raises is whether the supposed incredibility of the story of the Gadarene swine involves the general untrustworthiness of the story of the Gospels; and his conclusion is that it involves the incredibility of the story of the Gadarene swine. A more complete evasion of his own question it would be difficult to imagine. As Professor Huxley almost challenges me to state what I think of that story, I have only to say that I fully believe it, and moreover that Professor Huxley, in this very article, has removed the only consideration which would have been a serious obstacle to my belief. If he were prepared to say, on his high scientific authority, that the narrative involves a contradiction of established scientific truth, I could not but defer to such a decision, and I might be driven to consider those possibilities of interpolation in the narrative, which Professor Huxley is good enough to suggest to all who feel the improbability of the story too much for them. But Professor Huxley expressly says:–

> I admit I have no *à priori* objection to offer. . . . For anything I can absolutely prove to the contrary, there may be spiritual things capable of the same transmigration, with like effects. . . . So I declare, as plainly as I can, that I am unable to show cause why these transferable devils should not exist.

Very well, then, as the highest science of the day is unable to show cause against the possibility of the narrative, and as I regard the Gospels as containing the evidence of trustworthy persons who were contemporary with the events narrated, and as their general veracity carries to my mind the greatest possible weight, I accept their statement in this, as in other instances. Professor Huxley ventures 'to doubt whether at this present moment any Protestant theologian, who has a reputation to lose, will say that he believes the Gadarene Story.' He will judge whether I fall under his description; but I repeat that I believe it, and that he has removed the only objection to my believing it.

However, to turn finally to the important fact of external evidence. Professor Huxley reiterates, again and again, that the verdict of scientific criticism is decisive against the supposition that we possess in the four Gospels the authentic and contemporary evidence of known writers. He repeats, 'without the slightest fear of refutation, that the four Gospels, as they have come to us, are the work of unknown writers.' In particular, he challenges my allegation of 'M. Renan's practical surrender of the adverse case;' and he adds the following observations, to which I beg the reader's particular attention:–

> I thought (he says) I knew M. Renan's works pretty well, but I have contrived to miss this 'practical' – (I wish Dr. Wace

had defined the scope of that useful adjective) – surrender. However, as Dr. Wace can find no difficulty in pointing out the passage of M. Renan's writings, by which he feels justified in making his statement, I shall wait for further enlightenment, contenting myself, for the present, with remarking that if M. Renan were to retract and do penance in Notre Dame to-morrow for any contributions to Biblical criticism that may be specially his property, the main results of that criticism, as they are set forth in the works of Strauss, Baur, Reuss, and Volkmar, for example, would not be sensibly affected.

Let me begin then by enlightening Professor Huxley about M. Renan's surrender. I have the less difficulty in doing so as the passages he has contrived to miss have been collected by me already in a little tract on the *Authenticity of The Gospels*,[1] and in some lectures on the *Gospel and its Witnesses*;[2] and I shall take the liberty, for convenience' sake, of repeating some of the observations there made.

I beg first to refer to the preface to M. Renan's *Vie de Jésus*.[3] There M. Renan says:–

As to Luke, doubt is scarcely possible. The Gospel of St. Luke is a regular composition, founded upon earlier documents. It is the work of an author who chooses, curtails, combines. The author of this Gospel is certainly the same as the author of the Acts of the Apostles. Now, the author of the Acts seems to be a companion of St. Paul – a character which accords completely with St. Luke. I know that more than one objection may be opposed to this reasoning; but one thing at all events is beyond doubt, namely, that the author of the third Gospel and of the Acts is a man who belonged to the second apostolic generation; and this suffices for our purpose. The date of this Gospel, moreover, may be determined with sufficient precision by considerations drawn from the book itself. The twenty-first chapter of St. Luke, which is inseparable from the rest of the work, was certainly written after the siege of Jerusalem, but not long after. We are, therefore, here on

[1] Religious Tract Society.

[2] John Murray, 1883.

[3] 15th edition, p. xlix.

solid ground, for we are dealing with a work proceeding entirely from the same hand, and possessing the most complete unity.

It may be important to observe that this admission has been supported by M. Renan's further investigations, as expressed in his subsequent volume on *The Apostles*. In the Preface to that volume he discusses fully the nature and value of the narrative contained in the Acts of the Apostles, and he pronounces the following decided opinions as to the authorship of that book, and its connection with the Gospel of St. Luke (p. x *sq.*):−

> One point which is beyond question is that the Acts are by the same author as the third gospel, and are a continuation of that Gospel. One need not stop to prove this proposition, which has never been seriously contested. The prefaces at the commencement of each work, the dedication of each to Theophilus, the perfect resemblance of style and of ideas, furnish on this point abundant demonstrations.
>
> A second proposition, which has not the same certainty, but which may, however, be regarded as extremely probable, is that the author of the Acts is a disciple of Paul, who accompanied him for a considerable part of his travels.

At a first glance, M. Renan observes, this proposition appears indubitable from the fact that the author, on so many occasions, uses the pronoun 'we,' indicating that on those occasions he was one of the apostolic band by whom St. Paul was accompanied. 'One may even be astonished that a proposition apparently so evident should have found persons to contest it.' He notices, however, the difficulties which have been raised on the point, and then proceeds as follows (p. xiv):−

> Must we be checked by these objections? I think not; and I persist in believing that the person who finally prepared the Acts is really the disciple of Paul, who says 'we' in the last chapters. All difficulties, however insoluble they may appear, ought to be, if not dismissed, at least held in suspense, by an argument so decisive as that which results from the use of this word 'we.'

He then observes that MSS. and tradition combine in assigning the third Gospel to a certain Luke, and that it is scarcely conceivable that a name in other respects obscure should have been attributed to so important a work for any other reason than that it was the name of the real author. Luke, he says, had no place in tradition, in legend, or in history, when these two treatises were ascribed to him. Mr. Renan concludes in the following words; 'We think, therefore, that the author of the third Gospel and of the Acts is in all reality Luke, the disciple of Paul.'

Now let the import of these expressions of opinion be duly weighed. Of course M. Renan's judgments are not to be regarded as affording in themselves any adequate basis for our acceptance of the authenticity of the chief books of the New Testament. The Acts of the Apostles and the four Gospels bear on their face certain positive claims, on the faith of which they have been accepted in all ages of the Church; and they do not rest, in the first instance, on the authority of any modern critic. But though M. Renan would be a very unsatisfactory witness to rely upon for the purpose of positive testimony to the Gospels, his estimates of the value of modern critical objections to those sacred books have all the weight of the admissions of a hostile witness. No one doubts his familiarity with the whole range of the criticism represented by such names as Strauss and Baur, and no one questions his disposition to give full weight to every objection which that criticism can urge. Even without assuming that he is prejudiced on either one side or the other, it will be admitted on all hands that he is more favourably disposed than otherwise to such criticism as Professor Huxley relies on. When, therefore, with this full knowledge of the literature of the subject, such a writer comes to the conclusion that the criticism in question has entirely failed to make good its case on a point like that of the authorship of St. Luke's Gospel, we are at least justified in concluding that critical objections do not possess the weight which unbelievers or sceptics are wont to assign to them. M. Renan, in a word, is no adequate witness to the Gospels; but he is a very significant witness as to the value of modern critical objections to them.

Let us pass to the two other so-called 'synoptical' Gospels. With respect to St. Matthew, M. Renan says in the same preface (*Vie de Jésus*, p. lxxxi):–

To sum up, I admit the four canonical Gospels as serious documents. All go back to the age which followed the death of Jesus; but their historical value is very diverse. St. Matthew evidently deserves peculiar confidence for the discourses. Here are 'the oracles,' the very notes taken while the memory of the instruction of Jesus was living and definite. A kind of flashing brightness at once sweet and terrible, a Divine force, if I may so say, underlies these words, detaches them from the context, and renders them easily recognisable by the critic.

In respect again to St. Mark, he says (p. lxxxii):-

The Gospel of St. Mark is the one of the three Synoptics which has remained the most ancient, the most original, and to which the least of later additions have been made. The details of fact possess in St. Mark a definiteness which we seek in vain in the other Evangelists. He is fond of reporting certain sayings of our Lord in Syro-Chaldaic. He is full of minute observations, proceeding, beyond doubt, from an eye-witness. There is nothing to conflict with the supposition that this eye-witness, who had evidently followed Jesus, who had loved Him and watched Him in close intimacy, and who had preserved a vivid image of him, was the Apostle Peter himself, as Papias has it.

I call these admissions a 'practical surrender' of the adverse case, as stated by critics like Strauss and Baur, who denied that we had in the Gospels contemporary evidence, and I do not think it necessary to define the adjective, in order to please Professor Huxley's appetite for definitions. At the very least it is a direct contradiction of Professor Huxley's statement (p. 175) that we know 'absolutely nothing' of 'the originator or originators' of the narratives in the first three Gospels; and it is an equally direct contradiction of the case, on which his main reply to my paper is based, that we have no trustworthy evidence of what our Lord taught and believed.

But Professor Huxley seems to have been apprehensive that M. Renan would fail him, for he proceeds, in the passage I have quoted, to throw him over and to take refuge behind 'the main results of Biblical criticism, as they are set forth in the works of Strauss, Baur, Reuss, and Volkmar, for example.' It is scarcely comprehensible how a writer, who has acquaintance enough with this subject to venture on Professor Huxley's sweeping assertions, can have ventured to couple together those four names for such a purpose. 'Strauss, Baur, Reuss, and Volkmar!' Why, they are absolutely destructive of one another! Baur rejected Strauss's theory and set up one of his own; while Reuss and Volkmar in their turn have each dealt fatal blows at Baur's. As to Strauss, I need not spend more time on him than to quote the sentence in which Baur himself puts him out of court on this particular controversy. He says,[4] 'The chief peculiarity of Strauss's work is, that it is a criticism of the Gospel history without a criticism of the Gospels.' Strauss, in fact, explained the miraculous stories in the Gospels by resolving them into myths, and it was of no importance to this theory how the documents originated. But Baur endeavoured, by a minute criticism of the Gospels themselves, to investigate the historical circumstances of their origin; and he maintained that they were *Tendenz-Schriften*, compiled in the second century, with polemical purposes. Volkmar, however, is in direct conflict with Baur on this point, and in the very work to which Professor Huxley refers,[5] he enumerates (p. 18) among 'the written testimonies of the first century' – besides St. Paul's Epistles to the Galatians, Corinthians, and Romans, and the Apocalypse of St. John – 'the Gospel of Jesus Christ, the Son of God, according to John Mark of Jerusalem, written a few years after the destruction of Jerusalem, between the years 70 and 80 of our reckoning – about 75, probably; to be precise, about 73,' and he proceeds to give a detailed account of it, 'according to the oldest text, and particularly the Vatican text,' as indispensable to his account of Jesus of Nazareth. He treats it as written (p. 172) either by John Mark of Jerusalem himself, or by a younger friend of his. Baur, therefore, having upset Strauss, Volkmar proceeds to upset Baur; and what does Reuss do? I quote again from that splendid French edition of the Bible, on which Professor Huxley so much relies. On page 88 of Reuss's Introduction to the Synoptic Gospels, he sums up 'the results he believes to have been obtained by critical analysis,' under thirteen heads; and the following are some of them:–

[4] *Kritische Untersuchungen über die kanonischen Evangelien*, 1847, p. 41.

[5] *Jesus Nazarenus und die erste christliche Zeit*, 1882.

2. Of the three synoptic Gospels one only, that which ecclesiastical tradition agrees in attributing to Luke, has reached us in its primitive form.

3. Luke could draw his knowledge of the Gospel history partly from oral information; he was able, in Palestine itself, to receive direct communications from immediate witnesses. . . . We may think especially here of the history of the passion and the resurrection, and perhaps also of some other passages of which he is the sole narrator.

4. A book, which an ancient and respectable testimony attributes to Mark, the disciple of Peter, was certainly used by St. Luke as the principal source of the portion of his Gospel between chap. iv. 31 and ix. 50, and between xviii. 15 and xxi. 38.

5. According to all probability, the book of Mark, consulted by Luke, comprised in its primitive form what we read in the present day from Mark i. 21 to xiii. 37.

It seems unnecessary, for the purpose of estimating the value of Professor Huxley's appeal to these critics, to quote any more. It appears from these statements of Reuss that if 'the results of Biblical criticism,' as represented by him, are to be trusted, we have the whole third Gospel in its primitive form, as it was written by St. Luke; and in this, as we have seen, Reuss is in entire agreement with Renan. But besides this, a previous book written by Mark, St. Peter's disciple, was certainly in existence before Luke's Gospel, and was used by Luke; and in all probability this book was, in its primitive form, the greater part of our present Gospel of St. Mark.

Such are those 'results of Biblical criticism' to which Professor Huxley has appealed; and we may fairly judge by these not only of the value of his special contention in reply to my paper, but of the worth of the sweeping assertions he, and writers like him, are given to making about modern critical science. Professor Huxley says that we know 'absolutely nothing' about the originators of the Gospel narratives, and he appeals to criticism in the persons of Volkmar and Reuss. Volkmar says that the second Gospel is really either by St. Mark or by one of his friends, and was written about the year 75. Reuss says that the third Gospel, as we now have it, was really by St. Luke. Now Professor Huxley is, of course, entitled to his own opinion: but he is not entitled to quote authorities in support of his opinion when they are in direct opposition to it. He asserts without the slightest fear of refutation that 'the four Gospels, as they have come to us, are the work of unknown writers.' His arguments in defence of such a position will be listened to with respect: but let it be borne in mind that the opposite arguments he has got to meet are not only those of orthodox critics like myself, but those of Renan, of Volkmar, and of Reuss – I may add of Pfleiderer, well known in this country by his Hibbert Lectures, who in his recent work on original Christianity attributes most positively the second Gospel in its present form to St. Mark, and declares that there is no ground whatever for that supposition of an *Ur-Marcus* -- that is an original groundwork – from which Professor Huxley alleges that 'at the present time there is no visible escape.' If I were such an authority on morality as Professor Huxley, I might perhaps use some unpleasant language respecting this vague assumption of criticism being all on his side, when it, in fact, directly contradicts him; and his case is not the only one to which such strictures might be applied. In *Robert Elsmere*, for example, there is some vapouring about the 'great critical operation of the present century' having destroyed the historical basis of the Gospel narrative. As a matter of fact, as we have seen, the great critical operation has resulted, according to the testimony of the critics whom Professor Huxley himself selects, in establishing the fact that we possess contemporary records of our Lord's life from persons who were either eyewitnesses, or who were in direct communication with eyewitnesses, on the very scene in which it was passed. Either Professor Huxley's own witnesses are not to be trusted, or Professor Huxley's allegations are rash and unfounded. Conclusions which are denied by Volkmar, denied by Renan, denied by Reuss, are not to be thrown at our heads with a superior air, as if they could not be reasonably doubted. The great result of the critical operation of this century has, in fact, been to prove that the contention with which it started in the persons of Strauss and Baur, that we have no contemporary records of Christ's life, is wholly untenable. It has not convinced any of the living critics to whom Professor Huxley appeals; and if he, or any similar writer, still maintains such an assertion, let it be understood that he stands alone against the leading critics of Europe in the present day.

Perhaps I need say no more for the present in reply to

Professor Huxley. I have, I think, shown that he has evaded my point; he has evaded his own points; he has misquoted my words; he has misrepresented the results of the very criticism to which he appeals; and he rests his case on assumptions which his own authorities repudiate. The question he touches are very grave ones, not to be adequately treated in a Review article. But I should have supposed it a point of scientific morality to treat them, if they are to be treated, with accuracy of reference and strictness of argument.

"COWARDLY AGNOSTICISM"
A WORD WITH PROFESSOR HUXLEY
[W. H. Mallock]

"The Bishop of Peterborough departed so far from his customary courtesy and self-respect as to speak of "Cowardly Agnosticism." – Professor Huxley, *Nineteenth Century*, February, 1889, p. 170.

I welcome the discussion which, in this Review and elsewhere, has been lately revived in earnest as to the issue between positive science and theology. I especially welcome Professor Huxley's recent contribution to it, to which presently I propose to refer in detail. In that contribution – an article with the title "Agnosticism," which appeared a month or two since in *The Nineteenth Century* – I shall point out things which will probably startle the public, the author himself included, in case he cares to attend to them.

Before going further, however, let me ask and answer this question. If Professor Huxley should tell us that he does not believe in God, why should we think the statement, as coming from him, worthy of an attention which we certainly should not give it if made by a person less distinguished than himself? The answer to this question is as follows. We should think Professor Huxley's statement worth considering for two reasons. Firstly, he speaks as a man pre-eminently well acquainted with certain classes of facts. Secondly, he speaks as a man eminent, if not pre-eminent, for the vigour and honesty with which he has faced these facts, and drawn certain conclusions from them. Accordingly, when he sums up for us the main conclusions of science, he speaks not in his own name, but in the name of the physical universe, as modern science has thus far apprehended it; and similarly, when from these conclusions he reasons about religion, the bulk of the arguments which he advances against theology are in no way peculiar to himself, or gain any of their strength from his reputation; they are virtually the arguments of the whole non-

Christian world. He may possibly have, on some points, views peculiar to himself. He may also have, certain peculiar ways of stating them. But it requires no great critical acuteness, it requires only ordinary fairness, to separate those of his utterances which represent facts generally accepted, and arguments generally influential, from those which represent only some peculiarity of his own. Now all this is true not of Professor Huxley only. With various qualifications it is equally true of writers with whom Professor Huxley is apparently in constant antagonism, and who also exhibit constant antagonism amongst themselves. I am at this moment thinking of two especially – Mr. Frederic Harrison and Mr. Herbert Spencer. Mr. Harrison, in his capacity of religious teacher, is constantly attacking both Mr. Spencer and Professor Huxley. Professor Huxley repays Mr. Harrison's blows with interest; and there are certain questions of a religious and practical character as to which he and Mr. Spencer would be hardly on better terms. But underneath the several questions they quarrel about, there is a solid substructure of conclusions, methods, and arguments, as to which they all agree – agree in the most absolute way. What this agreement consists in, and what practical bearing, if taken by itself, it must have on our views of life, I shall now try to explain in a brief and unquestionable summary; and in that summary, what the reader will have before him is not the private opinion of these eminent men, but ascertained facts with regard to man and the universe; and the conclusions which, if we have nothing else to assist us, are necessarily drawn from those facts by the necessary operations of the mind. The mention of names, however, has this signal convenience. It will keep the reader convinced that I am not speaking at random, and will supply him with standards by which he can easily test the accuracy and the sufficiency of my assertions.

The case, then, of science or modern thought against theological religion or theism, and the Christian religion in particular, substantially is as follows.

In the first place, it is now an established fact that the physical universe, whether it ever had a beginning or no, is at all events of an antiquity beyond what the imagination can realise; and also, that whether or no it is limited, its extent is so vast as to be equally unimaginable. Science may not pronounce it absolutely to be either eternal or infinite, but science does say this, that so far as our faculties can carry us, they reveal to us no hint of either limit, end, or beginning.

It is further established that the stuff out of which the universe is made is the same everywhere and follows the same laws – whether at Clapham Common or in the farthest system of stars – and that this has always been so to the remotest of the penetrable abysses of time. It is established yet further that the universe in its present condition has evolved itself out of simpler conditions, solely in virtue of the qualities which still inhere in its elements, and make to-day what it is, just as they have made all yesterdays.

Lastly, in this physical universe science has included man – not alone his body, but his life and his mind also. Every operation of thought, every fact of consciousness, it has shown to be associated in a constant and definite way with the presence and with certain conditions of certain particles of matter, which are shown, in their turn, to be in their last analysis absolutely similar to the matter of gases, plants, or minerals. The demonstration has every appearance of being morally complete. The interval between mud and mind, seemingly so impassible, has been traversed by a series of closely consecutive steps. Mind, which was once thought to have descended into matter, is shown forming itself, and slowly emerging out of it. From forms of life so low that naturalists can hardly decide whether it is right to class them as plants or animals, up to the life that is manifested in saints, heroes, or philosophers, there is no break to be detected in the long process of development. There is no step in the process where science finds any excuse for postulating or even suspecting the presence of any new factor.

And the same holds good of the lowest forms of life, and what Professor Huxley calls "the common matter of the universe." It is true that experimentalists have been thus far unable to observe the generation of the former out of the latter, but this failure may be accounted for in many ways, and does nothing to weaken the overwhelming evidence of analogy that such generation really does take place or has taken place at some earlier period. "Carbonic acid, water, and ammonia," says Professor Huxley, "certainly possess no properties but those of ordinary matter . . . . But when they are brought together under certain conditions they give rise to protoplasm; and this protoplasm exhibits the phenomenon of life. I see no breach in this series of steps in molecular complication, and I am unable to understand why the language which is applicable to any one form of the series may not be used to any of the others."[1]

So much, then, for what modern science teaches us as to the Universe and the evolution of man. We will presently consider the ways, sufficiently obvious as they are, in which this seems to conflict with the ideas of all Theism and Theology. But first for a moment let us turn to what it teaches us also with regard to the history and the special claims of Christianity. Approaching Christianity on the side of its alleged history, it establishes the three following points. It shows us first that this alleged history, with the substantial truth of which Christianity stands or falls, contains a number of statements which are demonstrably at variance with fact; secondly, that it contains others which, though very probably true, are entirely misinterpreted through the ignorance of the writers who recorded them; and thirdly, that though the rest may not be demonstrably false, yet those amongst them most essential to the Christian doctrine are so monstrously improbable and so utterly unsupported by evidence that we have no more ground for believing in them than we have in the wolf of Romulus.

Such, briefly stated, are the main conclusions of science in so far as they bear on theology and the theologic conception of humanity. Let us now consider exactly what their bearing is. Professor Huxley distinctly tells us that the knowledge we have reached as to the nature of things in general does not enable us to deduce from it any absolute denial either of the existence of a personal God or of an immortal soul in man, or even of the possibility and the actual occurrence of miracles. On the contrary, he would believe to-morrow in the miraculous history of Christianity if only there were any evidence sufficiently cogent in its favour; and on the authority of Christianity he would believe in God and in man's immortality. Christianity, however, is the only religion in the world whose claims to a miraculous authority are worthy of serious consideration, and science, as we have seen, considers these claims to be unfounded. What follows is this – whether there be a God or no, and whether He has given us immortal souls or no, Science declares bluntly that He has never informed us of either fact; and if there is anything to warrant any belief in

[1] *Lay Sermons, Essays, and Reviews*, pp. 114, 117.

either it can be found only in a study of the natural Universe. Accordingly to the natural Universe science goes, and we have just seen what it finds there. Part of what it finds bears specially on the theological conception of God, and part bears specially on the theological conception of man. With regard to God, to an intelligent creator and ruler, it finds him on every ground to be a baseless and a superfluous hypothesis. In former conditions of knowledge it admits that this was otherwise – that the hypothesis then was not only natural but necessary; for there were many seeming mysteries which could not be explained without it. But now the case has been altogether reversed. One after another these mysteries have been analysed, not entirely, but to this extent at all events, that the hypothesis of an intelligent creator is not only nowhere necessary, but it generally introduces far more difficulties than it solves. Thus, though we cannot demonstrate that a creator does not exist, we have no grounds whatever for supposing that he does. With regard to man, what science finds is analogous. According to theology he is a being specially related to God, and his conduct and his destinies have an importance which dwarfs the sum of material things into insignificance. But science exhibits him in a very different light; it shows that in none of the qualities once thought peculiar to him does he differ essentially from other phenomena of the universe. It shows that just as there are no grounds for supposing the existence of a creator, so there are none for supposing the existence of an immortal human soul; whilst as for man's importance relative to the rest of the universe, it shows that, not only as an individual, but also as a race, he is less than a bubble of foam is when compared with the whole sea. The few thousand years over which history takes us are as nothing when compared with the ages for which the human race has existed. The whole existence of the human race is as nothing when compared with the existence of the earth; and the earth's history is but a second and the earth but a grain of dust in the vast duration and vast magnitude of the All. Nor is this true of the past only, it is true of the future also. As the individual dies so also will the race die; nor would a million of additional years add anything to its comparative importance. Just as it emerged out of lifeless matter yesterday, so will it sink again into lifeless matter to-morrow. Or to put the case more briefly still, it is merely one fugitive manifestation of the same matter and force, which, always obedient to the same unchanging laws, manifest themselves equally in a dung-heap, in a pig, and in a planet – matter and force which, so far as our faculties can carry us, have existed and will exist everywhere and for ever, and which nowhere, so far as our faculties avail to read them, show any sign, as a whole, of meaning, of design, or of intelligence.

It is possible that Professor Huxley, or some other scientific authority, may be able to find fault with some of my sentences or my expressions, and to show that they are not professionally or professorially accurate. If they care for such trifling criticism they are welcome to the enjoyment of it; but I defy any one to show, putting expression aside and paying attention only to the general meaning of what I have stated, that the foregoing account of what science claims to have established is not substantially true, and is not admitted to be so by any contemporary thinker who opposes science to theism, from Mr. Frederic Harrison to Professor Huxley himself.

And now let us pass on to something which in itself is merely a matter of words, but which will bring what I have said thus far into the circle of contemporary discussion. The men who are mainly responsible for having forced the above views on the world, who have unfolded to us the verities of nature and human history, and have felt constrained by these to abandon their old religious convictions – these men and their followers have by common consent agreed, in this country, to call themselves by the name of Agnostics. Now there has been much quarrelling of late amongst these Agnostics as to what Agnosticism – the thing which unites them – is. It must be obvious, however, to every impartial observer, that the differences between them are little more than verbal, and arise from bad writing rather than from different reasoning. Substantially the meaning of one and all of them is the same. Let us take for instance the two who are most ostentatiously opposed to each other, and have lately been exhibiting themselves, in this and other Reviews, like two terriers each at the other's throat. I need hardly say that I mean Professor Huxley and Mr. Harrison.

Some writers, Professor Huxley says, Mr. Harrison amongst them, have been speaking of Agnosticism as if it was a creed or a faith or a philosophy. Professor Huxley proclaims himself to be "dazed" and "bewildered" by the statements. Agnosticism, he says, is not any one of these things. It is simply – I will give his definition in his own words –

> "a method, the essence of which lies in the vigorous application of a single principle. . . . Positively, the principle may be expressed; In matters of the intellect, follow your reason as far as it will take you, without regard to any other consideration. And negatively: In matters of the intellect, do not pretend that conclusions are certain which are not demonstrated or demonstrable. That I take to be the Agnostic faith, which if a man keep whole and undefiled, he shall not be ashamed to look the universe in the face, whatever the future may have in store for him."

Now anything worse expressed than this for the purpose of the discussion he is engaged in, or indeed for the purpose of conveying his own general meaning, it is hardly possible to imagine. Agnosticism, as generally understood, may, from one point of view, be no doubt rightly described as "a method." But is it a method with no results, or with results that are of no interest? If so, there would he hardly a human being idiot enough to waste a thought upon it. The interest resides in its results, and its results solely, and specially in those results that affect our ideas about religion. Accordingly, when the word Agnosticism is now used in discussion, the meaning uppermost in the minds of those who use it is not a method, but the results of a method, in their religious bearings; and the method is of interest only in so far as it leads to these. Agnosticism means, therefore, precisely what Professor Huxley says it does not mean. It means a creed, it means a faith, it means a religious or irreligious philosophy. And this is the meaning attributed to it not only by the world at large, but in reality by Professor Huxley also quite as much as by anybody. I will not lay too much stress on the fact, that in the passage just quoted, having first fiercely declared Agnosticism to be nothing but a method, in the very next sentence he himself speaks of it as a "faith." I will pass on to a passage that is far more unambiguous. It is taken from the same essay. It is as follows:

> " 'Agnosticism [says Mr. Harrison] is a stage in the evolution of religion, an entirely negative stage, the point reached by physicists, a purely mental conclusion, with no relation to things social at all.' I am [says Professor Huxley] quite dazed

by this declaration. Are there then any 'conclusions' that are not 'purely mental'? Is there no relation to things social in 'mental conclusions' which affect men's whole conception of life? . . . 'Agnosticism is a stage in the evolution of religion.' If . . . Mr. Harrison, like most people, means by 'religion' theology, then, in my judgment, Agnosticism can be said to be a stage in its evolution only as death may be said to be the final stage in the evolution of life."

Let us consider what this means. It means precisely what every one else has all along been saying, that Agnosticism is to all intents and purposes a doctrine, a creed, a faith, or a philosophy, the essence of which is the negation of theologic religion. Now the fundamental propositions of theologic religion are these. There is a personal God, who watches over the lives of men; and there is an immortal soul in man, distinct from the flux of matter. Agnosticism, then, expressed in the briefest terms, amounts to two articles – not of belief, but of disbelief. *I do not believe in any God, personal, intelligent, or with a purpose; or, at least, with any purpose that has any concern with man. I do not believe in any immortal soul, or in any personality or consciousness surviving the dissolution of the body.*

Here I anticipate from many quarters a rebuke which men of science are very fond of administering. I shall be told that Agnostics never say "there is no God," and never say "there is no immortal soul." Professor Huxley is often particularly vehement on this point. He would have us believe that a dogmatic atheist is, in his view, as foolish as a dogmatic theist; and that an Agnostic, true to the etymology of his name, is not a man who denies God, but who has no opinion about him. But this – even if true in some dim and remote sense – is for practical purposes a mere piece of solemn quibbling, and is utterly belied by the very men who use it whenever they raise their voices to speak to the world at large. The Agnostics, if they shrink from saying that there is no God, at least tell us that there is nothing to suggest that there is one, and much to suggest that there is not. Surely, if they never spoke more strongly than this, for practical purposes this is an absolute denial. Professor Huxley, for instance, is utterly unable to demonstrate that an evening edition of the *Times* is not printed in Sirius; but if any action depended on our believing this to be true, he would certainly not hesitate to declare that it was a foolish and fantastic falsehood. Who would think the better of him – who would not think the worse – if in this matter he gravely declared himself to be an Agnostic? And precisely the same may be said of him with regard to the existence of God. For all practical purposes he is not in doubt about it. He denies it. I need not, however, content myself with my own reasoning. I find Professor Huxley himself endorsing every word that I have just uttered. He declares that such questions as are treated of in volumes of divinity, "are essentially questions of lunar politics . . . not worth the attention of men who have work to do in the world:" and he cites Hume's advice with regard to such volumes as being "most wise" – "Commit them to the flames, for they can contain nothing but sophistry and illusion."[2] Quotations of a similar import might be indefinitely multiplied; but it will be enough to add to this the statements quoted already, that Agnosticism is to theological religion what death is to life; and that physiology does but deepen and complete the gloom of the gloomiest motto of Paganism – 'Debemur morti.' If then Agnosticism is not an absolute and dogmatic denial of the fundamental propositions of theology, it differs from an absolute and dogmatic denial in a degree that is so trivial as to be, in the words of Professor Huxley himself, "not worth the attention of men who have work to do in the world." For all practical purposes and according to the real opinion of Professor Huxley and Mr. Harrison equally, Agnosticism is not doubt, is not suspension of judgment; but it is a denial of what "most people mean by religion' – that is to say, the fundamental propositions of theology, so absolute that Professor Huxley compares it to their death.

And now let us pass on to the next point in our argument, which I will introduce by quoting Professor Huxley again. This denial of the fundamental propositions of theology "affects," he says, "men's whole conception of life." Let us consider how. By the Christian world, life was thought to be important owing to its connection with some unseen universe, full of interests and issues which were too great for the mind to grasp at present, but in which, for good or evil, we should each of us one day share, taking our place amongst the awful things of eternity. But at the touch of the Agnostic doctrine this unseen universe bursts like a bubble, melts like an empty dream; and

---

[2] *Lay Sermons, Essays, and Reviews*, p. 125.

all the meaning which it once imparted to life vanishes from its surface like mists from a field at morning. In every sense but one, which is exclusively physical, man is remorselessly cut adrift from the eternal; and whatever importance or interest anything has for any of us, must be derived altogether from the shifting pains or pleasures which go to make up our momentary span of life, or the life of our race, which in the illimitable history of the All is an incident just as momentary.

Now supposing the importance and interest which life has thus lost cannot be replaced in any other way, will life really have suffered any practical change and degradation? To this question our Agnostics with one consent say Yes. Professor Huxley says that if theologic denial leads us to nothing but materialism, " the beauty of a life may be destroyed," and "its energies paralysed;"[3] and that no one not historically blind, "is likely to underrate the importance of the Christian faith as a factor in human history," or to doubt that some substitute genuine enough and worthy enough to replace it will arise."[4] Mr. Spencer says the same thing with even greater clearness: whilst as for Mr. Harrison, it is needless to quote from him; for half of what he has written is an amplification of these statements.

It is admitted, then, that life in some very practical sense, will be ruined if science, having destroyed theologic religion, cannot put, or allow to be put, some other religion in place of it. But we must not content ourselves with this general language. Life will be ruined, we say. Let us consider to what extent and how. There is a good deal in life which obviously will not be touched at all, that is to say, a portion of which is called the moral code. Theft, murder, some forms of lying and dishonesty, and some forms of sexual license, are inconsistent with the welfare of any society; and society, in self-defence, would still condemn and prohibit them, even supposing it had no more religion than a tribe of gibbering monkeys. But the moral code thus retained would consist of prohibitions only, and of such prohibitions only as could be enforced by external sanctions. Since, then, this much would survive the loss of religion, let us consider what would be lost along with it. Mr. Spencer, in general terms, has told us

---

3   *Lay Sermons, Essays, and Reviews*, p. 127.

4   "Agnosticism," *Nineteenth Century*, February, 1889, p. 191.

plainly enough. What would be lost, he says, is, in the first place, "our ideas of goodness, rectitude, or duty," or, to use a single word, "morality." This is no contradiction of what has just been said, for morality is not obedience, enforced or even instinctive, to laws which have an external sanction, but an active co-operation with the spirit of such laws, under pressure of a sanction that resides in our own wills. But not only would morality be lost, or this desire to work actively for the social good; there would be lost also every higher conception of what the social good or of what our own good is; and men would, as Mr. Spencer says, "become chiefly absorbed in the immediate and the relative."[5] Professor Huxley admits in effect precisely the same thing when he says that the tendency of systematic materialism is to "paralyse the energies of life," and "to destroy its beauty."

Let us try to put the matter a little more concisely. It is admitted by our Agnostics that the most valuable element in our life is our sense of duty, coupled with obedience to its dictates; and this sense of duty derives both its existence and its power over us from religion, and from religion alone. How it derived them from the Christian religion is obvious. The Christian religion prescribed it to us as the voice of God to the soul, appealing as it were to all our most powerful passions – to our fear, to our hope, and to our love. Hope gave it a meaning to us, and love and fear gave it a sanction. The Agnostics have got rid of God and the soul together, with the loves, and fears, and hopes by which the two were connected. The problem before them is to discover some other considerations – that is some other religion – which shall invest duty with the solemn meaning and authority derivable no longer from these. Our Agnostics, as we know, declare themselves fully able to solve it. Mr. Spencer and Mr. Harrison, though the solution of each is different, declare not only that some new religion is ready for us, but that it is a religion higher and more efficacious than the old; whilst Professor Huxley, though less prophetic and sanguine, rebukes those "who are alarmed lest man's moral

---

5   "Since the beginning Religion has had the all-essential office of preventing men from being chiefly absorbed in the relative or the immediate, and of awaking them to a consciousness of something beyond it." – *First Principles*, p. 100.

nature be debased," and declares that a wise man like Hume would merely "smile at their perplexities."[6]

Let us now consider what this new religion is – or rather these new religions, for we are offered more than one. So far as form goes, indeed, we are offered several. They can, however, all of them be resolved into two, resting on two entirely different bases, though sometimes, if not usually, offered to our acceptance in combination. One of these which is called by some of its literary adherents Positivism or the Religion of Humanity, is based on two propositions with regard to the human race. The first proposition is that it is constantly though slowly improving, and will one day reach a condition thoroughly satisfactory to itself. The second proposition is that this remote consummation can be made so interesting to the present and to all intervening generations that they will strain every nerve to bring it about and hasten it. Thus, though Humanity is admitted to be absolutely a fleeting phenomenon in the universe, it is presented relatively as of the utmost moment to the individual; and duty is supplied with a constant meaning by hope, and with a constant motive by sympathy. The basis of the other religion is not only different from this, but opposed to it. Just as this demands that we turn away from the universe, and concentrate our attention upon humanity, so that other demands that we turn away from humanity and concentrate our attention on the universe. Mr. Herbert Spencer calls this the Religion of the Unknowable; and though many Agnostics consider the name fantastic, they one and all of them, if they resign the religion of humanity, consider and appeal to this as the only possible alternative.

Now I have already in this Review, not many months since, endeavoured to show how completely absurd and childish the first of these two religions, the Religion of Humanity, is. I do not propose, therefore, to discuss it further here, but will beg the reader to consider that for the purpose of the present argument it is brushed aside like rubbish, unworthy of a second examination. Perhaps this request will sound somewhat arbitrary and arrogant, but I have something to add which will show that it is neither. The particular views which I now aim at discussing are the views represented by Professor Huxley; and Professor Huxley rejects the Religion of Humanity as com-

[6]   *Lay Sermons*, pp. 123, 124.

pletely as I do, and with a great deal less ceremony, as the following passage will demonstrate.

"Out of the darkness of pre-historic ages man emerges with the marks of his lowly origin strong upon him. He is a brute, only more intelligent than the other brutes; a blind prey to impulses which, as often as not, lead him to destruction; a victim to endless illusions which, as often as not, makes his mental existence a terror and a burden, and fill his physical life with barren toil and battle. He attains a certain degree of physical comfort, and develops a more or less workable theory of life, in such favourable situations as the plains of Mesopotamia or Egypt, and then, for thousands and thousands of years, struggles with varying fortunes, attended by infinite wickedness, bloodshed, and misery, to maintain himself at this point against the greed and the ambition of his fellow-men. He makes a point of killing or otherwise persecuting all those who try to get him to move on; and when he has moved on a step foolishly confers post-mortem deification on his victims. He exactly repeats the process with all who want to move a step yet further. And the best men of the best men of the best epoch are simply those who make the fewest blunders and commit the fewest sins. . . . I know of no study so unutterably saddening as that of the evolution of humanity as it is set forth in the annals of history; . . . [and] when the Positivists order men to worship Humanity – that is to say, to adore the generalized conception of men, as they ever have been and probably ever will be – I must reply that I could just as soon bow down and worship the generalized conception of a 'wilderness of apes.' "[7]

Let us here pause for a moment and look about us, so as to see where we stand. Up to a certain point the Agnostics have all gone together with absolute unanimity, and I conceive myself to have gone with them. They have all been unanimous in their rejection of theology, and in regarding man and the race of men as a fugitive manifestation of the all-enduring something, which always, everywhere, and in an equal degree, is behind all other phenomena of the Universe. They are unanimous also in affirming that, in spite of its fugitive character, life can afford us certain considerations and interests, which will still make duty

---

7   "Agnosticism," *Nineteenth Century*, February 1889, pp. 191, 192.

binding on us, will still give it a meaning. At this point, however, they divide into two bands. Some of them assert that the motive and the meaning of duty is to be found in the history of humanity, regarded as a single drama, with a prolonged and glorious conclusion, complete in itself, satisfying in itself, and imparting, by the sacrament of sympathy, its own meaning and grandeur to the individual life, which would else be petty and contemptible. This is what some assert, and this is what others deny. With those who assert it we have now parted company, and are standing alone with those others who deny it – Professor Huxley amongst them, as one of their chief spokesmen.

And now addressing myself to Professor Huxley in this character, let me explain what I shall try to prove to him. If he could believe in God and in the divine authority of Christ, he admits he could account for duty and vindicate a meaning for life; but he refuses to believe, even though for some reasons he might wish to do so because he holds that the beliefs in question have no evidence to support them. He complains that an English bishop has called this refusal "cowardly" – "has so far departed from his customary courtesy and self-respect as to speak of 'cowardly Agnosticism.' " I agree with Professor Huxley that, on the grounds advanced by the bishop, this epithet "cowardly" is entirely undeserved; but I propose to show him that, if not deserved on them, it is deserved on others, entirely unsuspected by himself. I propose to show that his Agnosticism is really cowardly, but cowardly not because it refuses to believe enough, but because, tried by its own standards, it refuses to deny enough. I propose to show that the same method and principle which is fatal to our faith in the God and the future life of theology, is equally fatal to anything which can give existence a meaning, or which can – to have recourse to Professor Huxley's own phrases – "prevent our 'energies' from being 'paralyzed,' and ' life's beauty' from being destroyed." I propose, in other words, to show that his agnosticism is cowardly, not because it does not dare to affirm the authority of Christ, but because it does not dare to deny the meaning and the reality of duty. I propose to show that the miserable rags of argument with which he attempts to cover the life which he professes to have stripped naked of superstition are part and parcel of that very superstition itself – that, though they are not the chasuble and the embroidered robe of theology, they are its hair shirt, and its hair shirt in tatters –

utterly useless for the purpose to which it is despairingly applied, and serving only to make the forlorn wearer ridiculous. I propose to show that in retaining this dishonoured garment, Agnosticism is playing the part of an intellectual Ananias and Sapphira; and that in professing to give up all that it cannot demonstrate, it is keeping back part, and the larger part of the price – not however from dishonesty, but from a dogged and obstinate cowardice, from a terror at facing the ruin which its own principles have made.

Some no doubt will think that this is a rash undertaking, or else that I am merely indulging in the luxury of a little rhetoric. I hope to convince the reader that the undertaking is not rash, and that I mean my expressions to be taken in a frigid and literal sense. Let me begin then by repeating one thing, which I have said before. When I say that Agnosticism is fatal to our conception of duty, I do not mean that it is fatal to those broad rules and obligations which are obviously necessary to any civilised society, which are distinctly defensible on obvious utilitarian rounds, and which, speaking generally, can be enforced by external sanctions. These rules and obligations have existed from the earliest ages of social life, and are sure to exist as long as social life exists. But so far are they from giving life a meaning, that on Professor Huxley's own showing they have barely made life tolerable. A general obedience to them for thousands and thousands of years, has left "the evolution of man, as set forth in the annals of history," the "most unutterably saddening study" that Professor Huxley knows. From the earliest ages to the present – Professor Huxley admits this – the nature of man has been such that, despite their laws and their knowledge, most men have made themselves miserable by yielding to "greed" and to "ambition," and by practising "infinite wickedness." They have proscribed their wisest when alive, and accorded them a "foolish" hero-worship when dead. Infinite wickedness, blindness, and idiotic emotion have then, according to Professor Huxley's deliberate estimate, marked and marred men from the earliest ages to the present; and he deliberately says also, that "as men ever have been, they probably ever will be."

To do our duty, then, evidently implies a struggle. The impulses usually uppermost in us have to be checked, or chastened, by others; and these other impulses have to be generated, by fixing our attention on considerations which lie somehow beneath the surface. If this were not so, men would always have done their duty; and their history would not have been "unutterably saddening," as Professor Huxley says it has been. What sort of considerations, then, must those we require be? Before answering this question, let us pause for a moment, and with Professor Huxley's help, let us make ourselves quite clear what duty is. I have already showed that it differs from a passive obedience to external laws, in being a voluntary and active obedience to a law that is internal; but its logical aim is analogous – that is to say the good of the community, ourselves included. Professor Huxley describes it thus – "to devote oneself to the service of humanity including intellectual and moral self-culture under that name;" "to pity and help all men to the best of one's ability;" "to be strong and patient," "to be ethically pure and noble;" and to push our devotion to others "to the extremity of self-sacrifice." All these phrases are Professor Huxley's own. They are plain enough in themselves; but to make what he means yet plainer, he tells us that the best examples of the duty he has been describing, are to be found amongst Christian martyrs, and saints such as Catherine of Sienna, and above all in the ideal Christ – "the noblest ideal of humanity," he calls it, "which mankind has yet worshipped." Finally he says that religion, properly understood, is simply the reverence and love for [this] ethical ideal, and the desire to realise that ideal in life, which every man ought to feel." That man "ought" to feel this desire, and "ought to act on it, "is," he says, "surely indisputable," and "Agnosticism has no more to do with it than it has with music or painting."

Here then we come to something at last which Professor Huxley, despite all his doubts, declares to be certain – to a conclusion which Agnosticism itself, according to his view, admits to be "indisputable." Agnosticism, however, as he has told us already, lays it down as a "fundamental axiom" that no conclusions are indisputable but such as are "demonstrated or demonstrable." The conclusion, therefore, that we ought to do our duty, and that we ought to experience what Professor Huxley calls "religion," is evidently a conclusion which, in his opinion, is demonstrated or demonstrable with the utmost clearness and cogency. Before, however, enquiring how far this is the case, we must state the conclusion in somewhat different terms, but still in terms which we have Professor Huxley's explicit warrant for using. Duty is a thing which men in general, "as they always have been, and probably ever will be," have lamentably failed to do, and to do which is very difficult, going as it does against some of the strongest and most victorious instincts of our nature. Professor Huxley's conclusion then must be expressed thus: "We ought to do something which most of us do not do, and which we cannot do without a severe and painful struggle, often involving the extremity of self-sacrifice."

And now, such being the case, let us proceed to this crucial question – What is the meaning of the all-important word "*ought?*" It does not mean merely that on utilitarian grounds the conduct in question can be defended as tending to certain beneficent results. This conclusion would be indeed barren and useless. It would merely amount to saying that some people would be happier if other people would for their sake consent to be miserable; or that men would be happier as a race if their instincts and impulses were different from "what they always have been and probably ever will be." When we say that certain conduct ought to be followed, we do not mean that its ultimate results can be shown to be beneficial to other people, but that they can be exhibited as desirable to the people to whom the conduct is recommended – and not only as desirable, but as desirable in a pre-eminent degree – desirable beyond all other results that are immediately beneficial to themselves. Now the positivists, or any other believers in the destinies of Humanity, absurd as their beliefs may be, still have in their beliefs a means by which, theoretically, duty could be thus recommended. According to them our sympathy with others is so keen, and the future in store for our descendents is so satisfying, that we have only to think of this future and we shall burn with a desire to work for it. But Professor Huxley, and those who agree with him, utterly reject both of these suppositions. They say, and very rightly, that our sympathies are limited; and that the blissful future, which it is supposed will appeal to them, is moonshine. The utmost, then, in the way of objective results, that any of us can accomplish by following the path of duty, is not only little in itself, but there is no reason for supposing that it will contribute to anything great. On the contrary, it will only contribute to something which, as a whole, is "unutterably saddening."

Let us suppose then an individual with two ways of life open to him – the way of ordinary self-indulgence, and the way of pain, effort, and self-sacrifice. The first seems to him obviously the most advantageous; but he has heard so much fine talk in favour of the second, that he thinks it at least worth considering. He goes, we will suppose, to Professor Huxley, and asks to have it demonstrated that this way of pain is preferable. Now what answer to that could Professor Huxley make – he, or any other Agnostic who agrees with him? He has made several answers. I am going to take them one by one; and whilst doing to each of them, as I hope, complete justice, to show that they are not only absolutely and ridiculously impotent to prove what is demanded of them, but they do not even succeed in touching the question at issue.

One of the answers hardly needs considering, except to show to what straits the thinker must be put who uses it. A man, says Professor Huxley, ought to choose the way of pain and duty, because it conduces in some small degree to the good of others; and to do good to others ought to be his predominant desire, or, in other words, his religion. But the very fact in human nature that makes the question at issue worth arguing, is the fact that men naturally do not desire the good of others, or, at least, desire it in a very lukewarm way; and every consideration which the Positivist school advances to make the good of others attractive and interesting to ourselves Professor Huxley dismisses with what we may call an uproarious contempt. If, then, we are not likely to be nerved to our duty by a belief that duty done tends to produce and hasten a change that shall really make the whole human lot beautiful, we are not likely to be nerved to it by the belief that its utmost possible result will be some partial and momentary benefit to a portion of "a wilderness of apes." The Positivist says to the men of the present day, "Work hard at the foundation of things social; for on these foundations one day will arise a glorious edifice." Professor Huxley tells them to work equally hard, only he adds that the foundation will never support anything better than pig-sties. His attempt, then, on social grounds, to make duty binding, and give force to the moral imperative, is merely a fragment of Mr. Harrison's system, divorced from anything that gave it a theoretical meaning. Professor Huxley has shattered that system against the hard rock of reality, and this is one of the pieces which he has picked up out of the mire.

The social argument, then, we may therefore put aside, as good perhaps for showing what duty is, but utterly useless for creating any desire to do it. Indeed, to render Professor Huxley justice, it is not the argument on which he mainly relies. The argument, or rather the arguments, on which he mainly relies have no direct connection with things social at all. They seek to create a religion, or to give a meaning to duty, by dwelling on man's connection, not with his fellow-men, but with the universe, and thus developing in the individual a certain ethical self-reverence, or rather, perhaps, preserving his existing self-reverence from destruction. How any human being who pretends to accurate thinking can conceive that these arguments would have the effect desired – that they would either tend in any way to develop self-reverence of any kind, or that this self-reverence, if developed, could connect itself with practical duty, passes my comprehension. Influential and eminent men, however, declare that such is their opinion; and for that reason the arguments are worth analysing. Mr. Herbert Spencer is here in almost exact accord with Professor Huxley; we will therefore begin by referring to his way of stating the matter.

"We are obliged," he says, "to regard every phenomenon as a manifestation of some Power by which we are acted on; though Omnipresence is unthinkable, yet, as experience discloses no bounds to the diffusion of phenomena, we are unable to think of limits to the presence of this power; whilst the criticisms of science teach us that this Power is Incomprehensible. And this consciousness of an Incomprehensible Power, called Omnipresent from inability to assign its limits, is just that consciousness on which religion dwells."[8] Now Professor Huxley, it will be remembered, gives an account of religion quite different. He says it is a desire to realise a certain ideal in life. His terminology therefore differs from that of Mr. Spencer; but of the present matter, as the following quotation will show, his view is substantially the same.

"Let us suppose," he says, "that knowledge is absolute, and not relative, and therefore that our conception of matter represents that which really is. Let us suppose further that we do know more of cause and effect than a certain succession; and I for my part do not see what escape there is from utter materialism and necessarianism." And this materialism, were it really what science forces on us, he admits would amply justify

---

[8] *First Principles*, p. 99.

the darkest fears that are entertained of it. It would "drown man's soul," "impede this freedom," "paralyze his energies," "debase his moral nature," and "destroy the beauty of his life."[9] But, Professor Huxley assures us, these dark fears are groundless. There is indeed only one avenue of escape from them; but that avenue Truth opens to us.

> "For," he says, "after all, what do we know of this terrible 'matter,' except as a name for the unknown and hypothetical cause of states of our own consciousness? And what do we know of that 'spirit' over whose extinction by matter a great lamentation is arising . . . except that it also is a name for an unknown and hypothetical cause of condition of states of consciousness? . . . And what is the dire necessity and iron law under which men groan? Truly, most gratuitously invented bugbears. I suppose if there be an 'iron' law it is that of gravitation; and if there be a physical necessity it is that a stone unsupported must fall to the ground. But what is all we really know and can know about the latter phenomena? Simply that in all human experience, stones have fallen to the ground under these conditions; that we have not the smallest reason for believing that any stone so circumstanced will not fall to the ground; and that we have, on the contrary, every reason to believe that it will so fall. . . . But when, as commonly happens, we change *will* into *must*, we introduce an idea of necessity which . . . has no warranty that I can discover anywhere. . . . Force I know, and Law I know; but who is this Necessity, save an empty shadow of my own mind's throwing?"

Let us now compare the statements of these two writers. Each states that the reality of the universe is unknowable; that just as surely as matter is always one aspect of mind, so mind is equally one aspect of matter; and that if it is true to say that the thoughts of man are material, it is equally true to say that the earth from which man was taken, is spiritual. Further, from these statements each writer deduces a similar moral. The only difference between them is, that Mr. Spencer puts it positively, and Professor Huxley negatively. Mr. Spencer says that a consciousness of the unknowable nature of the universe, fills the mind with religious emotion. Professor Huxley says that

---

[9] *Lay Sermons*, pp. 122, 123, 127.

the same consciousness will preserve from destruction the emotion that already exists in it. We will examine the positive and negative propositions in order, and see what bearing, if any, they have on practical life.

Mr. Spencer connects his religion with practical life thus. The mystery and immensity of the All, and our own inseparable connection with it, deepen and solemnize our own conception of ourselves. They make us regard ourselves as "elements in that great evolution of which the beginning and the end are beyond our knowledge or conception;" and in especial they make us so regard our "own innermost convictions."

> "It is not for nothing," says Mr. Spencer, "that a man has in him these sympathies with some principles, and repugnance to others. . . . He is a descendant of the past; he is a parent of the future; and his thoughts are as children born to him, which he may not carelessly let die. He, like every other man, may properly consider himself as one of the myriad agencies through whom works the Unknown Cause: and when the Unknown Cause produces in him a certain belief, he is thereby authorized to profess and act with this belief."[10]

In all the annals of intellectual self-deception, it would he hard to find anything to outdo, or even to approach this. What a man does or thinks, what he professes or acts out, can have no effect whatever, conceivable to ourselves, beyond such effects as it produces within the limits of this planet; and hardly any effect, worth our consideration, beyond such as it produces on himself and a few of his fellow-men. Now, how can any of these effects be connected with the evolution of the universe in such a way as to enable a consciousness of the universe to inform us that one set of effects should be aimed at by us rather than another? The Positivists say that our aim should be the progress of man; and that, as I have said, forms a standard of duty, though it may not supply a motive. But what has the universe to do with the progress of man? Does it know anything about it? or care anything about it? Judging from the language of Mr. Spencer and Professor Huxley, one would certainly suppose that it did. Surely, in that case, here is anthropomorphism with a vengeance. "It is not for nothing,"

[10] *First Principles*, p. 123.

says Mr. Spencer, "that the Unknowable has implanted in a man certain impulses." What is this but the old theologic doctrine of design? Can anything be more inconsistent with the entire theory of the Evolutionist? Mr. Spencer's argument means, if it means anything, that the Unknowable has implanted in us one set of sympathies in a sense in which it has not implanted others: else the impulse to deny one's belief, and not to act on it, which many people experience, would be authorised by the Unknowable as much as the impulse to profess it, and to act on it. And according to Mr. Spencer's entire theory, according to Professor Huxley's entire theory, according to the entire theory of modern science, it is precisely this that is the case. If it is the fact that the Unknowable works through any of our actions, it works through all alike, bad, good, and indifferent, through our lies as well as through our truth-telling, through our injuries to our race as well as through our benefits to it. The attempt to connect the well-being of humanity with any general tendency observable in the universe, is in fact, on Agnostic principles, as hopeless as an attempt to get, in a balloon, to Jupiter. It is utterly unfit for serious men to talk about; and its proper place, if anywhere, would be in one of Jules Verne's story-books. The destinies of mankind, so far as we have any means of knowing, have as little to do with the course of the Unknowable as a whole, as the destinies of an ant-hill in South Australia have to do with the question of Home Rule for Ireland.

Or even supposing the Unknowable to have any feeling in the matter, how do we know that its feeling would be in our favour, and that it would not be gratified by the calamities of humanity, rather than by its improvement? Or here is a question which is more important still. Supposing the Unknowable did desire our improvement, but we, as Professor Huxley says of us, were obstinately bent against being improved; what could the Unknowable do to us, for thus thwarting its wishes?

And this leads us to another aspect of the matter. If consciousness of the Unknowable does not directly influence action, it may yet be said that the contemplation of the universe as the wonderful garment of this unspeakable mystery, is calculated to put the mind into a serious and devout condition, which would make it susceptible to the solemn voice of duty. How any devotion so produced could have any connection with duty I confess I am at a loss to see. But I need not dwell on that point, for what I wish to show is this, that contemplation of the Unknowable, from the Agnostic's point of view, is not calculated to produce any sense of devoutness at all. Devoutness is made up of three things, fear, love, and wonder; but were the Agnostic's thoughts really controlled by his own principles (which they are not) not one of these emotions could the Unknowable possibly excite in him. It need hardly be said that he has no excuse for loving it, for his own first principles forbid him to say that it is lovable, or that it possesses any character, least of all any anthropomorphic character. But perhaps it is calculated to excite fear or awe in him. This idea is more plausible than the other. The universe as compared with man is a revelation of forces that are infinite, and it may be said that surely these have something awful and impressive in them. There is, however, another side to the question. This universe represents not only infinite forces, but it represents also infinite impotence. So long as we conform ourselves to certain rules we may behave as we like for anything it can do to us. We may look at it with eyes of adoration, or make faces at it, and blaspheme it, but for all its power it cannot move a finger to touch us. Why, then, should a man be in awe of thus lubberly All, whose blindness and impotence are at least as remarkable as its power, and from which man is as absolutely safe as a mouse in a hole is from a lion? But there still remains the emotion of wonder to be considered. Is not the universe calculated to excite our wonder? From the Agnostic point of view we must certainly say No. The further science reveals to us the constitution of things the feeling borne in on us more and more strongly is this, that it is not wonderful that things happen as they do, but that it would be wonderful if they happened otherwise: whilst as for the Unknown Cause that is behind what science reveals to us, we cannot wonder at that, for we know nothing at all about it, and if there is any wonder involved in the matter at all, it is nothing but wonder at our own ignorance.

So much, then, for our mere emotions towards the Unknowable. There still remains, however, one way more in which it is alleged that our consciousness of it can be definitely connected with duty; and this is the way which our Agnostic philosophers most commonly have in view, and to which they allude most frequently. I allude to the search after scientific truth and the proclamation of it, regardless of consequences. Whenever the Agnostics are pressed as to the consequences of their principles it is on this conception of duty that they invariably fall back. Mr. Herbert Spencer, on his own behalf, expresses the position thus –

> "The highest truth he sees will the wise man fearlessly utter, knowing that, let what may come of it, he is thus playing his right part in the world, knowing that if he can effect the change [in belief] he aims at, well; if not, well also; though not *so* well."[11]

After what has been said already it will not be necessary to dwell long on this astonishing proposition. A short examination will suffice to show its emptiness. That a certain amount of truth in social intercourse is necessary for the continuance of society, and that a large number of scientific truths are useful in enabling us to add to our material comforts is, as Professor Huxley would say, "surely indisputable." And truth thus understood it is "surely indisputable" that we should cultivate. The reason is obvious. Such truth has certain social consequences, certain things that we all desire come of it; but the highest truth which Mr. Spencer speaks of stands, according to him, on a wholly different basis, and we are to cultivate it, not because of its consequences, but in defiance of them. And what are its consequences, so far as we can see? Professor Huxley's answer is this. "I have had, and have, the firmest conviction that . . . the *verace via*, the straight road, has led nowhere else but into the dark depths of a wild and tangled forest." Now if this be the case what possible justification can there be for following this *verace via*? In what sense is the man who follows it playing "his right part in the world?" And when Mr. Spencer says, with regard to his conduct, " it is well," with whom is it well, or in what sense is it well? We can use such language with any warrant or with any meaning only on the supposition that the universe, or the Unknowable as manifested through the universe, is concerned with human happiness in some special way, in which it is not concerned with human misery, and that thus our knowledge of it must somehow make men happier, even though it leads them into a wild and tangled forest. It is certain that our devotion to truth will not benefit the universe;

---

11   *First Principles*, p. 123.

the only question is, will knowledge of the universe, beyond a certain point, benefit us? But the supposition just mentioned is merely theism in disguise. It imputes to the Unknowable design, purpose, and affection. In every way it is contrary to the first principles of Agnosticism. Could we admit it, then devotion to truth might have all the meaning that Mr. Spencer claims for it: but if this supposition is denied, as all Agnostics deny it, this devotion to truth, seemingly so noble and so unassailable, sinks to a superstition more abject, more meaningless, and more ridiculous than that of any African savage, grovelling and mumbling before his fetish.

We have now passed under review the main positive arguments by which our Agnostics, whilst dismissing the existence of God as a question of lunar politics, endeavour to exhibit the reality of religion, and of duty, as a thing that is "surely indisputable." We will now pass on to their negative arguments. Whilst by positive arguments they endeavour to prove that duty and religion are realities, by their negative arguments they endeavour to prove that duty and religion are not impossibilities. We have seen how absolutely worthless to their cause are the former; but if the former are worthless, the latter are positively fatal.

What they are the reader has already seen. I have taken the statement of them from Professor Huxley, but Mr. Spencer uses language almost precisely similar. These arguments start with two admissions. Were all our actions linked one to another but mechanical necessity, it is admitted that responsibility and duty would be no longer conceivable. Our "energies," as Professor Huxley admits, would be "paralysed" by "utter necessarianism." Further, did our conception of matter represent a reality, were matter low and gross, as we are accustomed to think of it, then man, as the product of matter, would be low and gross also, and heroism and duty would be really successfully degraded, by being reduced to questions of carbon and ammonia. But from all of these difficulties Professor Huxley professes to extricate us. Let us look back at the arguments by which he considers that he has done so.

We will begin with his method of liberating us from the "iron" law of necessity, and thus giving us back our freedom and moral character. He performs this feat, or rather, he thinks he has performed it, by drawing a distinction between what *will* happen and what *must* happen. On this distinction his entire position is based. Now in every argument used by any sensible man there is probably some meaning. Let us try fairly to see what is the meaning in this. I take it that the idea at the bottom of Professor Huxley's mind is as follows. Though all our scientific reasoning presupposes the uniformity of the universe, we are unable to assert of the reality behind the universe, that it might not manifest itself in ways by which all present science would be baffled. But what has an idea like this to do with any practical question? So far as man, and man's will, is concerned, we have to do only with the universe as we know it; and the only knowledge we have of it, worth calling knowledge, involves, as Professor Huxley is constantly telling us, "the great act of faith," which leads us to take what has been as a certain index of what will be. Now, with regard to this universe, Professor Huxley tells us that the progress of science has always meant, and "means now more than ever," "the extension of the province of . . . causation, and . . . the banishment of spontaneity."[12] And this applies, as he expressly says, to human thought and action as much as to the flowering of a plant. Just as there can be no voluntary action without volition, so there can be no volition without some preceding cause. Accordingly, if a man's condition at any given moment were completely known, his actions could be predicted with as much or with as little certainty as the fall of a stone could be predicted if released from the hand that held it. Now Professor Huxley tells us that, with regard to certainty, we are justified in saying that the stone will fall; and we should, therefore, be justified in saying similarly of the man, that he will act in such and such a manner. Whether theoretically we are absolutely certain is no matter. We are absolutely certain for all practical purposes, and the question of human freedom is nothing if not practical. What then is gained – is anything gained – is the case in any way altered – by telling ourselves that though there is certainty in the case, there is no necessity? Suppose I held a loaded pistol to Professor Huxley's ear, and offered to pull the trigger, should I reconcile him to the operation by telling him that though it certainly would kill him, there was not the least necessity that it should do so? And with regard to volition and action, as the result of preceding causes, is not the case precisely similar? Let Professor Huxley turn to all the past

---

12   *Lay Sermons*, p. 123.

actions of humanity. Can he point to any smallest movement of any single human being, which has not been the product of causes, which in their turn have been the product of other causes? Or can he point to any causes which, under given conditions, could have produced any effects other than those they have produced, unless he uses the word *could* in the foolish and fantastic sense which would enable him to say that unsupported stones could possibly fly upwards? For all practical purposes the distinction between *must* and *will* is neither more nor less than a feeble and childish sophism. Theoretically no doubt it will bear this meaning – that the Unknowable might have so made man, that at any given moment he could be a different being: but it does nothing to break the force of what all science teaches us – that man, formed as he is, cannot act otherwise than as he does. The universe may have no necessity at the back of *it*; but its present and its past alike are a necessity at the back of *us*; and it is not necessity, but it is doubt of necessity, that is really "the shadow of our own mind's throwing."

And now let us face Professor Huxley's other argument, which is to save life from degradation by taking away the reproach from matter. If it is true, he tells us, to say that everything, mind included, is matter, it is equally true to say that everything, matter included, is mind; and thus, he argues, the dignity we all attribute to mind, at once is seen to diffuse itself throughout the entire universe. Mr. Herbert Spencer puts the same view thus.

> "Such an attitude of mind [contempt for matter and dread of materialism] is significant not so much of a reverence for the Unknown Cause, as of an irreverence for those familiar forms in which the Unknown Cause is manifested to us.[13] . . . But whoever remembers that the forms of existence of which the uncultivated speak with so much scorn . . . are found to be the more marvellous the more they are investigated, and are also found to be in their natures absolutely incomprehensible . . . will see that the course proposed [a reduction of all things to terms of matter] does not imply a degradation of the so-called higher, but an elevation of the so-called lower."

[13]   *First Principles*, p. 556.

The answer to this argument, so far as it touches any ethical or religious question, is at once obvious and conclusive. The one duty of ethics and of religion is to draw a distinction between two states of emotion and two courses of action – to elevate the one and to degrade the other. But the argument we are now considering, though undoubtedly true in itself, has no bearing on this distinction whatever. It is invoked to show that religion and duty remain spiritual in spite of all materialism; but it ends, with unfortunate impartiality, in showing the same thing of vice and of cynical worldliness. If the life of Christ is elevated by being seen in this light, so also is the life of Casanova; and it is as impossible in this way to make the one higher than the other as it is to make one man higher than another by taking them both up in a balloon.

I have now gone through the whole case for duty and for religion, as stated by the Agnostic school, and have shown that as thus stated, there is no case at all. I have shown their arguments to be so shallow, so irrelevant, and so contradictory, that they never could have imposed themselves on the men who condescend to use them, if these men, upon utterly alien grounds, had not pledged themselves to the conclusion which they invoke the arguments to support. Something else, however, still remains to be done. Having seen how Agnosticism fails to give a basis to either religion or duty, I will point out to the reader how it actively and mercilessly destroys them. Religion and duty, as has been constantly made evident in the course of the foregoing discussion, are, in the opinion of the Agnostics, inseparably connected. Duty is a course of conduct which is more than conformity to human law; religion consists of the emotional reasons for pursuing that conduct. Now these reasons on the showing of the Agnostics themselves, are reasons that do not lie on the surface of the mind. They have to be sought out in moods of devoutness and abstraction, and the more we dwell on them, the stronger they are supposed to become. They lie above and beyond the ordinary things of life; but after communing with them, it is supposed that we shall descend to these things with our purposes sharpened and intensified. It is easy to see, however, if we divest ourselves of all prejudice, and really conceive ourselves to be convinced of nothing which is not demonstrable by the methods of Agnostic science, that the more we dwell on the Agnostic doctrine of the universe, the less and not the more shall duty seem to be binding on us.

I have said that Agnosticism can supply us with no religion. Perhaps I was wrong in saying so, for if we will but invert the supposed tendency of religion, it can and it will supply us with a religion indeed. It will supply us with a religion which, if we describe it in theological language, we may with literal accuracy describe as the religion of the devil – of the devil, the spirit which denies. Instead of telling us of duty, that it has a meaning which does not lie on the surface, such meaning as may lie on the surface it will utterly take away. It will indeed tell us that the soul which sins shall die; but it will tell us in the same breath that the soul which does not sin, shall die the same death. Instead of telling us that we are responsible for our actions, it will tell us that if anything is responsible for them it is the blind and unfathomable universe; and if we are asked to repent of any shameful sins we have committed, it will tell us we might as well be repentant about the structure of the solar system. These meditations, these communings with scientific truth, will be the exact inverse of the religious meditations of the Christian. Every man, no doubt, has two voices – the voice of self-indulgence or indifference, and the voice of effort and duty; but whereas the religion of the Christian enabled him to silence the one, the religion of the Agnostic will for ever silence the other. I say for ever, but I probably ought to correct myself. Could the voice be silenced for ever, then there might be peace in the sense in which Roman conquerors gave the name of peace to solitude. But it is more likely that the voice will still continue, together with the longing expressed by it, only to feel the pains of being again and again silenced, or sent back to the soul saying bitterly, I am a lie.

Such then is really the result of Agnosticism on life, and the result is so obvious to any one who knows how to reason, that it could be hidden from nobody, except by one thing, and that is the cowardice characteristic of all our contemporary Agnostics. They dare not face what they have done. They dare not look fixedly at the body of the life which they have pierced.

And now comes the final question to which all that I have thus far urged has been leading. What does theologic religion answer to the principles and to the doctrines of Agnosticism? In contemporary discussion the answer is constantly obscured, but it is of the utmost importance that it should be given clearly. It says this: If we start from and are faithful to the Agnostic's fundamental principles, that nothing is to be regarded as certain which is not either demonstrated or demonstrable, then the denial of God is the only possible creed for us. To the methods of science nothing in this universe gives any hint of either a God or a purpose. Duty, and holiness, aspiration, and love of truth, are "merely shadows of our own mind's throwing," but shadows which, instead of making the reality brighter, only serve to make it more ghastly and hideous. Humanity is a bubble; the human being is a puppet, cursed with the intermittent illusion that he is something more, and roused from this illusion with a pang every time it flatters him. Now from this condition of things is there no escape? Theological religion answers, There is one, and only one, and this is the repudiation of the principle on which all Agnosticism rests.

Let us see what this repudiation amounts to, and we shall then realise what, in the present day, is the intellectual basis which theological religion claims. Theologic religion does not say that within limits the Agnostic principle is not perfectly valid and has not led to the discovery of a vast body of truth. But what it does say is this: that the truths which are thus discovered are not the only truths which are certainly and surely discoverable. The fundamental principle of Agnosticism is that nothing is certainly true but such truths as are demonstrated or demonstrable. The fundamental principle of theologic religion is, that there are other truths of which we can be equally or even more certain and that these are the only truths that give life a meaning and redeem us from the body of death. Agnosticism says nothing is certain which cannot be proved by science. Theologic religion says, nothing which is important can be. Agnosticism draws a line round its own province of knowledge, and beyond that it declares is the unknown void which thought cannot enter, and in which belief cannot support itself. Where Agnosticism pauses, there Religion begins. On what seems to science to be unsustaining air, it lays its foundations – it builds up its fabric of certainties. Science regards them as dreams, as an "unsubstantial pageant;" and yet even to science Religion can give some account of them. Professor Huxley says, as we have seen, that "from the nature or ratiocination," it is obvious that it must start "from axioms which cannot be demonstrated by ratiocination;" and that in science it must start with "one great act of faith" – faith in the uniformity of nature. Religion replies to science: "And I too start with a faith in one thing. I start with a faith which you too profess to hold – faith in the meaning of duty and the infinite importance of life; and out of that faith my whole fabric of certainties, one after the other, is reared by the hands of reason. Do you ask for proof? Do you ask for verification? I can give you one only, which you may take or leave as you choose. Deny the certainties which I declare to be certain – deny the existence of God, deny man's freedom and immortality, and by no other conceivable hypothesis can you vindicate for man's life any possible meaning, or save it from the degradation at which you profess to feel so aghast." "Is there no other way," I can conceive Science asking, "no other way by which the dignity of life may be vindicated, except this – the abandonment of my one fundamental principle? Must I put my lips, in shame and humiliation, to the cup of faith I have so contemptuously cast away from me? May not this cup pass from me? Is there salvation in no other?" And to this question, without passion or preference, the voice of reason and logic pitilessly answers "No."

Here is the dilemma which men, sooner or later, will see before them, in all its crudeness and nakedness, cleared from the rags with which the cowardice of contemporary Agnosticism has obscured it; and they will then have to choose one alternative or the other. What their choice will be I do not venture to prophesy; but I will venture to call them happy if their choice prove to be this: To admit frankly that their present canon of certainty, true so far as it goes, is only the pettiest part of truth, and that the deepest certainties are those which, if tried by this canon, are illusions. To make this choice a struggle would be required with pride, and with what has long passed for enlightenment; and yet when it is realised what depends on the struggle, there are some at least who will think that it must end successfully. The only way by which, in the face of science, we can ever logically arrive at a faith in life, is by the commission of what many at present will describe as an intellectual suicide. I do not for a moment admit that such an expression is justifiable, but if I may use it provisionally, and because it points to the temper at present prevalent, I shall be simply pronouncing the judgment of frigid reason in saying that it is only through the grave and gate of death that the spirit of man can pass to its resurrection.

ARE AGNOSTICS IN GOOD FAITH?
A THEOLOGICAL ENQUIRY
[Charles Coupe]

Ever since the religion of Jesus Christ first reached its adult stature and stood four-square to resist the winds of adverse teachings, there has never perhaps been a period when reasoned unbelief in God was wider spread and deeper seated than in these latter days. Atheism has, indeed, ere this been louder and more obtrusive. It has never been more subtle or more seductive. The 18th century was certainly blatant in its unbelief – violent, intolerant, unmeasured. It tore down the altar of "the incorruptible God," and bowed the knee before the altar of an only too corruptible woman. It broke in pieces the figures of Christ and demolished the images of saints, while it guillotined those who practised the religion of Christ and emulated the holiness of the saints. But the unbelief of the 18th century made no lasting impression on the European mind. It was too gross and repulsive to last. It enthroned indeed a "goddess of Reason," but its foundation was ridicule rather than reason, and when the whirlwind of passion that had fanned it into fierce life subsided, it was smothered out beneath the load of its own grotesque and indecent extravagances. But the Agnosticism of our age prides itself on being, above all things, moderate, forbearing, reasonable, refined. It professes to entertain no prejudice against God – if He exist; and to have no disposition to deny His existence – if it can be proved. Modern unbelief, in England at least, is calm and dispassionate. It will weigh evidence as well for, as against, God. It aspires to the character of judge, and disclaims the attitude of counsel. And, indeed, such is its large impartiality that it brings the rush-light of its intelligence to the quest for data to establish the existence of the Almighty, and sorrows like another Diogenes when, lantern in hand at noonday, he sought in the market-place of Athens for a man, and bemoaned his inability to find one. English Agnosticism is, then, a tolerant philosophy.[1] It interferes with no man's religious belief; nay, rather it inclines to envy him his capacity to believe. So far from seeking by force to abolish faith in Christ or to prevent the practice of the Christian worship, it professes to feel an earnest respect for the one and to find a real utility in the other. For it holds that the man Jesus – though deluded by a dream that he was God – worked with a well-directed enthusiasm at the mental, moral, and social regeneration of the world, and thus deserved a niche amid the best and noblest of Humanity's sons;[2] while of his religion it may be said that the pomp and pageantry of its gorgeous ceremonial minister to that sentimental craving for ritual, implanted by a capricious evolution in the sensuous part of human nature.

The unbelief, then, of to-day, compared on its negative side with the unbelief of the 18th century, is a subtler influence and a stronger power for good or evil, because it is so moderate and so liberal and so tolerant of opinions that clash with its own. That it is, in some degree a power for good we English Catholics must needs allow. For we now meet with a large measure of liberty formerly denied to us, and are left to worship God in our own fashion, unvexed and unmolested. The Catholic Church in England and America is prosperous and not afflicted; while the Catholic Church, on the Continent – under a régime of Liberty, Fraternity, and Equality – is, on every side, brutally plundered and trampled under foot. This fair treatment English speaking Catholics owe in great part to Agnosticism. Let us be grateful for it. Not that Agnosticism loves us; it is merely indifferent towards us. Yet if indifferentism in the sphere of religion is doing huge harm, that is no reason to deny that it is also doing, indirectly, great good. And of this good we are reaping the benefit.

Modern unbelief, then, by its moderation allays opposition. But it does more. There are elements in it well calculated to make for it, if not partizans, at any rate friends even among nominal opponents. For it appeals to human respect and to

---

[1] But it sometimes forgets its gentleness. "Ultramontanism is demonstrably the enemy of society, and must be met with resistance, merely passive if possible, but active if necessary, by the whole power of the State." – Huxley: "Critiques and Addresses," p. ix.

[2] A curious view, truly of Jesus Christ! Surely as Catherine Elsmere said, He was either a miracle-working God or an infamous impostor. In neither case should He occupy the niche in question.

human sympathy. It appeals to human respect; for a Christian needs to have courage and the strength of his convictions to express dissent from the popular views of the men who represent Agnosticism in this country – men of splendid gifts and brilliant position – men who claim to be freed from the thraldom of prejudice – intellectual Dictators, who, consciously or unconsciously, assume a lofty tone of mental superiority, and from their pedestals, like so many Stylites, look down on the everyday worshippers of common clay below who continue to adore God in the ancient, orthodox, obsolete fashion. For has not Evolution "selected" the agnostic as the "fittest" for advanced development and endowed him with a mind to think more clearly, and a will to will more strongly than the vulgar rank and file of his own generation? And it appeals to human sympathy; for the agnostic has found that life is not worth the living, and hence there is begotten in him a more than Byronic melancholy that has about it for many people an attraction of its own. He is the victim of clear thought. He has sacrificed all in pursuit of pure unadulterated Truth, and, having found it, is very unhappy. For, as he will tell you, his philosophy in destroying the primitive childlike delusions about things – about God, and the human soul, and the eternity of punishment and reward, and the other "fascinationes nugacitatis' or witcheries of nonsense that so long have amused and beguiled men – has robbed life of its pleasantnesses, of all that gave it substance and solemnity, of all that cheered and gladdened it, of all its warmth and charm and colouring, and has left to its votary little to live for in the present, and nothing to hope for in the future, has left him as one only dreary inheritance to travail in weariness of spirit for the benefit of that airy nothing called Posterity, for which very possibly he cares hardly anything at all, and which most certainly will care absolutely nothing for him. So that behind the Agnostic sits Black Care, and he frankly confesses that the dry light of pure intellect is but a feeble substitute for that thick mental atmosphere in which the benighted believer bows the knee and prays, with bated breath, to the invisible intangible fetish, whom, in reverence, he calls Almighty God.

The agnostic, then, is so magnanimously regretful at his own advantages, mental and moral, and laments in so touching a strain the position of profound hopelessness to which – as he loves to put it – inexorable logic has reduced him that a tendency is noticeable, even among practising Christians, to admire and sympathise with the know-nothing philosophy, and to hint that it perhaps has a good deal to say for itself, and at least ought not to be too lightly condemned. I propose, therefore, to examine to what extent theology may be said to justify this sympathy, and to consider in the light of revelation how far an agnostic can fairly be regarded as in good faith and as conscientious in his unbelief. The arguments to be brought forward are, in the main, such as all denominations of Christians must admit to be valid; and even a fair-minded opponent in the agnostic camp, though he may refuse to receive revelation as the Word of God, will not deny a considerable value to what we call the inspired writers and the Fathers of the Church – the greatest intellects as well of the Old Dispensation as of the New. Finally, if in this paper hard words are applied to unbelievers the writer desires to point out that they are not his, but are those of the authorities he quotes. The agnostic claims to condemn us on his principles. He will not refuse us the right to judge him on ours.

It is necessary, however, at the very outset to forestall a preliminary objection. Theology, it will be said, can in no sense be a witness against Agnosticism. Theology has simply no *locus standi* in the case. The formal object of theology, the source from which it derives its premises and argues to its conclusions, is revelation; but how prove the existence of a revelation unless you first prove there is a God to reveal? Theology claims to be a science of which the primary subject-matter is God. Now a science or an art postulates, it does not demonstrate, the existence of its subject-matter. The geometrician, given a radius and a circumference, will work out, according to the rules of geometrical science, the relation of radius to circumference. The shoemaker, given a pair of feet requiring shoes, will measure and shoe them according to approved rules of sutorial art. Similarly the theologian, given God, will explain the nature and attributes of divinity; but the theologian assumes the divine existence just as much as the geometrician assumes the existence of a circle and the shoemaker the existence of feet to be shod. In one word, protests the adversary, theology presupposes God's existence and can therefore have no claim to sit in judgment on the agnostic who denies that existence. Theology has no jurisdiction in the matter.

This objection, it is fair to allow, is based on truth, but not on the whole truth. For the philosophical arguments, drawn from pure reason to prove the divine existence, may be viewed in a two-fold way – directly and reflexively. They are studied *directly* when we consider the nature of contingent beings, their mingled perfections and imperfections, the dependence of the universe as well as the arrangement of its parts and the co-ordination of these parts to an end, the absolute and ineradicable power of the moral law to impose moral obligations, and, in a less degree, to coerce the conscience and enforce the moral dictates; and thus we are led by our unaided reason, by the intellectual light connatural to the mind of man, to understand how there must exist a Non-contingent, Necessary Being, the creative Cause of these manifold effects, a Being All-powerful, All-wise, Most-perfect, Supreme, Unchanging, just and holy Upholder and Legislator, Origin, and End of all things. In this way is God's existence studied directly in the light of *à posteriori* reasoning. But we can also study the reasoning itself and weigh the value of the arguments adduced. The rational arguments for God's existence are viewed *reflexively* when we examine into the general question as to whether man's mind is endowed with the faculty to arrive by its own unaided natural light, and that, too, with certainty, at a knowledge of God's existence; and, more in particular, whether human reason, of itself and without supernatural aid, can ascend from the existence of the creature to the existence of the Creator, from the existence of the Made can deduce the existence of the Maker, and can prove Him to be a Supreme and Divine Being – God, one, true, personal, distinct from the rest of the material and spiritual universe. This reflex study belongs to the spheres of both reason and revelation, of both philosophy and theology – but to each in a different way. In philosophy, the direct and reflex considerations are so intimately connected that in the direct demonstration we have a solution of the reflex question; for it is universally true that human reason, when it knows an object with certainty, knows also by virtue of its very constitution that its knowledge is true. A very superficial self-introspection will make this clear. When, for example, the student has learnt that the square on the hypotenuse of a right-angled triangle is equal to the sum of the squares on the other two sides, he knows implicitly that he knows this truth, and he knows implicitly that he knows it truly. Hence it is an axiom of sound philosophy that there is no true knowledge unless, knowing, you know that you know; for knowledge is that resplendent intellectual light which illuminates and reveals, not only other things, but also itself. It would be superfluous to add that this implicit, reflex, philosophical knowledge may of course be made explicit, may be made more perfect and rendered more distinct by a formal analysis of the arguments involved.

This judgment, implicit or explicit, which human reason passes on its own natural capacity to know God, and on the rational demonstration by which it knows Him, does not exclude a supernatural utterance and declaration on the possibility and moral necessity of acquiring this knowledge. There is nothing inconsistent in this, that God, the author of the light of reason, should have delivered to us a supernatural revelation declarative of man's faculty of knowing Him, and of the precise manner of exercising this faculty. In a word, if the Creator has endowed man with reason, and has opened a channel, through creatures, by which man may exercise that reason to acquire an *à posteriori* knowledge of his Maker's existence, it is not difficult to understand that God should, by revelation, recall these facts to man's mind, and should chide man for his denial of the Creator who gave him being. To study this revelation is to study *reflexively and theologically* the rational arguments for the divine existence.

After this necessary vindication of the general claim of theology to testify to – to state, and weigh, and declare – the value of the rational arguments for God's existence, we can pass on to the particular question as to whether, in fact, it does so testify. Is there, in reality, a revelation in which God *theoretically* indicates the way in which man, by the unaided light of reason, can and ought to attain to a knowledge of Himself; by which He *practically* declares that rational demonstrations of His existence, based on the fact of the existence of the Universe, are valid and sufficient?

These questions have not seldom been answered in the negative. Even within the pale of the Church they have been answered in the negative. Supernaturalists asserted the absolute necessity of internal supernatural grace to strengthen the intellect for its acquisition of a knowledge of God. Traditionalists held that arguments from reason can do no more than corroborate and confirm the primitive supernatural revelation, handed down by tradition to our own day, concerning the existence of God.

Chief among the Supernaturalists Luther railed at Catholic theologians for recognizing a natural faculty of the intellect competent to argue to a knowledge of God. His heresy was the very opposite to that of Pelagius. The latter so over-rated man's natural powers as to deny the necessity for grace even in the supernatural order. The former so under-rated man's natural powers as to assert the necessity for grace even in the natural order. Sin, Luther contended, has warped and weakened both intellect and will so that in his fallen nature man can no longer connaturally either know or love God.[3] Calvin and the other sectaries followed suit and denied the possibility of a knowledge of God without supernatural grace.[4] Then the Jansenists undertook the defence of this error, and went even further in their depreciation of man's natural powers. Among the famous 101 propositions culled from the works of the notorious Jansenist, Pasquier Quesnel, and condemned as heretical by Pope Clement XI,[5] were the two following:-

All knowledge of God, even natural knowledge, even that possessed by the Pagan philosophers, can come only from God; and without grace begets only presumption, vanity, and opposition to God.

And again:-

What else can there be in us but darkness, wandering, and sin, if we have not the light of faith, &c.

This error has died hard, if it can even now be said to be dead. On the 8th September, 1840, pressure was put on Bautain, a priest and professor of theology at Strasburg, to subscribe to the following thesis, of which he had been publicly teaching the contradictory:-

The use of reason precedes faith, and leads man to faith by aid of revelation and grace.

---

[3] Cf. Doellinger, "Reformation," i., 437.

[4] Cf. Bellarmine, "Controv. de gratia et lib. arb.," iv., 2.

[5] In the Bull *Unigenitus*, on September 8th, 1713.

Among the later Traditionalists Cardinal de Bonald[6] maintained that the human race has not, and cannot have, any rational knowledge of God, except such as was implanted in it with the gift of speech and has been handed down by tradition. The basis of this opinion was the curious view that ideas spring from words, not words from ideas. The unhappy Lamennais taught that all natural knowledge of God and of the moral order springs from a primitive revelation, and that the medium by which to gauge the contents of this revelation, and the one criterion of the truth of it, is the consensus of the race.[7] Ventura modified this opinion so far as to allow that God's existence can be proved from reason, but only if faith has preceded – understanding by 'faith' an assent based on the word of our elders.[8] Finally, M. Bonnetty, the learned editor of the *Annales de philosophie chrétienne*, having in his defence of Traditionalism branded as veiled rationalism the common teaching of Catholic theologians as to the natural power of man's unaided reason to attain to a knowledge of God, had submitted to him for signature (June 15th, 1855) the following proposition:–

> The method used by St. Thomas, St. Bonaventure, and by other subsequent scholastics does not lead to rationalism; neither was it the cause why in the Schools of to-day philosophy borders of Naturalism and Pantheism, &c.[9]

After this brief historical summary which will help to clear the ground, we can now address ourselves directly to the question under discussion. Does theology then declare there are rational arguments to prove God's existence? And, if so, does it teach

---

6 Recherches philosophiques sur les premiers objets des connaissances morales, 1840.

7 Essai sur l'indifférence en matière de religion.

8 *La ragion e filosafica et la ragione cattolica*. Conferenze del Gioacchino Ventura.

9 The Church has condemned the doctrine of the *absolute and physical* necessity of revelation for a knowledge of God. But to prevent misconception it may be well to add that the Vatican Council defined the *moral* and *relative* necessity of it, in these words:– *To divine revelation is due the fact that, about those things concerning God which are not of their own nature above the reach of human reason, all men can, in the present condition of mankind, have knowledge that is easily acquired, perfectly certain, and unmixed with error. Nevertheless, revelation is not, on this account to be called absolutely necessary.* – Constit I. Cap 2, De Revel.

that these proofs are of such a nature as, of themselves, to produce certainty? Finally, does it affirm that every man lies under a strict moral obligation to know and accept these proofs? To these questions theology – Scripture, the Fathers, the Councils – replies with a most unmistakable and emphatic affirmative.

And first as to the declarations of Scripture. Two classes of arguments are put forward in Holy Writ as leading to a knowledge of God, the historical and the cosmological.

The historical argument – which I do not propose to dwell on here – was used at least twice by St. Paul; once, when preaching to the men of Lystra:–

. . . God who made the heaven, and the earth, and the sea, and all things that are in them; who in times past suffered all nations to walk in their own ways. Nevertheless, he left not himself without testimony, doing good from heaven, giving rains and fruitful seasons, filling our hearts with food and gladness.[10]

And again in the Areopagus at Athens:–

God it is who giveth to all life and breath and all things, and hath made of one, all mankind to dwell upon the face of the earth, determining appointed times and the limits of their habitation, that they should seek God if haply[11] they may feel after Him or find Him, although He be not far from every one of us; for in Him we live and move and are.[12]

---

[10]   Acts xiv., 14–16.

[11]   Acts xvii., 25–28.

[12]   Bengel writes on "if haply": – "The way lies open. God is ready to be found, but He does not compel a man. He wishes him to be free in such a way as that when a man seeks and finds God, this in respect to God may be in some measure so to speak, a contingent act. The particle implies that the attempt is easy."
　　The verb "feel after him" implies a groping in the dark along the wall. Rosenmüller says:– "If haply they may feel after Him, *i.e.*, if perchance they may grasp Him with the hand. He made all these things to give them an opportunity of finding Him, as it were, by touch. For from the works of creation it is with the greatest ease that the existence of the Creator and All-Ruler can be known." This natural knowledge of God from creatures is obscure, not absolutely but relatively; that is, as compared with the immediate vision of God in heaven. "We see now through a glass in a dark manner, but then face to face." (I. Cor. xiii., 12). If a man gropes along the wall, he is certain to reach the door at last.

In these texts St. Paul had in mind the secondary causes of the physical order, which in the guiding hand of God minister to the preservation and well-being of mankind. These things without intellect move towards an end, and, in the main, towards the best end.[13] This is evident from the uniformity of their operation. It is equally evident that motion towards an end must have an intellectual superintending cause. What is this cause? It cannot be the non-intellectual brute creation, animate or inanimate. This cause can only be God. St. Paul had also in mind the history of the nations of the earth, a history so ordained by God that in the course of events men could not but see the divine element underlying and showing through the human. "Who in times past suffered all nations to walk in their own ways; *nevertheless he left not Himself without testimony*." What was this testimony? "Doing good from heaven, giving rains and fruitful seasons, filling our hearts with food and gladness." And this with the purpose that men "should seek God if haply they may feel after or find Him." Lastly, the apostle alludes to the benevolent Providence of God that guides and directs the life of each individual man; "He is not far from each of us, for in Him we live, and move, and are." St. Paul therefore sets forth a triple aspect of God's paternal guardian-ship of man; He guides the brute creation, animate and inanimate to a definite end for the good of man; He moulds this history of nations; He shapes the life of the individual. The conclusion to be drawn from all this is too obvious to need expression, and the Apostle does not express it. Man is shown to be a dependent being; he has a guardian, and is therefore a ward – with the duties and obligations of a ward. And he knows his own dependence, for in every man, in full possession of his reason, there is begotten – as it were spontaneously and inevitably – an obscure and confused knowledge of a Supreme Being watching over and caring for him, so that he is led to grope after God and to find Him more clearly and more explicitly through a consideration of the manifold blessings of Divine Providence.

We now pass on to a consideration of the Scriptural testimony to the value of the physical or cosmological

---

13   It should be borne in mind that in the finite order there is no such thing as an absolute best. God, in Genesis, saw that creation was "very good," – but not the best. Nothing but the infinite can be the best, and no creature, inasmuch as it is a creature, can be infinite.

argument for God's existence. The primary classical text on the subject is Romans i., 18–25:–

> 18. For the wrath of God is revealed from heaven against all ungodliness and injustice of those men that detain the truth of God in injustice. 19. Because that which is known of God is manifest in them. For God hath manifested it unto them. 20. For the invisible things of Him, from the creation of the world, are clearly seen, being understood by the things that are made; His eternal power also and divinity; so that they are inexcusable. 21. Because that, when they knew God, they have not glorified Him as God, or given thanks; but became vain in their thoughts, and their foolish heart was darkened. 22. For professing themselves to be wise they became fools. 23. And they changed the glory of the incorruptible God into the likeness of the image of a corruptible man, and of birds and of four-footed beasts, and of creeping things. 24. Wherefore God gave them up to the desires of their heart unto uncleanness to dishonour their own bodies among themselves. 25. Who changed the truth of God into a lie; and worshipped and served the creature rather than the Creator, who is blessed for ever. Amen.

And the Old Testament (Wisdom xiii., 1–10) makes a similar declaration not less conclusive:–

> But all men are vain in whom there is not the knowledge of God; and who, by these good things that are seen, could not understand Him that is, neither by attending to the works have acknowledged who was the workman. 2. But have imagined either the fire, or the wind, or the swift air, or the circle of the stars, or the great water, or the sun and moon, to be the gods that rule the world. 3. With whose beauty if they being delighted took them to be gods; let them know how much the Lord of them is more beautiful than they; for the first author of beauty made all those things. 4. Or if they admired their power and their effects, let them understand by them that He that hath made them is mightier than them. 5. For by the greatness of the beauty, and of the creature, the Creator of them may be seen, so as to be known thereby. 6. But yet [it may be objected] as to these they are less to be blamed. For they perhaps err, seeking God and desirous to find Him. 7. For being conversant among His works, they search; and they are persuaded that the

things are good which are seen. 8. But then again [it is answered] they are not to be pardoned. 9. For if they were able to know so much as to make a judgment of the world: how did they not more easily find out the Lord thereof. 10. But unhappy are they and their hope is among the dead . . .[14]

These texts speak for themselves. They are certainly cogent and convincing enough. However, to draw them out a little, four things should be made clear from them. The Traditionalists, as has been said, contend that the rational arguments for God's existence do not prove, but only confirm, the supernatural revelation of that existence; and that human reason, apart from

[14] These two texts are so alike that it is difficult to believe St. Paul had not this chapter of Wisdom in mind when he penned his first chapter to the Romans. The following arrangement shows the parallelism:–

WISDOM XIII	ROMANS I
Verse	Verse
1. All men are vain in whom there is not the knowledge of God.	18. For the wrath of God is revealed from heaven against . . . men who detain the truth of God in injustice.
1-2. Who by these good things that are seen could not understand Him that is, neither by attending to the works hath acknowledged who was the workman; but have imagined either the fire, &c., to be the gods that rule the world.	22-23-28. Professing themselves to be wise they become fools. And they changed the glory of the incorrupt-ible God into the likeness of the image of a corruptible man, and of birds, &c. And they liked not to have God in their knowledge.
3-4. With whose beauty if they being delighted took them to be gods, let them know how much the Lord of them is more beautiful than they . . . or if they admired their power and their effects, let them understand by them that He that made them is mightier than they.	19. Because that which is known [knowable] of God is manifest in them. For God hath manifested it unto them.
5. For by the greatness of the beauty, and of the creature, the Creator of them may be seen so as to be known thereby.	20. For the invisible things of Him, from the creation of the world, are clearly seen, being understood by the things that are made, &c.
8. They are not to be pardoned.	20. They are inexcusable.
9. For if they were able to know so much as to make a judgment of the world [to make a thorough study of the visible world], how did they not more easily find out the Lord there-of? The introductory proposition of Wisdom (verse 1) is identical with the final conclusion of Romans (verse 21) – viz., that ignorance of God is *vanity*.	21. Because that when they knew God, they have not glorified Him as God, or given thanks; but became vain in their thoughts, and their foolish heart was darkened.

revelation, is incompetent to refute Pantheism. The first point then to make good is that, in these texts, the inspired writers understand by "God," a Supreme Being endowed with intellect and will, distinct from the world, to whom the rational creature owes divine honour. In one word, a personal God must be the material object of the demonstration. Again, the Ontologists maintain that our knowledge of God is immediate and intuitive – a false and delusive philosophy destructive of the position it is meant to defend. The second point, therefore, to establish is that the rational arguments for God's existence are à *posteriori* and deductive, are an intellectual ascent from creature to Creator. That is, the created universe must be the objective principle of the demonstration. Furthermore, against Supernaturalists holding the intrinsic incapacity of man's mind to know God at all, if not fortified by internal supernatural grace, it must be proved thirdly that the sacred writers postulate no such grace but confine themselves to the natural order pure and simple. Hence the subjective principle of the demonstration must be the connatural unaided light of human reason. Fourthly and lastly it remains to be shown that the Sacred Scriptures claim for these rational arguments adduced to prove God's existence, not merely that they have a presumption in their favour, not merely that they have about them a show and semblance of truth, not merely that they are reasonable, or plausible, or specious, or highly probable; but that they are practically and overwhelmingly certain.

I. The material object of the demonstration is a personal, not a pantheistic God. This indeed is evident from the context as well as from the drift and purpose of the writers. For St. Paul lays down, not only that the Gentiles had the means to know God generically "by the things that are made," but also specifically that they could make acquaintance with His Eternity and Power and Divinity, "His eternal power also and divinity" (v. 20). Moreover the apostle (v. 21) upbraids the nations for not having glorified God nor given Him thanks – an unreasonable complaint if the God of St. Paul were an entity indistinct from creation, void both of intellect and of will. Indeed the very point of the complaint was that the recognition, glory, and worship due to the personal God had been transferred to impersonal, brute, and inanimate deities, "And they changed the glory of the incorruptible God into the likeness of the image of a corruptible man, and of birds, &c. . . . And they changed the truth of God into a lie and worshipped and served the creature rather than the Creator."

Nor is the Wise Man less emphatic in his account of the personal character of the Creator. He calls God, "Him that Is" (*i.e.* Essential Being)[15] – the "Artificer of the world" (v. 1), "the Lord of the world" (v. 9) – predicates that effectually differentiate God from the world created by God. Like St. Paul, he sets off this Artificer against the spurious deities whom the world worshipped, jibing with infinite contempt and scorn at these soulless divinities, "But unhappy are they and their hope is among the dead who have called gods the work of the hands of men, gold and silver, the inventions of art, and the resemblances of beasts, or an unprofitable stone the work of an ancient hand." (v. 10). Such worshippers "are not to be pardoned." Hence against pantheistic views he speaks with no faltering tongue. Blameworthy and stuffed with folly he holds them to be who confound God with the world and identify Him with things made, who close their eyes to the patent fact that the Creator is distinct from the work of His own hands.

II. The objective principle of the demonstration is the world, and not supernatural revelation. This meaning is demanded by the obvious sense of St. Paul. For the purpose of the apostle is to show that all men, Jew and Gentile, are alike guilty before God. All, he argues, had it in their power to know God and to know the Moral Law, and yet they had failed to honour and worship the one or to regulate human life according to the dictates of the other. Then, to forestall an objection of the Gentiles that they, having received no revelation like the Jews, had sinned from ignorance, St. Paul puts aside the excuse and emphatically declares that God and His Law are naturally knowable from created things alone without any supernatural manifestation.

Nor is this sense less evident in "Wisdom." The drift of the writer is this; All men are blameworthy who know not God – *all*, even those who live under no light of supernatural revelation. For it is an easy thing for all men to find out God. It is a plain ascent from visible things that are good to the

---

15 Cf the etymological meaning of Jehovah; as also Apoc. I. 4. "Him that is and that was, and that is to come;" and Exod. iii., 14. "God said to Moses: *I am who am.*"

Invisible Good, to "Him who Is" (v. 1) – from works to workman – from reflected beauty to the Source of beauty (v. 3) – from recreated power to Power Increate (v. 4) – from creature to Creator (v. 5).

To express this in another way. An object of knowledge can be actually known only in so far as it actually manifests itself to the mind. Without this self-exhibition it might be knowable, it would not be known. To the ancients who thought the earth was flat the antipodes were knowable, but unknown. Now this self-manifestation may be made in two ways. An object may be its own evidence, by itself, immediately – as, for example, a fire when you look into it. And it may manifest itself only mediately through another, through the medium of something else previously known – as smoke reveals the presence of fire, or, in general terms, as an effect reveals the existence of its cause. The Scriptures plainly teach that God is naturally evident to human reason; not indeed immediately, for the immediate vision of God "not as in a glass darkly, but face to face" is a supernatural grace bestowed only in the Beatific Vision; but mediately through creatures as such, by knowing them as an effect and thus ascending to a knowledge of their Cause, the Creator; "That which is known is manifest in them," that which is objectively knowable becomes subjectively known, "for God hath manifested it unto them," hath made Himself actually known. And the Apostle tells us the manner of this manifestation. "for the invisible things of Him are clearly seen, being understood by the things that are made."[16] Hence God who of Himself and in His substance is naturally unintelligible to weak human reason, – not from defect but

---

[16] Many modern commentators (v.g. Alford) understand "from the creation of the World" to refer to *time*; for this reason that, if it referred to the *cause* of man's knowledge of God, the words "by the things that are made" would be tautological. The reason assigned seems incorrect. It is a view at least tenable that "from the creation" (meaning from created things) is the starting point, the terminus a quo, of cognition; while, "by the things that are made," is epexegetical of "creation," is the formal cause of cognition, and expresses the precise aspect under which "creation" must be apprehended, namely, as an effect. For the mind can rise from "creation" to "Creator," only on condition that it knows "creation" as such, i.e., as a thing (or collection of things) "*made*." In this very obvious sense was the text interpreted by the Greek Fathers who may be allowed to have understood their own tongue, by Basil, *ep 235 ad Amphil*; Theodoret *in h.l*; Cyril of Alex, in *Is. 13. 12. p. 515*; Gregory of Nyssa, *c. Eunom. 12. 346*; Chrysostom. *De Diab. Tent. Hom 2. n 3.*.

from excess of intelligibility,[17] manifests Himself and His attributes – His Eternity, His Power, His Divinity – by the intelligible effects of which He is the cause. Now, it is the very point of the complaint made by the apostle and by the author of "Wisdom" that man has prostituted his reason and refused to see that 'creation' is an effect, is the synthesis of "things that are made." For "these good things that are seen" ("Wisdom," xiii., 1) are defective and therefore caused. The "works" participate in reality, but only the "Workman" is pure reality ("He who Is"). For the "works" are limited, and pure reality is without limit. Creatures are, for example, living; but they are not life. The brute has the life of brute animality, but it is a life restricted to this particular grade, it is non-intellectual life, it is life limited in excellence, limited in duration. It shares largely in reality, but it shares more largely still in unreality. There is much that it has; but here is incalculably more that it has not. Where then is the fountain-head of reality whereof each creature is a rill? What is the reason that limited being is real, but not reality; living, but not life; powerful, just, merciful, wise, but not power, nor justice, nor mercy, nor wisdom? When then, is the cause of limited being? Not limited being itself. For, because it is limited, it is not self-existent; not self-existent, and therefore not its own cause. Limited being has, therefore, a cause outside itself, self-existent, unlimited, infinite. And such a cause in [is] God.

In the study we are engaged on, two distinct questions present themselves for solution, and are solved in different ways. "Is there a God?" "What is God?" As we have seen, the imperfection of the creature solves the former question, for the finite implies the Infinite. To answer the latter, we must turn from the negative to the positive side of creation, from what the creature is not, to what the creature is, from its imperfections to its perfections. For as these imperfect things, by virtue of their very imperfection, point to One more perfect, higher and nobler than themselves, and clamour (like Paul and Barnabas to the Lycaonians) "We are not thy God; seek higher;" so on the other hand, do they, by virtue of their perfection – by their

---

17   Aristotle distinguishes between "things more knowable in themselves" and "things more knowable to us." (*Prior. Anal. 1. 2*) and points out that the more an object is intelligible in itself the less is it intelligible to us because further removed from sensile perception. The sun at mid-day is a plain object to see, but not to the owl.

beauty, or power, or wisdom, or justice, or love – point the finer to One from whom all these attributes are derived, and in whom all these qualities are combined, who is Absolute Beauty, Absolute Power, Absolute Wisdom, and Justice and Love.[18] This is the drift of the Wise Man's discourse:

> With whose beauty if they being delighted took them (creatures) to be gods, let them know how much the Lord of them is more beautiful than they. If they admired their power . . . He that made them is mightier than they (v. 3. 4.)

The perfections of these imperfect "works" are but a shadow of the infinite excellence, and yet a shadow revealing substance.

> Ask now the beasts and they will teach thee; and the birds of the air, and they shall tell thee. Speak to the earth and it shall answer thee, and the fishes of the sea shall tell. Who is ignorant that the hand of the Lord hath made all these things.[19]

This twofold aspect of creatures, their perfection and their imperfection, is alluded to in that most beautiful verse of the psalm (xviii., 1).

> The heavens [by their magnificence] show forth the glory of God; and the firmament [by its want of absolute perfection] declareth the work of his hands.

In all this neither inspired writer speaks of, or pre-supposes, or implies a primitive supernatural revelation made to man by God about Himself. The Scriptures give no jot or tittle of support to Traditionalism.

III. The subjective principle of the demonstration of God's existence is, not supernatural grace, but the natural light of the human understanding. This is roundly asserted by St. Paul in so many words; "for the invisible things of him are clearly seen, being understood by the things that are made;" so that between God and the world made by God, there is that intimate link, bond, and connection by virtue of which the existence of God is legitimately inferred from the existence of the world – a nexus so obvious that those who shut their eyes to it "are inexcusable" (v. 20.) And the Wise Man is equally positive on the point, as a glance at the scope of his chapter will show. St.

---

[18] "God is love." I John 4 8.

[19] Job xii., 7–9.

Paul had contented himself with the general statement that man can, and ought, from the existence of the creature to argue by the natural light of reason to the existence of the Creator. But the author of "Wisdom" goes into detail; he sketches out the main outlines of the argument. The proposition he sets himself to prove is this, "All men are nought who know not God," (v. 1.)[20] and in support of his thesis he contends that a knowledge of the existence and perfections of the universe can and ought to lead to a knowledge of the existence and perfections of God. He shows us what the starting point is from which the mind sets out to investigate, insists on the simplicity of the process, and indicates the goal at which it quickly arrives.

STARTING POINT		TERMINUS
These good things that are seen (v. 1.) lead man		to understand Him who Is. (v. 1)
Attending to the "works" (v. 1.) leads man		to acknowledge the "work-man" (v. 1).
Delight in the world's beauty (v. 3) leads man		to know how much more beautiful is the Lord of the world (v. 3).
Admiration at the power and efficacy of created things (v. 4)	leads man	to grasp the idea how their Maker is mightier than they (v. 4).

And having thus set forth the logical connection between this visible universe and the invisible Maker thereof, the Wise Man concludes (as did St. Paul) that those who worship the creature, bewitched by the beauty of it, are without excuse (v. 8). Unhappy are they and their hope is among the dead (v. 10); because the same reasoning faculty that enabled them to study and appreciate the universe should have led them, still more easily, to a knowledge of the existence and perfections of the Lord of this universe; for if they were able to know so much as to make a judgment of the world, how did they not more easily find out the Lord thereof (v. 9).

Supernaturalism – or the doctrine that man without supernatural help cannot know God – has, therefore, no basis in Scripture.

---

20 The Greek text reads, "Fools are all men by nature in whom there is habitual ignorance of God;" "by nature" that is, "by abuse of the natural faculty of reason." This is parallel with St. Paul's "became vain (the Greek is *became fools*) in their thoughts." v. 21.

IV. On the fourth point – that Scripture claims real certainty for the rational arguments in proof of God's existence – there is no need to dwell. According to St. Paul the reasoning in question is in its evidence so convincing and entirely irresistible that the unbelievers "who professed themselves to be wise, became fools," and were "inexcusable." And the New Testament does but, on this point, re-echo the Old for the Wise Man had beforehand said of them that they were "inane," "unhappy," their "hope is among the dead," "they are not to be pardoned."

Such is the emphatic teaching of Scripture. The same doctrine is put forward in a not less uncompromising way, and if possible still more emphatically, by the Greek and Latin Fathers. To a student of patristic learning, the traditional teaching on the following heads will be abundantly clear; first, that this visible universe is a natural manifestation of God, appealing to man's unaided reason; secondly, that this objective manifestation, and the subjective power of the mind to grasp, realise, and appropriate it, are of such a character that in all men, arrived at the full use of reason, there arises – as it were, spontaneously – a knowledge of God at least confused and indistinct; thirdly, that to develop this primitive cognition, to make it full and explicit, to render it clear and distinct, there are ample means at hand – whether we consider the native powers of the human understanding itself or the traces of God in creation – to enable the mind to mount from creature to Creator.

But it may be well to recall to mind that the Fathers recognize and insist on two separate and distinct stages in the natural knowledge of God; the one, obscure, confused, and more or less spontaneous, which impels a reasoning man to examine further; the other, clear, distinct, reflex and philosophical. Of course this philosophical knowledge presupposes a trained and educated mind. It presupposes an intellect cultured enough to grasp the essential dependence of the universe, to understand what contingent being is, and to realise how the finite, imperfect, created implies of necessity the Infinite, Perfect, Self-existent. It presupposes a power to appreciate the "greatness of the beauty of the world," its unity in multiplicity, the marvellous subordination of the vast and the tiny, the gigantic and the microscopic to their proximate, mediate, and final ends. It presupposes a capacity to analyze and synthesize the "works," and thus elaborate and "pick out" a clearer notion of the "Workman." Such a study is not necessarily a process merely à posteriori. For when the existence of a First Cause has once been demonstrated à posteriori from contingent being, than by an à priori method, by a study of the intrinsic and essential constitution of Necessary Being, we can arrive at a more elaborate and explicit knowledge of God. The subtle-minded Augustine, when he fell to the contemplation of "What God is," betook himself to the metaphysical order; he sifted eternal and immutable truth as it reveals itself in mathematics and the other sciences; he analyzed the ideas of wisdom, justice, truth, goodness; he examined into the metaphysical laws which - rooted in the divine essence, though independent of all will, even the divine - rule and govern not only the actual but the possible; and by these means he strove to gain an extended view of the Truth, Wisdom, and substantial Goodness which are the foundation and exemplar of the whole metaphysical and notional order, as well as the Cause of the light of reason by which we understand that order. Such a study is obviously beset with difficulties and though within the *physical* competence of all men it is within the *moral* and practical capacity of few. Hence the reasonableness of the dogmatic decree of the Vatican Council.[21] That to supernatural revelation it is due that *all* men can know God *easily, with certainty, and without admixture of error.*

But it is with the non-philosophical knowledge of God we are here concerned. The Fathers teach, with striking unanimity, that, besides and prior to the knowledge of God acquired by scientific demonstration, there is a knowledge of the divine existence common to all men who have not quenched the torch of reason within them. That in a paper like this there is not space for more than a few specimen passages from patristic writings, such as strike the keynote of tradition on the subject, is sufficiently obvious. For the argument to the existence of God is repeated, inculcated, and driven home on every possible occasion by practically every Father from Justin to Bernard, and a complete catena would fill a volume.[22]

The Fathers pre-suppose the existence of God as a first principle, which no man in his wits would question. Clement of

21   Quoted above, p. 3, note S.

22   Cf. Petavius "De Deo," 1. 1; Kleutgen, "Theologie der Vorzeit," tom 2.

Alexandria, who (be it noted) had a perfect acquaintance with the life, manners, and literature of contemporary Paganism, writes:–

> Peradventure the proof of God's existence ought not even to be undertaken, since His Providence is plain to be seen from a glance at His works – works full of art, and wisdom, and order, and method. But He who gave us being and life gave us also reason, and willed us to live according to that reason (and not to ignore our Maker).

And again:–

> God, our Parent and the Creator of all things, is seen in all things through the inborn power of the mind and without instruction, by all men, Greeks and foreigners. But no class of men – bucolic, nomad, or city resident – can fail to have their minds filled with one and the same primitive conviction of the being of Him who set up the world.[23]

The Fathers again testify most unmistakably to the value of the theistic argument. St. John Chrysostom, commenting on the classical passage from St. Paul to Romans,[24] writes:–

> Whence, O Paul, is it known that God implanted this knowledge of Himself in the nations? Because (saith he) *that which is known of God is manifest in them*. This, however, is assertion, not proof. But do thou demonstrate to me and make it clear that the knowledge of God was manifest in them, and that with open eyes they turned aside. Whence, then, was it manifest? Did He send them a voice from above? Not at all. But he made what attracted more than any voice. He created and set this universe before their eyes, so that wise man and witling, Scythian and barbarian, being penetrated through sight with the beauty of things seen, could mount up to God. Wherefore he hath it: *the invisible things*. &c. What, too, saith the prophet? *The heavens declare the glory of God*. What excuse, then, shall the nations make in the day of wrath? We knew Thee not? Knew Me not! Heard ye nought, then, telling of Me? Not the firmament proclaiming Me by its aspect? No harmonies and symphonies of the trumpet-tongued universe? None of the

23   "Strom." v., 547–612.
24   "Hom." 3.

unchanging, everstable laws of day and night, with the fixed and goodly order of winter, spring, and the other seasons, together with the sea, ever tractable amid all its billows and its turbulence? Knew ye not of all these things, abiding in their order, preaching aloud the Creator by their beauty and their magnificence? All this, forsooth, and more doth the text of Paul sum up as in a nutshell.

Theophilus of Antioch enforces the same doctrine by an apt similitude:-

As the soul of man is itself invisible to men, but is perceived by the movement of the body; so, in like manner, God cannot be seen by the human eye, but is known by His providence and His works.

The Fathers moreover teach, with equal clearness, that this knowledge of God's existence is easy and accessible to all men who have not warped and debased their reason. So Augustine:-

Such is the force of true divinity that from the rational creature with full use of his faculties God cannot be wholly and entirely hidden; for, (excepting a few in whom human nature is too degraded) the whole race of men confesses God the Maker of the world.[25]

Gregory the Great puts it pithily:-

Every rational man – from the very fact that he is rational – ought to gather from reason that his Maker is God.[26]

And Chrysostom, with his golden eloquence:-

Silent is the firmament, but its very aspect is more than trumpet-tongued in its appeal, not to ear but to eye. Scythian and barbarian, Indian and Egyptian, and every earth-treading man will hear this voice . . . and whithersoever he goeth, by gazing on the sky, will find instruction enough in the look of it.[27]

Nor can a man, according to patristic teaching, shut his eyes to God's existence. He can debauch and prostitute his reason and thus in the end cheat and deceive himself, but as Tertullian emphatically expresses it:-

[25]   In Jo. 106, n. 4.

[26]   Moral 1 27, c. 5, n. 8.

[27]   Hom. 9, ad pop, Antioch n. 2.

No man denies – for no man is blind to what nature itself suggests – that God made the universe.[28]

And in the same sense Gregory Nazianzen uses words almost too strong for the politeness of modern ears:–

That God exists as the chief and primal Cause, Originator, and Preserver of all things is a fact made patent both by external nature and by natural law . . . Too dull and drivelling assuredly is the man who does not by himself attain to this degree of knowledge.

As a natural corollary of this teaching the Fathers hold the knowledge of God to be universal. This is sufficiently apparent from the foregoing extracts which may, however, be supplemented by another from Tertullian, where addressing pagans on the proofs of God's existence, he says:–

I call in a fresh witness . . . Stand thou forth, O soul, in open court . . . Not thee do I summon who hast been formed in the schools, trained in libraries, a frequenter of porches and academies, a babbler of crude wisdom. I address a soul, simple rustic, unpolished, homely such a soul as they have who have only thee; such a soul as we meet on the road, in the highways, at the shops of artizans. I have need of thy inexperience . . . Thou art not, I know, a Christian . . . Nevertheless Christians now demand of thee a testimony. . . . *We* give offence when we preach God as the One God, under the one name of God, from whom are all things and on whom the universe depends. Bear then witness thou to this description of God, if thou knowest it to be true. For thee too we hear saying openly, at home and abroad, with a freedom denied to us, *May God grant it,* and *If God wills it.* In such like words dost thou declare there is some God and makest confession of His Omnipotence to whose will thou dost appeal; and at the same time thou dost deny the rest of them to be gods in that thou callest them by their proper names, Saturn, Jove, Mars, Minerva. . . . Thou affirmest also that He alone is God whom alone thou callest by the name of God. . . . Neither art thou ignorant of the nature of God whom we preach; *God is good* is thine own expression.[29]

28   De Spectac., c. 2.

29   *De testimon. animae* c. i. 7.

Many Fathers go even further still. In teaching that the existence of God can be deduced from His works they seem so to exaggerate the facility and universality of the deduction as to reduce it almost to a simple intuition. They speak of this knowledge as "innate." Tertullian says:–

> Evidence of a soul *naturally* Christian! The soul's consciousness of God from the beginning is a *gift*.[30]

And John Damacene:–

> Not, however, in ignorance of Himself, utter and entire, hath God suffered us to be wrapped. For there is no man alive in whom the knowledge of God hath not been *naturally* implanted.[31]

Not of course that the word "innate" is used in the Kantian sense of "subjective form," nor yet in that of the School of "Innate Ideas." The word is a rhetorical exaggeration to express the simple, easy, and almost imperceptible process of reasoning which leads up to the knowledge of God. That the fathers never meant to deny that there is some process of reasoning, and therefore an *acquisition* of this knowledge, the foregoing citations amply prove. "Innate" therefore in this patristic sense is opposed, not to "acquired" but rather to that reflex, philosophical knowledge begotten of study and meditation, and especially to that fuller, surer, and more perfect knowledge of God imparted to the world by supernatural revelation.

The teaching then of patristic theology touching the value of the arguments for God's existence is most emphatic and unmistakable. The Fathers declare the knowledge of God to be accessible to all men, to be easily acquired, to be all but innate; and for the agnostic they can hardly find strong enough words of condemnation. Their teaching then reiterates, explains, and developes the teaching of Holy Writ.

Moreover precisely the same doctrine is inculcated by the great Doctors and Theologians, by the Franciscan Bonaventure,[32] by the Dominican Aquinas,[33] by the Jesuit

---

30   "Apol." c. 17.

31   "Fid. Orthod." I.1.

32   "In. Sent." 1.3.2.

33   "Cont. Gent." 1, 12.

Suarez.[34] St. Thomas stigmatises the opposite opinion as "falsity and error."

And last of all the teaching formulated in Scripture, elaborated by the fathers, explained by the Doctors of the Church and defended by her Theologians, is enunciated also in the Councils. The Vatican Council defined as follows:–

> Holy Mother Church holds and teaches that God – Beginning and End of all things – can, through created things, be known, with certainty, by the natural light of human reason. *For the invisible things of Him, &c.* (Rom. I. 20.)[35]

And again in the first canon appended to the chapter of which the above is part:–

> If anyone should say that God – One and True, our Creator and Lord – cannot be known, with certainty, by the things that are made, through the natural light of human reason, let him be anathema.

It will hardly be denied that these two dogmatic declarations are to the point. Short, clear-cut, unambiguous, they clinch the argument and leave no margin for cavil or evasion. As far as Catholics are concerned they have given the deathblow to Traditionalism and Supernaturalism. These opinions are now formally heretical.

And now we have the theological evidence before us on which to ground a judgment as to whether or not an agnostic can, in his Agnosticism, be conscientious and in good faith. But first let us put the issue simply and clearly. Let us put aside complicating and subordinate considerations. We are not, then, here debating at what age the full use of reason is reached and the obligation incurred of acknowledging God. We do not here deny there may be individuals, or even whole nations, so brutalised and degraded as to be adult indeed in body, but dwarfed and stunted in mind below the normal stature of man, and thus exempt from the responsibilities of men. Nor do we here enter on the further enquiry whether for a brief period after reaching the full use of reason a man can, without sin, be ignorant of God. But let the question be limited to this. Does theology recognize the possibility that a man can be in good

---

[34]   "Metaph." D. 27. S.3.

[35]   "Const." I. c., 2.

faith who disbelieves in God, with open eyes and after consideration, and that actually and at heart and for a considerable time; in a society such as we know it; in a society which affords a great variety of aids and helps, human and divine, external and internal, to acquire a knowledge of God; where he has consciously before him the order, beauty, and design of the universe; where he is impelled by introspection, or by self-examination, or by wonder, or by terror, or by penury, or by sickness, or by danger, or by sorrow, or by qualms of conscience to propose to himself these questions: "Where did this universe spring from?" "Who and what am I?" "Whence came I?" "Whither am I going?" What then is the verdict of theology on the good faith of such an atheist, or – to use the fashionable jargon – of such an agnostic, for new agnostic is but old atheist writ large? And what degrees of sympathy does theology allow us to extend to the unbeliever who declares he has not sufficient data to argue to God's existence, but proclaims:–

> There is nothing irrational in contending that the evidences of Theism are inconclusive, that its doctrines are unintelligible, or that it fails to account for the facts of the universe or is irreconcilable with them.[36]

The verdict of theology on such an one is undoubtedly an unqualified condemnation. The Scriptures condemn him. The Doctors concur in the condemnation. All the great theologians emphasize the condemnation. The Fathers condemn and upbraid him. The Councils condemn and anathematize him. He may plead "not guilty," but the plea is disallowed. His advocate may ransack the heavens above and the earth beneath for "extenuating circumstances," but they are waived aside as fictitious. In neither Testament, Old or New, is there any trace or shadow of excuse to be found for him. Not a word of it in the long catena of the Fathers. No mention of it in the Doctors. No faint allusion to it in the carefully qualified decisions of the Church. In the Old Testament "all men are nought in whom there is ignorance of God . . . unhappy are they and their hope is among the dead . . . they are not to be pardoned." The New Testament on this head reproduces and enforces the teaching of the Old. The Sophists of Greece and the philosophers of Rome,

---

[36]   "Huxley's Hume." I. 60.

when they ignored God, "professing themselves to be wise, became fools," for in reality " they knew God but glorified him not as God, nor gave him thanks, but became vain in their thoughts and their foolish heart was darkened."

Brief had been the sentence pronounced in "Wisdom" on all unbelievers; "they are not to be pardoned." Equally pithy is that pronounced by St. Paul "they are inexcusable." The Fathers concur. To Augustine a man who knows not God has "a warped and distorted nature:" to Gregory Nazianzen he is "a dullard and a driveller": to Cyprian and Tertullian he is "the crown and summit of wickedness."[37] Finally the Church, cautious to a degree and ever slow to condemn, confirms the verdict by its declaration and anathema.

So much then for the speculative aspect of Agnosticism. A word now on its practical side. Does theology allow that an agnostic can save his soul? Again the answer must be an emphatic negative. A natural and certain knowledge of God is a necessary condition, preliminary, and foundation of faith, and without faith there is no salvation. An absolutely essential condition of the credibility of faith is God's existence; for faith is assent to God's word and how can there be supernatural assent to the word of one of whose existence we are not naturally certain? That faith is a prerequisite of salvation is a primary truth of Christianity; "Without faith it is impossible to please God. But he that cometh to God must believe that He is."[38]

But, it will be asked, may there not be, if not a supernatural, at least a natural beatitude for the agnostic who observes faithfully all the precepts of the natural law? If he can have no part in the Beatific Vision, can never be an "adopted son of God," can never "see God face to face," may he not at least expect a share in the happiness of those who, though never raised by sanctifying grace to the supernatural order, yet at the same time have never offended God by a grievous and deliberate violation of the law of natural morality? May not the agnostic of pure life expect after death to enjoy a place at least, in the Limbo of unbaptized infants? Again the answer can only be in the negative. For the adult – adult in mind as in body – there is no middle place between Hades and Heaven. The

---

37 Tertul. Apol. c. 17: Cyprian De Idol Vanit. c. 9.

38 Heb. 11. 6.

question is based on a false supposition. To be an agnostic is, in itself, by the very fact, the most grievous of all violations of the Moral Law. For the primary precept of the Natural Law is to recognise the existence of the Lawgiver and "it is the very zenith and apex of depravity not to know Him whom thou canst not ignore."[39] God wills all men to be saved and to come to a knowledge of the truth.[40] And hence He, of necessity, gives to each the graces natural and supernatural to acquire that knowledge. Whoso therefore neglects this will of God commits grievous sin and shuts himself out from all reward, natural or supernatural.

Whether agnostics are to be taken at their word and regarded as men who in the main do keep the Commandments, and live moral and upright lives, is a question which this is not the place to discuss.[41] A theologian would probably say that as, in practice, so few men constantly observe the law of God even when helped by the more abundant graces given to believers, it becomes morally and practically impossible to keep it for any length of time without that assistance. It is needless to say that as to the state of conscience of this or that individual we have no right at any time to hazard conjectures. Each is answerable, in his own heart, to God alone. But by agnostics as a body, in the general, and viewed precisely as agnostics, the words of St. Paul, in the chapter quoted so often, deserve to be carefully pondered. Writing of a state of society so nearly akin to our own, of the Romans of the age of Nero, learned, cultured, and unbelieving, he says:-

> And as they liked not to have God in their knowledge, God delivered them up to a reprobate sense, to do those things which are not convenient.

What these "inconvenient things" were a reference to the chapter will show. And this "reprobate sense" the Apostle describes precisely as a consequence of their sin of unbelief:-

> "*Wherefore* God gave them up to the desires of their heart, &c.

[39]   St. Cyprian quoted above.

[40]   I. Tim. 2. 4.

[41]   F. Kleutgen, a theologian of broad and liberal views, says:- "The knowledge of God is so easily acquired, and so certain that ignorance or doubt on the subject cannot be explained except as springing *from guilty frivolity or arrogant obstinacy.*" Philosophie der Vorzeit, vol. i., n. 227.

And again:-

> They served the creature rather than the Creator. *For this cause* God delivered them up to shameful affections. &c.

They "liked not to have God in their knowledge," and on that account were "delivered up to a reprobate sense." They were abandoned to the "evil desires of their heart," and they fell into the sensualism of despair. And how could it, logically, be otherwise? For if there be no God, no moral law, no obligations, no sanctions, no eternity of punishment or reward, it is hard to see what else than self-indulgence an agnostic has to care for. His life, at beast, can be but very dreary – a mere desert of despair. And he must serve, – man is made to serve – if not the Creator, then the creature. The agnostic replies that he serves his race, lives for the improvement of his race! And what a will-o'-the-wisp this improvement of his race is! John Stuart Mill had set up this Jack-o'-lantern as his guiding star in life, and think how he wrote of it in his Autobiography, with what cynicism and bitterness of disappointment! "Suppose," he once said to himself, "all your objects in life were realised, that all the changes in institutions and opinions which you are looking forward to could be completely effected at this very instant, would this be a great joy and happiness to you? And an irrepressible self-consciousness distinctly answered, No."[42] If man, or Mankind – the Grand-être of Auguste Comte – be the highest attainable object of human hopes and human aspirations, what greater misery than to be haunted by visions of what is better and nobler than man; by glimpses of a truth and goodness and beauty never to be possessed; by strivings after an object which neither earth nor humanity can bestow? If these ideals are a dream, and these longings a delusion, intangible shadows never to be grasped either here or hereafter, there are but two conclusions open to us; either the hopeless and degrading conclusion of German Pessimism that life is a bad thing and cannot too soon be made away with; or that gayer and more popular conclusion – adopted by the Romans about whom St. Paul wrote – that there is nothing better for us than to frolic through life, sipping the passing pleasure of the hour, in the mood of that Epicurean singer who, having set his heart in turn on wealth, on love, on war, on travel, and on

---

[42] Autob. 133.

sounding fame, and having tasted the insipidity of them all, concluded - with an older and a greater singer than himself - that they are all vanity and affliction of spirit:-

Now I've set my heart upon nothing you see;
    Hurrah!
And the whole wide world belongs to me;
    Hurrah!
The feast begins to run low no doubt,
But at the old cask we'll have one good bout,
    Come, drink the lees all out.[43]

Among the ancient Egyptians there flourished a custom, described by Herodotus[44] in some such words as these. When a banquet was well advanced and the appetite of the guests was cloyed with abundant meat and their thirst slaked from goodly stores of wine and the revel ran high, a slave entered and carried round to each feaster in turn an open coffin wherein lay a wooden figure carved and painted to represent a corpse; and pointing to this counterfeit presentment he whispered into each reveller's ear, "*Looking on this, drink and be merry; such in death shalt thou become.*"

And not only the worshipper of Isis but the prophet of the Old Law,[45] and the apostle of the New,[46] ask of the unbeliever what happiness in life there can be for him except that very mournful *drink and be merry*. The author of "Wisdom"[47] with his keen insight into human nature, has summed up in the same sense the Epicurean reasonings of unbelievers:-

They said, reasoning with themselves, but not right, the time of our life is short and tedious and in the end of a man there is no remedy . . . for we are born of nothing, and after this we shall be as if we had not been; for the breath in our nostrils is smoke; and speech is a spark . . . which being put out, our body shall be ashes and our spirit shall be poured abroad as soft air, and our life shall pass away as the trace of a cloud, and shall be dispersed as a mist which is driven away

43 Goethe's *Song of Life*.
44 Euterpe 78.
45 Isaias 22, 13; 56, 12.
46 1 Cor. 15, 32.
47 II 1-9.

by the beams of the sun. And our name in time shall be forgotten and no man shall have any remembrance of our works. For our time is as the passing of a shadow . . . Come, therefore, and let us enjoy the good things that are present, and let us speedily use the creatures as in youth. Let us fill ourselves with costly wine . . . and let not the flower of the time pass by us. Let us crown ourselves with roses before they are withered . . . Let none of us go without his part in luxury; let us everywhere leave tokens of joy. For this is our portion and this is our lot.

St. Paul told the Corinthians:-

If in this life only we have hope in Christ we are of all men most miserable.[48]

For the agnostic who has hope neither in Christ nor in God, neither in this life nor in the life to come, these lines of the poet Fletcher aptly point the moral of his existence:-

The word's a labyrinth where unguided men
Walk up and down to find their weariness.
No sooner have they measured with much toil
The crooked path, with hope to gain their freedom,
But it betrays them to a new affliction.[49]

[48]   1 Cor. 15, 9.
[49]   The Night-Walker, 4, 6.

PROFESSOR HUXLEY'S CREED
[William Barry]

Art. VII. – 1. *Collected Essays*. By T. H. Huxley, F.R.S.
London, 1894.
2. *Essays on Controverted Questions*. By the Same. London,
1892.
3. *The Life and Letters of Charles Darwin*. By Francis Darwin.
London, 1887.
4. *Reden*. Von Du Bois Reymond. Leipzig, 1887.
5. *Epitome of the Synthetic Philosophy of Herbert Spencer*. By
F. Howard Collins. London, 1894.

To the average citizen who reads as he runs, and who is
unacquainted with any tongue save his native British, it may
well appear that the Gospel of Unbelief, preached among us
during the last half-century, has had its four Evangelists – the
Quadrilateral, as they have been called, whose works and
outworks, demilunes and frowning bastions, take the public
eye, while above them floats the agnostic banner with its
strange device, 'Ignoramus et Ignorabimus.'

These pillars of the faith unorthodox which sums itself up as
Nescience, rest on one foundation, but are each characteristic
and unlike their fellows. Mr. Herbert Spencer may be termed
the 'Great Philosopher,' who, by cohesions and correspondences, binds worlds and eons together in sesquipedalian
chains, with a fullness of language so overpowering that he
almost persuades us to look upon all things in heaven and earth
as 'necessary results of the persistence of force, under its forms
of matter and motion.' Such is the triplicity which, manifesting
the Unknowable, finds in the 'Apostle of the Understanding' a
fervent though critical worshipper. Again, Mr. Darwin,
though, as he was fain to admit, 'bewildered' in questions
metaphysical, nor given to dwelling on the mechanism of the
universe, tells us with gentle iteration that if we grant, by way
of commencement, simply 'a mud-fish with some vestiges of
mind,' he will thence deduce all vertebrate animals,

including man, and build up science, civilization, and morality, yet not upon sand. Over this astonishing creed, Mr. Tyndall, who by temperament had in him much of the poet, has flung a veil of religious melancholy, adorning with his utmost skill of eloquence, and celebrating with unction, the pithecoid origin of our race which he did not desire to conceal. Mr. Tyndall was a mystic who touched with dreamy colour the harsh and staring outlines of Darwin's biology, and the vast and vague of Spencer's all-embracing world-nebula. The finest qualities, whether of prophet, philanthropist, or man of science, he was willing to trace back through the ranges of zoology, and farther still, to the fires which are blazing, in the sun.

Last of all, but the most effective, as he is undoubtedly the most popular, of the Four, comes Professor Huxley, – 'all the while sonorous metal breathing martial sounds,' as Milton has it, – to do battle, like a champion armed in complete steel, with creeds and clericals, in 'untiring opposition' to the enemies of science, be they bishops or biologists, cardinals or followers, of Hegel, Prime Ministers in office or out, and orthodox Christians wheresoever found. Always incisive and dogmatic, and, as Darwin observed, writing with a pen dipped in aqua-fortis, he has been a man of war from his youth up. And now, when he might take his ease in honourable retirement, having 'warmed both hands at the fire of life,' he seems not unwilling to fight his battles over again, by collecting in a general view the records of this many encounters, and republishing his Essays with scarcely the change of a syllable.

They are lively but delusive reading. Of the Gospel which is thus in pungent style commended to our attention, we remark at the outset that it is calculated, in spite of its obvious frankness, or because of it, to entrap the unwary. If we may borrow an expression from the author, this latest message of science – misleadingly so called – is woven of 'ideal cobwebs' stretched above the abyss of Mr. Spencer's Unknowable, and shining prettily enough in the sun. Who first hung them out before mankind? We do not pretend to know; but David Hume, 'the prince of agnostics,' certainly did so a hundred and fifty years ago, smiling at his own cleverness, and with such an innocent air that he seemed rather to be taking for granted what everyone thought, than transforming into hopeless enigmas the beliefs men had cherished concerning God, the Soul, and Immortality. Now, since the animated discussions in which Kant led the way, those who are skilled in metaphysics have learnt that Hume's polite and flowing rhetoric needs to be sharply scanned, its terms sifted to the bottom, and its assumptions pointed out. The majority of readers, however, cannot do this for themselves. They are not, nor ever will be metaphysicians; they listen in good faith to the specious language of demonstration, and their – we had almost said incurable – naïveté in the presence of celebrated teachers makes them ready victims whenever ambiguities which really hold the key of the position are inflicted upon them.

Professor Huxley's doctrine is by its nature and essence double-seeming; it takes the sovereign words, and plays upon them, and makes them of two colours. Outwardly it is Science, inwardly Nescience. It has given a mighty impetus to Materialism. Yet Professor Huxley affirms with scornful vehemence that he is no Materialist. It has marshalled squadrons against free-will, and all that is called 'spirit and spontaneity.' But the author protests that free-will has not been ousted by science, and that a drawn battle in this region is all one with giving the victory to the old and orthodox banner. It is couched in terms that make a man the merest automaton, that deny any possible effect in the physical world to his volition. Yet, marvellous to relate, when a timid Bishop proposes that Christians shall confine their petitions to things spiritual, Professor Huxley steps forward, and in language clear as day, and with felicitous illustration, supplies to embarrassed spirits an argument which restores all that the prelate had too speedily surrendered. Darwinism appeals to scientific observers especially on the ground that it puts an end to final causes, silences Paley, and throws back theologians upon an uncertain à priori demonstration. At once the Professor replies that 'evolution has no more bearing upon Theism than has the First Book of Euclid.' To crown all, Hume being confessedly as much of a Pyrrhonist, or absolute sceptic, as any man can be whose reason is not totally in abeyance, and Professor Huxley delighting to stand by him, we yet find with equal pleasure and amazement that the latter values truth so highly, and is so convinced of its objective worth, that sooner than give it up at the bidding of an evil fiend, though omnipotent, he is prepared to undergo the worst such fiend can do upon him, be the torture as intolerable as it may, and its duration everlasting. If this be not to confess the 'transcendental,' to know what is at the heart of the universe and to worship it as known, we do not understand the meaning of words. Yet, in the very height and ecstasy of his passion for the truth, irrespective of utilitarian reckonings whether in regard to himself or the race (for what he would dare on behalf of virtue, the Professor would surely recommend to every living mortal), this most heroic of self-contradictors tells us in an aside, that his worship is chiefly of the silent sort, and at the altar of the Unknown, which, when he first made its acquaintance, was the Unknowable.

Such flashes from a higher light, and revelations, as unexpected as they are welcome, of what German philosophy has called the Absolute, lend a charm to the Professor's eloquence that no want of logic, however manifest, can wholly dissolve. They betoken the change that is passing over science no less than literature, – the new spirit and the wider views towards which men are moving as they realize how inadequate, how much resembling a mere 'verbal mystification,' is the Materialism of the Comtes and the Häckels, in whose eyes 'the Unknown and the Unknowable are but more or less advanced stages of a mathematical problem.' True it is, in the words of the thoughtful student whom we have just been quoting, Mr. Henry Coke, that 'perhaps hardly any living writer has contributed so much to the common scepticism, – the crass unbelief of the day, – as Professor Huxley.' Nevertheless, we may, with the same critic, allow or insist that 'this is rather the misfortune of the ignorant pupils, than the fault of the brilliant teacher.' Must we lay on him the blame if words, which for the wise man are but counters, become in the hands of the less wise current coin, stamped at the royal mint, and possessing the value which is inscribed on their surface? Well, that is a question for casuists, and involves many delicate issues. One thing is sure. When we challenge Professor Huxley to declare the worth of his seeming gold pieces, he answers that they are bare tokens and 'useful symbols,' devices and tricks of the intellect to facilitate its operations; that science is nothing but a relative aspect of things which in themselves we do not apprehend, – an algebra, a calculus, employed by the mind because it has been found to work, – but as human as the oldest or newest of religions, and no whit, so far as we can judge, more akin to the Absolute. It is a *fable convenue*, but with this advantage that the learned and not the ignorant have agreed to take it as genuine history.

Nine men out of ten, as soon as they hear the name of science, believe that a real knowledge of objective facts and their laws and causes must be thereby meant. Professor Huxley, too, often speaks as though such were the case; but from time to time he throws out a *caveat*, and writes in the margin that all-multiplying coefficient, the unknowable. The rough garments of Esau the Materialist suit by no means well with the smooth tones of Idealist Jacob. But so incongruous a mixture denotes mystery, 'and,' as the amiable poet warns us, 'things are not what they seem.' Does the simple reader who shrinks from creeds and formularies on the ground of their supposed contradictions, turn to science, dreaming that he shall find therein nothing but clearly ascertained facts, experience always verifiable, and no problems which defy solution? Let him not be deceived. The shadow of the transcendental looms above these lights; beneath is the great abyss; and that rounded whole in which he walks with comfort, as a little world germane to his thoughts and level with his understanding, is merely 'the phenomenal,' – an allegory or parable, the play of unknown forces, agents, powers, – call them by what name we may, – which exist beyond his ken. Such is the moral which Professor Huxley enforces throughout these pages. He describes himself as an agnostic, but, in admitting that there is a region into which science has never penetrated, he leaves scope and room for another method, which may accomplish the task that has fallen from his hands. In one word, scientific Reason, thus confessedly bounded, and impotent to answer the questions of eternal life, seems by its very helplessness to call for Revelation and to demand its aid.

Again and again, in reading these fragments, – the shortcomings of which, had they been moulded into a book, must have struck the most careless, – we are reminded of the famous Professor at Berlin, Du Bois Reymond, whose 'Addresses' we have set at the head of our article. Alike the English and the German writer display such technical knowledge as but few among their contemporaries boast; and it is clothed by them in a vesture of well-chosen, clear, and definite language, in the best sense popular, because not only precise but idiomatic. Both disdain scholastic pedantry, and are indebted for the influence which they wield outside museums and lecture-halls to that literary skill whereby they have added the graces of culture to their learning. In keenness of temper, in unbounded self-confidence, in vivacity of feeling, and in a combative spirit, these eminent persons would probably yield no jot the one to the other. They mingle much autobiography in their discourses; and the prophet countersigns his message with not undisguised satisfaction. Both are avowedly partisans, good haters, and delight in their beak and claws as congenial weapons of offence. Like the war-horse in Job, the neck of each is clothed with thunder, and he saith among the trumpets, 'Ha, ha.' Certainly, none of the Homeric chieftains could have taken more pleasure in a tourney with the Trojans than do these in setting upon their chosen adversaries. They give and receive wounds with the courage of Sioux warriors, and, however they mean to be philosophical and well-balanced, their temperament, as a rule, is too much for their philosophy; the dissertation ends in a war-whoop; scalpels are exchanged for tomahawks, and the reviewer of their doughty deeds is too often compelled to break off with the lively indication, 'Left fighting.'

Professor Huxley's favourite Latin verb is 'Nego, – I say No.' But with such vehemence does he say No, that the negative of this captain-general of unbelievers sounds desperately like an affirmative. Mr. Spencer, with an eye to affinities of disposition which depend hardly at all on identity of doctrine, has suggested, – so we learn from the amusing piece of self-portraiture prefixed to these Essays, – that Professor Huxley was intended by nature to be a clergyman. Let us say rather that every sect has its apostles and its propaganda; that the tone of authority, the indicative and imperative moods in which our author indulges, the somewhat peremptory humour, disdain of those who do not agree with him, sarcastic touches, and challenging voice, mark him out as a priest of the new hierarchy which assumes a Creed of Science for its Thirty-nine Articles, and would substitute for religion fresh 'laws of conduct' established upon the 'laws of comfort' and by them authenticated. Somewhere in Professor Huxley lurks the mystic whose ears are open towards the spiritual world, and whose utterances every now and then come across the harmonies of Materialism, with bewildering effect. But the emphasis which is laid upon science in opposition to orthodoxy, strikes the keynote in these discussions. And thus we discern a clericalism *à l'inverse* in the almost episcopal charges which it has pleased him to issue against tradition Hebrew and Christian, to the intended discomfiture of Christians to whatever communion belonging, and as a renewal of the eighteenth-century campaign whose war-cry was 'Écrasez l'infâme.'

Our Professor, then, to his other qualities adds that of a belated Voltairean. With British doggedness he sets himself to fabricate shafts of wit against the many things held sacred by his countrymen; and the method of Zadig is frequently combined with the method of the French Mephistopheles. As a scientific man he welcomes la Mettrie's *L'homme-machine*, well pleased to be an automaton or skeleton-clock, wound up by the unknown Powers and striking the hours correctly. As a partisan in the guerrilla warfare against Christianity, this latest of the unbelieving apostles, born out of due time, rehearses with varying success the jibes and sneers of the *Aufklärung*, and treats the recognized creed of Europeans and Americans with less respect than he would bestow upon the waste products of a soap-factory. The finest criticism always implying sympathetic insight, we are now accustomed to hold that Goethe saw more deeply into the Christian Religion – though in the main by virtue of his artistic, and not his ethical faculty – than Voltaire, whose keen sense of the ridiculous never broadened into genial or tolerant humour. Science has no enmities, and the study of those varied elements which enter into religious belief is not only compatible with an even temper, but demands it, unless we are to take our dead analysis for the miraculous life on which nations have thrived, and to lose the spirit, – *das geistige Band*, – neglecting which we fall into the great but widespread sophism, that the chemical constituents displayed in flasks at the South Kensington Museum make the whole man. On this deluding method, and not seldom with a bluntness of speech that hurts his opponents less than himself, Professor Huxley has brought his engines to bear on the New as well as the Old Testament.

But in this procedure we are not minded to follow him. And as the Christian principle is to return good for evil, it appears to us that a fair and impartial summary of his teaching may be of service, not only to those who refuse it by very instinct, but also to the many in whose judgment so accomplished a writer and so highly-praised a physicist cannot be utterly in the wrong. 'Castigatque auditque dolos' is Rhadamanthine justice, which fallible mortals must not imitate. Let us hear first and pass sentence afterwards. When we have suffered Professor Huxley to speak on his own behalf, and to put his arguments with the utmost force of which he is capable, we may find in his science and his nescience grounds whereon to conclude, as he does, that natural knowledge 'is as little atheistic as it is materialistic'; that it has no quarrel with Religion; and that symbols or ideas which deal with things unseen and spiritual have as real a value as those in virtue of which we manipulate the evidence of things tangible into laws and formulas, and subdue to ourselves the universe of sense.

The drift of our exposition may be stated in the words, as classic as they are significant, which Du Bois Reymond uttered on a well-known occasion. Science is concerned with experience, indeed, but runs up of necessity into abstractions. On the other hand, no Religion has either charm or influence which does not issue in personal communion between the worshipper and the Supreme: 'Cor ad cor loquitur' is the touching sentence which Cardinal Newman wrote upon his shield, and which sums up all the grace of all aspiration towards the Infinite since prayer was first breathed. Now then, says Du Bois Reymond with point and precision, 'The tendency in virtue of which our intellect personifies its ideas is just as normal and inevitable as that whereby it abstracts and universalizes.' Does any one call Religion a dream? Then let him call Science a dream too. But is natural knowledge valid, true so far as it goes, not an empty symbol, but an acquisition proving its reality by conforming to experience, and enabling us to move along an ascending scale of facts in which we feel ourselves more and more at home? All this may be said of Religion; it is the proof by power, by life, by the spirit to which, and not to bare syllogisms, mankind have ever appealed, when their paramount beliefs were in question. Or, as Mr. Herbert Spencer proclaims, although with a deeper significance than he has hitherto realized, 'We cannot but conclude that the most abstract' (he means the most real) 'truth contained in Religion, and the most abstract truth contained in Science, must be that in which the two coalesce. It must be the ultimate fact of our intelligence.'

However, let not the reader be alarmed. We propose to go up these heights by easy steps, and to pause now and then for the view. All we require at the beginning is granted, nay pressed upon our acceptance, by Professor Huxley. Science, he affirms, agrees with mediaeval scholasticism (a great and rare saying!) in postulating the rational order of the universe; it would commit suicide unless it did so; and we must always assume that 'every part of matter is a realm of law and order.' Thus we banish the irrational, the chaotic, as an impossibility and a contradiction; it neither does nor can exist. Goethe, with his simple and profound genius, puts the truth in a nutshell, 'Alles factische ist schon Theorie,' – in other words, 'Give me a fact, and I will show you a thought behind it.' The world is the manifestation, the embodiment of ideas. Professor Huxley says so, too. Not by disposition a naturalist, what is it that has fascinated him all these years? 'I never collected anything,' he tells us, 'and species work was always a burden to me: what I cared for was the architectural and engineering part of the business, – the working out the wonderful unity of plan in the thousands and thousands of diverse living constructions, and the modification of similar apparatus to serve diverse ends.' We seem to be listening to the famous Archdeacon of Carlisle, and a nineteenth-century Pope might be tempted, as he reads, to murmur, 'What a Paley was in Huxley lost!' Physiology, the Professor repeats, took his imagination, and no wonder, since he defines it as 'the mechanical engineering of living machines.' But a machine without a plan is inconceivable; it exhibits and contains what Plato and all theologians have described as a purpose, an end, a final cause; it is there to do something, and, if it could speak as well as work, it would cry out with the king in the tragedy, 'For this was I ordained.' Thus are we already within sight of Darwin, and the sound of battle reaches us where we stand.

Few chapters in the history of science are more interesting, or so little understood by the crowds who style themselves Darwinians, as the relation of Professor Huxley to that patient but strangely limited framer of hypotheses. The 'architectural' idea, to which reference is made in the foregoing quotation, has never ceased to haunt the Professor's mind. Not at once did he accept Natural Selection; to the last he has held it on his own terms; and while, in reviewing Häckel, he is tenderly cautious not to set down his 'Story of Creation' as the romance which Du Bois Reymond openly declares it to be, his sense of logic and belief in Reason as the ground of science lead him to assert over and over again that the 'primordial teleology,' or plan in the nature of things, remains unaffected by any process which biologists may discover, so to speak, in the act. As we cannot too often remind ourselves, Darwin was quite aware of

> 'the extreme difficulty, or rather impossibility, of conceiving this immense and wonderful universe, including man with his capacity of looking far backwards and far into futurity, as the result of blind chance or necessity.'

He tells us further that,

> 'when thus reflecting, I feel compelled to look to a First Cause having an intelligent mind in some degree analogous to that of man, and I deserve to be called a Theist. This conclusion was strong in my mind about the time, as far as I can remember, when I wrote "The Origin of Species." '

Yet, while recording this suggestive statement, he declares that

> 'the old argument from design in Nature, as given by Paley, which formerly seemed so conclusive, fails, now that the law of Natural Selection has been discovered. We can no longer argue that, for instance, the beautiful hinge of a bivalve shell must have been made by an intelligent being, like the hinge of a door by man. There seems to be no more design in the variability of organic beings, and in the action of Natural Selection, than in the course which the wind blows.'

A pretty decided antithesis to the conclusion that was strong within him during the period of his greatest vigour!

The reply shall be given by Professor Huxley. First, as regards Paley's argument, we are directed to the chapter in his 'Natural Theology' where this far-sighted, though narrow apologist, has left room for Evolution, and anticipated the reasoning which it demands. 'There may be many second causes, and many courses of second causes, one behind another,' says the Archdeacon, 'between what we observe of nature and the Deity; but there must be intelligence some-where.' Variations, appetencies, gradual development, the tendency on which Professor Tyndall has remarked, of particles to marshal themselves into definite forms, – all these, and as many more wheels as you please, may be granted in the machinery; they will neither move in order to an effect, nor be capable of producing it, unless design has impressed upon them the direction in which they shall concur. What does Professor Huxley add to this but a notable confirmation, when he writes, 'It is necessary to remember that there is a wider teleology which is not touched by the doctrine of Evolution, but is actually based upon the fundamental proposition of Evolution'? 'The belief in chance and the disbelief in design' are 'in no sense appurtenances' of this great doctrine, and must be 'got rid of'; for, indeed, 'the more purely a mechanist the speculator is,' the more firmly 'does he assume a primordial molecular arrangement of which all the phenomena of the universe are consequences.' This corresponds to Paley's 'trains of mechanical dispositions fixed beforehand by intelligent appointment and kept in action by a power at the centre,' and thus it is that the mechanist, as Professor Huxley declares, is 'at the mercy of the teleologist, who can always defy him to disprove that this primordial molecular arrangement was not intended to evolve the phenomena of the universe.' So, then, the law of Natural Selection which made Darwin an agnostic, has in itself no such tendency. Moreover, if we give ear to this same ardent disciple, but neither fool nor fanatic of Evolution, 'the theological equivalent of the scientific conception of order is Providence,' and the determinate mechanism, which on both views must be granted, will be as consistent with the attributes of Deity working in the past and at the centre of things, as with the laws, or the ascertained sequences, which science goes upon.

But Darwin still objects: 'There seems to be no more design in variability and selection than in the course of the wind that blows.' The implication is that 'Chaos rules the fray,' and that order, if anywhere visible, comes by accident. Let such a votary of blind fortune, cries Professor Huxley in a passage of rare emotional eloquence, go down to the seashore, and, when a heavy gale is blowing, watch the scene; let him note the infinite variety in the tossing waves, mark the flakes of foam driven hither and thither by the wind, note the play of colours which answers a gleam of sunshine as it falls upon them, and will he not be tempted to say that chance is supreme? Yet 'the man of science knows that here, as everywhere, perfect order is manifested'; that 'there is not a curve of the wave, not a note in the howling chorus, not a rainbow-glint on a bubble, which is other than a necessary consequence of the ascertained laws of nature'; and that, 'with a sufficient knowledge of the conditions, competent physico-mathematical skill could account for, and indeed predict, every one of these "chance" events.'

Order is there in the midst of the hurly-burly; and Darwin's appeal to the wind's caprice and seeming unreason has suggested its own refutation. For where prophecy may be, design will furnish a true cause for it.

Over such passages, surprising at first sight to the readers of Professor Huxley, as the blessings uttered by Balaam son of Beor must have sounded in the ears of the Moabites, David Hume would have shaken his head dubiously. These 'primordial arrangements' call for a mind to arrange them; and 'necessary' consequences which may be predicted thousands of years before they come to pass, stop the mouth of Epicurus, with whose fortuitous clashings and cohesions Hume, despite his argument against miracles, felt a constitutional sympathy. 'The existing world,' nevertheless, affirms our 'retrospective prophet,' did lie 'potentially in the cosmic vapour,' and an intelligence well enough versed in the nature of its molecules could have written out in advance 'the state of the fauna in Britain,' – not excluding that of its political parties, – at any given moment from the landing of Julius Caesar to Mr. Gladstone's retirement. Surely we may agree that, whatever becomes of Darwin and his vacillations, nothing but an 'immortal fallacy' could charge Professor Huxley with having consented to 'reinstate the old pagan goddess, Chance.' He believes in what the Germans describe as 'die rein-mechanische Welt-construction,' but only as a process; he never takes it to be the last word that might be spoken, if we could see through the mechanism and explain the allegory of which it is a prose account. Never, did we say? It is merely the 'algebra by which we interpret Nature,' he repeats. But the mechanical symbols do often blind him to the meaning beyond. Although he maintains that they, like all abstract ideas, are, in the language of du Bois Reymond, 'purely formal notions, and signify no real existence'; although, to the dismay of the Materialists, he laughs at Matter when submitted for his acceptance as an 'entity,' and will not acknowledge Force, except by way of a working or temporary supposition, yet, bring him face to face with the believer in self-conscious spirit, whether finite or infinite, and he gives forth sayings which the crudest of the followers of La Mettrie could not better. At one time he concludes warningly, 'The philosopher who is worthy of the name knows that his personified hypotheses, such as law, and force, and ether, and the like, are merely useful symbols, while the ignorant and the careless take them for adequate expressions of reality.' This offence against logic he denounces in terms of deep reprobation as idolatry and shadow-worship. With dogmatic idols he will have no fellowship. Yet those of us who remember the controversies arising out of the Professor's readings on 'Yeast' and 'The Physical Basis of Life,' or who have taken the trouble to make a list for themselves of his pronouncements regarding matter and motion, will have already been confronted with the dilemma which either robs his utterances of definite meaning, or reduces the Ego to a nullity, destroys moral freedom, and makes the dependence of mind upon material phenomena absolute.

We must dwell a little upon this remarkable and perplexing situation. To begin with, the Professor, no less than his compeer at Berlin, holds the final confession of natural science to be 'Nescimus'; with the sword of experiment it never has, and never will, cut through the Gordian knot. As, therefore, Evolution leaves theology intact, so, by parity of reasoning, it should not meddle with the Ego or Self, which, as a lesser deity, abides within the material but living frame. 'Les dés de la Nature sont pipés,' said Galiani; and in the loading of the dice lies hidden the event: Evolution necessitates a previous Involution, which may explain the laws or process of world-building. Now does not all this apply to the Self, the agent or spiritual power that in man's organism binds the elements together, weaves the tissues, assigns or directs the functions, and governs its little human world, its microcosm, with intention? We put aside the vague word Vitalism. We speak of a person, not an abstraction which hides behind the phenomena, but the agent who controls them to whatever extent facts may determine. And we say that he transcends mechanism by the very force of his being able to direct it, his presence or absence making the essential difference between living or dead muscle, bone, and brain, precisely as it is the design put into the world-machine which hinders it from falling asunder and tumbling into chaos. Function implies purpose; without the adaptation of means to ends it becomes simply impossible. And protoplasm is the clay, the marble, or the bronze which the sculptor fashions to his own ideas of use and beauty. Itself it could not fashion, much less may we suppose that, by some absolute contradiction, it could fashion the artist who moulds it into form.

Nor does Professor Huxley fail to allow room for the Ego. 'In the first place,' he observes, 'it seems to me pretty plain that there is a third thing in the universe, to wit, consciousness, which, in the hardness of my heart or head, I cannot see to be matter or force, or any conceivable modification of either.' Furthermore, relying on Descartes and Berkeley, to him it seems that 'our one certainty is the existence of the mental world, and that of *Kraft und Stoff* falls into the rank of, at best, a highly probable hypothesis.' So that, between atoms and forces on the one side, and consciousness on the other, there is an impassable gulf fixed. But is not experience the ground of science? And have we any experience so deep and intimate as that of the living self-determined Ego which is the implied subject to every statement that we put forth? Can a man say truly, 'I think, therefore I am,' unless the verb is taken with the pronoun which alone makes it intelligible?

No, replies the Professor, that would be mediaeval Realism and pseudo-Science. There is no Self, only states of Self; and 'the assumed substantial entity, spirit,' is not even a necessary fiction. Why? we ask with astonishment. Because, says our teacher, when we abstract 'the phenomena of consciousness,' not so much as a 'geometrical ghost' is left behind. We rub our eyes and read the sentence again. Did any man who upheld the reality of his open existence suppose that, if it could be caught alone, it would exhibit the forms of geometry, – an isosceles triangle, for instance, or a hollow square? And are the 'phenomena of consciousness' – to let an ill-sounding expression pass – anything else than the very mode by which the Ego is made known to itself? Truly, these slips in reasoning lead us to be more suspicious of the Professor's logical acumen than we would wish. At all events, let it be clearly understood as an article in Professor Huxley's creed that no substantial Ego has ever been apprehended by him, or, so far as he can tell, exists within his own 'fleshy tabernacle,' or in that of any of his fellows.

This provision made, in rushes Materialism with energy irresistible. Between the attractions and repulsions of physical forces, and the highest degree of consciousness, the Professor now sees no break. Not only will the progress of science banish 'spirit and spontaneity' from the universe, and 'the physiology of the future gradually extend the realm of matter and law (as though these terms were identical!) until it is co-extensive with knowledge, with feeling, with action' – not only, again, may we hope to reach the 'mechanical equivalent' of thought, as, thanks to Joule and Clerk Maxwell, we have already attained to that of heat or electricity, – but consciousness and self-consciousness must be regarded as 'products,' direct or collateral, of the physical forces at work in the machine. For 'molecular changes are the cause,' – not a mere condition, or sign, or antecedent in their own distinct order, – but 'the cause of psychical phenomena'; and these, we have been repeatedly told, are all the Ego we can claim. An unbroken series of causes and effects leads up from matter to the philosophers' theorizing, the poet's ideal, the saint's intuitions of righteousness.

Unbroken, in spite of the 'impassable gulf'! There is no conceivable transition from 'molecules' to 'motives' in one section – the water-tight compartment, as we may term it, of Professor Huxley's philosophy. But go below where the foundations of the world are laid, and you shall watch how the *Bathybius Häckelii* – mere shred of protoplasm – emerges from mechanical combinations of forces into a life that may be everlasting. Darwin's mud-fish required at least 'some vestiges of mind,' wherewith to start upon its adventurous upward journey towards the Raphaels and the Shakesperes, into which it was one day to evolve. But 'the primitive, undifferentiated, protoplasmic living things,' – how like a swinging line this reads from one of the choric songs in Aristophanes! – 'whence the two great series of plants and animals have taken their departure,' can scarcely have begun with a particle of mind, unless we choose to imagine that the lowliest forms of algae or sea-weed not only are alive, but possess some fragment of feeling which they cannot manifest. So that, 'If the properties of water may be said to result from the nature and disposition of its component molecules,' – as they may – 'I,' exclaims our lecturer, 'can find no intelligible ground for refusing to say that the properties of protoplasm,' viz. 'the phenomena of life,' which include all thought, volition, and seemingly spiritual operations, 'result from the nature and disposition of its molecules.'

Now, 'a solution of smelling salts in water, with an infinitesimal proportion of some other saline matters,' would contain all the elementary bodies that enter into protoplasm; and in none of these, single or combined, do we meet with any trace of feeling. Is life, then, the 'direct result' of such, with no fresh principle *sui generis* brought in to account for psychical phenomena? Professor Huxley resolves 'every form of human action into 'muscular contraction'; and thought itself, on this showing, is, if an activity, muscular, if among the functions or results of life due, in the last analysis, to the complicated grouping of elements themselves summed up in a chemical formula. Shall we be wronging the essayist if we remind him of Condillac's statue, which began as marble but ended as man? It was a transformation without miracle, so Condillac asserted; no fresh creative act kindled the spirit in those eyes, no life came down into the heart, or thought substantial took the brain for its instrument. All was a mere change in the grouping of elements already there, as by mixing colours we produce a novel tint or shading. But the French Pygmalion who thus accounted for his Galatea did not deny himself. He never, to borrow a phrase from Newmarket, hedged when he had made his book, by quietly defining the substantive 'matter' as 'a name for the unknown and hypothetical cause of states of our own consciousness.' Mr Spencer has stopped this earth in which his friend would fain take refuge, by the well-warranted declaration that, 'if Idealism is true, science is a dream.' The dream-figure of ammonia, carbonic acid, and the rest, will doubtless leave spirit uninjured. What we are called upon to deal with, however, is not a phantom of the imagination, but the perfectly definite and necessarily real thing known as a chemical element. Does this, in union with other elements of like properties, and with none of unlike properties, give rise to that which we know as the self-conscious? That is the question to which Professor Huxley replies first Yes and then No, as he is thrust with either horn of the dilemma created by his own Agnosticism.

Thus these innocent algebraic symbols turn out to have a formidable meaning. Interpret them we must and we do. 'The errors of *systematic* Materialism may paralyze the energies and destroy the beauty of a life,' concludes the preacher as he descends from his pulpit in Edinburgh. Will the errors of hypothetical Materialism work less disaster? Suppose we reduce a question of metaphysics to a question of mechanics, talk about expressing consciousness in foot-pounds, and land ourselves in the conclusion that this and all other deductions of science are made by machinery, shall we escape the charge of transforming thought into matter by suggesting that machinery may be a form of thought? It has been said, as tersely as admirably, that 'matter is annihilated if it be identified with mind.' Yet, unless it be thus identified, Professor Huxley stands committed to the amazing doctrine – less easy of credence than all the fables in Alcoran, as Bacon has said of atheism – that a little smelling-salts in water, with infinitesimal quantities of phosphorus and so forth added, will produce the godlike being of man, complete psychically and ethically, as we view him in the history of the world. As the electric force and light-waves are expressions of molecular changes, 'so consciousness is, in the same sense,' an expression of the same changes, taking place in nervous matter. To cap the climax, while we are told on one page that 'man is not the centre of the living world, but one amid endless modes of life,' another we read that he *is* 'the centre and standard of comparison.' that all these various 'modes' are merely forms of his consciousness; and yet again, that, so far as each individual is concerned, 'those manifestations of intellect, of feeling, and of will which we rightly name the higher faculties,' are known 'to everyone but the subject of them' 'only as transitory changes in the relative position of parts of the body.' Confusion of thought can no farther go; the whole is a bewildering kaleidoscope where, the moment we attempt to fix our gaze upon an object, it turns into its opposite.

Criticism, says the Professor gaily is a commodity for lack of which he has never suffered. Can we marvel, seeing how deep his language cuts, how strong are its asseverations, with what loud anathemas furnished, and the slight extent to which they differ in oracular obscurity from the dogmas they undertake to overthrow? Those who glory, like himself and Du Bois Reymond, in making a humble acknowledgment and confession of intellectual impotence, whose Credo is Nescio, and who lift their devoutly sealed eyes to the unknown God, should be willing to allow that theirs is an Orphic song responding in its intelligibility to the nature of the Object celebrated. But no; so convinced is Professor Huxley that he writes a clear style, not only when dealing with coal and chalk, but as he passes with lightning quickness from neurosis to psychosis and back again, that he disdains to alter at the critic's suggestion so much as a paragraph. 'What I have written, I have written,' he says with Pilate. An amusing chapter might be composed on 'the silence of Professor Huxley' when hard-pressed by difficulties.

Do you hold out to him the bottle of smelling-salts, or vinaigrette, and, having ascertained that no vital principle hides within, beg him to show you how the Homunculus of the alchemist can arise in it. *Presto*, he strikes it with an idealizing wand, darkness falls, and by muttering the magic words, 'modes of consciousness,' lo, he has evoked the miracle! You are neither enlightened nor satisfied, but the game is at an end, the fee demanded. Homunculus steps down as an automaton, molecular and mechanical, with consciousness thrown in by way of result, but – mark it well – 'as completely without any power of modifying that working' which we call action, and whereby we judge a man's moral character, 'as the steam-whistle which accompanies the work of a locomotive engine.'

It is little to observe with the late Mr. Herbert, that by such affirmations 'states of consciousness' are made the 'regular effects of physical antecedents, but do not become causes in their turn.' The bad logic of Professor Huxley's automaton is a vanishing quantity in comparison with its ethical outcome. If the lower series can produce the higher, certainly there should be no insuperable hindrance to the higher reacting on the lower; and it might seem that the law of the conservation of energy required as much. But, leaving this point, we remark how the disciple who takes Professor Huxley at his word, may under pretext of 'Law' behave as though an Antinomian; for the steam-whistle, to which man's spirit has been likened, would surely, could it understand its relation to the steam-engine, be painfully aware of its helplessness. And in morals, he that thinks himself to be impotent is lost. In molecules, whether as causes or effects, righteousness has neither place nor meaning. The fall of a stone towards the centre, and of a character into what would be crime, were the agent responsible, must, if both are but complex motions of atoms, be esteemed equally devoid of moral interest; for what are they at last except facts reducible to a system of pushings and pullings? Neither let us imagine, with the Professor, that an automaton, however conscious, will recognize as a duty the performance of acts which it cannot help doing: – the Imperative on which Kant has established his belief in God demands as its correlative freedom. When conscience speaks, it does not say, 'Thou must,' but 'Thou oughtest.' And therefore, it is a fresh and very significant paralogism on the author's part when he makes 'the safety of morality' to depend, not on a conviction that we are subjects of the Living Righteousness, but on 'a real belief in the order of Nature which sends social disorganization upon the track of immorality as surely as it sends physical disease after physical trespasses.' If the automaton cannot help its immorality why should it be punished? If it can, it is no automaton. Moreover, has physical science such insight, denied to ordinary mortals, as to perceive this exquisite adaptation of penalties to offences, and is Providence thus triumphantly vindicated in the world below? Disease may reward virtue as well as vice; and the social catastrophe smites good and bad together, as bullets on a battlefield show no respect of persons. Did 'consequences' here and now avenge the violation of the Commandments, that trial of faith which Professor Huxley's adjectives in this sentence covertly acknowledge, when he urges that it should be 'real and living,' would be altogether spared us.

Great, indeed, is the difference between him who, with Mohammed or Calvin, looks up to a Righteous Deity disposing all things according to His will, and the modern who exclaims that 'the doctrine of free-will is now demolished, the men must reconcile themselves to the fact that they are automata.' If they must, they will, and advice so to do is superfluous. The determinist, however, who believed in God, knew that he moved about in a world spiritual and supernatural, – if, in some mysterious way, he was necessitated, yet he denied that he was coerced, and his sin was his own, not the act of the Supreme. Much simpler, and far more terrible, is the case of one who finds himself urged by blind mechanical forces, masquerading as motives, to actions that something within him reprobates and condemns. Professor Huxley is content if wound up to virtue and benevolent without choice: would he be quite as cheerful were the winding up of another sort, and the outcome, apparently, a criminal? Once more, there is a well-known, and alas too familiar state, which we call temptation against the moral law. Who is more likely to issue victorious from that contest, – the man in whose mind it is deeply fixed that he must go with the stronger force, or one to whom his freedom has been revealed by the very fact of the struggle? These are not otiose questions. As an observant traveller and citizen of the world, Professor Huxley must have remarked on the growing tendency, perceptible in all classes, to surrender at the call of inclinations which a less agnostic generation would have stamped out. The increase of suicide, no less marked in London than in Paris and Berlin, denotes a lessened confidence in the power of men and women to resist impulse. Trained upon such reading as the Essays before us, but in a dialect and with a colouring adapted to the million, unhappy creatures will talk of 'destiny' where the Professor writes of 'molecular arrangements' and, though he declares with proud independence, 'Fact I know, and Law I know, but what is this Necessity?' those whom he has thrown back upon mechanism for their code of conduct and key to the universe, may interpret the helplessness of the will which he admits as its defeat by circumstances, and a justification, in their anguish, for self-murder.

At any rate, the multitude will believe it to be an excuse for self-indulgence. What need have they to ascribe Righteousness to the Unknown? By supposition, it has no qualities which we can define or even guess at. The world which we see is all we are ever likely to experience; for Professor Huxley does not shrink from telling us that, 'like jesting Pilate,' when he has asked the question, 'Is man immortal?' he shall not think it worth his while to await an answer. We may, therefore, take such comfort as this fresh enigma supplies; the question of immortality belongs to 'lunar politics,' and the wise man will act without reference to what passes on the other side of the moon. Is Professor Huxley, then, a Positivist? Mindful of a most trenchant dissertation upon Auguste Comte, we dare not say so. And yet, all the morality which he recognizes in his sum of belief – the Prologue to his 'Controverted Questions,' – is a social product, it is bounded by the limits of human society, without acknowledgement of a Divine Conscience, or any relation to the transcendental even as Unknown. 'The desire to do what is best for the whole' is its highest conceivable form; and its sanction is tribal, for to break the law will ruin the social organism. This – if we may venture to whisper it – is precisely Comte's teaching, which George Eliot in her stories has so gloriously exalted.

But the social sanction is absurdly unequal to the burden which Professor Huxley, or Comte, or Mr. Herbert Spencer, would lay upon it. And signs are by no means wanting of a serious attempt, in widely-separated parts of the Old World and the New, to relax the bonds of morality by lowering the sanction, – a plain proof that, stripped of the transcendental qualities which have hitherto clothed it in majesty, the public conscience is liable to be perverted or even led captive by growing licence. Society does not show its former quickness to reprobate suicide, because the notion that it is an offence against the Everlasting has, in various circles, become palpably weaker. The traditional Christian feeling which fenced domestic purity round about has been satirized and flouted, or, in the very name of science, denounced as superstition. Forms of vicious indulgence hitherto severely kept down, but in Pagan epochs rampant and unashamed, have found their advocates. The automaton surrenders to impulse, and 'states of consciousness,' not centred in the Spiritual Ego, tend to disintegration, with emergence into disastrous activity of the lower faculties. In brief, thanks to Professor Huxley's accommodating 'molecules,' and the substitution of darkness impenetrable for the light from Heaven, Morality, which was in its nature Divine, and in its sanction infinite, has become finite, temporal, fluctuating, – a thing of fashion, race, and opinion, a department of police, and a function to be regulated by its foreseen utility. In practice, it should tend more and more to resolve itself into the strength of the strong and the cunning of the weak; for those who can govern consequences may despise them, and those who know how to escape penalties will laugh at them. Must we, then, go back to Hobbes and Lucretius, to the world in which 'Homo homini lupus,' and the Beast Epic usurped the place of the Human Tragedy? Our Professor, with an eye towards the primeval forest, talks firmly enough of the 'rights of tigers,' which are synonymous and co-extensive with their 'mights.' Not only does he scorn Rousseau, but, if we may judge from his various pronouncements *in re politica*, the startling dictum that 'all tigers have an equal natural right to eat all men,' is not so much a paradox facetiously stated, as a parable intended to sanctify the strong hand. In fact, the 'Law of Nature' thus exemplified is the struggle for existence; and whether force or fraud prevails, the victory of either is its justification.

'Nay,' it may be said, 'you are too hasty; the ethical agnostic goes on to distinguish between "natural right" and "moral right," which, in his view, may even be opposed to each other.' Doubtless, and what, pray, are these 'moral rights,' after all? Simply the interest of the larger organism – of society – overpowering the interest of the smaller, and the individual made subject, by a contract express or implied, to the 'tiger' a thousand times magnified – the 'Leviathan' of our afore-named Hobbes – which, armed with teeth and claws, can rend him in pieces the moment he declines to obey. It is all a matter of expediency founded upon the association of man with his fellows; and an incidental remark of Professor Huxley's will prove that, in his idea, there can be no moral transgression where Society happens not to be injured by the individual's procedure, though it were as monstrous as fancy may suggest. 'The solitary, individual man,' he says, 'living under the law of nature, cannot sin.' Sin is, therefore, a social offence; it is treason, not to God, but to humanity; and its bounds are assigned by tribal considerations. Suppose the tribe does not know, or has no power to punish, does morality cease and is the individual lawless? It would seem so. Then our ethics become a trial of strength between the leonine and the vulpine types among mankind; and whereas prophets have eloquently descanted upon the 'infinite nature of duty,' they must now yield to mathematicians who shall calculate the probabilities of a judicious investment in murder, lust, or cheating, whensoever these hold out a sufficient premium to run the blockade of social sanctions.

But the attentive reader who has come thus far along with us, will here spy out a contradiction. Has not Professor Huxley, in words to which we made reference at the beginning, defied, like the man-loving Titan upon Caucasus, all the thunderbolts of an Evil Deity, rather than prove disloyal to the truth? How, then, limit his ethics to social sanctions? For such a Deity would be more than a match for any tiger or Leviathan, and an omnipotent disorganizer of our little systems. Most true; but, as the Professor does not revise, we are compelled to take him with all his contradictions on his head, admiring the sturdy heroism, a remnant of discarded but not wholly forgotten Christian teaching (Stoical too, if he pleases), which flings foul scorn at mere brutal strength and invokes a law wherewith molecular combinations have no thrill in common. Like Tertullian upon a similar occasion, we can but exclaim, 'O testimonium animae naturaliter (Christianae!)' The agnostic's theory is naught; his personal nobleness revolts against it, and, amid the imagined shock of world, he defines Satan, though seated upon the throne of the universe, and wielding all the might of 'consequences.' Our automaton has suddenly proved that he can 'choose' to some purpose; were he willing to be a craven, how easy to worship falsehood and cringe before the Everlasting No! But the same delightful inconsistency which led Stuart Mill to prefer honesty in hell to the greatest happiness of the greatest number in a hypocritical heaven, drives his utilitarian brother to as brave, though as self-contradictory, an act of martyrdom. He will not 'shore up tottering dogmas' at the expense of truth; and in saying so with transcendent energy, not only has the Professor immolated his agnosticism upon the altar of the Absolute, but in the same moment he has ruined the morality of expediency from summit to base.

Unhappily, these splendid interludes pass unheeded by the many. As they take Darwin for a Heaven-storming giant who pulls down the Zeus of sovereign Law to set up Chance in his stead, and as, when Mr. Spencer bids them adore the Unknowable, they translate his mystic meaning into a mechanism without God, so, despite Professor Huxley's absolute morality in such passages we have quoted, they are prone to rely upon the 'laws of comfort' as determining for them the 'laws of conduct,' and to 'still their spiritual cravings' by such 'natural knowledge' as will, *e.g.*, enable them to enjoy alcohol in the hope of escaping its sad consequencs by the use of chloral, or, if that turn out a mistake in therapeutics, they can endow research until the requisite antidote has been discovered. The 'new morality' looks to medicine rather than repentance as ministering to a mind diseased; the doctor, and not the divine, attends upon Lady Macbeth, a detergent for the crimson spot in his waistcoat pocket; and if good digestion wait on appetite, there is no reason why Vitellius should not prolong the banquet, or Nero sleep less soundly when his entertainments in the Vatican gardens have ended and his living torches burnt down to a snuff.

Pernicious logic, but, granting the premises to which Professor Huxley clings in his materialistic mood, not unwarrantable! Why should a steam-engine feel remorse, though mangled limbs lie upon its pathway? Can it arrest its own movement or leave the track along which it is driven? Consciousness may prompt a groan, as conscience may tell us that we are free, – delusions both, and the groan mere sentiment, a variation in the music of the steam-whistle! We are not free, 'and there's an end on't.'

Neither did we come to our present state of religious convictions, so we learn, under the guiding hand, the all-seeing eye, of a Providence which has shaped the world's course. And, therefore, in the same spirit of criticism, satirical, dissolvent, and negative, whereby man has been split asunder into heaps of chipwood, misnamed by his foolish vanity the immortal soul, Professor Huxley undertakes, but with redoubled enthusiasm, to dislocate, to unhinge, and to lay level with the ground, that temple of the ages known as the Christian Religion. Were it a freshly tabulated form of fetish-worship from Eastern Africa, his curiosity as a man of science would temper his disdain, and we should be warned that we must deal with its peculiarities, however strange, as at least interesting survivals, or perhaps as important aids towards the insight we so greatly need into our common nature. But mention the 'cosmogony' of the 'semi-barbarous Hebrew,' and you will be told with heightened voice that it is 'the incubus of the philosopher and the opprobrium of the orthodox.' Why should the Professor's soul be so deeply vexed? Would it not be more worthy of him to explain than to render railing for railing? What though we grant, for instance, that the Hebrew conception of God and religion has resemblances or affinities in numerous points with the Babylonian or the Phoenician, how comes it that from Hebrews and not from other Semitic tribes, though mentally as well as racially akin to them, has risen over mankind the ideal of character and conduct in which the Bible-story culminates? It is an ideal, we are elsewhere told in these pages, with which men may, possibly, never be able to dispense, – as near an imitation, therefore, of the moral Absolute, though clad in human garments, as the sum of our knowledge is ever likely to attain. How account for this 'variety' among religious beliefs, so weighed down and fettered as the argument declares by 'monstrous survivals from savage superstitions,' having subdued to itself the most unruly elements, exalted one God, the Living and True, above idols, amulets, and base ignoble teraphim, lighted upon the law of righteousness hidden away beneath mountains of prehistoric drift and dross, baptized millions into a life of virtue, consecrated the lowliest things to divine uses, and, notwithstanding the stubborn blindness of many among its adherents, lived on until it might challenge criticism, as it does, to show in the moral world a principle of redemption or progress which is not already written on the Christian heart?

To furnish, not an apology but an explanation of this, by far the greatest and most momentous fact in history, would have been an achievement shedding lustre on the closing days of a philosopher and a searcher-out of Evolution. For is it not the crown and high prophetic scope to which development attains? And are we dealing with it philosophically when we break up the living whole, overlook the spirit whence all its portions derive their *raison d'être*, and shut our eyes to the fact which Butler has in so masterly a fashion exhibited, that here is, not a chaos of isolated fragments, but a dispensation the stages of which lead onward and upward, until the entire pattern is wrought upon the loom of time, the rudimentary lines filled out, the prophecy accomplished, and the earlier scaffolding, so to speak, taken away as the building grows to perfection? Of this, surely not unscientific, method, the only one adapted to an immense and complicated historical drama, what instance does professor Huxley afford? His manner of approaching the Christian system is, we had almost said, to represent it as a clerical intrigue, or, at least, as in the main an exhibition of tyranny, ignorance, and self-seeking on the part of Churchmen. Would he approve, did one of his students decline to acknowledge the relation between the imperfect being of man at early stages of his existence, and the full-grown adult, on the ground that such beginnings were so very undeveloped? Everywhere, from the problems with which Natural Selection busies itself to the scheme of Church and Bible, it is the same question, – Can we understand if we leave out design and turn away our thoughts from the final cause, the determining purpose, that, as professor Huxley is compelled to admit, may have been present all through?

The multiplied coincidences all entering into a world-wide plan, whose outcome is perfection, whether physical as in man's frame, mental in his genius, or moral in the pattern of life which he conceives and according to which his Master in the New Testament has acted, will be the result of chance only when the universe itself is Lucretian dice-play. Now, apply this method to Christianity and Judaism as they grow before the eyes of the historian. Look from the tendency to the event which limits and explains it; watch how the type leads on to its fulfilment; how the higher spiritual principle breaks out of its sheath, and the mystery is a germ of light; how the personal becomes an incarnation of ethics according to its measure, the history a disclosure of heavenly laws, and sense itself a handmaiden to spirit. By the bare teaching of morals no great human change has ever been brought to pass; but the Christian martyrs have founded an everlasting kingdom, a public polity, and have revolutionized the only progressive races of mankind. If these things lay hid in the cosmic vapour, who was it that gave to it such power and potency? Shall we talk of 'molecular combinations' any more? It would be the height of unreason. But if we recognize a foreseeing Mind, is the whole of this wonderful story to be degraded into nonsense, because Professor Huxley, fastening on a record, neither announced as complete nor a modern précis of evidence, and still less (in the intention of the writers) to be detached from that encompassing tradition which they called the Christian Faith, is not satisfied with the witnesses? Paley himself here becomes inadequate by reason of the very qualities which gave to his 'Natural Theology' its keenest edge. The method of argument in physical science is not that whereby great historians, dramatists, and moral teachers have sounded the human heart, or given us a picture of human events. It fails in subtlety, in the insight of emotion, in the sympathy which alone can interpret the music of these tones.

For the argument on behalf of Christianity is cumulative and practical, and is a matter, in the first place, of true historical induction, addressed to those who are willing to taste of its benefits, and to enter into its spirit. Though we could not prove it directly, in what more evil case would it be than the theory of development, the strength of which, as Darwin maintained, lay in its supplying a key to phenomena otherwise disconnected and insoluble? Of such a system the life is at once in the whole and in every part. Ridicule and satire, which are so eminently anthropomorphic, have little purchase on Nature and her productions; the acute angles of our wit lose themselves in her great circle, where the grotesque itself has a serious meaning, as the imperfect is prized not for its achievement but in the light of a step to something higher. When we regard the Christian history with such an experienced eye as Aristotle recommends the wise man to acquire if he would judge, most of the criticism that Professor Huxley spends on its documents will appear to be no less beside the point than needlessly envenomed. For it is the work of a man who seems to blot out the centuries with a sponge, and according to whose tactics the details are never to be interpreted by the organism they subserve. Isolated facts, miracles divorced from their purpose, and a sort of physical calculus applied to things of the spirit, make an ill preparation for understanding the Gospels. Though Professor Huxley should multiply his rationalist queries a hundredfold, and cover the pages of the New Testament with objections, that divine palimpsest would not lose its charm. As a keen judge, the late Mark Pattison, observes, men have never given up their beliefs on account of the difficulties raised against them; they will not plunge into a vacuum. And until that new creed is forthcoming, objections may perplex, sarcasm irritate, special pleading cast a cloud of dust, but the ancient doctrine will hold its own. For what, after all, is gained by negative criticism? When we close the book, its sharp sayings will not enable us to do our duty; they have answered no questions; they have propounded more riddles than they can solve; and the wilderness into which they drive mankind lies all before us while the Paradise, which was an inspiring vision of the world's childhood, melts into a mirage. Will 'cohesions and correspondences' atone for the disenchantment? And must we close with them?

Certainly not so long as Professor Huxley shows himself to be a Nisi Prius lawyer, who asks for legal evidence, but does not insist upon the impossibility of the Gospel narratives. The entire spiritual view of things, as he often grants, involves no contradiction. If we keep to the analogy of what is known, we can easily 'people the universe with entities in an ascending scale, until we reach something practically indistinguishable from omnipotence, omnipresence, and omniscience.' Would not, by the way, an omniscient 'something' be, of necessity, a Person? Nay, 'analogy might justify the construction of a naturalistic (that is to say, of a strictly scientific) theology and demonology not less wonderful than the current Supernatural.' And, by way of clinching these admissions, the Professor, when assailing with every engine of irony and ridicule certain narratives selected by him for animadversion from the Gospels, begins his attack by conceding that phenomena, like those of hypnotism as exercised on the brute creation, forbid his taking up a position – which Voltaire and his disciples most certainly would have occupied – in the region of the *à priori*, or questioning, not only the alleged facts, but their possibility.

Therefore, as distinguished from the vulgar herd, he does not say, 'These are impostures which reason scorns'; while in opposition to Hume, he is prepared to consider the evidence which may be tendered in proof of them. It shall no longer be thought the shortest way to write outside the Bible, 'Omnis homo mendax'; and then fling the volume aside. For the continuity of what is known as the Supernatural cannot be called in question. Its nature and meaning lie open to various theories; but the events themselves must no longer be dismissed with a sneer. Not that Professor Huxley has any intention to 'march to the spiritual city Sarras.' He will not even practise telepathy, or be present at a dark *séance*. Nevertheless, Braid and Charcot have strangely perplexed the rules of the game of Rationalism. Old superstitions are reviving; the question of wizardry vexes practical statesmen; Science discovers that its dry light leaves whole provinces unexplored; and no sooner is thought declared to be a function of the brain, than it shows its independence by migrating under trance to the solar plexus. Once more, the untutored intuitions of the child and the savage bear a likeness, all the stronger that it is often a caricature, to the moods of genius, as these in their turn show an ever-recurring affinity with religion. Molecules seem likely, therefore, to sink into their former place; and, whereas our Professor would not allow that the conscious or the Ego was anything more than a collateral product of forces, we have now the strongest grounds for asserting that forces are governed, and their results to an amazing degree modified, by 'states of consciousness.' The tables have been turned upon Materialism.

Thus it is that the rationalizing critic has lost ground in proportion as experience is cross-questioned. We are rapidly leaving behind the shallow 'enlightenment,' whose rule of thumb was the obviously intelligible. Materialism, ashamed of itself, puts on the agnostic's disguise; it wears the mask of Nescience, and 'with bated breath and whispering humbleness' assures us that the language it cannot but employ is altogether metaphorical. The bold ruffianism, of 'matter and motion,' to which man's highest principles were no more sacred than the instincts of swine or the appetites of the carnivora, blanches and is silent as physiology, fumbling about after the soul, stumbles upon the 'threshold of consciousness,' and shuts up its case of instruments on the approach of the medium and the mesmerizer. If Professor Huxley drags in the primeval savage as a witness against religion, the medicine-man with his incantations seems likely to prove an embarrassment to the College of Surgeons. Science is now confronted by phenomena which it can neither explain nor suppress. And Rationalism, already despoiled of its antecedent objections to the creed of the Bible, when it asks for evidence may find to its disgust that more than it demands is forthcoming.

Pascal has said in a famous epigram, 'Nature confounds the Pyrrhonist, and Reason the Dogmatist.' We may believe that in our day he would have written, 'Nature rebukes the agnostic, and Science the materialist.' Which horn of the dilemma will Professor Huxley choose? Escape is for such an one, who declines to revise, impossible. Science postulates the existence of matter, but is already reaching beyond it to that which gives matter its laws and subdues it to design. This alone is Evolution; take away purpose, and the eternal rain of atoms into a fathomless gulf can produce neither the cosmic cloud nor its ordered molecules. But it is precisely the denial of purpose that constitutes Materialism; and if we may believe Professor Huxley, that system of baseless assumptions is doomed. He has fled for refuge to Agnosticism. Will that mere negative help him to trench round about Evolution, or to put a wall of brass between the new theories of development and Religion? Surely not, while the master-principle which selects and evolves can make its necessity felt in sound logic. Variations upon lines of tendency alone will account for issues so beautiful and in every fibre adapted to each other as the world exhibits. And the higher we ascend in the scale, so much the more evident is that need of a co-ordinating Providence. When at length we perceive that an ethical universe emerges above the mud and slime of formations which gave no promise of it, we are compelled to look round until we discern a present Deity, under whose law the human qualities may be trained to their highest, and time and eternity shall be reconciled in one great scheme of Righteousness.

Here, then, is the demand of science for a reasonable account of things splendidly fulfilled, the chief lines of an eternal order made manifest, and the conscience established in its sovereign place. What, in exchange for these things, does Professor Huxley hold out? Let him gather into one view the principles he has laid down, exhibit them side by side, and enable us to judge the doctrine which he would substitute for a Christianity put to shame. He will, we make bold to affirm, be no less amazed than his readers, at the tissue of contradictions thus unfolded. For, as he is by turns agnostic and materialist, he weaves such a web of Penelope as, even in an age of confusion, the world has rarely seen. Mind is an effect of matter; but matter is a property of mind. The will counts for something in conduct; yet conduct is the response of an automaton to molecular stimulus. Morality goes by calculation, though we ought to defy consequences and let an omnipotent Devil do his worst. Between consciousness and mechanical movement yawns an impassable gulf; nevertheless, an unbroken chain binds the two as cause and effect, provided always we do not imagine that mind can act upon molecules. We ought to explain the known by means of that which we know already; still, if from the effects of mind which our innermost sense perceives, we go on to argue that in the world at large like phenomena must involve like causes, and that there is an Objective Reason, we exceed our warrant and fall into superstition. Science postulates that for the whole of Nature there must be somewhere an explanation which will make of it an intelligible and coherent system; when, however, we speak of Providence as looking before and after, we are told to beware of anthropomorphic delusions. Evidence for the marvels of Christian history is demanded; we point to the Religion as an existing fact, and our critic fastens upon passages in the Gospels which do not satisfy his sense of the trustworthy, nor will budge until we have accepted principles of argumentation that applied in similar circumstances to the events of secular story would yield no result.

In fine, the test of science being verified experience, and causes proving their reality by the effect which they produce, when we ask what Agnosticism can do for mankind, we receive the assurance that its power is wholly destructive, its outcome the practical negation of God and Immortality, its temper so sceptical that the thinking substance which every man knows himself to be is dealt with as an obsolete fiction, and we are left as mere bubbles on the stream of progress to be swallowed up ere long in the Unknown. To quote the poetical but exact language of Jean Paul, 'The immeasurable universe has become but the cold mask of iron which hides an eternity without form and void.'

Such is Professor Huxley's triumphant Nescio, chanted with a sense of exultation which would not be unbefitting were he St. Paul declaring that Death is swallowed up in victory. His scientific knowledge, his grace and dexterity of speech, his wide reading, and even his not unkindly feeling on occasion, all must serve to adorn and beautify this dissolving strain, to set a crown upon this skull into which he has fashioned the universe, and to bid us keep cheerful and work for progress though it end in the great abyss. What can be said of it all which shall not read like satire? But even Mephistopheles in an ordered system has his function; and we will end by consoling ourselves with the thought of Professor Huxley as, in his own way, doing that for metaphysics and religion which Natural Selection does for species. He is a critic who would fain eliminate whatsoever can be destroyed in the Christian system. Yet how much, by his own confession, is left standing? Will any less eloquent and well-furnished agnostic do more? If not, we may feel grateful to the man who, with an unbought zeal and the industry of years in many departments, has but succeeded in showing that now, since the growth of Science has made of Materialism a baseless absurdity, the reign of Reason, culminating in the Righteousness that rules the world, can be the only sound issue of age-long controversies. The agnostic perceives that matter and motion have not resolved 'the terrible problems of existence.' Yet a solution there must be; and when Religion gives personality to the mind which Science is continually employing but so often fails to interpret, we may expect that, instead of a haughty and most unfruitful 'Ignoramus,' we shall hear from the lips of those whom it has trained to knowledge, the Te Deum which philosophy justifies and duty demands.

NATURALISM AND AGNOSTICISM
[James Ward]

LECTURE I

Introduction

The attitudes towards Theism of Newton and Laplace: the latter has become the common attitude of 'Science.' This illustrated.

The polity of Modern Science claims to be in idea a complete and compacted whole. 'Gaps,' in what sense admitted, and how dealt with.

The dualism of Matter and Mind: 'Science' decides to treat the former as fundamental, the latter as episodic.

Professor Huxley on the situation: his admissions and advice – a blend of Naturalism and Agnosticism. These doctrines complementary: they react upon each other. According to the one, Natural Theology is unnecessary; according to the other, Rational Theology is impossible.

Examination of the position that Science forms a self-contained whole. No sharp boundary between 'science and nescience.' Mr. Spencer betrays science.

Tyndall's suggestion of an Emotional Theology.

Sir Isaac Newton concludes his famous *Principia* with a general scholium, in which he maintains that "The whole diversity of natural things can have arisen from nothing but the ideas and the will of one necessarily existing being, who is always and everywhere, God Supreme, infinite, omnipotent, omniscient, absolutely perfect." A little more than a hundred years later Laplace began to publish his *Mécanique Céleste*, which may be described as an extension of Newton's *Principia* on Newton's lines, translated into the language of the differential calculus. When Laplace went to make a formal presentation of his work to Napoleon, the latter remarked: "M. Laplace, they tell me you have written this large book on the system of the universe and have never even mentioned its Creator." Whereupon Laplace drew himself up and answered bluntly: "Sire, I had no need of any such hypothesis."[1] Since that interview another century has almost passed. Sciences that were then in their infancy – such as chemistry, geology, biology, and even psychology – have in the meantime attained imposing proportions. Any one who might now have the curiosity to compare the treatises of their best attested exponents with the great work of Laplace would find that work no longer singular in the omission which Napoleon found so remarkable, an omission which Newton, by the way, in his famous letters to Bentley, had already pronounced to be absurd.

Of course, it is not to be forgotten, the increasing specialisation brought about by the growth of knowledge justifies and even necessitates far greater restriction in the scope of any given branch of it than was customary a couple of centuries ago. People talked then, not of this or that natural science, but of 'natural philosophy'; and psychology, as we know, even in our own day, is often lumped together with metaphysics as 'mental philosophy.' It was incumbent on men styling themselves philosophers to define their attitude towards the notions of a necessarily existent Being, a First and Absolute Cause, and not to confine themselves merely to contingent existences and to causes that are in turn conditioned. The sharp division which Christian Wolff brought into vogue between empirical and rational knowledge was then ignored, if not unknown. But nowadays, at all events, the absence from a work on natural science of all reference to the supernatural would be no proof that the author disavowed the supernatural altogether.

Still, this is not the point. what we have to note is the existence in our time of a vast circle of empirical knowledge in the whole range of which the idea of a Necessary Being or a First Cause has no place. Towards this result religious and devout men like Cuvier or Faraday have contributed as much as atheists such as Holbach or Laplace. Like many another result of collective human effort, it was neither intended nor foreseen. But there it is nevertheless; and it is all the more impressive because it has grown with humanity, and is not the

[1]   W. W. Rouse Ball, *Short History of Mathematics*, 1888, p. 388.

work of a one-sided sect or school. If modern science had a voice and were questioned as to this omission of all reference to a Creator, it would only reply: I am not aware of needing any such hypothesis.

God made the country, they say, and man made the town. Now we may, as Descartes did, compare science to the town. It is town-like in its compactness and formality, in the preëminence of number and measurement, systematic connexion, and constructive plan. And where science ends, they say too, philosophy and faith may begin. But where *is* science to end? All was country once, but meanwhile the town extends and extends, and the country seems to be ever receding before it. Let us recall a few familiar instances by way of illustration. To Bentley's inquiry, how the movements and structure of the solar system were to be accounted for, Newton replied: "To your query I answer that the motions which the planets now have could not spring from any natural cause alone, but were impressed by an intelligent Agent. . . . To make this system with all its motions required a cause which understood and compared together the quantities of matter in the several bodies of the sun and planets and the gravitating powers resulting from thence, . . . and to compare and adjust all these things together in so great a variety of bodies, argues that cause to be not blind and fortuitous, but very well skilled in mechanism and geometry."[2] But now, in place of this direct intervention of an intelligent Agent, modern astronomy substitutes the nebular hypothesis of Kant and Laplace. Think again of the remarkable instances of special contrivance and design collected by Paley in his *Natural Theology*, published at the beginning of the century, or of those of the *Bridgewater Treatises* a generation later – works from which some of us perhaps got our first knowledge of science. Nobody reads these books now, and nobody writes others like them. Such arguments have ceased to be edifying, or even safe, since they cut both ways, as the formidable array of facts capable of an equally cogent dysteleological application sufficiently shews. But, in truth, special adaptations have ceased to lie on the confines of science, where natural causes end. "Sturmius," says Paley, "held that the examination of the eye was a cure for atheism."[3]

---

[2] Bentley's *Works*, Dyce's edition, vol. iii, pp. 204–206.

[3] *Natural Theology*, ch. iii, Tegge's edition of the *Works*, p. 263.

Yet Helmholtz, who knew incomparably more about the eye than half a dozen Sturms, describes it as an instrument that a scientific optician would be ashamed to make: and Helmholtz was no atheist.[4] Again the immutability and separate creation of species, which Cuvier and other distinguished naturalists long stoutly maintained, are doctrines now no longer defensible. And without them the unique position assigned to man in the scale of organic life – for the sake of which, it is not too much to say, Cuvier and his allies held out so desperately – can be claimed for man no more. "The grounds upon which this conclusion rests," says Darwin, the conclusion, *i.e.*, that man is descended from some less highly organised form, "will never be shaken, for the close similarity between man and the lower animals in embryonic development as well as in innumerable points of structure and constitution, both of high and of the most trifling importance, – the rudiments which he retains, and the abnormal reversions to which is he occasionally liable, – are facts which cannot be disputed."[5] And certainly the unanimity with which this conclusion is now accepted by biologists of every school seems to justify Darwin's confidence a quarter of a century ago. And not merely man's erect gait and noble bearing, but his speech, his reason, and his conscience too, are now held to have been originated in the course of a vast process of evolution, instead of being ascribed, as formerly, to the inspiration and illumination of the Divine Spirit directly intervening.

But vast as the circuit of modern science is, it is still of course limited. On no side does it begin at the beginning, or reach to the end. In every direction it is possible to leave its outposts behind, and to reach the open country where poets, philosophers, and prophets may expatiate freely. However, we are not for the present concerned with this extra-scientific region – the metempirical as it has been called: what we have to notice is rather the existence of serious gaps *within* the bounds of science itself. But over these vacant plots these instances of *rus in urbe*, science still advances claims, endeavouring to occupy them by more or less temporary erections, otherwise called working hypotheses. Concerning such gaps more must be said presently. Meanwhile, it may suffice to refer to one or two in

4   *Popular Lectures*, 1893, vol. i, p. 194.
5   *The Descent of Man*, 1871, vol. ii, p. 385.

passing, as our immediate concern is only to understand the claim of science to include them within its domain, though it can only occupy them provisionally.

There is first the great gap between the inorganic and the organic world. Even if astronomical physics will carry us smoothly from chaotic nebulosity to the order and stability of a solar system, and if again "it does not seem incredible that from . . . low and intermediate forms, both animals and plants may have been developed";[6] still what of the transition from the lifeless to the living? There is no physical theory of the original of life. Nothing can better shew the straits to which science is put for one than the reception accorded to Lord Kelvin's forlorn suggestion that possibly life was brought to this planet by a stray meteorite! But, on the other hand, taking living things as there, science finds nothing in their composition or in their processes physically inexplicable. The old theory of a special vital force, according to which physiological processes were at the most only analogous to – not identical with – physical processes, has for the most part been abandoned as superfluous. Step by step within the last fifty years the identity of the two processes has been so far established, that an eminent physiologist does not hesitate to say "that for the future, the word 'vital' as distinctive of physiological processes might be abandoned altogether."[7] It is allowed that life has never been found to arise save through the mediation of already existing life – in spite of many a long and arduous search. Yet, on the ground that vital phenomena furnish no exceptions to purely physical laws, it is assumed that life at its origin – if it ever did originate – formed no break in the continuity of evolution. This instance may perhaps be taken as a type of the scientific treatment of existing lacunae in our empirical knowledge. Wherever there are reasons for maintaining that a natural explanation is *possible*, though none is, in fact, forthcoming, there actual discontinuity and the supernatural are held to be excluded.

But this principle is put to a far severer trial when we pass from the physical aspect of life to the psychical. The coarse and shallow materialism that disposed of this difficulty with an

---

6 *Origin of Species*, sixth edition, p. 425.

7 Professor Burdon Sanderson, *Opening Address* to the Biological Section, British Association, 1889. *Nature*, vol. xl, p. 522.

epigram, "The brain secretes thought as the liver secretes bile," only served to set the problem in a clearer light. For it is just the hopelessness of the attempt to resolve thought into a physiological function that is the difficulty. And accordingly, within twenty years after Karl Vogt's flippant utterance, we find the physiologist, Du Bois-Reymond, answering this 'riddle,' not merely with an *Ignoramus*, but with an *Ignoribimus*. Indeed, nowadays there is nothing that science resents more indignantly than the imputation of materialism. For, after all, materialism is a philosophical dogma, as much as idealism. It professes to start from the beginning, which science can never do; and, when it is true to itself, never attempts to do. Modern science is content to ascertain coexistences and successions between facts of mind and facts of body. The relations so determined constitute the newest of the sciences, psychophysiology or psychophysics. From this science we learn that there exist manifold correspondence of the most intimate and exact kind between states and changes of consciousness on the one hand, and states and changes of brain on the other. As respects complexity, intensity, and time-order the concomitance is apparently complete. Mind and brain advance and decline *pari passu*; the stimulants and narcotics that enliven or depress the action of the one tell in like manner upon the other. Local lesions that suspend or destroy, more or less completely, the functions of the centres of sight and speech, for instance, involve an equivalent loss, temporary or permanent, of words and ideas. Yet, notwithstanding this close and undeviating parallelism, between conscious states and neural states, it is admitted, as I have already said, that the two cannot be identified. It is possible, no doubt, to regard a brain change as a case of matter and notion, but the attempt to conceive a change of mind in this wise is allowed to be ridiculous.

But though these two sets of facts cannot be identified, as the physical and physiological may be, yet, since they vary concomitantly, may not causal connexion at all events be safely affirmed of them? Yes, it is said, if that means merely that the connexion is not casual. When, however, the attempt is made to determine an event in either as the cause or the effect of the concomitant event in the other, the difficulties seem insuperable. There is not merely the difficulty that the two are strictly coincident in time, so that all question of sequence is excluded – although this difficulty is one on which stress had been laid.

But, in addition, the series of neural events – being physical – is already, so to say, closed and complete within itself, each neural state is held to be wholly the effect of the neural state immediately preceding it, and the entire cause of that directly following. In other words, the master generalisation of the physical world, that of the conservation of energy, would be violated by the assumption that energy could appear or disappear in one form without at once disappearing or reappearing to a precisely equivalent amount in another. Brain changes could not then be transformed into sensations, or volitions be transformed into brain changes, without a breach of physical continuity; and of such a breach there is supposed to be no evidence.

The position, then, of science in the present day as regards what I have called the gap between the psychical and the physical is briefly this: If the mechanical theory of the material world including the modern principle of energy is not to be impugned, then there is no natural explanation of the parallelism that exists between processes in brain and processes in consciousness; the gap is one across which no causal links can be traced. This amount of dualism science seems content to admit rather than forego the strict continuity and necessary concatenation of the physical world. But it is not regarded as the sort of discontinuity that sets empirical generalisation at defiance or points directly to supernatural interference. True, the gulf is such that the utmost advance on the physical side would not, of itself, help on psychology in the least, nay would not even suggest to the physicist, pure and simple, the existence of the psychical side at all. True, again, the gap is such that psychology, keeping strictly to its own domain, gives no hint of the existence of that physical mechanism of brain, nerve, and muscle, by which it is so intimately shadowed, or – as many very arbitrarily prefer to say – which it so intimately shadows. But this very concomitance is itself a uniformity of nature, a uniformity of coexistence, and no limit can be assigned to the extent to which psychophysics may succeed in determining its details. Inasmuch as supernatural intervention is not invoked by physiology or psychology severally, psychophysics can obviously dispense with it in merely correlating the two. As a result of our brief survey, then, we find that "the ideas and the will of the one necessarily existing Being," to which Newton referred, do not figure even as a working hypothesis anywhere within the range of that systematic exposition of "the whole diversity of natural things," that calls itself modern science.

This summary of existing knowledge about whatever comes to be is confessedly meagre in the extreme. To many it will suggest objections and to some it may seem obscure. I shall myself have objections in plenty to make and to meet, as best I may, later on; as to the obscurity, this I fear could only be remedied by an elaboration of detail which would call for more time than we can spare. Moreover, this defect is made good already in sundry well-known essays and addresses by men like Huxley, Tyndall, Clifford, Helmholtz, Du Bois-Reymond, and others. Besides, it is precisely the broadest and most general characteristics, not the details, of the current science of nature, that I wish to emphasise. Let me then, before attempting to advance further, ask your patience while I try to restate them in another way.

We note first of all the old dualism of Matter and Mind, or rather – since a duality of substances is nowadays neither asserted nor denied – the dualism of so-called material and mental phenomena. As to material phenomena – that is to say wherever there is matter in motion, whether planets revolving round a sun or molecules vibrating in a living frame, over all these – certain mechanical laws are held to be supreme; that a single atom should deviate from its predetermined course were as much a miracle as if Jupiter should break away from its orbit and set the whole solar system in commotion. Matter and energy are the two fundamental conceptions here. The amount of both is constant, and even independent, in so far as matter cannot be raised to the dignity of energy nor energy degraded to the inertness of matter. But the energy of any given body or material system may vary indefinitely, provided only every increase or decrease shall entail always an equivalent decrease or increase by transfer to or from other bodies or systems. Thus the continuity and solidarity of the material world is complete; but there is no limit to the diversities which it may assume, provided its physical unity and concatenation are strictly conserved.

When we turn to what are called mental phenomena we find nothing answering to this quantitative constancy, inviolable continuity, and strict reciprocity. Minds are not a single conservative system as matter and energy are. What one mind gains in ideas, feeling, strength of will, another does not necessarily lose. We have here a number of separate individuals, not a single continuum. But on the other hand we know nothing of minds without a living body and without external environment. Between each living body and this environment there is a continuous exchange of material – the metabolism of physiologists – accompanied by a constant give and take of energy. While the organism gains in this exchange, it thrives and developes, goes up in the world; as it loses it begins to decline and perish, to go down in the world. But, as all organisms collectively, together with their environments, constitute the constant and continuous physical system, indefinite increase and advance all round are impossible. Sooner or later what we describe as struggle must ensue, leading to 'the survival of the fittest,' as its result. But conscious life is found to rise and fall with organic efficiency and position, so that (completely isolated and distinct as the consciousness of A is from that of B), all minds are indirectly connected; each is yoked to its own body and through this body to the one material world. Of other connexions and relations that minds may have wholly independent of this physical connexion, we have so far no experience; all intercourse, all tradition, is mediated through the one physical world.

So then the concomitance of mind with body is invariable; concomitance of body with mind on the other hand is not certainly more than occasional, even exceptional. Moreover, keeping strictly to the psychological standpoint, we can never get beyond qualitative description and rough classification, natural history in a word, not natural science. And this would be true even though in *individual* cases, quantitative determinations were possible, which however they are not. For there are certainly no *common* psychological units of intensity or duration; no mind-stuff fixed in amount; no psychical energy that must be conserved. Thus, on the physical side we have a single system, unvarying law, quantitative exactness, complete concatenation of events – in a word, one vastly complex, but rigidly adjusted, mechanism. But on the psychical side we have as many worlds as there are minds, connected indeed, yet independent to an indefinite extent; a series of partial and more or less disparate *aperçus* or outlooks; each for itself a centre of experience, but all without any exact orientation in common. Psychology, pure and simple, has always been individualistic and accepted, tacitly at least, the *Homo Mensura* doctrine. Again, on the physical side the elements with which we deal are held to be indestructible and unalterable, the same always and everywhere. Whereas minds, so far as we know them, are the subjects of continual flux while they last; and seem to arise and melt away like streaks of morning cloud on the stable firmament of blue. But though all these unique and transient centres of thought and feeling are psychologically as isolated and individual as mountain summits, oases in a desert, or stars in space, yet they are indirectly related through physical organisms, which are integral parts of the one great mechanism. To set out, then, from this one permanent material scheme and to trace its working through the fleeting multitude of vital sparks, as one follows the stem of a tree up into its branches with their changing leaves and fruit – that is a sure, synthetic, and direct method. But to attempt, setting out from these sporadic and shifting complexities, to reach an abiding and fundamental unity, is as precarious as analytic and inverse methods always are; and possibly it is altogether hopeless. In brief, then, we are to conclude that, in proportion as psychological facts are physiological interpretable, and in proportion again as their physiological concomitants are physically explicable, in that same proportion will every fact of mind have a definite and assignable place as an epiphenomenon or concomitant of a definite and assignable physical fact, and our empirical knowledge approximate towards a rounded and complete whole.

No doubt such consummation of natural science is indefinitely far off. But it is an ideal. Let me cite a single and very eminent witness. "Any one who is acquainted with the history of science," says Professor Huxley, "will admit, that its progress has, in all ages, meant, and nor more than ever means, the extension of the province of what we call matter and causation, and the concomitant gradual banishment from all regions of human thought of what we call spirit and spontaneity. . . . And as surely as ever future grows out of past and present, so will the physiology of the future gradually extend the realm of matter and law until it is coextensive with knowledge, with feeling, and with action. The consciousness of this great truth," Mr. Huxley believes, "weighs like a nightmare upon many of the best minds of these days. They watch what they conceive to be the progress of materialism in such fear and powerless anger as a savage feels, when, during an eclipse, the great shadow creeps over the face of the sun. The advancing tide of matter threatens to drown their souls; the tightening grasp of law impedes their freedom."[8]

The alarm and perplexity are, in Professor Huxley's opinion, alike needless; the "strong and subtle intellect" of David Hume, if only we would ponder his words and accept his "most wise advice" would, he thinks, soon allay our fears and give us heart again. The advice is well-known, but as it will fitly introduce a new trait in the modern scientific attitude, the main features of which it is our present business to characterise, I will ask leave to re-quote it. It was in the *Inquiry concerning the Human Understanding* that Hume wrote: "If we take in hand any volume of divinity, or school metaphysics, for instance, let us ask, Does it contain any abstract reasoning concerning quantity or number? No. Does it contain any experimental reasoning concerning matter of fact and existence? No. Commit it then to the flames; for it can contain nothing but sophistry and illusion." How this advice is to dispel perplexity at "the advancing tide of matter and the tightening grasp of law," and how it is to reassure those who are alarmed lest man's moral nature should be debased by the increase of his knowledge, are perhaps not straightway obvious! Well, the comfort consists simply in saying: *After all the knowledge is very superficial and must always remain so.* As Professor Huxley puts it: "What, after all, do we know of this terrible 'matter' except as a name for the unknown and hypothetical cause of states of our own consciousness? And what do we know of that 'spirit' over whose threatened extinction by matter a great lamentation is arising, . . . except that it is also a name for an unknown and hypothetical cause, or condition, of states of consciousness? And what is the dire necessity and 'iron' law under which men groan? Truly, most gratuitously invented bugbears. . . . Fact I know, and Law I know; but what is this necessity save an empty shadow of my own mind's throwing – something illegitimately thrust into the perfectly legitimate conception of law?" "The fundamental doctrines of materialism," continues Professor Huxley, "like those of spiritualism and most other 'isms' lie outside the limits of philosophical inquiry; and David Hume's great service to

[8]   *Collected Essays*, Eversley edition, vol. i, pp. 159 ff.

humanity is his irrefragable demonstration of what these limits are."

In this deliverance of Professor Huxley we have a fragment of that particular 'ism' for which he is proud to be sponsor and which he has christened Agnosticism. It is in fact that doctrine that has led modern science, as I have already remarked, to separate itself from the pronounced materialism and atheism so common in scientific circles half a century or so ago. But it is only in its bearing on the ideal of knowledge just described that agnosticism concerns us at present. Professor Huxley – in this point following the lead of Mr. Herbert Spencer – concludes the consolatory reflections he derives from Hume and returns to his first position in this wise: "It is in itself of little moment whether we express the phenomena of matter in terms of spirit, or the phenomena of spirit in terms of matter – each statement has a certain relative truth. But with a view to the progress of science, the materialistic terminology is in every way to be preferred. For it connects thought with the other phenomena of the universe, . . . whereas, the alternative, or spiritualistic, terminology is utterly barren, and leads to nothing but obscurity and confusion of ideas. Thus there can be little doubt, that the further science advances, the more extensively and consistently will all the phenomena of Nature be represented by materialistic formulae and symbols."

This 'nightmare' theory of knowledge, as regards its exclusion of everything supernatural or spiritual, thus closely resembles the doctrines which in the seventeenth century they called Naturalism. And the name has recently been revived. But it is important to bear in mind the difference already noted. Naturalism in the old time tended dogmatically to deny the existence of things divine or spiritual, and dogmatically to assert that matter was the one absolute reality. But Naturalism and Agnosticism now go together; they are the complementary halves of the dominant philosophy of our scientific teachers. So far as knowledge extends all is law, and law ultimately and most clearly to be formulated in terms of matter and motion. Knowledge, it is now said, can never transcend the phenomenal; concerning 'unknown and hypothetical' existences beyond and beneath the phenomenal, whether called Matter or Mind or God, science will not dogmatise either by affirming or denying. This problematic admission of undiscovered country beyond the polity of science has tended powerfully to promote the consolidation of that polity itself. Release from the obligation to include ultimate questions has made it easier, alike on the score of sentiment and of method, to deal in a thoroughly regimental fashion with such definite coexistences, successions, resemblances, and differences as fall within the range of actual experience. The eternities safely left aside, the relativities become at once amenable to system. All this is apparent in the passages just quoted from Professor Huxley.

But I pass now to a new point. Agnosticism, we have just seen, has reacted upon naturalism, inducing in it a more uncompromising application of scientific method to all the phenomena of experience. And it will be found that naturalism in its turn has reacted upon agnosticism, inducing in that a more pronounced scepticism, or even the renunciation of higher knowledge as a duty, in place of the bare confession of ignorance as a fact. The contrast between the certainty of science, with its powers of prediction and measurement, and the uncertainty of philosophic speculation, forever changing, but never seeming to advance, has been one source of this agnostic despondency. The long record of attempts that can only appear as failures, the many highly gifted minds, as it seems, uselessly sacrificed in the forlorn enterprise of seeking beneath the veil of things for the very heart of truth – this, when contrasted with the steady growth of scientific knowledge, might well, as Kant puts it, "bring philosophy, once the queen of all sciences, into contempt, and leave her, like Hecuba forsaken and rejected, bewailing: *modo maxima rerum, tot generis natisque potens – nunc trahor, exul, inops.*"[9] But since Kant's day the position of philosophy has become still more desperate. That agnosticism – for such we might call it – by which he himself supplanted the bold but baseless metaphysics of his rationalistic predecessors, is now in turn scouted as transcendental and surreptitious; is charged, that is with borrowing from experience the very forms on whose strictly *a priori* character it would rest the possibility of experience. By the advance of what has been called metageometry, still more by the advance of experimental and comparative psychology, and by the wide reach of the conception of evolution, science has encroached upon what Kant regarded as the province of the *a priori*. He allowed that all our knowledge begins with

[9] *Critique of Pure Reason*, first edition, Pref., p. 3.

experience and is confined to experience. He allowed that if the several particulars of that experience had been different, as they conceivably might have been, our *a posteriori* generalisations would have varied in like manner. But a spontaneous generation of knowledge from sense particulars without the aid of *a priori* formative processes, was to him as inconceivable as the spontaneous generation of a living object from lifeless matter without the aid of a vital principle. But now that the physical origin of life is regarded as not merely credible but certain, *a priori* forms of knowledge are out of fashion. Kant's position, in a word, is held to be out-flanked. There can be no science without self-consciousness; but then this very self-consciousness, it is said, has been evolved by natural processes. Nature herself has polished, and apparently is still polishing, the mirror in which she sees herself reflected. Kant's dialectic against dogmatic metaphysics is thankfully accepted; but his theory of knowledge is held to be superseded by a better psychology and a better anthropology. All this, of course, really amounts to saying that there can be no theory of knowledge at all as distinct from an account of the natural processes by which, as a fact in time, knowledge has come to be. The *solvitur ambulando* procedure is at once the most effective and the most summary method of dealing with this position, and we shall have to try our best at it later on.

Meantime one or two remarks on this unreflective, uncritical, character of modern science may serve to complete this preliminary sketch of its attitude towards the problem of theism. We have seen that, on the one hand, it allows no place of Natural Theology or such knowledge of God as the constitution of nature may furnish; and that, on the other, it denies the title of Knowledge to Rational Theology, or such knowledge of God as philosophy may claim to disclose. We have seen further that these negations have two main grounds: first, the Laplacean *dictum*, which Naturalism adopts, that science has no need of the theistic hypothesis; and secondly, the Humean, or ultra-agnostic, *dictum*, that what is neither abstract reasoning concerning quantity or number, nor yet experimental reasoning concerning matter of fact or existence, can only be sophistry or illusion. Disregarding Hume's somewhat rhetorical phraseology, these two statements amount to saying, first, that there is no knowledge save scientific knowledge, or knowledge of phenomena and of their relations, and secondly, that this knowledge is non-theistic. It is worth our while to note that in a sense both these propositions are true, and *that* is the sense in which science in its every-day work is concerned with them. But again there is a sense in which, taken together, these propositions are not true, but this is a sense that will only present itself to the critic of knowledge reflecting upon knowledge as a whole. Thus it is true that science has no need, and indeed, can make no use, in any particular instance, of the theistic hypothesis. That hypothesis is specially applicable to nothing just because it claims to be equally applicable to everything. Recourse to it as an explanation of any specific problem would involve just that discontinuity which it is the cardinal rule of scientific method to avoid. But, because reference to the Deity will not serve for a physical explanation in physics or a chemical explanation in chemistry, it does not therefore follow that the sum total of scientific knowledge is equally intelligible whether we accept the theistic hypothesis or not. Again, it is true that every item of scientific knowledge is concerned with some definite relation of definite phenomena and with nothing else. But, for all that, the systematic organisation of such items may quite well yield further knowledge which transcends the special relations of definite phenomena. In fact, so surely as science collectively is more than a mere aggregate of items or 'knowledges,' as Bacon would have said, so surely will the whole be more, and yield more, than the mere sum of its parts.

And the strictly philosophical term 'phenomenon,' to which science has taken so kindly, is in itself an explicit avowal of relation to something beyond that is not phenomenal. Mr. Herbert Spencer who, more perhaps than any other writer, is hailed by our men of science as the best exponent of their first principles, is careful to insist upon the existence of this relation of the phenomenal to the extra-phenomenal, noumenal, or ontal. His synthetic philosophy opens with an exposition of this "real Non-relative or Absolute," as he calls it, without which the relative itself becomes contradictory. And when Mr. Spencer speaks of this Absolute as the Unknowable, it is plain that he is using the term 'unknowable' in a very restricted sense. I say this, not merely because he devotes several chapters to its elucidation, for these might have been purely negative; but also because it is an essential part of Mr. Spencer's doctrine to maintain that "our consciousness of the Absolute, indefinite

though it is, is positive and not negative";[10] that "the
Noumenon everywhere named as the antithesis of the Phenomenon, is throughout necessarily thought of as an actuality";[11]
that, "though the Absolute cannot in any manner or degree be
known, *in the strict sense of knowing*, yet we find that its
positive existence is a necessary datum of consciousness; that
so long as consciousness continues, we cannot, for an instant,
rid it of this datum; and that thus the belief which this datum
constitutes, has a higher warrant than any other whatever."[12]
In short the Absolute or Noumenal according to Mr. Spencer,
though not known in the strict sense, that is as the phenomenal
or relative is known, is so far from being a pure blank or
nonentity for knowledge that this phenomenal, which *is* said to
be known in the strict sense, is inconceivable without it. It is
worth noting, by the way, that 'this actuality behind appearances,' without which appearances are unthinkable, is by Mr.
Spencer identified with that 'ultimate verity' on which religion
ever insists. His general survey of knowledge then has led this
pioneer of modern thought, as he is accounted to be, to reject
both the Humean dictum that there is no knowledge save
knowledge of phenomena and of their relations, as well as the
Laplacean dictum that this knowledge is non-theistic.

But it might be maintained that the several relations among
phenomena may suffice in their totality to constitute an
Absolute. Possibly it may be so; this much remains for the
present an open question. But even so, it would still be true that
any knowledge of this Absolute would not be phenomenal
knowledge. Science, which is chary of all terms with a
definitely theistic implication, talks freely of the Universe and
of Nature; but I am at a loss to think of any single *scientific*
statement that has been, or can be, made concerning either the
one or the other. By scientific statement I mean one that having
a real import is either self-evident or directly proved from
experience.[13]

There is till another possibility, some seem to think, which,
however, has not yet been realised, and which indeed, it seems
to me, never can be realised. It might conceivably have

[10]   *First Principles*, stereotyped edition, p. 92.

[11]   *o.c.*, p. 88

[12]   *o.c.*, p. 98.

[13]   Kant's discussion of the cosmological antinomies is instructive here in its
method even more than in its results.

happened, they say, that our finite knowledge of phenomena proved to be a complete and rounded whole as far as it went, a sort of microcosm within the macrocosm; a model of the whole universe on a scale appropriate to our human faculties, rather than a fragment with hopelessly 'ragged edges.' And spite of the many obstinate questionings that show the contrary, it is far from unusual to find scientific men talking as if this preferable ideal, as some perhaps think it, was the sober fact. Thus Mr. Spencer, though controverting all such views, nevertheless describes "science as a gradually increasing sphere," such that "every addition to its surface does but bring it into wider contact with surrounding nescience." True, this with Mr. Spencer is only a metaphor, whereas for Comte it was a doctrine; but as metaphor or as doctrine it is widely current and most misleading. Our knowledge is not only bounded by an ocean of ignorance, but intersected and cut up as it were by straits and seas of ignorance; the *orbis scientiarum*, in fact, if we could only map out ignorance as we map out knowledge, would be little better than an archipelago, and would show much more sea than land.

Of course the rejoinder will be made, We admit the intervening streaks and shallows; but here our ignorance, like our knowledge, is only relative, whereas, of the illimitable ocean beyond, our ignorance is absolute and profound. By the help of postulates and generalisations which our perceptive experience confirms, and by the help of hypotheses congruent with our present experiences and verifiable by experiences yet to come, we have completed the circle of the sciences and built up a *Systema Naturae*. I have endeavoured to describe this system of natural knowledge, as it is commonly conceived by those whose genius and enterprise we have to thank for it. The said fundamental postulates and unrestricted generalisations, the various assumptions consciously or unconsciously made, the hypothetical abstractions by which this unity is secured – to all these we must give our best attention later. For the moment I am concerned only with this one conceit: that the several sciences by their mutual attraction, if I might so say, together form a single whole, *totus teres atque rotundus*, floating in "an interminable air" of pure nescience. But unless we are prepared to repudiate logic altogether, this sharp severance of known and unknown, knowable and unknowable, must be abandoned, so radical are the contradictions that beset it. Where nescience is absolute, nothing can be said; neither that there is more to know nor that there is not. But if science were verily in itself complete, this could only mean that there was no more to know; and then there could be and would be no talk of an environing nescience.

Again, if nescience is real, – is such, I mean, that we are conscious of it, – we must at least know that there is more to know. But how can we know this? To say that we know it because of the incompleteness of the phenomenal relations actually ascertained, may be true enough; but of course such an admission gives up at once the *solid* unity of science as it is and the *utter* vacuity of the opposed nescience. We must suppose then that phenomenal knowledge is regarded as *ideally complete* – the fragments sufficing at least to suggest an outline of the whole, helped out by ultimate generalisations such as the conservations of matter and energy, the principle of evolution, and the like. And if it is still held that there is an endless and impalpable envelope of nescience beyond this ideally perfect sphere of positive knowledge, this can only be because the phenomenal implicates the noumenal; the known and knowable, as Mr. Spencer and others teach, being necessarily related to the 'unknowable,' which means, we must remember, the not strictly knowable. But this doctrine too is fatal to any thoroughgoing dualism of science and nescience; on the contrary, it amounts to a dualism of knowledge. As Mr. Spencer himself says: "The progress of intelligence has throughout been dual. Though it has not seemed so to those who made it, every step in advance has been a step toward both the natural and the supernatural. The better interpretation of each phenomenon has been, on the one hand, the rejection of a cause that was relatively conceivable in its nature but unknown in the order of its actions, and, on the other hand, the adoption of a cause that was known in the order of its actions but relatively inconceivable in its nature. . . . And so there arise two antithetical states of mind, answering to the opposite sides of that existence about which we think. While our consciousness of Nature under the one aspect constitutes Science, our consciousness of it under the other aspect constitutes Religion."[14]

Finally, if on the other hand, it be held that phenomenal knowledge, when ideally complete, will be clear of these

[14]   *First Principles*, p. 106 *fin.*

noumenal and supernatural implications, then this position again is incompatible with a dualism between science and nescience. For if the sphere of science were so complete as to be clear of all extra-scientific implications, then, as I have already said, there would be no nescience. If, however, there must be nescience so long as science is finite and relative, then *so long* the metaphysical ideas of the Absolute and the Infinite will transcend the limits of actual science, and yet will have a place within the sphere of science ideally complete. In other words, ideally complete science will become philosophy. This conceit or doctrine of an absolute boundary between science and nescience and the endeavour to identify with it a like sharp separation between empirical knowledge and philosophical speculation may then, we conclude, be both dismissed as "sophistical and illusory." Nevertheless, as I have said, these notions are widely current in one shape or other, save among the few in these days, who have even a passman's acquaintance with the rudiments of epistemology. One of the most plausible and not least prevalent forms of this doctrine is embodied in the shallow Comtian 'Law of Development,' according to which there are three stages in human thought, the theological, the metaphysical, and the positive; the metaphysical superseding the theological and being in turn superseded by the positive or scientific. A glance at the past history of knowledge would shew at once the facts that make these views so specious and yet prove them to be false.

And now to resume what has been said, and to conclude: I have tried to present an outline sketch of that polity of many mansions, which we may call the Kingdom of the Sciences, and the mental atmosphere in which its citizens live. As the constant inhabitants of large towns, though familiar with shops supplying bread and beef, know nothing of the herds in the meadows or the waving fields of wheat, so the mere *savant* is familiar with 'phenomena and their laws' and with the methods by which they are severally measured and ascertained, but rarely or never thinks of all that 'phenomena' and 'law' and 'method' imply. As a knowledge of what is thus beyond his purview cannot be attained by experiment or calculation, it should surprise us as little to find him associate it with nescience as it surprises us to find the urchins in a slum confusing with the tales of fairy-land what we may try to tell them of the actual facts of country life.

Indeed the resemblance in the two cases is closer than at first it seems. For it is very common for those who decline to recognise Natural or Rational Theology to speak with fervour of what I think we might fairly call Æsthetic Theology. Tyndall, for example, in his once famous Belfast Address to the British Association, spoke thus to the assembled representatives of science: "You who have escaped from these religions into the high-and-dry light of the intellect may deride them; but in so doing you deride accidents of form merely, and fail to touch the immovable basis of the religious sentiment in the nature of man. To yield this sentiment reasonable satisfaction is the problem of problems at the present hour."[15] It seems clear that in Tyndall's opinion this reasonable satisfaction could not need, at any rate, must not have, an intellectual basis either 'high-and-dry,' or otherwise. For he proceeds to describe this religious sentiment as "a force, mischievous, if permitted to intrude on the region of *knowledge*, over which it holds no command, but capable of being guided to noble issues in the region of *emotion*, which is its proper and elevated sphere." Yet a page or two further on Tyndall brings his address to a close with these words: "The inexorable advance of man's understanding in the path of knowledge, and those unquenchable claims of his moral and emotional nature which the understanding can never satisfy, are here equally set forth. The world embraces not only a Newton, but a Shakespeare – not only a Boyle, but a Raphael – not only a Kant, but a Beethoven – not only a Darwin, but a Carlyle. Not in each of these, but in all, is human nature whole. They are not opposed, but supplementary; not mutually exclusive, but reconcilable. And if, unsatisfied with them all, the human mind, with the yearning of a pilgrim for his distant home, will still turn to the Mystery from which it has emerged, seeking so to fashion it as to give unity to thought and faith; so long as this is done, not only without intolerance or bigotry of any kind, but with the enlightened recognition that ultimate fixity of conception is here unattainable, and that each succeeding age must be held free to fashion the Mystery in accordance with its own needs – then, casting aside all the restrictions of Materialism, I would affirm this to be a field for the noblest exercise of what, in contrast with the *knowing* faculties, may be called the *creative* faculties of man."

[15]   Reprint of Address, 1874, p. 60.

I am really at a loss to know whether this is to be taken for climax or anti-climax, pathos or bathos. But of one thing I am sure: tried by the "high-and-dry light of the intellect – this specimen of Professor Tyndall's "eloquence and scientific fire," as the *Saturday Review* called it, is almost too flimsy for derision.

Surely the late professor must have thought lightly of his own teaching, to be ready under the influence of an emotional yearning to cast aside the doctrine to which an "intellectual necessity" (p. 55) had led him, the doctrine by which he discerned in matter "the promise and potency of all terrestrial life"; nay, further, to be ready to refashion the Mystery from which the human mind has emerged so as to give unity to thought and faith. If religious sentiments must not be permitted to intrude on the region of knowledge, how is the refashioning in the interests of this unity to begin? And if nothing short of *creative* faculties can satisfy this sentiment, what about 'the danger' and 'the mischief' to the work of the *knowing* faculties when such sentiment does intrude?

Professor Tyndall does not tell us where he went for his psychology. But Mr. Spencer, to whom he frequently refers, would have taught him that no sentiments are entirely without a cognitive basis, the religious perhaps least of all. This cognitive element in religious sentiment is of necessity amenable to intellectual challenge, just because it is itself of necessity intellectual. No doubt, "ultimate fixity of conception is here unattainable"; but when Professor Tyndall tells us this, has he forgotten that on the very same page he has also declared "it certain that [scientific] views will undergo modification"? In fact, just as religious sentiment implies knowledge, so too do the high-and-dry constructions of the intellect involve "creative faculties"; finality will be impossible and reconstruction a necessity in both regions so long as we only "know in part." But why do I talk of the regions of knowledge? The semblance of two regions, one pure fact, the other pure fancy, one all science, the other all nescience, is just the error that I have been trying to expose and to which this utterly unscientific notion of an emotional theology is due.